Commemorations

Studies in Christian Thought and History

Commemorations

Studies in Christian Thought and History

by

Alan P.F. Sell

Wipf and Stock Publishers
150 West Broadway • Eugene OR 97401
1998

Commemorations: Studies in Christian Thought and History

By Sell, Alan P. F.

ISBN: 1-57910-129-1

Printed by *Wipf and Stock Publishers* 1998
150 West Broadway • Eugene OR 97401

Previously Published by University of Calgary Press, 1993.

Contents

Preface ix

Part One: Anniversaries and Anticipations

I. Newman, Spurgeon, Martineau and the Problem of Authority 3
II. Richard Baxter and the Unity of the Church 31
III. Fox and Wesley: Experience and Evangelism 61
IV. The Martyrs of 1593, the Church and the State 91

Part Two: Occasional Commemorative Studies

V. Through Suffering to Liberty: 1689 in the English and Vaudois Experience 119
VI. Robert Barclay (1648-1690), the Fathers and the Inward, Universal Saving Light: A Tercentenary Reappraisal . . . 147
VII. The Message of the Erskines for Today 165
VIII. Revival and Secession in Early Nineteenth-Century Geneva: The British Connection 183
IX. The Pembrokeshire Congregational Magazine 211
X. In the Wake of the Enlightenment: The Adjustments of James Martineau and Alexander Campbell Fraser 219
XI. J.H.A. Bomberger (1817-1890) *versus* J.W. Nevin: A Centenary Reappraisal 249
XII. Harley College and its Congregational Alumni 275
XIII. Theology for All: The Contribution of H.F. Lovell Cocks 303
XIV. Rhetoric and Reality: Theological Reflections on Congregationalism and its Heirs 341

Index 373

To our ministers

Robert Cruickshank, Jean Morris and Kirk Summers

and to our friends at

Varsity Acres Presbyterian Church, Calgary, Canada

Preface

This book is a collection of commemorative papers in which I probe, and reflect theologically upon, aspects of Christianity's intellectual and historical heritage. With two exceptions (VII and IX) the papers were written during my tenure of the Chair of Christian Thought in the University of Calgary (1988–92). Among the duties of the Chairholder is that of delivering regular public lectures which are expected to be scholarly and publishable and, at the same time, to interest a remarkably diverse audience. My first series of such lectures was published under the title *Aspects of Christian Integrity*; my second and final series, delivered under the title "Anniversaries and Anticipations," comprises Part One of the present volume. It occurred to me that during the 1990s the anniversaries of a number of prominent Christians would be commemorated, and that the study of some of these would raise questions which the churches need to address with renewed zeal as they anticipate Christianity's third millennium.

As before, the Public Lectures are named in honour of some who were prominent in the establishment of the Chair. Lectures I and III were delivered on the University campus; Varsity Acres Presbyterian Church and Foothills Mennonite Church were hosts for lectures II and IV. I should like to thank the Reverends Robert Cruickshank and John Lenshyn and their church officers for their cordial hospitality; and my University colleagues, Dr. Merlin B. Brinkerhoff, Associate Vice-President (Research), and Dr. Ronald W. Neufeldt, Head of Religious Studies, for chairing the series of lectures.

A version of the first lecture was presented as one of the four Staley Distinguished Christian Scholar Lectures which I was privileged to deliver at Union College, Kentucky, in March 1991. I should like to thank President Jack C. Phillips for his kind invitation, and the Reverend Amy L. Fisher and Dr. Andelys Wood and colleagues for the warmth of their welcome.

Part Two contains seven papers which have previously been published in widely scattered places, and three which appear here for the first time. They are all of a commemorative nature. Paper V was delivered at an international tercentennial conference held at Torre Pellice, Italy, in September 1989. It concerns the tercentenary of England's so-called Toleration Act of 1689, and "The Glorious Return" from exile of the Waldensian Protestants in the same year. I am most grateful to the officers of the Società di Studi Valdesi for their kind invitation and generous hospitality. The sixth paper marks the 300th anniversary of the death of Robert Barclay, Quakerism's major early theologian. The paper on the Erskines (VII) was delivered at Erskine Theological Seminary, South Carolina, on 10 February 1987, as part of the 150th anniversary programme of that institution. I am grateful to Dr. Randall T. Ruble, Dean of the Seminary, for his kind invitation and cordial welcome. The following paper on Geneva, dedicated to my former colleague Dr. Edmond Perret, sometime General Secretary of the World Alliance of Reformed Churches (Presbyterian and Congregational), marks a happy period of service in the city of his birth. If the 150th anniversary of the founding of *The Pembrokeshire Congregational Magazine* (IX) is now past, the centenary of Martineau's death in 1900 (X) will as surely be noted when the new millennium dawns, as was that of Bomberger (XI) in 1990. I thank the officers of The Mercersburg Society for the opportunity of addressing their convocation on the Bomberger–Nevin controversy at Mercersburg, Pennsylvania, on 4 June 1990. The paper on Harley College (XII) both tells the story of a little-known institution, and appears as a tribute to James Alfred Kaye, a prominent minister of my youth, while that on Lovell Cocks (XXIII) provides the first account of a highly respected theologian, the centenary of whose birth will fall in 1994. The final item (XIV) is my Congregational Lecture of 1991, which was delivered in London on 13 November of that year. I was honoured to be invited to give this lecture, and I thank the Board of the Memorial Hall Trust for their confidence and generosity. The lecture commemorates not an event, or a person, but a tradition, much of which has now flowed into united churches in many parts of the world, but whose legacy is, I believe, of considerable importance to the Church of the future. It also marks the fortieth anniversary of my reception on 2 December 1951 as a member at Perry Hill Congregational Church (now United Reformed), Worplesdon, England.

I should like to thank the officers of the respective publications and bodies for permission to reprint the following materials, which first appeared under their auspices: "Through Suffering to Liberty: 1689 in the English and Vaudois Experience," in *Dall' Europa Alle Valli Valdesi*, ed. Albert De Lange, Turin: Claudiana, 1990, 215–36; "Robert Barclay (1648–1690), the Fathers and the Inward, Universal Saving Light: A Tercentenary Reappraisal," *The Journal of the Friends' Historical Society*, LVI, no. 3, 210–26; *The Message of the Erskines for Today*, Due West, SC: Erskine Theological Seminary, 16pp., reprinted in *The Evangelical Quarterly*, LX, no. 4, October 1988, 299–316; "The Pembrokeshire Congregational Magazine," *The Journal of the United Reformed*

Church History Society, IV, no. 2, May 1988, 98–103; "In the Wake of the Enlightenment: The Adjustments of James Martineau and Alexander Campbell Fraser," *Enlightenment and Dissent*, IX, 1990, 63–92; "J.H.A. Bomberger (1817–1890) *versus* J.W. Nevin: A Centenary Reappraisal," *The New Mercersburg Review*, VIII, Autumn 1990, 3–24; *Rhetoric and Reality: Theological Reflections on Congregationalism and its Heirs* [The Congregational Lecture for 1991], London: The Congregational Memorial Hall Trust (1978) Ltd., 1991, 29pp.

Research for some of the papers herein was funded by The Social Sciences and Humanities Research Council of Canada, and to this body I am much indebted. Grants towards the cost of publication were received from the Special Projects Fund, Research Services, the office of the Vice-President (Research), the Faculty of Humanities and the Department of Religious Studies—all of the University of Calgary. I am most grateful to Professor Murray Fraser (President of the University), Dr. Emlyn Jessop (Director of Research Services), Dr. Merlin B. Brinkerhoff (Associate Vice-President, Research), Dr. Ronald B. Bond (Dean of Humanities) and Dr. Ronald W. Neufeldt (Head of the Department of Religious Studies) for their willing support of this venture. All of these colleagues have been to the fore in their encouragement of the work of the Chair of Christian Thought To all of them, and to many others who have helped to make my tenure of the Chair such an enjoyable experience, I return thanks.

Many librarians and others have assisted me in my work, and some of these are thanked in the following pages. Special tribute must, however, be paid to Mr. John Creasey and his staff at Dr. Williams's Library, London. It has been a pleasure to discuss most of the papers in this book with Dr. Geoffrey F. Nuttall, from whom I never cease to learn. Linda Cameron, Shirley Onn and their colleagues at the University of Calgary Press have once again married competence with courtesy.

It remains to elucidate the cover design, which depicts the tower of the former Lancashire Independent College, Manchester. No commemorative paper in this book concerns that worthy establishment, but since the volume will appear in 1993 and the College was founded in 1843, I have thought it fitting to mark pictorially the 150th anniversary of the institution I entered in 1953. The drawing is reprinted by kind permission of the Reverend Dr. R.J. McKelvey, Principal of Northern College, Lancashire's successor.

Alan P.F. Sell
Calgary, Alberta
September 1992

I

Anniversaries and Anticipations

Newman, Spurgeon, Martineau and the Problem of Authority

Some of you may recall the sad day on which the Old Grey Donkey, Eeyore, lost his tail. Determined to find it for him, Winnie-the-Pooh set off for Hundred Acre Wood in order to seek the guidance of Owl: "'if anyone knows anything about anything,' said Bear to himself, 'it's Owl who knows something about something,' he said, 'or my name's not Winnie-the-Pooh,' he said. 'Which it is,' he added. 'So there you are.'"[1]

There you have Owl cast in the role of an authority figure. Nor are such figures confined to the animal kingdom: we all regularly encounter them. Knowledge, status, power—all of these in various mixtures go into the making of authority figures. Hence the headmaster who greeted his new intake of pupils with the words, "The first thing to remember is that in this school I'm the biggest;" hence the music hall ditty, "If you want to know the time, ask a p'liceman;" and hence the music critic's cliché: "The maestro wielded the baton with his customary authority."

Of course, authority figures can, and sometimes do, abuse their power, as when headmasters terrorise the innocent, or policemen allow themselves to be moved by prejudice rather than by evidence, or when conductors exhaust their musicians with painful and idiosyncratic interpretations which the composer could never have envisaged. On the other hand, those under authority often seem able to neutralise some of the worst effects of their position. School children persist in smoking in the lavatories; those victimised by the police have recourse to the law or the press; and members of an end-of-the pier orchestra have been known to feel better when, paying no heed to the conductor at all, they play selections from *The*

1 A.A. Milne, *Winnie-the-Pooh*, London: Methuen, 2nd edn., 1926, 45.

Merry Widow as it were on automatic pilot, whilst actually reading the racing results.

The plot really begins to thicken, however, when authorities conflict. This they can do in many fields of human interest and endeavour, but since our concern is with Christianity, let us draw an example from the *Reminiscences* of the Anglican scholar, A.H. Sayce. He tells of his first Sunday in Oxford as an undergraduate. The year was 1865. He attended the morning service in St. Mary's, the University Church: the very pulpit from which John Henry Newman had proclaimed the distinctive doctrines of Anglo-Catholicism thirty years before. The preacher on this occasion, Mark Pattison, concluded his sermon with these words: "It will be an ill day for the Church of England when dogma and authority gain the upper hand, and reason is denied its rightful place as the cornerstone of all religion." On the same day Sayce returned to the same church and heard the afternoon preacher, the Anglo-Catholic H.P. Liddon. Liddon began his sermon with these words: "Dogma and authority, authority and dogma—these two form the keystone in the arch of our holy faith."[2] Here we have two authorities flatly contradicting one another; and had there been an evening service Sayce might well have been able to hear a third preacher declare that the cornerstone of religion is the Bible, or the individual conscience, or religious experience, or even the nobler moral sensitivities of the race. Indeed, the future bishop, Mandell Creighton, a contemporary of Sayce, did hear Dean Stanley preach in St. Mary's on another occasion. Describing the sermon in a letter of 22 April 1871, he wrote, "There was a certain amount of general moral enthusiasm, to the intent that it was desirable to be good rather than bad; but I had previously gathered that from other sources."[3]

What makes all of this an especially interesting thickening of the plot is the fact that the three authority-figures named are themselves resting upon distinct authorities: reason, dogma and tradition, and natural law. This raises our question in a clamant way: "Where is the locus of authority in Christianity?" I just described this as "our question"—but is it? After all, the preachers I have quoted were all holding forth in the 1860s, and times have changed. Indeed they have; but in the first place, we ought not to rule out the possibility of learning from the past; and secondly, if anything the question of the locus of authority in Christianity is posed more dramatically now that it was during the nineteenth century. There

2 A.H. Sayce, *Reminiscences*, London: Macmillan 1923, 35.

3 Louise Creighton [wife], *Life and Letters of Mandell Creighton*, London: Longmans 1904, I, 92.

are two main reasons for this. First, as a result of population movements over the last hundred years, and in some cases as a result of the missionary activity of those who are not Christians, we of the western world are faced by many more belief options than were our forebears. What is more, not all of the world views on offer are religious (however much some of them, with their banners, songs and processions, may assume the trappings of religion, and claim a quasi-religious commitment from their supporters). Thus, where John Henry Newman declared in the nineteenth century that "the trials which lie before us are such as would appal and make dizzy even such courageous hearts as St. Athanasius, St. Gregory I or St. Gregory VII . . . [because] Christianity has never yet had the experience of a world simply irreligious,"[4] we should have to say that until now Christianity has never confronted a world as bewilderingly and interestingly irreligious and multireligious. In a word, we can no longer legitimately make the assumptions of Christendom which our forebears did. In some ways our situation is much more like that faced by the earliest theologians of the Church, who had to forge their thought in a multi-faith intellectual climate characterised by ideas ranging from the noble to the utterly bizarre, than it is like that of Luther, Calvin or Schleiermacher, all of whom could understandably, if not altogether justifiably, take it for granted that Christianity was the right religious option—indeed, that there were no other viable options. This point is so obvious that it could be doubted only by a student who deems my course on Patristics irrelevant!

The second reason for the urgency of the question of authority is that the churches seem to be more muddled about it than they were a hundred years ago. Their confusion is partly attributable to the proximity of the other options to which I have alluded, but for the rest of this lecture I shall be concerned with the muddles internal to the churches. It would do nothing but good if, as they approach a new millennium, the churches would strive for clarity as to the authoritative centre of their faith and ground of their claims.

It is all too easy to illustrate the kind of muddles I have in mind. For example, we have the Roman Catholic Church, whose *magisterium* is charged with the reponsibility of informing the faithful what is to be believed, and how, accordingly, life is to be lived. In fact, as we all know—and I take no pleasure in reminding you of this—in a major way since the advent of the birth control pill, and in connection with some of the liberation theologies, many Roman Catholics are questioning, and even repudiating, the authoritative teaching

4 J.H. Newman, *Catholic Sermons*, London: Burns & Oates 1957, 121, 123.

which is presented to them. This, in turn, provokes a response from the *magisterium*. Thus, in answer to 163 European Roman Catholic theologians who criticised the way in which the present Pope is applying his teaching authority, the Pope declared that "If the theologian is first of all and thoroughly a believer, whose Christian Faith is faith in the Church of Christ and in the Magisterium, his theological work must remain faithfully bound to his ecclesial faith, whose authentic and definitive interpreter is the Magisterium."[5] Again, in March 1990 thirty-three Roman Catholic bishops from the United States, concerned about the contextualizing of the Gospel in their land, had an audience with the Pope. During the proceedings Cardinal Ratzinger, Prefect of the Congregation for the Doctrine of the Faith, lamented that "dissident theologians have taken the place of the bishops as teacher, causing uncertainty and confusion."[6] In the summer of 1990 the document, *Instruction on the Ecclesial Vocation of the Theologian*, was published by the Vatican. It cautioned theologians against opposing the Church's teaching, and urged collaboration between theologians and bishops. Many have welcomed the idea of collaboration, but as to the caution, Hans Küng, Edward Schillebeeckx and twenty others signed *The Tübingen Declaration*. They complained that the Vatican document "seeks to suppress the pluralism of theological opinions by banning dissent and demanding obedience . . . [so that] . . . only the voice of the *magisterium* can be heard."[7] In so far as the Vatican is making this attempt, it would seem to be consistent with Pope Pius X's encyclical of 1906: "The one duty of the multitude is to allow itself to be led, and, like a docile flock, to follow the Pastors."[8]

I do not think that "docile" would be the most apt adjective with which to characterize some members of the flock of the United Church of Canada at the present time. For here too, underlying all the perplexity and agonizing over the place properly to be accorded within the Church to practising homosexuals, is the same question which is posed within the Roman Catholic Church: What is the locus of authority within the Church? Thus, some United Church Christians uphold the Bible as *the* authority: "the supreme rule of faith and practice," to use the classical language of that Church's tradition. But then these same Christians interpret the Bible in radically different ways. Others make an appeal to natural law, and

---

5 Quoted by Alfred de Manche, [Canadian] *Catholic Register*, 22 April 1989.

6 Report in *Newsweek*, 20 March 1990, 60.

7 Quoted in the [Canadian] *Anglican Journal*, September 1990, 16.

8 *Encyclical Vehementer* 11 February 1906; in *The Papal Encyclicals 1903–1939*, ed. Claudia Carlen, Ann Arbor, MI: The Pierian Press 1990, 48.

so persuade themselves that homosexual acts are strictly unnatural and hence wrong. Still others appeal selectively to Scripture and/or are moved by sincerely held convictions regarding love, openness and inclusiveness. Their opponents are liable to accuse them of having been swamped by a genial humanism which sits loose to the fact that the moral law has been fulfilled by Christ but not abrogated, and which forgets that God's love, though welcoming and inexhaustible, is at the same time holy and righteous.

My diagnosis is thus that there is a serious muddle—some would say a crisis—concerning authority within the Church. My prescription is that we retreat from the heat of the moment and take our bearings from three Christians who died between ninety and one hundred years ago. They are John Henry Newman, who by living sufficiently long managed to spend forty-five years in the Church of England and forty-five years in the Roman Catholic Church; Charles Haddon Spurgeon, who was raised in Congregationalism, but became the most prominent Baptist preacher of his day; and James Martineau, the thinker and liturgist, who was never anything other than a Unitarian, but who led much of the Unitarianism around him away from widely prevalent naturalism towards a more spiritual approach to the faith. It is an interesting aside that Newman and Martineau had Huguenot blood in their veins, and that Newman and Spurgeon shared Dutch ancestry, Spurgeon's forebears having left the Netherlands during the persecutions of the Duke of Alva. More important for our present purpose is the fact that Newman, Spurgeon and Martineau lived in a period of rapid social, political and economic change; science, manufacturing and commerce were burgeoning against a background of poverty, social deprivation and disease; and the foundations of Christianity were being shaken by evolutionary thought, the blossoming of modern biblical criticism, naturalistic and agnostic philosophy, and ecclesiastical rivalry.[9]

I select these three because they represent, at first sight, three very different ways of approaching the question of authority in the Church. I say "at first sight" because although they differ in emphasis, approach and final result, there are more links between them than might be expected given their diverse ecclesiastical backgrounds. But let us go step by step, expecting Newman to uphold the authority of the Church, Spurgeon the authority of the Bible, and Martineau the authority of the individual conscience.

---

9 For a fuller account of some of these trends see Alan P.F. Sell, *Theology in Turmoil: The Roots, Course and Significance of the Conservative-Liberal Debate in Modern Theology*, Grand Rapids: Baker Book House 1986.

I

John Henry Newman, the centenary of whose death fell on 11 August 1990, was born in 1801 and, as he tells us, converted at the age of fifteen in the autumn of 1816. The impression which his conversion experience made upon him never left him: it was, he said, "more certain than that I have hands and feet."[10] This experience was evangelical in type, its doctrinal framework Calvinistic, and this despite the impact of William Law's *A Serious Call to a Devout and Holy Life* (1728) upon the youthful mind. Among the influences upon Newman during the next few years was that of Thomas Scott, the biblical commentator, who had worked his way out of Priestleyan, necessarian Unitarianism, and into devoutly trinitarian Anglicanism.

Following studies at Oxford University Newman was ordained to the ministry of the Church of England on Trinity Sunday 1824. For the next six years he was involved with such evangelical and interdenominational bodies as the Church Missionary Society and the British and Foreign Bible Society. Having circulated an anonymous pamphlet showing how Nonconformist domination of the CMS could be broken, he was dismissed from his position as local secretary of that organization. Three months later he opted out of the Bible Society, and with that his formal connections with the Evangelical party in the Church ceased.

Newman became an increasingly ardent student of patristics, and the conviction of the Church's continuity through the ages grew upon him. In the early 1830s, convinced that the Roman Catholic faith was polytheistic, degrading, and idolatrous, he began to strive with such like-minded colleagues as E.B. Pusey to demonstrate and defend the view that the Church of England was continuous with the Church of the ages, and truly within the apostolic succession. From these endeavours flowed the *Tracts for the Times*, the first of which, written by Newman, appeared in 1833; and from the title of this series came the name "Tractarian" by which Newman and his friends were designated. Without doubt Newman's most famous and provocative tract was the ninetieth, published in 1841, in which he argued to the satisfaction of some and the dismay of many that the Anglican Articles of Religion were opposed only to doctrinal and ritualistic perversions of Roman Catholicism, and not to the Roman Catholic faith as such.

10 J.H. Newman, *Apologia Pro Vita Sua*, ed. Martin J. Svaglic, Oxford: Clarendon Press 1967, 17.

After considerable spiritual agony which, as he tells us, gave him stomach-ache, and having been on his "death-bed as regards my membership of the Anglican church" since 1841, Newman, in 1843, published a retraction of his earlier harsh criticisms of Rome, and resigned the living of St. Mary's, Oxford, to which he had been presented in 1828. Early in 1845 he began to write his *Essay on the Development of Christian Doctrine*, and as his manuscript grew, so his remaining objections to Roman Catholicism fell away. On 9 October 1845 Newman was received into the Roman Church; in February 1846 he was ordained in Rome, and had the degree of Doctor of Divinity conferred upon him by the Pope. Thereafter he lived for most of the rest of his life in Birmingham at the Oratory which, commissioned by the Pope, he founded in 1847. In 1878 Pope Pius IX, who had retained lingering suspicions of Newman, died, and on 12 May Newman was created a cardinal by the new Pope, Leo XIII.

There can be no question that a prominent factor in Newman's conversion to Rome was his urgent desire to find an answer to the question of the locus of authority in the Church. His developing ideas concerning churchmanship and tradition seemed to him to have their only justifiable terminus in Rome. We should, however, note in passing that just as Newman posited a constant amid Christianity's earthly vicissitudes and doctrinal changes, so there were things about himself which survived his transition to Rome. Sheridan Gilley has pointed out, for example, that temperamentally Newman remained an Evangelical of the rigorist-otherworldly type (as contrasted with the holy worldliness of the Evangelicals of the Clapham Sect).[11] This temperamental continuity would seem to be borne out by the remark of the artist Edward Burne-Jones, who recalled his youthful contact with Newman in Birmingham thus: "In an age of sofas and cushions he taught me to be indifferent to comfort; and in an age of materialism he taught me to venture all on the unseen . . . so if this world cannot tempt me with money or

11 See S. Gilley, "Newman and prophecy, Evangelical and Catholic," *The Journal of the United Reformed Church History Society*, III, no. 5, March 1985, 170. Thus while agreeing with Thomas Morris ("Did Newman preach a Gospel of gloom?" *The Irish Theological Quarterly*, L, nos. 2–4, 1983–4, 198–211) that A.B. Calkins presented a seriously one-sided case in his article, "Newman's Gospel of gloom" (Ib., XLIX, no. 3, 1982, 184–94), we may perhaps suggest that while the "kindly light" was ever ahead and ultimately unquenchable, the "encircling gloom" was never less than real to Newman.

luxury, and it can't, . . . it is most of all because he said it in a way that touched me—not scolding nor forbidding nor much leading—walking with me a step in front."[12]

Returning to Newman's quest of authority, we must not overlook the negative stimulus provided by those whom he called liberals. Like "evangelical," "liberal" is a slippery term, but when he used it Newman had in mind those Christians who sat loose to dogma and maintained that "there is no positive truth in religion, but that one creed is as good as another."[13] Such liberals succumbed to what another convert to Rome, G.K. Chesterton, was later somewhere to call "the tyranny of taste." In the person of his own brother Francis, Professor of Latin at University College, London, Newman had a striking example of the results of ungrounded thought, for Francis had attached himself to one intellectual novelty after another, baulking only at spiritualism. By contrast, "From the age of fifteen," writes John Henry, "dogma has been the fundamental principle of my religion . . . religion, as a mere sentiment, is to me a dream and a mockery."[14] Accordingly, he castigated the liberal doctrine, so widely prevalent to this day, that "truth and falsehood in religion are but matter of opinion; that one doctrine is as good as another . . . that there is no truth . . . that no one is answerable for his opinions . . . that it is enough if we sincerely hold what we profess. . . ."[15] All of which, he might have noted, is a prize example of *dogma!*

A further charge which Newman levelled against the liberals was that they manifested "irreverence towards Antiquity,"[16] and seemed to live, intellectually, only for the passing moment. To Newman, however, the continuity of the faith was of supreme importance, and the key to understanding it was the notion of development under infallible authority.[17] The fact of doctrinal change could not be denied—any honest scrutiny of history would testify to it. Moreover, such change had been essential as Christians

12 Francis Horner, *Times Remembered*, London: Heinemann 1933, 120.

13 J.H. Newman, *My Campaign in Ireland*, Aberdeen: A. King 1896, 395. This is from Newman's speech on receiving the Biglietto in Rome, 12 May 1879. For a helpful discussion of this theme see Thomas Morris, "Cardinal Newman and the liberals," *The Irish Theological Quarterly*, LIII, no. 1, 1987, 1–16.

14 Idem, *Apologia*, 54.

15 Idem, *An Essay on the Development of Christian Doctrine*, London: Toovey 1845, 345.

16 Idem, *Fifteen Sermons Preached before the University of Oxford*, London: Rivingtons, 3rd. edn., 1872, 174.

17 Idem, *Essay on Development*, 114–30.

reflected upon the implications of their faith, and as they stood against heresy. What had to be affirmed was that despite all the change, or, rather, in all the change, the original deposit of the faith was preserved and remained intact. It was only on the authority of the *magisterium*, itself open to the Word of God, that this affirmation could be made, and that the line could be drawn between what was acceptable and what was unacceptable doctrinal change. The Bible as such could not serve as the criterion of permissible change, for it was itself subject to wildly fluctuating interpretations. Which is to say that the attraction of the *magisterium* increased as Newman's confidence in the infallibility of Scripture, which Spurgeon was so forcefully to expound, diminished.

Does this mean that we are obliged to assent blindly to the teaching of the *magisterium*? By no means. Yet another of Newman's complaints against the liberals was that they were fixated upon the rational. To him, the human being was "a seeing, feeling, contemplating acting animal," not a reasoning one.[18] We are able to live, and we must live, by our conscience. Conscience, says Newman is "a messenger from above;"[19] it is not simply one means of knowing, it is "a connecting principle between the creature and his Creator."[20] It is the vehicle by which we hear the very voice of God. In all of this there is a prominent point of contact between Newman and Martineau.[21]

In his illuminating reflection upon all of this, my colleague Hugo Meynell has said, "Newman is surely quite right, that one very important condition that any alleged divine revelation must meet, is that it should confirm and enhance our natural moral sense,"[22] the latter being conceived as already God-given. The difficult part comes, however, when Newman relates this insight to that of papal authority. In his *Letter to the Duke of Norfolk* he argues that a person can, without contradiction, be a good Englishman and a

18 Idem, *Discussions and Arguments on Various Subjects*, London: Basil Montagu Pickering 1872, 294.

19 Idem, *Essay on Development*, 348.

20 Idem, *An Essay in Aid of A Grammar of Assent*,, ed. I.T. Ker, Oxford: Clarendon Press 1985, 81.

21 The first part of A.M. Fairbairn's aphorism is thus wide of the mark: "Newman was never happy in the presence of conscience; Martineau was never happy away from it." See his "James Martineau," *The Contemporary Review* LXXXIII, January–June 1903, 9.

22 Hugo Meynell, "Newman's Vindication of Faith in the *Grammar of Assent*," in *Newman after a Hundred Years*, eds. Ian Ker and Alan G. Hill, Oxford: Clarendon Press 1990, 254.

good Catholic. (You will recall that opposition to the restoration of the Catholic hierarchy in 1850 had been fuelled in part by the denial of this proposition). Nevertheless, continued Newman, if ever something said by the Pope went against the prayer-formed conscience, then conscience must take precedence. "Certainly," he wrote, "if I am obliged to bring religion into after-dinner toasts (which indeed does not seem quite the thing) I shall drink—to the Pope if you please—still, the conscience first, and to the Pope afterwards."[23]

In view of the fact that Newman wrote these words after the 1870 declaration of the first Vatican Council concerning papal infallibility; in view also of the fact that he had fought against that declaration on the ground of its historical difficulties and its potentially dissuasive effect upon otherwise likely converts; and despite his acquiescence in the dogma once it had been promulgated, we cannot forbear to ask, "What price now the *magisterium*?"

Did Newman perhaps think that a clash between conscience and the *magisterium* was so unlikely as not to be a possibility demanding serious consideration? It is difficult to say. Many Roman Catholics today, however, would invoke the distinction between the general *magisterium* and the infallible *magisterium*—that is, the relatively rare *ex cathedra* utterances of the Pope, and would say that while the latter, being matters of divine revelation, *cannot* contradict our moral sense,[24] the former very well may. In the case of such a conflict the Roman Catholic of integrity should abide by his or her conscience, acting, believing, and if so called protesting accordingly; but if a Roman Catholic's conscience were violated by the infallible *magisterium*, the action of integrity would be resignation from the Roman Church. However that may be, the *magisterium* itself is quite sure of its status. The Vatican II Dogmatic Constitution on Divine Revelation declares that "the task of giving an authentic interpretation of the Word of God, whether in its written form or in the form of Tradition has been entrusted to the living teaching office of the Church alone."[25]

Here we have a clear reference to Scripture and Tradition, and I do not think we shall reach anything approaching clarity unless we attempt to unpack the term "Tradition." This ambiguous term may denote the general Christian message as proclaimed in differ-

---

23 J.H. Newman, *Letter addressed to His Grace the Duke of Norfolk*, London: B.M. Pickering 1875, 66.

24 Cf. Idem, *A Grammar of Assent*, 269.

25 Austin Flannery (ed), *Vatican Council II. The Conciliar and Post Conciliar Documents*, Collegeville, MN: Liturgical Press 1975, 755.

ent accents from age to age; it may signify the diverse practices which the several Christian communions have developed through time; or, in the more technical sense which concerns us here, it may stand for a body of teaching developing through time, which is deemed to be consonant with, and equal in status to, Scripture. This, at any rate is one way of reading the historic usage of the term. Thus, for example, the Council of Trent spoke of two authoritative sources, Scripture and Tradition, declaring that these must be "received and venerated with equal piety, affection, and reverence." If these appear to conflict the *magisterium* must resolve matters.

This position was not arrived at overnight: on the contrary. Indeed, Oscar Cullmann argued strongly that "the infant Church itself made the distinction between apostolic tradition and ecclesiastical tradition, subordinating the latter clearly to the former."[26] His case in a nutshell, and in my own formulation, is that in the sub-apostolic age, with its variegated developing ecclesiastical traditions, its numerous disciplinary questions, and its manifold doctrinal emphases—some of them fantastic, it became necessary to take stock. The result was the biblical canon and the Apostles' Creed. In the absence of such norms as these it did not seem that it would be possible to maintain the apostolic tradition, because in so many ways the ecclesiastical tradition was militating against it. It thus transpired, says Cullmann, that "the Fathers of the Church who wrote *after* 150—Irenaeus, Tertullian—understood infinitely better [than most of the so-called Apostolic Fathers] the essence of the Gospel."[27] The conclusion is that the second-century Church opted for the witness of apostles and their immediate followers to Christ, over against the ecclesiastical tradition in its entirety which was developing all around.

Nevertheless, Vincent of Lérins, who died before 450, feels impelled to affirm that Christian faith is founded upon the Divine Law—the Scriptures—*and* Tradition, Tradition being required because Scripture "seems to be capable of as many interpretations as there are interpreters."[28] Eventually, as R.P.C. Hanson has it, "more and more external authorities came into being. Fathers, councils, doctors, popes, and the origin and extensive growth of a

---

26 O. Cullmann, "Scripture and Tradition," *Scottish Journal of Theology* VI, no. 2, June 1953, 124.

27 Ibid., 132.

28 Vincent of Lérins, *The Commonitorium*, 2, in *Nicene and Post-Nicene Fathers of the Christian Church*, Oxford: James Parker 1894, XI, 132.

codified Canon Law assisted this development. By the end of the Middle Ages the Church was supported by a vast system of external authority."[29]

Two points of importance must be added. First, some Roman Catholic scholars have argued against Cullmann's conclusion to the effect that his evidence *supports* their position that the Church determines what orthodoxy is. This, however, is to overlook the important distinction between the reaffirmation of the earliest apostolic Gospel, and the pronouncement that doctrinal developments which appear to be novel, and tenuously or obscurely related to the apostles' Gospel, are to be accorded the same weight as that Gospel. In a word, while Tradition may or may not be a medium of revelation, it is not the source of it.

Secondly, such twentieth century Roman Catholic theologians as Rahner, Congar, Küng and Tavard have set their faces against Bellarmine and others who have supported the Tridentine view of two sources of revelation; and some argue that, properly understood, that was never the Tridentine view. Be that as it may, Vatican II's *Dogmatic Constitution on Divine Revelation* declares that the "Magisterium is not superior to the Word of God, but is its servant. It teaches only what has been handed on to it. At the divine command and with the help of the Holy Spirit, it listens to this devotedly, guards it with dedication and expounds it faithfully. All that it proposes for belief as being divinely revealed is drawn from this *single deposit of faith*."[30]

This sounds hopeful to Protestant ears, though it must be said that the message does not appear to have been completely grasped by all to whom it was initially addressed. Thus the Reverend Robert Nash S.J. can write, "God knows that we need a competent teacher to explain to us the meaning of the written word. That teacher He has given to us in the Catholic Church and He promises that His Holy Spirit will be with her, endorsing her words."[31] This might suggest to the popular audience Nash was addressing that the role of the Spirit is simply to endorse what the Church teaches, to rubber-stamp, as it were, that which the Church has already determined to proclaim. Vatican II, however, insists that the Spirit, through the Word, gives the Church what it must say.

But these references to the Word of God in Scripture prompt me to turn to Charles Haddon Spurgeon.

---

29 R.P.C. Hanson, "Authority," in *A Dictionary of Christian Theology*, ed. Alan Richardson, London: SCM Press 1969, 27.

30 *Vatican Council II*, 756.

31 R. Nash in *The Sunday Press* (Dublin), 8 February 1981.

II

The centenary of Spurgeon's death fell on 31 January 1992. Although Newman and Martineau outlived him by more than thirty years, Spurgeon packed so much into his fifty-eight years that his influence, no less than theirs, lives on. Many of his sermons are still in print; the Pastors' College which he founded now bears his name, as do his homes for children.

Spurgeon, whose grandfather James and father John were Congregational ministers, was born at Kelvedon, Essex on 19 June 1834. Like Newman he had a dateable conversion experience, though unlike Newman's his occurred in a Primitive Methodist chapel. Also like Newman he changed his ecclesiastical allegiance, becoming a member of the Baptist church at Isleham on 3 May 1850. At the age of sixteen he preached his first sermon in a cottage at Teversham, near Cambridge. He was a great success and in 1852, at the age of only eighteen, and having received no formal ministerial training, he became pastor at Waterbeach, Cambridgeshire. Thence, in 1854, to New Park Street, Southwark. The almost empty chapel was soon bursting at the seams; it was enlarged, and soon burst again. The Surrey Gardens music hall was used for services, and congregations of ten thousand were normal. The Metropolitan Tabernacle, opened in 1861, became Spurgeon's base for the rest of his ministry.

Biblical exposition in forthright style, spliced with humour and peppered with shrewd comment on the affairs of the day was Spurgeon's forte. In a lecture to his trainee pastors he said,

> There are brethren in the ministry whose speech is intolerable; either they dun you to death, or else they send you to sleep. No chloral can ever equal their discourse in sleep-giving properties. No human being, unless gifted with infinite patience, could long endure to listen to them, and nature does well to give the victim deliverance through sleep. I heard one say, the other day, that a certain preacher had no more gifts for the ministry than an oyster, and in my own judgment this was a slander on the oyster, for that worthy bivalve shows great discretion in his openings, and he also knows when to close.[32]

He urged clarity in preaching: "If you look down into a well, if it be empty, it will appear to be very deep; but if there be water in it you

32 C.H. Spurgeon, *An All-Round Ministry. Addresses to Ministers and Students*, [1900], London: The Banner of Truth Trust 1960, 41.

will see its brightness. I believe that many 'deep' preachers are simply so because they are like dry wells with nothing whatever in them, except decaying leaves, a few stones, and perhaps a dead cat or two."[33] While valuing forcefulness in preaching, he reminded his hearers that "Nonsense does not improve by being bellowed."[34] Spurgeon followed his own advice, people of all types flocked to hear him, and not even *The Times* could ignore him.

The Metropolitan Tabernacle became a hub of activity. It sponsored no fewer than sixty-six organizations including a Police Mission and a Female Servants' Society. The premises, which were open on seven days each week from 7:00 a.m. to 11:00 p.m., were let out to other worthy bodies too—the Christian Butchers' Association always held their Annual General Meeting there. Here was an activist evangelicalism with a social conscience quite different in style from the otherworldly evangelicalism in which Newman had been reared; and it was all grounded in the Calvinistic conviction that God was sovereign Lord of the whole of life and of all creation too.

Which brings us to Spurgeon's concern for purity of doctrine. True to his conviction that "The plan of making things pleasant all round is a perilous as well as a wicked one,"[35] he provoked a wide-ranging controversy with his 1864 sermon on baptismal regeneration. He just could not find that doctrine in the Bible, and therefore it was not to be believed. The doctrine was, however, plainly presented for belief in the Book of Common Prayer of the Church of England. Were not Anglican evangelicals who, like himself, repudiated baptismal regeneration, at least inconsistent in remaining within that communion? Matching deeds to words, Spurgeon resigned from the Evangelical Alliance, which body drew much of its strength from the Low Church party in the Church of England, to which party Newman had once belonged.

As to his own denomination, he feared that many Baptists were becoming doctrinally lax. The influence of Arminianism, he thought, was tempting some to emphasise human ability in the matter of salvation; some were verging upon Arianism; some were emphasising the Incarnation of Christ at the expense of the Atonement, as if what saved was Christ's assumption of human flesh rather than his death upon the Cross.[36] Some were shying away from belief in the

33 Ibid., 42.

34 Ibid.

35 Ibid., 48.

36 See further, Alan P.F. Sell, *Aspects of Christian Integrity*, Calgary: University of Calgary Press 1990, and Louisville: Westminster/John Knox 1991, ch. II.

eternal punishment of the wicked. In this last connection an important catalyst was the book *Life in Christ*, published in 1846 by the Congregational minister Edward White, and soon the alternatives of future probation, conditional immortality, and universalism were all being proposed. None of these, thought Spurgeon, squared with Scripture.

What Spurgeon did find in Scripture, that he preached, however inconsistent some of the biblical teaching might appear to be. Thus, for example, concerning one of the cruces in the long-standing Calvinist-Arminian debate[37] he writes:

> Two truths cannot be contradictory to each other. If, then, I find in one part of the Bible that everything is fore-ordained, *that is true*; and if I find, in another Scripture, that man is responsible for all his actions, *that is true*; and it is only my folly that leads me to imagine that these two truths can ever contradict each other. I do not believe they can ever be welded into one upon any earthly anvil, but they certainly shall be one in eternity. They are two lines that are so nearly parallel, that the human mind which pursues them farthest will never discover that they converge, but they do converge, and they will meet somewhere in eternity, close to the throne of God, whence all truth doth spring.[38]

It should in fairness be pointed out that if Spurgeon trounced doctrines which he deemed unscriptural and false, he did not fall into the trap of erecting doctrinal tests as conditions of entry to the kingdom of heaven. Moreover he could be generous to the persons of opponents whilst roundly condemning their teaching. Thus in the same sermon from which I have just quoted he says,

> far be it from me even to imagine that Zion contains none but Calvinistic Christians within her walls, or that there are none saved who do not hold our views. Most atrocious things have been spoken about the character and spiritual condition of John Wesley, the modern prince of Arminians. I can only say concerning him that, while I detest many of the doctrines which he preached, yet for the man himself I have a reverence second to no Wesleyan. . . . I believe there are multitudes of men who cannot see [truths] in the

37 For which see further Alan P.F. Sell, *The Great Debate: Calvinism, Arminianism and Salvation*, Worthing: H.E. Walter (now Bletchley: Word Books) 1982, and Grand Rapids: Baker Book House 1983.

38 C.H. Spurgeon, *A Defense of Calvinism*, a sermon on Romans 2:4, reprinted Phoenix, Arizona: Reformation Press n.d., 12.

> way in which we put them, who nevertheless have received Christ as their Saviour, and are as dear to the heart of the God of grace as the soundest Calvinist in or out of heaven.[39]

With the passage of time modern biblical criticism made increasingly potent inroads into the received evangelical tradition. Against all rationalistically-inspired liberalism Spurgeon raised his voice no less determinedly than did Newman. Hear him tease the German pioneers of biblical "higher" criticism: "Our German friends have diligently made vast nets with which they have enclosed the sea of thought; and upon drawing them out, what a noise there has been, and what a sensation, and what a trembling and fainting among the old ladies of Christendom; but when we have seen their mighty catch, it has not been the tenth part of a sardine!"[40] Many were allowing themselves to be overcome by fashionable and false teaching: "Such and so varied are some men's beliefs and unbeliefs; an agglomeration of philosophic rags, metaphysical tatters, theological remnants, and heretical cast-offs. Certain thinkers have reached the blessed ultimatum of believing nothing at all with anything like certainty of belief."[41] Worst of all, some ministers were behaving as if "the truth of God were a variable quantity, a matter of daily formation, a nose of wax to be constantly reshaped, a cloud driven by the wind. So do not I believe! . . . Rest assured that there is nothing new in theology except that which is false. . . ."[42] Spurgeon was not sold on doctrinal development, nor on the need to acknowledge sources: the "nose of wax" is a transplant from John Locke.

There was only one thing to be done. The doctrinal Downgrade must resolutely be opposed—and with that word "Downgrade" we come to the controversy of that name.[43] Among Spurgeon's numerous enterprises was the magazine, *The Sword and the Trowel*, which he had founded in 1865, and of which he was the editor. In March and April 1887 two anonymous articles (in fact by Robert Shindler) were published entitled, "The Down Grade." The articles constituted

39 Ibid., 11.

40 C.H. Spurgeon, *An All-Round Ministry*, 143.

41 Ibid., 180.

42 Ibid., 10.

43 Recent studies of the Downgrade Controversy include: Ernest A. Payne, "The Down Grade controversy: A postscript," *The Baptist Quarterly*, XXVIII, October 1979, 146–58; J.H.Y. Briggs, "Charles Haddon Spurgeon and the Baptist denomination in nineteenth century Britain," ibid., XXI, January 1986, 218–40; Michael Nicholls, "The Downgrade Controversy: A neglected protagonist," ibid., XXXII, April 1988, 260–74; Mark T.E. Hopkins, "Spurgeon's opponents in the Downgrade Controversy," ibid., 274–94.

a protest against doctrinal laxity, and against those who "forgo the old for the sake of the new."[44] To them the editor appended a note: "Earnest attention is requested for this paper. . . . We are going downhill at breakneck speed."[45] In a subsequent article Spurgeon declared that, "A new religion has been initiated, which is no more Christianity than chalk is cheese. . . . The Atonement is scouted, the inspiration of Scripture is derided, the Holy Spirit is degraded into an influence, the punishment of sin is turned into a fiction, and the resurrection into a myth. . . ."[46] Matters were so serious that Spurgeon, an erstwhile staunch opponent of credal subscription, felt by 1887 that the Baptist Union should define its doctrinal position.[47] Since the Union showed no sign of doing this to Spurgeon's satisfaction, he wrote his letter of resignation from that body on 28 October 1887, declaring that "every hour of the day impresses upon me the conviction that I am moving none too soon."[48]

As we leave Spurgeon for the moment we need only remark that just as Newman expected a conscientious reponse to Tradition, so Spurgeon approached Scripture with an alert and receptive conscience. And with that word we come to Martineau.

III

James Martineau was born in Norwich on 21 April 1805, and died in his ninety-fifth year on 11 January 1900. Apprenticed in 1821 to Samuel Fox the civil engineer of Derby, he changed direction on the death of Henry Turner, the Unitarian minister in Nottingham, who had married Martineau's cousin Catherine Rankin. In 1822 he went to Manchester College, York, to train for the Unitarian ministry. William Turner, the philosophy tutor there, was wedded to the determinism of Hartley, and with this Martineau became increasingly ill at ease.

In 1827 Martineau became assistant at the school of the Unitarian Lant Carpenter in Bristol, and the following year saw him installed as assistant pastor at Eustace Street church, Dublin. There he remained until 1832, when he became John Grundy's colleague at Paradise Street chapel, Liverpool. Here he found time to

---

44 *The Sword and the Trowel*, 1887, 126.

45 Ibid., 122.

46 Ibid., 397.

47 See J.H.Y. Briggs, art. cit., 231.

48 Spurgeon's letter to S.H. Booth, General Secretary of the Baptist Union; quoted by J.J. Ellis, *Charles Haddon Spurgeon*, London: Nisbet 1891, 169.

lecture on chemistry at the Mechanics' Institution, and to take a lively part in the local Unitarian controversy. Although his opponents in this connection were for the most part Anglicans, it is interesting to note that the Wesleyans thought twice over their ministerial appointments to Liverpool, the local people deeming "the appointment of two steady-going, sedative Superintendential ministers to the same Circuit inexpedient, especially in the neighbourhood of . . . the brilliant Martineau."[49]

In 1840, without relinquishing his pastorate, Martineau became a professor at his *alma mater*, now back in Manchester and known as Manchester New College. In 1854 the College removed to London. After more than three years of commuting to give his lectures, Martineau resigned his pastorate in 1857 and became permanently resident in the capital. He was appointed principal of the College in 1869.

Martineau's interests were wide. He wrote and published hymns, liturgies, sermons and essays; and the substance of his college lectures was eventually published in a number of books—for the most part following his retirement in 1885. Pressure of pastoral and other duties had prevented earlier publication, and we thus have the interesting circumstance that apart from their being freshly mulled over, the ideas set down in Martineau's major works of the 1880s and 1890s differ little from those he was propounding half a century earlier.[50]

What Martineau had to say about the locus of authority in religion is summed up in his book, *The Seat of Authority in Religion* (1890), but our way into the question is *via* one of his earlier essays, in which he concisely distinguishes his approach from those we have already considered. While he thinks that in Newman's writings are to be found "the chief truths of Christian morals and faith;"[51] while generously allowing that in Newman's personality and publications we see "a great preponderance for good,"[52] he dismisses what he calls "Roman appendages"—the invocation of saints, Mariolatry and the Apostolic Succession—as being "chiefly remarkable for having raised up in their defence the obnoxious but highly

49 Benjamin Gregory, *Side Lights on the Conflicts of Methodism*, London: Cassell 1898, 247.

50 See further Ralph Waller, "James Martineau: The development of his thought," in *Truth, Liberty, Religion. Essays celebrating Two Hundred Years of Manchester College*, Oxford: Manchester College 1986, 225–64; and ch. X below.

51 James Martineau, *Essays Philosophical and Theological*, London: Trübner 1866, 358.

52 Ibid., 364.

important 'doctrine of development.' In the absence of any plausible support from Scripture [Spurgeon would say "Amen!"], it became necessary . . . to widen the source of doctrine, and give an interpreting and determining power to the church."[53] So to Martineau's adjudication between the Newmans and the Spurgeons, and to the statement of his own position. He writes:

> The assumption on both sides is, that *either* the Bible or the Church is impregnable . . . the only question is, *which* of the two it is. To put this to the test, each party tries to discredit the favourite refuge of the other. Dr. Newman does not scruple to discharge a volley into the intrenchment of Scripture. . . . [The Protestants] reply by a hot fire at his church-bastions, to convince him that they may be knocked about his head. Is it surprising if both are pretty well riddled; if neither is found to be designed for the purpose to which it has been applied; and if a change of the whole ground should be the clearly indicated result? By *no* documentary process, no construction of title-deeds, be they canonical or ecclesiastical . . . can you draw forth the oracular system which you seek. . . . For discriminating the true from the false, the accidental from the essential, in morals and religion . . . something more is needed than to draw an arbitrary line round a select group of books, or a favoured series of centuries. "Objective authority" in religion there doubtless is; but vested in a Person who is eternal, and not therefore a fixture of chronology; speaking to us through *all* the media of His life in humanity, and not therefore separable from the "subjective authority" of conscience, or discoverable without it; and though uniquely manifested in the "Word made flesh," yet owned by us even there only through the same Word in hearts already tinctured with the Christian consciousness.[54]

With this we come to Martineau's own view. "Conscience," he declares, "has a right to you through and through, and must be served without terms."[55] Indeed, he continues, "The deepest form of scepticism is seen in the mind which is in haste to believe; which resolves, by some violent spring, to make an end of darkness, whether the light attained be God's or not. . . . Something of this *un*faith lurks in the spirit of the new Catholic party. They recognize the ambassadorial credentials of Conscience, and show you on its casket of secrets the very signet of the King of kings:- on opening

53 Ibid., 361.

54 Ibid., 363–64.

55 Ibid., 365.

the despatch-box, you find they have stuffed in all the creeds."[56]

Over against Bible and Church, it was in conscience that Martineau found what he calls "the very 'Seat of Authority' of which I was in search."[57] To him, conscience is that faculty whereby we adjudicate the worth of conflicting motives or springs of action; the necessarian philosophy in which he had been reared left no room for such a faculty, nor for the moral governance of God.

Martineau's view has been criticised from many points of view, and I shall mention some of these in a moment. But first I wish to clear him of the oft-repeated charge of subjectivism in ethics. I have already quoted Martineau's affirmation of objective authority in religion, but against ill-judged criticism it is well to underline the point in his own words taken from four different books: "if the sense of authority means anything, it means the discernment of something *higher than we*, having claims on our *self*,—therefore no mere part of it. . . ."[58] "In the very constitution of the human soul there is provision for an immediate apprehension of God."[59] "Once bend before the authority of God, and you can reserve nothing from it: it covers every obligation: it is not that it creates another and separate sphere of duties, and adds a department to the claims upon the human will; but that it transfigures and elevates the work and affections of every relation, be it domestic, social, or political."[60] And finally: "We *cannot allow* the Conscience to resign for an instant its native right of immediate contact and audience with God: to delegate the privilege is treason; and to quit his eye is death."[61]

Martineau's psychology has been criticised—by J.S. Mackenzie, for example. "Modern Psychology," wrote Mackenzie, "treats the human mind as an organic unity, and repudiates any hard and fast distinction of faculties, such as seems implied in Martineau's

56 Ibid., 366.

57 Idem, *The Seat of Authority in Religion*, London: Longmans, Green 1890, vi.

58 Idem, *Types of Ethical Theory*, Oxford: Clarendon Press 1891, II, 104.

59 Idem, *The Seat of Authority in Religion*, 651.

60 Idem, *A Study of Religion*, Oxford: Clarendon Press, 2nd. revised edn., 1900, II, 47.

61 Quoted from Martineau's sermon on "The watch-night lamps" in James Drummond and C.B. Upton, *The Life and Letters of James Martineau*, London: Nisbet 1902, I, 200. N.H.G. Robinson would thus seem wide of the mark in listing Martineau among those who have discussed morality "in total independence of religion." See his *The Groundwork of Christian Ethics*, London: Collins 1971, 22.

list";[62] and the theologian P.T. Forsyth concurred: "Martineau had never really escaped from the old psychology which set one part or faculty of the soul to judge another. He had never really grasped the truer theory of conscience as the moral consciousness; *i.e.* as the self judging itself instead of one side or section of it judging another."[63] Moral philosophers—notably Henry Sidgwick[64]—repudiated Martineau's way of reaching ethical decisions *via* the internal appraisal of springs of interest, in favour of the consideration of the worth and likely consequences of contemplated and possible actions.

Others again found Martineau's approach too individualistic, and this despite his assertion of the way in which the acknowledgement of God in conscience fertilises all the relations of life. Thus A.S. Pringle-Pattison declared that "Martineau does scant justice to the social aspect of morality—the extent, that is, to which our actual conscience is the creature of authority, moulded by inherited institutions and customs, the product, in a word, of the age-long 'education of the human race.'"[65] Yet Pringle-Pattison quotes Martineau as saying, "If there is one modern tendency more than another against which I have striven through life with the united earnestness of natural instinct and deliberate conviction, it is the extreme individualism which turns our foremost politics, philosophy, and religion into a humiliating caricature."[66] On which Pringle-Pattison drily comments, "that merely shows how far the intellectual framework of a man's beliefs may come short of embodying the animating principle of his thought. . . ."[67] The truth of the matter would seem to be that there are two lines in Martineau's thought,[68] but that in the last resort the individual takes precedence over the social. Thus in the same book, *The Seat of Authority in Religion*, he can write, "God's part is done, when,

62 J.S. Mackenzie, *A Manual of Ethics*, London: University Tutorial Press, 6th edn., 1929, 107.

63 P.T. Forsyth, "Dr. Martineau," *The London Quarterly Review*, XCIII, N.S. vol. III 1900, 228.

64 See H. Sidgwick, *Lectures on the Ethics of T.H. Green, Mr. Herbert Spencer, and J. Martineau*, London: Macmillan 1902.

65 A.S. Pringle-Pattison, *The Philosophical Radicals and Other Essays*, Edinburgh: Blackwood 1907, 93–94.

66 J. Martineau quoted by Drummond and Upton, op. cit., I, 373; and by A.S. Pringle-Pattison, op. cit., 105.

67 A.S. Pringle-Pattison, op. cit., 105.

68 Cf. S.H. Mellone, "James Martineau as an ethical teacher," *International Journal of Ethics*, X, October 1899—July 1900, 386.

having made us free, he shows to us our best: ours now remains to pass on from illumination of the conscience to surrender of the will;"[69] and he can also ask concerning the multitude of other consciences by which we are surrounded in society, "How is it that they . . . work upon us? . . . Is it that they are principals in command, and we subordinates in service, that, accepting their will as sovereign, we are content to do their bidding? No: their function in this matter is, not to fill the post of authority, but to join us on the steps of submission below it. . . . And so, following out the moral authority of my solitary nature to human-kind, I only widen, and do not elevate, my position. . . ."[70] It would thus appear that despite the influence of nature, history and society as mediators of the sense of religion,[71] individuals, with conscience and God, are to be trusted to form moral judgments.

But can they be trusted? Here we approach the theological crux of the matter. Some have felt that Martineau himself was "too easily good." Thus, to Alexander Crauford Martineau's ethics "were rather too abstract and non-human. He assigned to the Categorical Imperative a dynamic force which it very often has not. To a large proportion of our race *mere* duty frequently seems more repulsive than attractive."[72] Others, more theologically inclined, have felt that he did not have a sufficiently acute sense of the radical effects of human sin, and of the radical remedy consequently required. As Martineau's contemporary, the Scottish theologian A.B. Bruce, put it: "He has not sufficiently borne in mind the veil that is on the face of the human soul, preventing it from seeing the light of God."[73] It is not that he had *no* sense of sin: he can speak of "the paralytic twist of sin."[74] But he too easily concludes concerning conscience that "In its retrospect . . . nay, in its very failures, it brings us to [God's] presence."[75] Does it always and necessarily do this? One of the characters in Oliver Goldsmith's novel, *The Vicar of*

69 J. Martineau, *The Seat of Authority in Religion*, 106.

70 Ibid., 67–68.

71 J. Martineau, *The Transient and the Permanent in Theology, a lecture delivered at the opening of the session of Manchester New College, London, on October 13 1862*, London: Charles Green 1862, 9–10.

72 Alexander H. Crauford, *Recollections of James Martineau*, Edinburgh: Morton 1903, 173.

73 A.B. Bruce, *Apologetics; or, Christianity Defensively Stated*, Edinburgh: T. & T. Clark 1892, 498.

74 J. Martineau, *Endeavours After the Christian Life*, (1843) 10th impression 1900, 20.

75 Idem, *A Study of Religion*, II, 35.

Wakefield, knew that it did not: "I quickly silenced [my conscience] by two or three specious reasons, which served to satisfy me and reconcile me to myself. The pain which conscience gives the man who has done wrong is soon got over. Conscience is a coward, and those faults it has not strength enough to prevent, it seldom has justice enough to accuse."[76]

Again, as the more recent Unitarian scholar Fred Kenworthy has remarked,

> it is possible for the mind to make mistakes and for the conscience to go wrong. It should never be forgotten that some of the most horrible excesses have been committed in the name of conscience, and in the best of men the line between conscience and prejudice may sometimes be finely drawn. Martineau seemed to assume that the utterances of conscience are far more clear than in fact they are to the average man, and he forgot, too, that when men see the good, and the right, they often lack the power to achieve it.[77]

In witness of this Kenworthy quotes Paul's classic cry, "For the good which I would I do not: but the evil which I would not, that I practise" (Romans 7:15). But what is Kenworthy's remedy for this predicament? He says, "Conscience, therefore, needs the help of inspiration and example."[78] What a let-down! This represents no advance upon Martineau's own position, namely, that "The exhibition of Christ as [God's] Moral Image has maintained in the souls of men a common spiritual type to correct the aberrations of their individuality, to unite the humblest and the highest, to merge all minds in one family,—and *that* the family of God."[79] We are thus left with the influence of an example, which may or may not be effective; we are not here offered a Saviour who will rescue us. No wonder Forsyth complained that Martineau "does not face the problem of revelation *to a guilty race*, which is only possible as redemption. He treats the matter as if the one thing needful were the removal of scales, instead of the restoration of the visual nerve, or even the treatment of the optic centres."[80] With this we come to

---

76 Oliver Goldsmith, *The Vicar of Wakefield*, London: Collins 1966, 88.

77 F. Kenworthy, *Freedom, Authority, and Liberal Christianity*, London: The Lindsey Press 1954, 20.

78 Ibid., 21.

79 J. Martineau, *Essays, Reviews and Addresses*, London: Longmans 1891, III, 50–51.

80 P.T. Forsyth, "Dr. Martineau," 233.

the authority of grace, and it is time briefly to survey the route we have travelled, and come to a conclusion.

IV

Newman stands for the authority of the Church, though he tempers his commitment by paying high regard to the claims of conscience. As far as the Church is concerned, Newman reminds us that Christianity is a social matter, and that the Church has and needs embodiment in this world. All of which is simply New Testament teaching. To be a Christian is to be a member (that is, a limb) of what Paul called Christ's body (I Corinthians 12:27); it is to be of what he also called the household of faith (Galatians 6:10). Christians, then, are expected and challenged to receive the Word of God declared in Scripture (this is Spurgeon's point) in fellowship. Paul hoped that Christians (saints) would be "strong to grasp, *with all God's people,* what is the breadth and length and height and depth of God's love in Christ. . ." (Ephesians 3:18).

This embodied fellowship—this ecclesial reality, if you like—extends through time and into eternity itself, and its witness, though often seriously flawed, has been present through all the Christian centuries. This long-standing witness, together with the circumstances of the day and the eternal operation of God the holy Trinity, comprise the context of the Church's reverent listening to the Word of God. There is, however blemished, a Christian tradition—with a small "t." Moreover, since Christian proclamation is not well served by fuzziness as to the central doctrines, there is everything to be said for the several Christian communions' setting down the things most commonly believed among them. Such declarations, however, are best regarded as provisional, revisible standards which are subordinate to Scripture, the primary witness to the apostles' faith; and assent to such statements (if it be demanded at all) should never be deemed the mode of entry to the kingdom of heaven.

But when the Church, conceived as an institution, is given, or acquires, magisterial functions, and where Tradition with a capital "t" is elevated into a source of truth alongside Scripture, I see warning lights. In fact in Newman's Church it is one group of persons alone which is given the magisterial function. They are the experts, who may seem to come between the individual Christian and the grace and truth the *magisterium* is supposed to proclaim and defend. Thus the consciences of many in the Church can be violated; the institution can hide itself from the prophetic voice it needs to hear; and it can become very difficult for the Church to admit error, and repent. In this way the institutional Church becomes the judge of the Gospel as surely as rationalistic deniers of the Gospel do. Above all, along this route the Church can convey the impression that the key to Christian living is obedience to the Church, rather than to Christ the Lord *of the Church*. I am the first to observe that the Vatican Council document *Dei Verbum* 10, 12, clearly states that the Church is under the Word, a position which Spurgeon would have applauded; but attempts to square Scripture and Tradition can be as tortuous as the Protestant fundamentalist's attempt to turn the Bible into a reliable textbook of science.

It goes without saying that the Jesuit Robert Nash would not share my qualms concerning the *magisterium* and Tradition with a capital "T." Against what he takes to be the Protestant alternative he argues that "the lack of such a guide [as the *magisterium*] is mainly responsible for the innumerable dissensions and contradictions which our separated brethren have to acknowledge among themselves and which Catholics view with deep sorrow. . . . In discussing a text of scripture, for instance, it is largely futile for him to insist that his interpretation must be the correct one. Why? Because all he has to go on is what he has thought out for himself. His Church allows him to accept or reject according to what seems right to himself."[81] It is somehow particularly sad when a Jesuit overlooks the Holy Spirit, who blows where he will, without so much as a "by your leave" from the *magisterium*. On the other hand, there is no smoke without fire, and some Protestants have been incautious to the point of heresy, and have given every appearance of making up the Gospel as they go along. Such Protestants, along with Fr. Nash, should write out Forsyth's words one hundred times: "as a matter of fact, the unlimited right of private judgment is not a fruit of the Reformation but of the Renaissance and of the Revolution in their wild individualism. It is Socinian and rationalist, it is not Protestant. The Reformation certainly made religion personal, but it did not make it individualist."[82] At their best the Reformers and their successors have known that the Word is discerned by the Spirit, through the Bible, in fellowship.

Together with other Christians, they have also upheld the indispensability of Scripture. In one of his satirical works, Henry Rogers, a contemporary of Newman, Spurgeon and Martineau, who was as strongly opposed to John Henry's Catholicism as he was to Francis Newman's rationalism, describes a dream of the character Mr. B.

---

81 Robert Nash in *The Sunday Press (Dublin)*, 8 February 1981.

82 P.T. Forsyth, *The Principle of Authority (1913)*, London: Independent Press 1952, 283.

Mr. B. dreams that all the pages of all Bibles have become blank! Calamity! We read that "There was universally . . . an interest in the Bible now it was *lost*, such as had never attached to it while it was *possessed*." People urgently began to try to recall the contents of Scripture. "All the ethical maxims, indeed, were soon collected; for though, as usual, no one recollected his own particular duties or infirmities, every one, as usual, kindly remembered those of his neighbours. Husbands remembered what was due from their wives, wives from their husbands. . . . Undertakers said there was 'a time to mourn;' and comedians that there was a 'time to laugh;' young ladies innumerable remembered that there was a 'time to love;' and people of all kinds that there was a 'time to hate;' everybody knew there was a 'time to speak;' but a worthy Quaker reminded them that there was also a 'time to keep silence.'"[83]

I can well imagine that Spurgeon would have enjoyed Rogers's depiction of the panic caused by a bookless revelation. And to such as Father Nash he might well have retorted in the words attributed to William Chillingworth: "The Bible, I say, the Bible only, is the religion of Protestants." Certainly *Sola Scriptura* is a prominent Reformation watchword. Over against a second authority, Tradition, equivalent in status to the Bible there is point in Chillingworth's expostulation. But in another sense the Bible is never as such the only authority which Protestants recognise. The witness of the Holy Spirit, the claims of conscience, the traditions (small "t") in which they find themselves—all of these weigh with Bible readers. The trouble, indeed, with some Protestants is that they really do seem to think that the Bible as a book is the sole authority, and then we have bibliolatry in all its legalistic ugliness. Any suggestion that biblical literalism is non-interpretive is ludicrous. Protestants, like everyone else, receive the Bible from and through the Church which determined its shape; its contents are already interpretations of the Christ event, and Protestants and others go on interpreting that event to this day. Thus, not only could Spurgeon repudiate many of the views of Newman and Martineau on biblical grounds, he also, on the same grounds, strongly dissented from the hyper-Calvinism of John Gill, his predecessor in his own Baptist pulpit. From the liberal side, during the Downgrade Controversy James Thew, also a Baptist, declared, "I *hope* I love the Holy Book, but I do not read it as Mr. Spurgeon reads it. The God of Mr. Spurgeon's theology is

---

83 Henry Rogers, *The Eclipse of Faith*, London: Longmans 1852, 231, 241–42. For Rogers, see Alan P.F. Sell, *Dissenting Thought and the Life of the Churches*, Lewiston, NY: Mellen Research University Press 1990, chs. XVII, XVIII.

not my God."[84] Small wonder that the Word needs to be received in fellowship—something which some of the more autocratic Protestant "princes of the pulpit" have been little inclined to do. When individualism undermines the body, you have interpretative anarchy. The Bible is the book of the people of God, and its authority is derived from that to which it is the chief earthly witness, the redemptive grace of God in Christ.

This grace, which called both Church and Bible into being, is the very power needed to rescue the maimed conscience, that capacity of moral appraisal, to which Newman and Martineau witnessed in their different ways, and which Spurgeon presupposed as he approached Scripture and took his conscientious stands. Hear Forsyth again: "The Reformation was not the rediscovery of the Bible chiefly, but of the Gospel in the Bible. And it stood not for the supremacy of conscience, but for the rescue of the conscience by the supremacy of Christ in it."[85] And the Christ who reigns within is the Christ who won the atoning victory in history. Hence the forceful words of the Primitive Methodist biblical scholar A.S. Peake: "Christianity is a *historical* religion, resting upon certain historical facts, and unless these facts are true the experience of which they speak is a delusion."[86] As Forsyth crisply put it, "The court is subjective, but the bench is not."[87]

I thus conclude that the supreme authority for Christians is the redemptive act of God in Christ. This authority puts all others in perspective. The Bible is rightly our supreme rule of faith and practice because it is the primary earthly witness to the saving deed, conveying to us the good news of God's deed, and the apostles' testimony to it. By this good news the Church was called forth; and the Church and our consciences, enabled by the Holy Spirit, witness to God's mighty act. Because they have rested upon this authority Christians have been enabled to resist all others—even to the death.[88] And in this authoritative act we have the content of our proclamation and the source of the unity of all things.

---

84 *Christian World*, 22 September 1887.

85 P.T. Forsyth, "The evangelical principle of authority," *Proceedings of the International Congregational Council*, II 1899, 60.

86 Letter of 9 December 1892 from Peake to his son Leslie; quoted by Leslie S. Peake, *Arthur Samuel Peake. A Memoir*, London: Hodder & Stoughton 1930, 258.

87 P.T. Forsyth, *The Principle of Authority*, 75.

88 Cf. Douglas John Hall, *Thinking the Faith. Christian Theology in a North American Context*, Minneapolis: Augsburg 1989, 433.

II

The Kaz Iwaasa Lecture

Richard Baxter and the Unity of the Church

Our century has been called the ecumenical century. There is some point in this when we recall the energy which has been expended with a view to reconciling and uniting the fragmented Church. The several Christian world communions, the World Council of Churches and the Roman Catholic Church (especially since the Second Vatican Council), have all attached great importance to Christian unity.

We should not, however, overlook the fact that Christian unity has been a concern of the Church from New Testament times onwards. Preoccupation with our own modern denominationalism should not obscure the fact that the great theological debates of the early Christian centuries, which resulted in the so-called ecumenical creeds of the Church, had as their objective unity of belief with a view to united church life and witness. This reference to the formative period of Christian theology reminds us that when we speak of ecumenism or of church unity we are not simply, or primarily, speaking of attempts to glue existing denominations together, or to engage in what has been called ecclesiastical joinery.

The truth is that *we* do not create or concoct the unity of the Church at all. The Church's unity resides in the Church's Lord. As Paul reminded the Ephesians, there is "one Lord, one faith, one baptism, one God and Father of all, who is over all and through all and in all."[1] We do not invent this unity: it is God's gift to his people. By his Spirit we are called through the Word to constitute God's reconciled people—a people reconciled to God by the saving work of Christ, and *therefore* reconciled to one another. To be "in Christ" at all is to be at one with all others who are "in Christ."

1 Ephesians 4:5.

This is by no means a call to flat and boring uniformity. Paul recognises that there are "varieties of gifts;" that the Church is a body with many limbs, none of which may say to any of the others, "we do not need you."[2] But it is very definitely a challenge to Christians to set their faces against sectarianism of all kinds. "Sectarianism," writes James Torrance, "arises when two things happen, first when any group or church makes an absolute identification between their formulations of the truth and the Truth, and then secondly says, 'We shall only accept you IF you accept our formulations!'"[3] I would add that sectarianism similarly results when any group or church elevates its own cherished practices into terms of fellowship, cutting off those who do things differently. It is not without significance that much of Paul's teaching as to the Church's given unity was called forth by sectarianism. At Corinth, you recall, he was repudiating factions and party spirit in the church. The Christians there were saying, "'I am Paul's man,' or 'I am for Apollos,' 'I follow Cephas,' or 'I am Christ's.'" In response Paul protests, "Surely Christ has not been divided among you!"[4] The point is that, do what they may, Christians *cannot* break the fundamental unity into which they have been called by God's grace. They can, however, render it opaque by sectarianism, and they must strive to manifest the unity in Christ which they have been given.

As the Puritan Thomas Shepard (1604–1649) wrote in his now quaint-sounding way, "It is the delight of Hell to set & see Churches at variance among themselves."[5] Few understood this more clearly, or worked more zealously for the manifestation of Christian unity than Richard Baxter: "We still profess before men and Angels," he wrote, "that we own no Religion but the Christian Religion, nor any Church but the Christian Church, nor dream of any Catholick Church but one, containing all the true Christians in the world, united in Jesus Christ the Head."[6] In further reflecting upon Christian unity we shall take our starting point from Baxter, the tercentenary of whose death falls this year.

---

2 I Corinthians 12:14–31.

3 James B.[incorrectly given as "D" *ad loc.*] Torrance, "Sectarianism and the Gospel of grace," *PACE*, XVIII, no. 1, Spring 1986, 3.

4 I Corinthians 12:12.

5 Thomas Shepard, *The Parable of the Ten Virgins opened and applied*, 1660, 8.

6 Richard Baxter, *Key for Catholicks*, 1659, Preface, 6.

I

Richard Baxter was born at his mother's home at Rowton, near Shrewsbury, Shropshire, on Sunday 12 November 1615. There he remained until the family removed about ten miles to Eaton-Constantine in the parish of Leighton-under-Wrekin. His father, also Richard, was converted from a dissolute life at about the time of Baxter's birth, and from that time forward was a good and upright Christian. Baxter received his early education from a succession of less than efficient Anglican curates, of whom only one was morally suited to his calling. He then proceeded, aged fifteen, to the endowed school at Wroxeter, where the master was John Owen. Though patchy, the education given would have sufficed to admit Baxter to Oxford, but Owen advised against this, recommending that Baxter become the one pupil permitted to Richard Wickstead, chaplain to the council at Ludlow. Consumed by the necessities of his own personal advancement, Wickstead was a neglectful tutor, but in the library of Ludlow Castle Baxter eagerly repaired the omissions in his education.

In 1633 Baxter allowed himself to be persuaded by Wickstead to embark upon the life of a courtier in London, but he could tolerate this for only one month. His mother's sickness hastened his return to Shropshire, and she died on 10 May 1634. By now Baxter was seriously inclined towards the Christian ministry, and he had already been impressed by a number of writings—especially those of such Puritans as Richard Sibbes and William Perkins. He began the serious study of theology under Francis Garbet, the incumbent of Wroxeter, and in 1638 the way opened for him to become a schoolmaster at Dudley. He was ordained by Bishop Thornborough of Worcester, and licensed to teach. Thence to Bridgnorth as assistant to William Madstard, and, in 1641, on as lecturer to Kidderminster, with which Worcestershire town he will be for ever associated.

Less than two years later the Civil War broke out, and though Baxter in principle favoured the monarchy, he felt that on this occasion right was on the side of the Parliament. He was thus in a precarious position in strongly royalist Worcestershire, and for most of the next three years he lived in comparative peace in Coventry, though he found himself in intense controversy with Anabaptist sectaries. Following the battle of Naseby (1645) he became a chaplain to Colonel Whalley's regiment.

Never robust, he suffered many periods of ill health. He spent one such period, in 1647, in the home of Lady Rouse, and whilst there wrote what has become a classic of Puritan spirituality, *The Saint's Everlasting Rest* (1650). In the meantime Baxter had returned to Kidderminster, where he preached, wrote pamphlets (some of them controversial), and catechised, visited and even doctored the flock. The rich harvest of his pastoral reflections is gathered in his book *Gildas Salvianus; or The Reformed Pastor* (1656), a work which continues in print to this day.

In 1660 Baxter removed to London, where he worked for the restoration of the King—a matter accomplished in the same year. He was made a chaplain to the King, and offered the see of Hereford, which he declined. His request to return to Kidderminster was not granted. On 13 May 1662, three days before the Act of Uniformity became law, he left the Established Church. The Act required all ministers of religion and schoolmasters to give their "unfeigned assent and content" to the *Book of Common Prayer* of the Church of England, or forfeit their livings. In view of his conviction that Scripture was the supreme rule of faith and order, and his opinion that some features of the Prayer Book were only doubtfully in accord with the Bible, if that, Baxter, like some two thousand other ministers between 1660–62 became a reluctant nonconformist, with all the legal impositions which that entailed.[7]

Baxter preached when circumstances permitted, and publications flowed from his pen. Like many others he was intermittently hounded by the authorities, and was for a time in prison. His was one of the kindlier prison régimes. He writes:

> My Imprisonment was at present no great Suffering to me, for I had an honest jaylor, who showed me all the Kindness he could; I had a large room, and the liberty of walking in a fair Garden; and my Wife was never so cheerful a Companion to me as in Prison, and was very much against my seeking to be released, and she had brought so many Necessaries that we kept House as contentedly and comfortably as at home, though in a narrower room, and I had the sight of more of my Friends in a day than I had at home in half a Year. . . . And the number of Visitors by day did put me out of hope of Studying, or doing anything but entertain them.[8]

Baxter's wife Margaret, whom he had married in 1662, was a saint indeed. Alexander Gordon, no sentimentalist, described her as a "delicately nurtured royalist gentlewoman who, in the freshness of her vivid powers, gave her once giddy heart to the outcast invalid of

---

7 See further ch. V below.

8 R. Baxter, *Reliquiae Baxterianae* (hereinafter referred to as RB), ed. M. Sylvester, 1696, III, 50–51, para. 119.

forty-seven, and having married him when his fortunes were at the lowest, identified herself with every interest of his, at first in a trembling diffidence, at length with an angelic courage."[9] On 14 June 1681 Margaret died, and in the same year Baxter wrote a most moving "Breviate" of her life.

Towards the end of his days Baxter was in prison once more—from 28 February 1684/5 to 24 November 1686. On his release he continued to preach and lecture as he was able; saw the accession of William and Mary in 1688, and, like many though not all others, was granted religious liberty by the Toleration Act of 1689; completed his autobiography, *Reliquiae Baxterianae*; and died on 8 December 1691. The funeral oration was delivered by the "silver-tongued" William Bates,[10] and Baxter was laid to rest beside his wife and her mother in Christ Church, London.

Such are the bare bones of the life and career of Richard Baxter—except that I have so far omitted his major concern: the unity of Christians and the peace of the Church. To this we must now turn.

II

From which ecclesiastical vantage point did Richard Baxter view the Church? The question sounds straightforward enough, but the answer to it is not immediately apparent. The difficulty can be demonstrated if we juxtapose the opening words of A.B. Grosart's *Dictionary of National Biography* article on Baxter with some of Baxter's own pronouncements upon himself. Grosart's article begins, "Baxter, Richard (1615–1691), presbyterian divine." Our confidence in this bold assertion is somewhat shaken by Baxter's refusal to be labelled by what he called "the odious Name."[11] There is the further complication of the meaning to be assigned to "Presbyterian." According to the English Presbyterian polity devised and defended by Thomas Cartwright and others, the governance of the local congregation was in the hands of its own session (comprising the elected elders); wider bodies such as classes and synods had advisory roles only. In Scottish Presbyterianism, by contrast, the higher courts of the church were deemed to be increasingly authoritative. By Baxter's time, in the English Presbyterianism of the period from the beginning of the Civil War to the Restoration of

9 A. Gordon, *Heads of English Unitarian History*, London: Philip Green 1895, 58.

10 For William Bates (1625–1699) see *The Dictionary of National Biography*.

11 Richard Baxter, RB I.ii. 373, para. 242.

the monarchy in 1660, the laity heavily outnumbered the ministers in church governance, whereas in Scotland they were supposed to serve in equal proportions. Baxter did not decidedly opt for either of these positions. He certainly upheld the authority of the minister, and was highly suspicious of congregationalist tendencies which, he thought, fostered sectarianism. He was in favour of the widest possible association of evangelical ministers whatever their favoured polity, though he himself preferred the old system of incumbent and church wardens. He was also known for his advocacy of "moderate Episcopacy."[12] In this he was in the line of Archbishop James Ussher (1581–1656), who had, on biblical grounds, argued for a pastoral, servant-like episcopacy over against a prelacy appointed and guaranteed by royal command and favour, and which alone was deemed competent to ordain. Baxter never wavered in his view. As late as 1680, in his reply to Henry Dodwell entitled, *A treatise of Episcopacy*, he distinguished between the older and the newer idea of bishops in favour of the former. Two years later, in a further pamphlet, *An answer to Mr. Dodwell and Dr. Sherlocke*, he trounced the notion of an *Universal Humane Church-Sovereignty, Aristocratical and Monarchial, as Church-Tyranny and Popery.*[13] By contending that ordination could be only at the hands of certain bishops, the new bishops and those who supported them were in effect unchurching the early Church and violating the Scriptures.[14] He did not hesitate to brand the prelates sectarians: "Whoever be the Sect-Masters, it is notorious, That the Prelates (tho' not they only) are the Sect-makers," he declared.[15] But he was equally zealous against those who separated from the Established Church: they also had imbibed the sectarian spirit. Prelates and sectaries alike were disrupting the peace of the Church. In walking the line he did, Baxter was open to attack from either side, and attacked he was. Indeed, his mediating way brought trouble upon him in other ways too, as we shall see. But for the moment we may agree with J.M. Lloyd Thomas, that Baxter "died as he lived, a moderate Episcopalian."[16] In Baxter's own words, "I am a CHRISTIAN, a MEER CHRISTIAN. . . . If the name Christian be not enough, call me a

---

12 Ibid., I.ii. 281, para. 120.

13 See ibid., III 189, para. 65; cf. 188.

14 Ibid., I.ii. 401, 403, paras. 323, 332.

15 Ibid., III.i.43, para. 99.

16 J.M. Lloyd Thomas, *The Autobiography of Richard Baxter*, London: J.M. Dent 1931, Introduction, xix.

CATHOLICK CHRISTIAN."[17] A year later he underlined the point: "You could not (except a Catholick Christian) have trulier called me, than an Episcopal-Presbyterian-Independent."[18]

Another of Baxter's self-descriptions was that he was "but a Pen in God's hand;"[19] and where the unity of Christans was concerned he was prolific: Christian Concord (1653); *Catholick Unity* (1660), and in the same year, *Universal Concord* and *The True Catholick and Catholick Church Described; The Cure of Church Divisions* (1670); *The True and Only Way of Concord* (1680); and *Catholick Communion Defended* (1684).

That Baxter was no armchair ecumenist is clear from numerous enterprises in which he was involved. "God," he wrote in 1653, "hath possessed my heart with such a burning desire after the peace & unity of the churches that I cannot forget it, or lay it by."[20] A year previously he had broached the possibility of an association of pastors and churches in Worcestershire, and in the following year the idea came to fruition. His colleagues invited him to draft the terms of a working agreement, and the result was his *Christian Concord: of the Agreement of the Associated Pastors and Churches of Worcestershire,* to which I have just referred. The Worcestershire Association was to be a voluntary association "adhering to no Faction; neither Episcopal, Presbyterian nor Independent, as to Parties; but desiring Union, and loving that which is good in all."[21] Something of the influence of the Association is revealed in the fact that, as Geoffrey Nuttall's researches have shown, "Within the first three years of [its] life as many as seventy-two ministers are known to have joined it,"[22] some of them from neighbouring counties. The bulk of the members were Episcopalians or Presbyterians. Baxter recalled that there were about five or six Independents only in the county, and of these just one joined the

17 R. Baxter, *Church-History of the Government of Bishops and their Councils abbreviated*, 1681, Preface, fol b1.

18 Idem, *Third Defence of the Cause of Peace*, 1681, I, 110.

19 William Bates, *A Funeral Sermon for . . . Richard Baxter . . . with some Account of His Life*, 1692, 125.

20 DWL Baxter MSS. Letters, VI, 94. Baxter to John Dury, 5 February 1652(3). I am grateful to Dr. Neil Keeble of the University of Stirling for checking this reference for me.

21 R. Baxter, RB I.i. 90, para. 137.

22 Geoffrey F. Nuttall, *Richard Baxter*, London: Nelson 1965, 68.

Association.[23] Monthly meetings were held at various Worcestershire towns, and there was a quarterly general meeting too. The ministers read, heard and discussed papers, and interested themselves in evangelisation and catechising. The Association's existence and success encouraged those of like mind in other parts of the country, though the several associations which were formed were not identical in every respect. Thus, for example, although Baxter favoured legislation to legalise ordinations performed by associations, the Worcestershire Association did not actually ordain ministers, whereas those of Cumberland and Westmorland and Devonshire did.

A bare list will indicate something of the range of Baxter's other activities towards unity. In 1654 he was among those appointed by Parliament to establish a list of the fundamentals of Christian belief to be adhered to by all whose religion was to be tolerated in the land. Baxter's view was that toleration should be granted to all who affirmed the creed, the Lord's Prayer and the decalogue.[24] Others retorted that this would include Papists and Socinians: "So much the better," declared Baxter. "If you are afraid of communion with *Papists* and *Socinians*," he continued, "it must not be avoided by making a new Rule or Test which they will not Subscribe to, or by forcing others to Subscribe to more than *they* can do, but by calling them to account whenever in Preaching or Writing they contradict or abuse the Truth to which they have Subscribed."[25] The formidable Independent, John Owen, disagreed, and a group of his colleagues, including Thomas Goodwin, Philip Nye and Sydrach Simpson, drafted a specific set of "The principles of faith," to which assent would be required. In the event, as Daniel Neal drily relates, "the parliament being abruptly dissolved, they were all buried in oblivion."[26]

In 1661 Baxter was involved in Prayer Book revision designed to make for peace in the Church, and in 1669 he was again in controversy with John Owen over the fundamentals of the faith.

---

23 Richard Baxter, RB, II. 148, para. 28. Though Dr. Nuttall has pointed out that in 1672 four members of the Association took out licenses as Congregationalists. See his "The Worcestershire Association: its membership," *Journal of Ecclesiastical History*, I, no. 2, 1950, 204.

24 Ibid., II.198, para. 52.

25 Ibid.

26 Not quite! They were certainly set aside, but Neal was able to reproduce them in his *History of the Puritans*, ed. J. Toulmin, 1793–1797, IV, 98–100. They are also in the British Library at "England: Churches and Religious Bodies: Committee of Divines, 1654."

Owen wished to make Scripture and the deliverances of the first four Councils of the Church the standard of orthodoxy on the ground that, despite Scripture, heresy had found its way into the early Church . . . Baxter persisted in his conviction that by increasing the number of "fundamentals" one fed sectarianism and promoted hypocrisy. He grounded on the principle of the sufficiency of Scripture and, using Owen's example of Socinianism, declared "If there be nothing against *Socinianism* in Scripture, it is no Heresie: If there be (as sure there is enough, and plain enough) Judge them by that Rule, and make not new ones."[27]

Throughout his life Baxter opposed the separatist principle, and he strongly repudiated the charge of separation when it was lodged against him in 1680 by Dr. Edward Stillingfleet. Writes Baxter, "Dr. *Stillingfleet* being made Dean of *Pauls* was put on as the most plausible Writer to begin the assault against us, which he did in a printed Sermon proving me and such Others Schismaticks and Separatists. To which I gave an answer which I thought satisfactory. . . . To all of which he wrote some what like a Reply. Against this I Wrote a second Defence, which he never answered."[28]

In the wake of the Toleration Act of 1689 (from the provisions of which Roman Catholics and anti-trinitarians were excluded), renewed attempts were made to unite the Independents or Congregationalists with the Presbyterians. Both parties were now legally outside of the Establishment, and they needed to build places of worship, and to fund and to train their ministers. Under the indulgence of 1672 they had already established a joint Lectureship at the Pinners' Hall, but now a more formal union was envisaged which would entail the dropping of their traditional ecclesiastical labels. A Common Fund was set up in 1691, and in the following year the *Heads of Agreement assented to by the United Ministers in and about London* was published. Though realising that such a union spelled the end of his hopes of comprehension within an Established Church, Baxter, on 23 April 1691, wrote an encouraging letter "To the United Protestant Nonconformists in London."[29]

Sadly, although the example of the London ministers was followed in some other parts of the land with more permanent results, the London union was soon in ruins and, for all his desire for union, Baxter was as much to blame as anyone else. Indeed, in view

---

27 Richard Baxter, RB, III.62, para. 143.

28 Ibid., III.187–88, paras. 54–55. See *Richard Baxters answer to Dr. Edward Stillingfleet's charge of separation*, 1680; idem, *A Second Defence of the Meer Nonconformists*, 1681.

29 It is added to the Preface of his *Church Concord*, 1691.

of his Pinners' Hall Lecture of 28 January 1690, it is remarkable that the ship of union was floated at all. Never the diplomat,[30] he there launched a stern attack on antinomianism—the doctrine that since we are saved by grace alone our actions, whether good or ill, can neither contribute to our salvation nor deprive us of it. Baxter had fought this doctrine for fifty years, and now here it was in public view once more through the posthumous publication of Tobias Crisp's sermons.[31] To Baxter, antinomianism fostered anti-rational, instinctive religion, and this he despised.[32] What made matters worse, according to Baxter, was that some of his trusted colleagues, including John Howe (who afterwards admitted that he had read neither the preface nor the sermons, and was known not to be an antinomian), had signed their names to the Preface. He could not understand why they had given their names "to be hanged up like a sign before the door of a House of Seduction."[33] Not altogether surprisingly, a later writer, looking back, referred to "the first Thunder-Clap of this Nature in Pinners' Hall."[34]

Again, Baxter's own mediating theology made him appear as a trimmer to some. To put a complicated matter bluntly: where the high Calvinists taught that the elect are saved by God's free, unmerited grace alone, while the non-elect are passed by; and the Arminians held that God's grace in Christ is sufficient for all if only they will to be saved—and they can so will; Baxter maintained that both free grace and free will must be held together, and that since the saved received more grace than the unsaved, they are competent to fulfil the new law of Christ. Into the complications of this view, sometimes called Baxterianism, sometimes Neonomianism, we need not enquire. Suffice it to say that Baxter's moderation appeared as vacillation to his opponents on the high Calvinist side. They charged him with having done more to advance the cause of popery than any papist: this, be it remembered, at a time when Rome was not only hated by many, but feared on political grounds.

---

30 In this connection it is instructive to compare the characters of Baxter and Cromwell. The latter's diplomacy appeared to Baxter as opportunism or insincerity. See F.J. Powicke, "Baxter and Cromwell," *Congregational Historical Society Transactions* X, no. 3, April 1928, 124–35.

31 For a fuller account of the doctrinal context, see Alan P.F. Sell, *The Great Debate: Calvinism, Arminianism and Salvation*, Worthing: H.E. Walter (now Bletchley: Word Books) 1982, Grand Rapids: Baker Book House 1983, ch. II.

32 R. Baxter, *The Scripture Gospel Defended*, 1690.

33 R. Baxter, Preface to part two of *The Scripture Gospel Defended*, 15 January 1689/90.

34 Joseph Hussey, *The Glory of Christ Unveil'd*, 1706, 209.

The third cause of strife was over church government. Baxter could not rest easily with the Congregational idea of the church as the company of gathered believers. In his opinion this view tended "to extirpate Godliness out of the Land; by taking a very few that can talk more than the rest, and making them the Church, and shutting out more that are as worthy, and by neglecting the Souls of all the Parish else, except as to some publick Preaching."[35]

Amid such tensions the London union could not survive (though, as I said, in other parts unions fared better), and within three years it was no more. Though Baxter did not live to see the break-up, it cannot be denied that his angularity fostered it. But if he was not always methodologically peaceable, we can only agree with his self-assessment that the "preaching of peace" between Christians was "the very drift of my doctrine and life, though I speak sharply against Peace-breakers."[36] Clearly, he was in advance of most in those partisan times. Many would simply not have understood his advice that "he that would procure the Welfare of the Church must do his best to promote all the *Truth* and Good which was held by every part, and to leave out all their Errors and their Evil; and not take up all that any party has espoused as their own."[37] Not surprisingly, he found himself in an uncomfortable position: "I will go sometimes on both sides the Hedge, though by so doing I be scratcht."[38] To change the metaphor: if Baxter sat on the fence he did so not out of apathy but from conviction and with a view to gathering others to join him. But few did, and so the greatest ecumenist of the seventeenth century was almost entirely isolated. Nevertheless, as he wrote, "The Gospel dieth not when I die: The Church dieth not: The Praises of God die not: the Word dieth not: . . . it may be some of the seed that I have sowen, shall spring up to some benefit of the dark unpeacable World when I am dead."[39]

35 R. Baxter, RB, III.67, para. 143.

36 Idem, *Plain Scripture Proof of Infants Church-Membership and Baptism*, 1653, Preface.

37 Idem, RB, II.141, para. 10.

38 Idem, *A Third Defence of the Cause of Peace*, 1681, II, 85.

39 Idem, *Richard Baxter's Dying Thoughts*, 1683, 115.

III

We may well imagine that some of the things that have happened since Baxter's day towards the manifestation of the Church's God-given unity would rejoice his heart. Building upon a good deal of earlier inter-denominational cooperation, of which the British and Foreign Bible Society (1804), the Y.M.C.A. (1844) and the Evangelical Alliance (1846) are examples; building upon the experience of the several modern confessional groupings, of which the World Presbyterian Alliance (1875) was the first to be constituted; and building also upon international meetings designed to promote mission, which were held in London in 1878 and 1888 and New York in 1900, considerable ecumenical advances have been made during the twentieth century.

In the wake of the World Missionary Conference held at Edinburgh in 1910 there was created the International Missionary Council (1921). Concerns for peace and justice prompted the convening of the Universal Christian Conference on Life and Work at Stockholm in 1925; and the first World Conference on Faith and Order was held at Lausanne in 1927. All of these generated continuing activity, and eventually Life and Work and Faith and Order coalesced in the World Council of Churches (1948), to be joined by the International Missionary Council in 1961.[40] In the meantime regional unions of churches had begun to take place in may parts of the world. Some of these were inner-family unions, as when many Scottish Presbyterians came together in 1929, English Methodists in 1932, and American Presbyterians in 1983. Other unions have crossed traditional confessional lines, as when Presbyterians and Congregationalists came together with Methodists in Canada (1925), Zambia (1965) and Australia (1977). The Church of North India (1970) has the most diverse heritage of all, encompassing as it does former Anglicans, Baptists, Brethren and Disciples, as well as Presbyterians, Congregationalists and Methodists. It would be quite wrong to present church union as a bed of roses, or to suppose that the results of every union are alike in all respects. A detailed scholarly comparative analysis of the several united churches is much to be desired, but at least we can say that the

40 For the history see *A History of the Ecumenical Movement 1517–1948*, eds. Ruth Rouse and Stephen Charles Neill, London: SPCK 1954; Norman Goodall, *The Ecumenical Movement: what it is and what it does*, London: OUP, 2nd edn., 1964.

task of union has been successfully completed in diverse parts of the world.

The Second Vatican Council (1962–1965)[41] gave further impetus towards Christian unity, for it led to the establishment of the Secretariat for Promoting Christian Unity, through which body the Roman Catholic Church has engaged in international bilateral dialogues with a number of Christian traditions. In turn, many non-Roman Catholic communions have engaged in international bilateral dialogue with each other, while the multilateral dialogue, sponsored by the Faith and Order Department of the World Council of Churches, and with Roman Catholic theologians as full participants, resulted in the publication of the booklet, *Baptism, Eucharist and Ministry* (1982).[42] This report both reveals important points of convergence on doctrinal matters and exposes certain neuralgic issues which clamour for further attention.[43] In addition to the international dialogues there have been many regional ones and the hope, sometimes realised, is always that wider and more local dialogues will mutually aid each other.

In response to the pessimistic lament that despite all the talk there is little theological advance, I may perhaps refer to just five recommendations from five dialogues in which my own Christian family has been involved.[44] These seem to me to constitute significant advances. First, in the Roman Catholic-Reformed international dialogue report the clear statement is made that "The sacrifice brought by Jesus Christ is his obedient life and death. (cf. Hebrews 10:5–10; Philippians 2:8). His once-for-all self-offering under Pontius Pilate is continued by him for ever in the presence of the

---

41 For the relevant documents see, e.g., *Vatican Council II. The Conciliar and Post Conciliar Documents*, ed. Austin Flannery, Collegeville, MN: Liturgical Press 1975.

42 Published Geneva: World Council of Churches.

43 See the series of official responses to the document, ed. Max Thurian *et al.*: Churches Respond to BEM, Geneva: World Council of Churches 1985, etc. For an account of the response of one communion to BEM, in which special attention is paid to matters requiring further treatment, see Alan P.F. Sell, "Some Reformed responses to *Baptism, Eucharist and Ministry*," *The Reformed World*, XXXIX, no. 3, September 1986, 549–65.

44 For a full-scale critical analysis along systematic lines of the theological contribution of the World Alliance of Reformed Churches from its inception to 1982 see Alan P.F. Sell, *A Reformed, Evangelical, Catholic Theology*, Grand Rapids: Eerdmans 1991.

Father in virtue of his resurrection."[45] This emphasis upon the once-for-all-ness of Christ's sacrifice should allay Reformed fears that Christ is believed to be sacrificed again every time the mass is observed. Secondly, among the nine recommendations of the Anglican-Reformed international dialogue report is the following: "We recommend that where churches of our two communions are committed to going forward to seek visible unity, a measure of *reciprocal* communion should be made possible; for communion is not only a sign of unity achieved, but also a means by which God brings it about."[46] We may hope that this will make it easier for Anglicans to respond to invitations to communion in Churches of the Reformed tradition when the two families are moving towards union. Unity in the Gospel, which is presupposed whenever pulpit exchanges are arranged, and in all local ecumenical projects, requires unity at the table. Thirdly, building upon the European *Leuenberg Agreement* (1973) the report of the international Lutheran-Reformed dialogue urges the participating bodies "to declare full communion with one another"—which means, among other things, "Establishing full pulpit and altar/table fellowship, with the necessary mutual recognition of ministers ordained for word and sacrament."[47] Were this recommendation acted upon around the world the four-hundred-year-old breach between two major branches of the Reformation tradition would be well on the way to being healed. Fourthly, the report of the international Reformed-Methodist dialogue declared that "the classical doctrinal issues [on which the two communions have differed] ought not to be seen as obstacles to unity between Methodists and Reformed,"[48] and it recommended attention to those parts of the world in which Reformed and Methodists are not yet united. Finally, the report of the international dialogue between the Reformed and the Disciples of Christ concluded: "we believe there are no theological or ecclesiological

45 *The Presence of Christ in Church and World. Dialogue between the World Alliance of Reformed Churches and the Secretariat for Promoting Christian Unity, 1970–77*, Geneva: WARC and Rome: Secretariat for Promoting Christian Unity 1977, 23.

46 *God's Reign and Our Unity. The Report of the Anglican-Reformed International Commission 1981–1984*, London: SPCK and Edinburgh: The Saint Andrew Press 1984, 82.

47 *Toward Closer Fellowship. Report of the Joint Commission of the Lutheran World Federation and the World Alliance of Reformed Curches*, Geneva: LWF and WARC 1989, 28.

48 *Reformed and Methodists in Dialogue. Report of the Reformed/Methodist Conversations (1985 and 1987)*, Geneva: WARC 1988, 14.

issues which need divide us as churches,"[49] and it proposed practical ways in which the unity in Christ of the two families could be expressed locally, regionally and internationally.

Encouraging though these recommendations are, it cannot be said that they have been taken up with enthusiasm around the world. At the most basic level, it is not easy to communicate dialogue findings in the multi-linguistic families of Christians to which they relate. Secondly, not much practical outcome can reasonably be expected in regions where one or other of the partners in an international dialogue is not present. Again, some regard ecclesiological discussions of this kind as a "Western" hobby which need not engage the attention of those of other cultures—this notwithstanding the Christian divisions and even multiple secessions which are evident in many non-Western places. Others, more loftily, declare that their concern is more with evangelism, or with pressing socio-political concerns—as if the evangel were not precisely that which makes Christans one and gives them a concern for the well-being of persons in all their relations and needs.[50] There is also the perennial problem to which John Locke referred in Baxter's time: "The dissenting congregations, are supposed by their teachers, to be more accurately instructed in matters of faith than the vulgar conformists. . . . But I ask them to tell me seriously, whether half their people have leisure to study? Nay, whether one in ten of those who come to their meetings in the country, if they had time to study, do or can understand the controversies at this time so warmly managed among them, about justification."[51]

When all allowances have been made, I continue to find it sad that in England, for example, little if any progress has been made with the Church of England over reciprocal intercommunion, and that in Canada the striking results of the international Lutheran-Reformed dialogue have not been more widely reported in the major Lutheran Church and the local Reformed Churches: the Presbyterian, Reformed and United. For the dialogues, far from being genial gatherings of *ad hoc* groups of ecumenical hobbyists, were officially sanctioned commissions, whose findings ought at the very least to be noted. There will always be a time-lag between paper theological

49 *Towards Closer Fellowship. Report of the Dialogue between Reformed and Disciples of Christ*, Geneva: WARC 1988, 14.

50 For a critique of the attitude which would seek to drive wedges between evangelism, ecumenism and social witness see *God's Reign and Our Unity*, 10–12, 19–22.

51 John Locke, *Reasonableness of Christianity*, ed. I.T. Ramsey, Stanford: Stanford University Press 1958, 76.

advances and their reception down to the grass roots—especially given the great internal diversity of the communions in dialogue. But we must ever draw a distinction between understandable delay and the wilful ignoring of possible lines of advance.

What most disturbs is the not altogether unfounded suspicion that in some cases the ignoring is a product of a sectarian spirit which is still too alive and well in Christian circles: indeed, it would seem that new temptations to sectarianism lie before us as we approach Christianity's third millennium. We shall, I think, do well to reflect with some care upon sectarian possibilities old and new.

IV

You will recall that at the outset I quoted James Torrance as saying that sectarianism results when a group decides that its *formulation* of the truth equals the whole truth, and when it then proceeds to unchurch those who see things differently. To this I added the thought that when a group decides that its favoured practices—rites or rituals—constitute the true Church, and that those who do not share them are lesser Christians if Christians at all, you have the same sectarian result. There is nothing new in any of this, and the pages of Christian history are sullied with the dire results of it. We find it in the New Testament itself: indeed, we might, as shorthand, attach the label "Galatian heresy" to the tendencies I have in mind. For why did Paul write so sternly to the Galatian Christians? Precisely because they were elevating non-essentials into criteria of the true Church, thereby making the Gospel of God's sheer grace appear inadequate or insufficient on its own to save and call the Church into being. In particular, Paul's Galatian opponents were saying that the way into the Church was by the pathway of Jewish tradition, of which circumcision was a prominent symbol. No, retorted Paul: that is another Gospel which is no Gospel at all. Salvation is by God's free grace in Christ plus nothing.[52]

There have been times in the history of the Church when it has been believed that unless a person was in fellowship with a specific Christian communion, that person could not be saved. Thus despite a variety of earlier more liberal statements on the matter, Pope Pius IX declared in 1854 that "it must be held as 'of faith' that outside the Apostolical Roman Church no one can be saved"; though he did go on to add that those in invincible ignorance of "the true religion"

52 See Galatians 1.

are not guilty in God's eyes.[53] Lest any should think that the Roman Church has the monopoly on such language, I draw your attention to an entry in the diary of the Welsh Calvinistic methodist, Howel Harris, for 10 March 1740. On that day his evangelistic itinerary took him to Glandwr, where hundreds gathered. He writes, "Heard dreadful things here of Rees Davies of the Anabaptists. . . . On receiving some to communion last time at Rhydwilym near here, they asked the young ones if they thought all were damned that were out of their persuasion, they said they thought they were damned."[54]

Generally today we are not so eager to claim such detailed knowledge of the eternal fate of individuals; but we certainly find that certain doctrines and/or practices are elevated into principles of exclusion from full fellowship—from fellowship at the Lord's table, for example. Nor does this come from just one wing of the Church. Thus, on the one hand we find Catholics (whether Roman or Anglican) who will say, "Until your ministerial orders are of a kind we can approve, we will not receive communion from you"—to which some add the clause, "and until you are in communion with us, you may not receive the sacrament in our church."[55] On the other hand, and as their mirror image, we find Protestants who will say, "Because you have not been baptised by immersion on profession of faith, you may not receive communion in our Church." All of which raises the question of polity, of church order. Time would fail to tell of the thousands of pamphlets which have been written to proclaim that episcopalianism, or presbyterianism, or congregationalism is the only defensible polity because it is the only biblical one. Two things may briefly be said. First, the reading of one's favoured polity out of Scripture cannot be done with integrity, for modern biblical scholarship has made it quite clear that while the New Testament gives a diversity of *hints* as to how the Church is to be governed, it lays down no one polity for all time. Thus, as somebody once said with respect to the Bible and polity, "Everyone has won, and all shall have prizes." Secondly, even when it has been agreed that there is only one defensible polity, the sectarian spirit has not been banished. Far from it: the secessionist spirit has often been

53 Allocution *Singulari quadam*, in D. Carl Mirbt, *Quellen zur Geschichte des Papstums und des römischen Katholizismus*, Tübingen: Mohr 1911, 349.

54 *Howell Harris's Visits to Pembrokeshire*, transcribed by Tom Beynon, Aberystwyth: The Cambrian News Press 1966, 24.

55 For a fuller discussion of ministry and sacraments vis-à-vis the Gospel see Alan P.F. Sell, *Aspects of Christian Integrity*, Calgary: University of Calgary Press 1990, and Louisville: Westminster/John Knox Press 1991, ch. III, espec. 93–96.

rife. Recall the tale of Presbyterian secessions in eighteenth-century Scotland, and note that such inner-Presbyterian sectarianism is not dormant to this day. It has been estimated that in the last thirty years more than fifty new Presbyterian denominations have been organised in South Korea. Nor are other Christian families immune from the secessionist spirit, however much they agree on polity. I heard recently of a believer-Baptist denomination in the United States which has fragmented into more than twenty-five branches. On all of which an impartial observer commented to my informant, "I don't know what you people put in your baptismal water: you all go down into the water peaceable and friendly, and you all come up arguing!"

Now it is perfectly possible and justifiable to believe that some ways of ordering the Church are more in keeping with biblical teaching than others. I happen to think that a church polity which does not take seriously the *corporate* priesthood of all believers is to that extent lacking. But I need not and should not unchurch those who order their churchly life differently; nor should I have to wait until I am in communion with them in a technical ecclestiastical sense before I can receive the Lord's Supper from them, or they from me. In the only sense which finally matters, if they and I have been called by God and given grace to acknowledge Christ as Lord and Saviour, we are already in communion whether we know it, agree with it, or like it, or not. The only proper response is to manifest that God-given union. As the wise Anglican friend of John Bunyan, William Dell wrote, "What wild and woful work do men make when they will have the Church of God thus and thus, and get the power of the magistrate to back them, as if the new heavens wherein the Lord will dwell must be the work of their own fingers, or as if the New Jerusalem must of necessity come out of the Assembly of Divines at Westminster."[56]

What Baxter wrote concerning creeds and confessions applies equally to orders and polity: indeed we may urge it against the Galatian heresy in whatever form it comes: "Two things have set the Church on fire, and been the plagues of it above one thousand years. 1. Enlarging our Creed, and making more fundamentals then ever God made. 2. Composing (and so imposing) Creeds and Confessions in our own words and phrases."[57] That fuel for fires can still be found is clear from the newer sectarian possibilities to which I now turn.

---

56 Quoted by John Brown, *John Bunyan. His Life, Times and Work*, London: Wm. Ibister 1885, 3rd edn., 79.

57 R. Baxter, *The Saint's Everlasting Rest*, 1652 II, Preface.

I speak carefully of "sectarian possibilities" because of a sincere desire not needlessly to offend, and because I wish to be heard. My point is that today, over and above the older sectarianisms which turn upon ministry, sacraments and polity, new possibilities of developing sectarian attitudes and adopting sectarian stances are afforded by current ways of approaching the Bible, ways of doing theology, and ways of responding to ethical challenges. I believe that as the new millennium approaches we need to be alive to these sectarian possibilities and, for the sake of manifesting the unity God has given his Church, we need to be zealous in resisting them. Let us look briefly in turn at the three potential problem areas.

I said earlier that during this century considerable ecumenical advance has been made. There has been doctrinal advance, so that, for example, on 17 November 1980 Pope John Paul II called upon German Protestants to "rejoice that we can affirm, not a partial consensus on some truths, but an agreement on the central truths of the faith. This allows us to hope that we shall attain unity in the spheres of our faith and our life where we are still separated."[58] There have also been actual unions of churches, as we saw. We must not be blind, however, to the fact that many millions of Christians are in no way involved in the mainstream ecumenical movement. Many of these would call themselves evangelicals; many of them would regard themselves as, in their own sense, ecumenical. But for them ecumenism means unity in the truth; the truth is declared in the Bible; and, since God, being a God of truth, does not mutter or mumble his word to us, or set out to deceive us, the Bible is inerrant in its original autographs. Those Christians who cannot agree on this are not to be consorted with. A major fountain-head of this approach is the Old Princeton of B.B. Warfield (1851–1921).[59] But, of course, we do not have access to the original

58 Quoted by Y. Congar, *Diversity and Communion*, London: SCM Press 1984, 176. The Roman Catholic ecumenist J.M.R. Tillard is, however, a little over-optimistic when he writes that as a result of inter-confessional dialogues we can say that "issues which were once stressed by one church and in the past became divisive—as, for instance, justification by faith, the eucharistic presence of Christ, the primacy of the bishop of Rome, and eucharistic *epiclesis*, now appear as essential facets of the Christian truth as such." That they do not so appear to all Christians, or even to all who engage in ecumenical dialogue, is, however, widely known: many find insistence upon the primacy of the bishop of Rome especially problematic. See J.M.R. Tillard, "The ecclesiological implications of bilateral dialogue," *Journal of Ecumenical Studies*, XXIII, no. 3, Summer 1986, 415.

59 See, e.g., B.B. Warfield, *The Inspiration and Authority of the Bible*, Philadelphia: Presbyterian and Reformed, 1948. For an illuminating discussion of inerrancy in the pre-Vatican II Roman Catholic context see J.K.S. Reid, *The Authority of Scripture*, London: Methuen 1957, 145–55.

autographs, and thus biblical inerrantists have no option but to interpret the Bible we do have. In doing this they divide among themselves. Some, the absolute inerrantists, declare that every biblical propositon—historical, scientific, religious—is literally true. Moderate inerrantists hold on the contrary that the Bible is literally true only in its account of the plan of salvation—over the components of which they sometimes differ. Thus, over against mainstream ecumenism they would all probably agree with the conservative evangelical writer who, convinced that in various ways the Roman Church, the Eastern Orthodox Churches and Protestant liberals deny the Gospel, concluded that "The price of ecumenical success is the surrender of the authority and sufficiency of Holy Scripture."[60] But when they focus attention upon themselves they appear relentlessly to divide. As the conservative evangelical theologian E.J. Carnell once put it, "When there are no modernists from which to withdraw, fundamentalists compensate by withdrawing from one another."[61] Certainly, it is the sad fact that entire new denominations, theological seminaries and the like, have been established because of inner-evangelical differences over the interpretation of Scripture.[62] It is difficult to believe that we do not have, in some cases, a failure of faith on our hands. The desire to have everything battened down and buttoned up can indicate a reluctance—even a refusal—to walk by faith: we prefer sight here and now. Walter Lippmann once noted that insecurity "welcomes manacles to prevent its hands shaking."[63]

Be that as it may, the mentality of what J.W. Nevin a century and a half ago called the "sect system," is still alive and well. Nevin examined the revivalist and other sectarianism of his time and repudiated the claim of sectarian leaders that they were standing upon the Bible and the right of private judgment. Hear his trenchant words:

> What sect in reality, allows the Bible and Private Judgment to rule its faith? Is it not notorious that every one of them has a scheme of notions already at hand . . . which is made to underlie all this

---

60 Donald Gillies, *Unity in the Dark*, London: The Banner of Truth Trust 1964, 14. It is believed that this writer subsequently modified his position.

61 E.J. Carnell, *The Case for Orthodox Theology*, London: Marshall, Morgan & Scott 1961, 117.

62 For a balanced treatment of inerrancy by one who is not committed to it see Gabriel Fackre, *The Christian Story. A Pastoral Systematics. II. Authority: Scripture in the Church for the World*, Grand Rapids: Eerdmans 1987, 63–69.

63 Quoted by G.T. Bellhouse, *Immortal Longings*, London: Epworth Press 1950, 69.

> boasted freedom in the use of the Bible, leading private judgment along by the nose, and forcing the divine text always to speak its own way? . . . [The sect] is loud for the Bible, an open Bible, the Bible *alone;* but only as read through the medium of its own theological habit, and wo to the wight who may presume to read it in any other way.[64]

That the same warning is appropriate concerning other than evangelical Christians will become clear as we turn to the second potential problem area: current approaches in theology.

To put it at its very lowest, the plethora of contextual theologies which have been developed over the past twenty years have given traditional theology a much needed shake-up![65] Theological voices from around the world are demanding a hearing, and it is all very exciting. Although in many of these theologies the idea of liberation is prominent, the authors—even within a specific type—are by no means all saying the same thing. Thus, whereas in some of the earlier liberation theologies of Latin America we find a good deal of attention paid to the concept of revolution, later liberationists who are identified with base Christian communities have placed greater emphasis upon the indigenization of the Gospel.[66] On the other hand, Latin American liberation theology has been slower off the mark in dealing with sexism, the specific form of oppression which rightly concerns the feminist theologians.

Feminist theology is also diverse. Some feminists are committed to remaining within the Church, and to working for change—for the ordination of women, for example, in those circles where at present this is not permitted. Others have felt unable to remain within the Church. Of these, some have urged recourse to mother goddess figures in order to counterbalance the image of God as male, while others decidedly have not.[67] Again, whereas in *Beyond God the*

64 J.W. Nevin, *The Sect System* (1849), reprinted in *Catholic and Reformed. Selected Theological Writings of John Williamson Nevin*, eds. Charles Yrigoyen Jr. and George M. (*sic*) Bricker, Pittsburgh: The Pickwick Press 1978, 141, 165.

65 For some reflections upon the analysis of "context" see Alan P.F. Sell, *Aspects of Christian Integrity*, 12–14.

66 See Juan Luis Segundo, "The shift within Latin American theology," *Journal of Theology for Southern Africa*, no. 52, September 1985, 17–29.

67 See Carol P. Christ and Judith Plaskow (eds.), *Womanspirit Rising*, San Francisco: Harper 1979, 10–11. Compare and contrast, for example, Mary Daly, *Beyond God the Father*, Boston: Beacon Press 1973; Letty M. Russell, *Human Liberation in a Feminist Perspective: A Theology*, Philadelphia: Westminster 1974; Rosemary Radford Reuther, *To Change the World: Christology and Cultural Criticism*, New York: Crossroads 1981; Daphne M. Hampson, *Theology and Feminism*, Oxford: Basil Blackwell 1990. I am well aware of the lapse of years between the Reuther

Father Mary Daly argued that the God of the Bible was irremediably and damagingly patriarchal, Mary Ann Tolbert, while exposing untoward patriarchalism in the biblical texts, also finds it possible to recover from the same texts emphases upon the religious, social and political contribution of women which have thus far been overlooked or underplayed.[68]

For its part, Afro-American theology has grown out of the experience of slavery and the social humiliation of men and women, boys and girls and, not surprisingly, the motif of the exodus has worked powerfully upon the minds of Afro-American theologians.[69] Like the Latin American liberation theologies, this complex of theologies have not paid great attention to sexism. Hence the comment of the feminist Rosemary Reuther, "If contemporary black American theology dealt with the integral relationship of sexism, paternalism, and slavery within patriarchy, it might find itself closer to the questions and issues of feminist theology."[70]

From the other side of the world comes the protest of the Korean Minjung theologians that, unlike their Latin American colleagues,

---

and the Hampson volumes, and of the considerable amount of writing done in the interim. I simply advert to some of the foundational works, and to a more recent contribution from a non-American quarter. On the alleged "maleness" of God, it ought in fairness to be pointed out that there exists a long tradition in Christian thought to the effect that to conceive of God as male (or, presumably, as female) is to break the commandment against the making of idols. No doubt in English our pronouns may mislead; but since it is of supreme importance for Christians to maintain that the Godhead is *personal* (albeit not male)—and this not least over against prevalent gnosticisms which would denude the divine of personhood—it is, I believe, preferable to use masculine pronouns of God rather than neuter ones: I cannot bring myself to think of the God I know in Christ as "it." On the other hand, were I suddenly to begin using feminine pronouns of God, some might mistakenly conclude that I had now decided that God is female! Lest it be thought that feminism is of concern only to theologians, we may note the philosophers Michèle le Doeuff and Elizabeth Grosz. In *L'Étude et le rouet: Des femmes, de la philosophie, etc.*, Paris: Seil, the former sees women as transforming philosophy from within, while in *Sexual Subversions: Three French Feminists*, Sydney: Allen & Unwin, the latter deems this a forlorn and misguided hope.

68 Mary Ann Tolbert, "Defining the problem: The Bible and feminist hermeneutics," *Semeia*, XXVIII, 1983, 119. Cf. Phyllis Trible, *God and the Rhetoric of Sexuality*, Philadelphia: Fortress Press 1978; idem, *Texts of Terror*, Philadelphia: Fortress Press 1984.

69 For Afro-American theology the writings of James H. Cone have been seminal. See, e.g., his *Black Theology and Black Power*, New York: Seabury 1969; *A Black Theology of Liberation*, Philadelphia: Lippincott 1970.

70 Rosemary Radford Reuther, "Re-contextualising theology," *Theology Today* XLIII, no. 1, April 1986, 23.

they have not for the most part had recourse to Marxist analysis of the social situation in which they find themselves. To them, "the people" is not a sociological "class" term in the way that "proletariat" is. It is more comprehensive in a this-worldly sense, and it is employed within a view of history which has a strong transcendentalist dimension.[71] This theology is rooted in the collective grief (*han*) of those who comprise "the underside of history." Suffused by their adverse political experiences, this grief is communicated through their stories, poems and expressive arts.

From Africa, and to speak in very general terms, come two significant strands of theological endeavour. On the one hand there is a concern to take traditional African religion seriously, to recover African culture and value systems—this with a view to relocating the Gospel and indigenizing it.[72] On the other hand the racial tensions within Southern Africa have provided fertile soil for liberation theologians who resemble much more their Latin American or Afro-American counterparts. Their questions have been bluntly encapsulated by Allan Boesak: "What does it mean to believe in Jesus Christ when one is black and living in a world controlled by white racists? And what if these racists call themselves Christians also?"[73]

I think that a rapid survey of exciting theological movements such as I have just attempted, though incomplete and in other ways inadequate, does at least bring home both the variety and the vitality of these approaches. While warning us not to make the mistake of regarding them as identical, it also makes plain the starting-point which many of them share: the experience of the oppressed. Here is an experience which cannot be ignored; here are voices which need to be contained within Christian theological and other debate. Above all, here are Christians whose word of challenge to the traditionalists in the Church must be taken with the utmost seriousness, and this not simply because much of what they say is important, but supremely because God has made us one in Christ. If we fail here we shall only foster the sectarian *possibilities* which such movements—like Catholicism, Evangelicalism, Barthianism, Thomism—can bring to reality.

In the case of the theologies I have briefly described, the danger

71 See the references to Marx and Marxism in *Minjung Theology. People as the Subjects of History*, ed. Commission on Theological Concerns of the Christian Conference of Asia, Maryknoll, NY: Orbis Books 1983.

72 See, e.g., J.W. Zvomunondita Kurewa, "The meaning of African theology," *Journal of Theology for Southern Africa*, no. 11, July 1975, 32–42.

73 Allan A. Boesak, *Farewell to Innocence. A Socio-Ethical Study on Black Theology and Black Power*, Maryknoll, NY: Orbis Books 1977, 1–2.

is that their exponents, either out of conviction or out of frustration with the rest of us, may get themselves into the position of saying, "Until you agree with us; or until you adopt our theological methodology," you cannot be a *bona fide* Christian or theologian. Such arrogance and incipient sectarianism are to be challenged in the name of the Gospel which makes us one whencesoever they come. Thus, I see the same kind of warning light when the feminist theologian Elisabeth Schüssler Fiorenza declares that "To truly understand the Bible is to read it through the eyes of the oppressed,"[74] as when a conservative evangelical Christian says, "Unless you have a dateable experience of being born again you will not truly understand the Bible." In both cases a particular experience is being elevated into a privileged norm of interpretation and, as Gabriel Fackre has said, this is a form of elitism. Such elitism, he continues, "declares that the text is available only to those properly credentialed—often meaning those with the right class, sex, race, condition, commitment, or skill. In all cases the text tends to be shut up in the hearer's context, precluding a Word that would be other than the word that accords with the interests or skills of the interpreter, that would enlarge or question them."[75] Fackre has elsewhere described the result as tribalism, concerning which he says,

> As truth is accessible in all tribalism only to those of common stock, relationships with outsider can only be polemical or calls to conversion. No *conversation* is conceivable, for that would undercut the assumption of privleged loci. Where imperial tribalism reigns, the theological forum, or the church, begins to look like an armed camp. The city of Beirut replaces the city of God. *Beirutization* is the end.[76]

Lest you are by now thinking that we have moved a long way from Richard Baxter, let me simply say that although he did not know the word "Beirutization," he spent most of his working life fighting traditional versions of the phenomenon designated by it.

Before turning to one more potentially sectarian possibility, I should like to recount an experience of mine which will round off the matter of varied theological methods. In an informal discussion

---

74 E. Schüssler Fiorenza, "Toward a feminist biblical hermeneutics: Biblical interpretation and liberation theology," reprinted in *A Guide to Contemporary Hermeneutics*, ed. Donald K. McKim, Grand Rapids: Eerdmans 1986, 369.

75 Gabriel Fackre, *The Christian Story* II, 56.

76 Idem, "Evangelical Cathclicity today," *The New Mercersburg Review*, VIII, Autumn 1990, 43.

in which I shared a theologian said, "Every theological seminary needs a Korean to teach Minjung theology, an Afro-American to teach that theology, a Hispanic to teach liberation theology, a woman to teach feminist theology—and so on." The reason he gave was that none of us *can* by any kind of imaginative leap "see" through the eyes of another. Our differing contexts and experiences preclude this. My response was threefold. To mention the lowest point first, I could not think of a seminary anywhere in the world which could afford to employ one of all conceivable kinds of theologian. More seriously, I felt that to tolerate the sectarianism implicit in his reasoning would be to sanction a most unfortunate schizophrenia within theological seminaries. For the pastoral theologians major on, and seek to foster, empathy; are the systematicians by their very organisational structure to deny that we can emphathise with anyone else? God forbid! But at the deepest level my point was that in the Gospel of his grace God has made us one; he has given us a relationship with all who name Christ; he has spoken a Word which judges all our partial experiences. Accordingly, it ill behoves us to draw exclusive boundaries of communication, or so to encapsulate others within their epistemologies or methodologies that, having labelled them, we feel justified in having nothing further to do with them.[77]

Ethical, social and political stances constitute the third potential source of new sectarianisms. Here I can be very brief, for the pattern of argument is identical with what has gone before, and the point is easy to illustrate. In some parts of the world churches have split, and new denominations have been formed because of apparently irreconcilable political convictions held by the members. Ought we to take care lest we put the party above the Gospel? Yes; but there may also be times when to concede too much to Caesar is to deny Christ. Those of my own Dissenting heritage have traditionally felt this to be the case, and hence my forebears in the faith

77 I deem it important that this discussion should be reflected in the way that the teaching of systematic theology is organised. I believe that a strong case can be made for saying that theological students should take rounded courses in systematics—courses in which the insights of the several theological movements and traditions are introduced *en passant* as appropriate—before they take more specialist courses on "The theology of Barth," or "Liberation theology," or "Feminist theology." Apart from any other consideration, it does not seem helpful that, for example, Hispanics should flock to courses on liberation theology in the belief that that is "their thing," while others should avoid it because of a conviction that it isn't theirs! It is one of a number of strengths of Gabriel Fackre's systematics, to which reference has here been made, that, in a lucid and balanced way, and as an integral part of his work, he subjects wide variety of approaches to close scrutiny.

refused to *opt into* the Anglican Establishment.[78] Elsewhere today some Christians have felt called to stand against an oppressive régime, and against their own church which appears to be, or actually is, siding with that régime. Such Christians, I believe, are *de facto* sectaries, but they need not be, and should not be sectarian on principle. They are in protest against a church sincerely believed to have gone wrong; and they should be the first to look for reunion when change in the parent body occurs; and for such change they should work and pray.[79]

As to socio-ethical issues, one illustration will suffice to make my point. A news broadcast during the 1988 American presidential election campaign showed two Christian groups meeting in the same town on the same day. Each group was holding open-air meetings, and each had its placard. One placard proclaimed human rights, favoured abortion on request, and wished to cut money spent on armaments. The other placard was "pro-life," and in favour of strong defences. The reporter asked the leaders of both meetings, "Do you think that Christians who advocate contradictory policies to your own have misunderstood the Christian message?" "Yes," they independently replied, "we do." "Can you imagine working together with those Christians?" "No," they independently replied, "we cannot." Here, then, is a sectarian spirit fostered not by questions of ministry, sacraments or polity; not by differences over theological method; and not enforced by political circumstance. Here is a sectarianism resulting from contradictory conclusions on socio-ethical-political issues of the day. And, as we know, people are cutting themselves off from fellowship, or are being made to feel unwanted, precisely because of issues of that kind. It is sad. Is the Gospel so impotent that sincerely held differences on such matters cannot be contained within the Church which God has made one in Christ?

I end this section with a warning to us all in the drily sardonic words of Robert Mackintosh: "Persons, who herd in corners with those who share their prejudices, are apt to take the whisperings of a coterie for the verdict of 'the civilised world,' or even of the

78 Cf. the observation of Bernard Lord Manning: "We of the Three Dissenting Bodies [i.e., Baptists, Congregationalists and Presbyterians] never 'left the Church.'. . . We did not take ourselves off in a fit of pious ill-temper as a result of some small difference with Anglicans—in 1662 or at any other date." See his *Essays in Orthodox Dissent*, London: Independent Press 1939, 132.

79 See further, Alan P.F. Sell, *Saints: Visible, Orderly and Catholic. The Congregational Idea of the Church*, Geneva: World Alliance of Reformed Churches and Allison Park, PA: Pickwick Publications 1986, 120.

Almighty."[80] Yes, and as soon as they begin unchurching those in other corners, they have fallen headlong into a sectarian denial of the Gospel.

V

To put it bluntly: those who are sectarian on principle need to have the Gospel preached to them. Those who are sectarian out of desperation ought to perform the salutary task of prodding the Church into wakefulness, so that it may open its ears to what it should have been hearing perhaps long ago. But those who persist in sectarianism once their point has been made and received violate the catholicity of the one Church.[81] Whenever we encounter sectarians, whether of the older kind with their concerns over ministry, sacraments and polity, or of the newer kind with their exaltation of specific human experiences, or ways of doing theology, or socio-ethical-political platforms, we need to challenge them in the words of P.T. Forsyth: "Is unity determined by the Gospel making the Church or by the Church developing the Gospel, by the source of Christian history or by its course and its canons?"[82] Genuine ecumenism is an implication of the Gospel by which we have been made one in Christ. For this Gospel we must be ever vigilant, allowing no sectarianism, old or young, to rend asunder what God in Christ has joined together. Even as we rejoice in the ecumenical advances of this century—and we are still too close to them to appreciate their full significance—we need to strive against everything which would continue to divide the people of God.

Roger Thomas, a Unitarian scholar who was not given to visions said, "I like to think of Baxter, Bunyan and George Fox meeting at the Golden Gate for I find it hard to think of them meeting on common ground anywhere else."[83] My vision is even bolder. It concerns the new millennium which is upon us. I have a vision of Orthodox Christians and Roman Catholics and Protestants and Evangelicals and feminists and liberationists and Barthians and social activists and political conservatives and all the rest gathered

80 Robert Mackintosh, *The Obsoleteness of the Westminster Confession of Faith*, 52; bound with his *Essays Towards a New Theology*, Glasgow: Maclehose 1889.

81 See Philip Schaff, *The Principle of Protestantism*, eds. Bard Thompson and George M. Bricker, Philadelphia: United Church Press 1964, 171–72.

82 P.T. Forsyth, *Congregationalism and Reunion*, London: Independent Press 1952, 21.

83 Roger Thomas, "The break-up of Nonconformity," in *The Beginnings of Nonconformity*, London: James Clarke 1964, 33.

around the table of the Lord in our imperfect earthly churches. They will not be around the Lord's Table because they agree on all points of doctrine, church order, biblical interpretation, theological method, or socio-ethical policy, though they will all agree with Richard Baxter's words of 1654: "I knew how ticklish a Business the Enumeration of Fundamentals was,"[84] and very often they will find themselves in radical disagreement. But they will be around the Table together—perhaps on the great Christian festivals—because they know that the fundamental thing is not the ten or twenty or fifty doctrines on which they have managed to agree, or the common polity which they have hit upon, or the shared theological or socio-political platforms on which they stand. They will rejoice that the unifying factor of fundamental importance is that God, in grace, has called them all; that they, by that same grace, have responded; and they will be witnessing to the fact that those who call Christ Lord cannot consistently exclude one another from the Table to the Lord. Accordingly, they will mind their manners and not argue at the Table. They will not refuse the bread and wine because the person presiding has not been episcopally ordained, or is a woman, or is black; they will not leave the Table because some present have not been baptised by immersion on profession of faith; they will not close their ears to the sermon because the preacher does not constantly reiterate their favoured "language of Canaan"—whether concerning "the blood of the Lamb" or concerning "God's preferential option for the poor;" they will not cease to pray if God is addressed as Father, and they will not seek to ban the Lord's Prayer from Christian worship for the same reason. In a word, they will not allow "Galatian" sectarianism to obscure the Good News of the triune God's redemptive once-for-all act in the Cross and Resurrection, on the basis of which they have been called by the Spirit, given new life, and made one in Christ. Rather, the fact that they are together around the one Table will witness to their conviction that the Gospel of God's grace, which is over and above them all in both mercy and judgment, not only transcends in importance all the neuralgic issues which keep Christians apart from one another, but is also the supreme healing agent. The only Christians who would be disturbed by such a communion service would be of the same mentality as those who looked askance at the open-hearted nineteenth-century Baptist pastor Thomas Hughes: they feared that "because he was not rigid, he was not decided; and that, where

84 R. Baxter, RB, II.197, para. 51.

there was no exclusiveness, there was no conviction."[85]

In the middle of the nineteenth century Dr. John Campbell sighed, "Would that all occasions of strife were at an end, and that the one family on earth (for after all it *is* one family) were more like the one family in heaven—a family of love."[86] Christians are one, but their unity is not yet fully manifested. Nevertheless Christian unity needs to be manifested not only for the sake of the Church, but for the sake of the world. When Jesus prayed for the unity of his followers in John's Gospel 17, he had in mind their mission to the world. Their unity was to facilitate the belief of others. After all, how can the unreconciled credibly preach a Gospel of reconciliation? It may well be that Christian unity in all its fulness will not be realised until the end of time. But this should not tempt us to take our ease. Instead, let us be challenged and encouraged by Richard Baxter's letter to Peter Ince: "Dear brother bottom uppon Christ & the great fundamentals. Unite in those with men of holiness & righteousness. Prosecute that union affectionately & unweariedly: & keep your eye uppon that glory where we shall be one."[87]

85 So William Jay, *The Autobiography of William Jay* (1854), Edinburgh: The Banner of Truth Trust 1974, 388.

86 Quoted by John Stoughton, *Reminiscences of Congregationalism Fifty Years Ago*, London: Hodder & Stoughton 1881, 70.

87 R. Baxter, Doctor Williams's Library, London, MSS., Letters, I.2, 21 November 1653.

Fox and Wesley: Experience and Evangelism

If "experience" is one of the most slippery terms in the philosophical and general vocabularies, "evangelism" is surely the term which in Christian circles prompts the widest variety of reactions—from the enthusiastic to the horror-struck. Whatever else may be said about these terms, it cannot be denied that they are in vogue at the present time. All around us people are in quest of experience—not least of religious experience. Westerners are turning to eastern religions, some Easterners are finding a new faith in the western heritage, whether religious or humanistic; there are the devotees of the New Age, some of whose pantheistic and monistic ideas seem anything but novel; there is the avenue to religious experience allegedly provided by drugs; there are the various forms of witchcraft; retreat centres are mushrooming and, in many cases, flourishing. The objectives of the quest are variously described as inner peace, meaning for life, a sense of unity with creation, contact with "the powers," a relationship with God. Whereas the sixteenth-century writer Roger Ascham declared that "Learning teacheth more in one yeare than experience in twentie"[1] today's seekers expect to learn by experience, and they would by no means be deterred by Oscar Wilde's Dumby who declared that "Experience is the name everyone gives to their mistakes."[2]

As to "evangelism," the (Anglican) Lambeth Conference of Bishops in 1988 declared the 1990s to be the Decade of Evangelism. As James Nikkel, the Executive Director of the Board of

1 R. Ascham (1518–1568), *The Scholemaster*, London: Bell and Daldy 1863, 54. It should, however, be noted that Ascham was extolling education, and that, if the rumour be true, he learned little from experience, dying in poverty owing to an addiction to cock-fighting and dicing.

2 Oscar Wilde, *Lady Windermere's Fan* (produced 1892; published 1893), Act II, Harmondsworth: Penguin Books 1954, 55.

Evangelism of the Canadian Mennonite Brethren Conference has put it: "The decade of the nineties is expected to be a decade of Christian advances with the year 2000 as the target date for many visions to be fulfilled. The year 2000 has become a rallying year for church challenge and aggressive planning."[3] Special attention is being paid to the needs of the Soviet Union now that that vast area is open to evangelistic activity as never before in recent history.[4] We thus find Christians—not least Canadians—praying as never before for the conversion of their neighbours; directors of evangelism are being appointed in many churches; new courses are being developed, and Wycliffe College within the Toronto School of Theology is establishing an Institute of Evangelism. All of this is accompanied by Christian dismay over some evangelistic styles and methods. The word "evangelism," declared the distinguished Methodist scholar Albert Outler, has "generated many a distorted image in many modern minds—abrasive zealots flinging their Bibles about like missiles, men (and sometimes women!) with a flat-earth theology, a monophysite Christology, a montanist ecclesiology and a psychological profile suggestive of hysteria. Every Saturday night . . .. there are advertisements for these characters—eyes ablaze, bodies coiled for the leap of faith, or for pouncing on the hapless sinner."[5]

We should not, however, let either the variety of religious experiences (some of them bizarre) or the many evangelistic styles (some of them grotesque) dissuade us from considering the important question, What, in Christian terms, is the relation between experience and evangelism? That there is a relationship I have no doubt: it was classically affirmed by Peter and John when confronted by unimpressed Jewish authorities: "We cannot possibly give up speaking of things we have seen and heard."[6] If their message is to be grounded and not to sound hollow, Christians need to be clear on this relationship as they prepare to enter Christianity's third millennium.

In accordance with the theme of this series of lectures I have chosen to address this subject through an anniversary commemoration of two Christians who most certainly had profound religious experiences and who were nothing if not evangelists: George Fox (who would not have appreciated an anniversary commemoration)

---

3 James Nikkel, "Transitions for the nineties," *Evangelism Canada*, VI, no. 3, September 1989, 1.

4 See "Historic Soviet evangelism declaration," Ibid., VIII, no. 2, June 1991, 1.

5 Albert C. Outler, *Evangelism in the Wesleyan Spirit*, Nashville: Tidings 1971, 34.

6 Acts 4:20.

and John Wesley. Fox died three hundred years ago, on 13 January 1691; Wesley died two hundred years ago, on 2 March 1791.

I

On Firbank Fell in the old county of Westmorland there is a spot which is to this day known as Fox's Pulpit. A tablet fixed to a massive rock reads as follows:

LET YOUR LIVES SPEAK

> Hear or near this rock George Fox preached to about one thousand seekers for three hours on Sunday June 13, 1652. Great power inspired his message and the meeting proved of first importance in gathering the Society of Friends known as Quakers. Many men and women convinced of the truth on this fell and in other parts of the northern counties went forth through the land and over the seas with the living word of the Lord enduring great hardships and winning multitudes for Christ.

This success was just what Fox had expected, for on his way north, on the top of another hill, Pendle in Lancashire, "I saw the Lancashire sea; and there atop of the hill I was moved to sound the day of the Lord; and the Lord let me see a-top of the hill in what places he had a great people to be gathered." That same night, while staying in an alehouse, "the Lord opened to me . . . and let me see a great people in white raiment by a river's side coming to the Lord, and the place was near John Blaykling's where Richard Robinson lived."[7] That is to say, it was near the point at which the river Rawthey runs into the Lune.

This passage from Fox's *Journal* underlines the point made on the Fox's Pulpit tablet: the seekers were already there and waiting. In many parts of the land groups of separatists were in quest of religious reality, opposed to religious hypocrisy, and silently awaiting a word from the Lord. In Westmorland the coming over to Fox of Francis Howgill of Grayrigg and John Audland of Crosslands, leaders of the Preston Patrick Seekers, was of decisive importance.[8] The result, in George Fox's own words, was that "The truth sprang

---

7 *The Journal of George Fox*, ed. John L. Nickalls, London: Religious Society of Friends 1975, 104. This edition is reprinted with minor corrections from the Cambridge University Press edition of 1952. Unless otherwise stated our references to Fox's *Journal* are to this edition.

8 See further Alan P.F. Sell, *Church Planting. A study of Westmorland Nonconformity*, Worthing: H.E. Walter (now Bletchley: Word Books) 1986, 15–17.

up first . . . in . . . Westmorland in 1652."[9] It had already sprung up elsewhere, for example in 1648 among the Nottinghamshire Children of the Light—a group whom Fox describes as "shattered Baptists and others."[10]

Not only was Fox able to gather to himself many scattered companies of Seekers, he was also indebted to the Lollard inheritance which still permeated his home county of Leicestershire, where, at Lutterworth, John Wyclif had been Rector. Now once again the English air was redolent with religion. King Charles I had been executed in 1642, and the saints had set up a godly commonwealth. The recent King James Bible was in the hands of the people and in their own tongue, and religious pamphleteering was rife. The Quakers were not backward in producing their tracts. Indeed, "In their first fifty years (1650–1700) . . . close to 650 Friends (at least 82 being women) wrote 'as each felt led,' and 3100 new writings were published, besides 650 reprints and memorials."[11] This heady atmosphere spawned numerous groups—the Diggers, the Muggletonians, the Ranters and others—whose members variously dreamed dreams, saw visions, went into ecstasies, proclaimed messages which were deemed revolutionary if not fantastic, and, after the Restoration of the monarchy in 1660, sometimes found themselves in gaol. Among all of these, George Fox's Society of Friends alone survives to this day. Who was this man whom William Penn described as "an original, being no man's copy"?[12]

Geoffrey F. Nuttall answers that question with *quasi*-Quaker-like directness: "He was a nobody: a weaver's son from an utterly undistinguished village in Leicestershire."[13] The village was Drayton-in-the-Clay (now Fenny Drayton). There Fox was born in July 1624 to Christopher Fox, a churchwarden known to his neighbours as "righteous Christer," and his wife Mary (née Lago). After a godly upbringing uninterrupted by overmuch schooling, Fox, though earmarked for holy orders by some of his relatives, was apprenticed

---

9 *A Collection of Many Select and Christian Epistles, Letters and Testimonies, Written on Sundry Occasions, by that Ancient, Eminent, Faithful Friend and Minister of Christ Jesus, George Fox*, London: T. Sowle 1698, II, pt. I, 2. (This book is called "The second volume" of a three-part publishing venture, of which the first was the *Journal*, and the (unspecified) third was *Gospel Truth*, 1706.

10 G. Fox, *Journal*, 25.

11 *Early Quaker Writings 1650–1700*, eds. Hugh Barbour and Arthur O. Roberts, Grand Rapids: Eerdmans 1973, 14.

12 William Penn, preface to Fox's *Journal*, London W. and F.G. Cash 1852, I, 31.

13 Geoffrey F. Nuttall, *The Puritan Spirit. Essays and Addresses*, London: Epworth Press 1967, 181; "Introduction" to Fox's *Journal*, xxiv.

to a shoemaker, whose customers quickly learned that "If George says 'Verily' there is no altering him."[14] One day his business took him to Atherstone fair, where he met his cousin Bradford and another man—both of them "professors"—that is, professing Christians. They invited Fox to drink beer with them, and from mere thirst-quenching the session developed into a series of toastings after the custom of the times. Fox was horrified that Christians should thus indulge themselves, put his groat on the table and walked off to a sleepless night during which the Lord said to him, "Thou seest how young people go together into vanity and old people into the earth; and thou must forsake all, both young and old, and keep out of all, and be as a stranger unto all."[15] In response Fox left his home in September 1643 and embarked upon a four-year period of wandering in search of forgiveness and peace of mind. He was regularly disappointed by religious professors, and received no help from "priests" (as he indiscriminately called them), whether of the Church of England or of Nonconformity. One of the former, Richard Abel of Mancetter, Warwickshire, advised Fox to "take tobacco and sing psalms." But, Fox ruefully records, "Tobacco was a thing I did not love, and psalms I was not in an estate to sing; I could not sing."[16]

From time to time Fox received what he called "openings" from the Lord. He came to see that mere outward religious profession and observance was a hollow sham, and that an education at Oxford and Cambridge was not enough to turn a man into a minister of Christ. Eventually, in 1647 at the age of twenty-two, he was able to write,

> And when all my hopes in [priests] and in all men were gone, so that I had nothing outwardly to help me, nor could tell what to do, then, Oh then, I heard a voice which said, "There is one, even Jesus Christ, that can speak to thy condition," and when I heard it my heart did leap for joy. Then the Lord did let me see why there was none upon the earth that could speak to my condition, namely, that I might give him all the glory; for all are concluded under sin, and shut up in unbelief as I had been, that Jesus Christ might have the pre-eminence, who enlightens, and gives grace, and faith, and power. Thus, when God doth work who shall let it? And this I knew experimentally.[17]

14 G. Fox, *Journal*, 2.

15 Ibid., 3.

16 Ibid., 5–6.

17 Ibid., 11.

In the strength of this experience (here stated in language characteristically replete with biblical allusions),[18] and despite the temptations which assailed him from time to time, Fox embarked upon his prophetic itinerant mission, counting it an honour to face misunderstanding, physical violence and imprisonment for Christ's sake.

II

If religious and political turbulence formed the backdrop to Fox's evangelistic mission, the air which Wesley breathed was heavy with reason and orderliness. While it would be a slight upon the effectiveness of the Independent Philip Doddridge (1702–1751), the Baptists Alvery Jackson (d. 1763), Benjamin Beddome (1717–1795), and others to say that there was no life in the churches,[19] there was widespread absenteeism among the Anglican clergy coupled with formalism in worship; the older Dissenters, officially tolerated since 1689, had in some cases all but fallen asleep in their meeting-houses; and the Quakers had entered their quietist phase of withdrawal from the sinful world. In reaction against seventeenth-century violence and rabid sectarianism many, of whom the Presbyterian divine John Aikin (1713–1780) was typical, viewed religious enthusiasm askance. At Aikin's funeral it was said that "Whilst he readily acknowledged the existence, and the powerful operation, of original principles in human nature, he was no advocate of that indolent philosophy (so well adapted to the spirit and manners of the present age) which has raised an unnatural contest between *Reason* and *Common Sense*, and instructed men to trust to their feelings rather than to their understandings."[20]

John Wesley, born on 17 July 1703 in the Rectory at Epworth, Lincolnshire, grew up in this intellectual atmosphere. In his case, however, the prevailing ways of thinking were tempered by his read-

18 See, for example, Romans 11:32; Galatians 3:23; Colossians 1:18; Isaiah 43:13. Against any representation of Fox as a free-wheeling "mystic," it is of great importance to advert to his biblical foundation and his scripturally-saturated language.

19 See further, Alan P.F. Sell, *The Great Debate. Calvinism, Arminianism and Salvation*, Worthing: H.E. Walter (now Bletchley: Word Books) 1982, Grand Rapids: Baker Book House 1983, 63, 83–84; idem, *Dissenting Thought and the Life of the Churches. Studies in an English Tradition*, Lewiston, NY: Mellen Research University Press 1990, 614–15.

20 William Enfield, *A Funeral Sermon, occasioned by the death of the late Rev. John Aikin, D.D., Professor of Divinity at the Academy in Warrington*, Warrington 1781, 8.

ing of mystical writers and his contact with the Moravians, and by the Puritan blood which flowed into his veins from his paternal grandmother's father, John White, vice-chairman of the Westminster Assembly; from Dr. Samuel Annesley, his maternal grandfather, who was ejected from his London living in 1662; and from his paternal great-grandfather and grandfather, Bartholomew and John Westley, both of whom were ejected from their Dorset livings in 1662.[21] Wesley's father, Samuel, and his mother, Susanna, had found their way into the Established Church—the church which John was to irritate by his innovations, but in which he lived and died.

The great incident of Wesley's early years was his rescue from the burning rectory on 9 February 1708/9, an escape which he construed as divinely ordained. After Charterhouse he proceeded to Christ Church, Oxford, graduating in 1724. In the following year, after reading Jeremy Taylor's *Rule and Exercises of Holy Living and Dying* Wesley underwent what is sometimes called his conversion to seriousness. He writes, "Instantly I resolved to dedicate all my life to God . . . being thoroughly convinced . . . that every part of my life (not some only) must either be a sacrifice to God, or myself, that is, in effect, the devil."[22] Following this decision Wesley was ordained deacon on 19 September 1725. After being elected a Fellow of Lincoln College on 17 March 1726, he became his father's curate in August 1727, and was ordained priest at Oxford on 22 September 1728. In the following year, while fulfilling the teaching duties of his fellowship, he became the leader of a group of young men nicknamed "methodists" because of their self-imposed rules of study and devotion, who soon earned the further nickname, "the holy club." Within this orbit Wesley pursued his quest of holiness, and engaged in self-examination, but gave little sign of evangelistic zeal. On the contrary, he was if anything self-absorbed. In a letter of 20 November 1734 his father reported John as having written thus: "The question is not whether I could do more good to others [at Epworth] or here; but whether I could do more good to myself: Seeing wherever I can be most holy myself, there I can most promote holiness in others. But I can improve myself more at Oxford than at any other place. . . ." To which father Samuel curtly replied,

21 For Annesley and the Westleys see *Calamy Revised*, ed. A.G. Matthews, Oxford: The Clarendon Press (1934) 1988.

22 John Wesley, *Works*, London: Wesleyan Conference Office 1872, XI, 366.

that when considering our vocation, the primary objective "is not dear self, but the glory of God. . . ."[23]

This was the Wesley who, with his brother Charles, Benjamin Ingham and Charles Delamotte, embarked upon a mission to Georgia on 14 October 1735. Their chief motive, Wesley wrote, was "to save our souls."[24] He was much impressed by the religious experience of the twenty-six Moravians on board, and whilst in Georgia he learned much from the Moravian leader, Augustus Gottlieb Spangenberg. One of their exchanges went like this: Spangenberg asked, "'Do you know Jesus Christ?' I paused, and said, 'I know He is the Saviour of the world.' 'True,' replied he, 'but do you know He has saved you?' I answered, 'I hope He has died to save me.' He only added, 'Do you know yourself?' I said, 'I do.' But I fear they were vain words."[25] During the voyage home Wesley wrote, "I who went to America to convert others, was never myself converted to God."[26] Although Wesley much later queried this remark, the fact remains that his mission to Georgia, quite apart from the scandal surrounding himself and Sophia Christiana Hopkey, was by no means a success. He had no assurance of salvation. As he had written on the homeward voyage, "The faith I want is, A sure trust and confidence in God, that through the merits of Christ, my sins are forgiven, and I reconciled to the favour of God . . . I want that faith which none can have without knowing that he hath it."[27] As Albert Outler remarks, Wesley "was an evangelical, all right—orthodox in doctrine, zealous in personal faith, self-righteous and overweening—but with next to nothing to show for thirty-six years of high-minded diligence."[28] That state of affairs was soon to change.

Six days after landing in England Wesley met the Moravian Peter Böhler, by some of whose recent converts Wesley was greatly impressed. Their personal testimonies prompted him to cry out, "Lord, help Thou mine unbelief!"[29] During the next two weeks Wesley resolved to forsake all attempts to find salvation by the performance of good works, and prayed hard for the assurance of

23 Joseph Priestley, *Original Letters by The Rev. John Wesley and his Friends*, Birmingham: Thomas Pearson 1791, 48.

24 J. Wesley, *Journal*, *Works* (1872), I, 17.

25 Ibid., 23.

26 Ibid., 25–26.

27 Ibid., 77.

28 Albert C. Outler, *Evangelism in the Wesleyan Spirit*, 17.

29 J. Wesley, *Journal*, *Works* (1872), I, 91. Cf. Mark 9:24.

saving faith. He received his answer on Wednesday 24 May 1738. He was consoled by his morning Bible reading; in the afternoon he attended service at St. Paul's Cathedral, and was encouraged by the anthem "Out of the depths have I called unto thee, O Lord" (William Croft), with its lines, "O Israel, trust in the Lord; for with the Lord there is mercy, and with Him is plenteous redemption."[30] Then in the evening, to quote his words which stand with Fox's among the classics of conversion narratives,

> I went very unwillingly to a society in Aldersgate Street, where one was reading Luther's Preface to the Epistle to the Romans. About a quarter before nine, while he was describing the change which God works in the heart through faith in Christ, I felt my heart strangely warmed. I felt I did trust in Christ, Christ alone for salvation; and an assurance was given me that he had taken away *my* sins, even *mine*, and saved *me* from the law of sin and death.[31]

Charles Wesley, converted three days earlier, was soon to write a hymn celebrating the One to whom they owed their common experience:

> And can it be that I should gain
> An interest in the Saviour's blood?
> Died He for me, who caused His pain,
> For me, who Him to death pursued?
> Amazing love! how can it be
> That Thou, my God, shouldst die for me!

There you have the experience—and the personal pronouns—on which Wesleyan Methodism was founded.[32]

It must, however, be pointed out that although the Aldersgate Street experience was of crucial importance—it allowed Wesley to feel the Gospel he preached, and it impelled him on his highly successful evangelistic journeys—he could still from time to time

30 Psalm 130:1, 7.

31 J. Wesley, *Journal, Works* (1872) I, 103. Cf. Luke 24:32; Romans 8:2.

32 Strictly construed, you also have a heresy in the last line of the stanza! It should be noted that Wesley's emphasis upon the personal was balanced by his concern for the whole world to a degree not always found among some who came after him.

doubt whether or not he was saved;[33] and although 1738 gave him his characteristic evangelical doctrines and assured him of their truth, he seldom afterwards referred to his personal experience as such. Again, although he was led to modify some of his earlier High Church opinions—his opposition to field preaching and his view of apostolic succession, for example—he never forsook his High Church eucharistic doctrine or his rigorous devotional practice.[34] More naturally cerebral than emotional, he knew his constant need of the fire of the Lord—another word which recurs in his brother's hymns:

> O Thou who camest from above,
> The pure celestial fire to impart,
> Kindle a flame of sacred love
> On the mean altar of my heart.
> There let it for Thy glory burn
> With inextinguishable blaze. . . .
> Still let me guard the holy fire,
> And still stir up Thy gift in me.

III

We must now turn from the historical circumstances in which Fox and Wesley came by their respective experiences to a closer consideration of the experiences themselves. One of the ways of approach is to enquire into their relations to mysticism—a subject on which much ink has been spilled.

Was George Fox a mystic? This question has prompted both positive and negative answers. The distinguished Quaker Rufus M. Jones was in no doubt that Fox "was a mystic, not a scholastic or a rationalist."[35] Certainly Fox had no patience with scholastic systems of theology which, he thought, did not have the essence of religion in them; and far from being a rationalist, he was opposed to "notions" to which one might assent and then live as if they never were. But was he a mystic—whatever that means? There can be no

---

33 See, e.g., his *Journal* entries of 29 May and 6 June 1738, *Works* I, 105, 106. See further Richard P. Heitzenrater, *The Elusive Mr. Wesley*, Nashville: Abingdon 1984, I, 96–97, 101–03, 198.

34 For a careful and authoritative account of Wesley's conversion see Henry D. Rack, *Reasonable Enthusiast. John Wesley and the Rise of Methodism*, London: Epworth 1989, ch. IV.

35 Rufus M. Jones, *The Faith and Practice of the Quakers*, London: Methuen 1927, 26.

doubt that the writings of such continental mystics as Jakob Boehme were known in the England of Fox's day. Indeed, Boehme's complete *Works* were translated into English between 1644 and 1662. Jones, following the second generation Quaker Robert Barclay, has claimed the influence of Boehme upon Fox in the latter's reference to "the flaming sword";[36] but Geoffrey F. Nuttall has pointed out that this phrase was used by other Quakers, and that in any case it is found in Genesis 3:24.[37] Further, Nuttall is particularly impressed by the absence in Boehme of a Christian doctrine of the Holy Spirit in Fox's sense.[38] It has similarly been suggested that Fox was indebted to his contemporaries the Cambridge Platonists. But their approach, though intuitive, was in the rationalist spirit, and whereas to Henry More the light within was his reason and conscience, to Fox it was the truth, the supernatural gift of Christ within, who quickens the "seed"—"that of God in every man"—that by which the serpent's head is bruised (Genesis 3:15)—and brings it to fruition.[39] Thus, in 1656 Fox argued, against John Owen, Vice-Chancellor of Oxford University, that the light was not a natural light but "divine and spiritual from Christ the divine and spiritual man"; and two years later, in Leominster, he reaffirmed the point to the incumbent John Tombes.[40]

But this characteristically Quaker language about truth, light, the seed, and that of God in every man requires further elucidation. Richenda Scott has well said that "The Inward Light or the Seed is dormant, a mere potentiality, until it is awakened and kindled by the coming of God to man in his own experience. And the Light has

---

36 G. Fox, *Journal*, 27.

37 See Rufus M. Jones, *Spiritual Reformers in the 16th and 17th Centuries*, Boston: Beacon Press 1914, 221–27; Geoffrey F. Nuttall, *The Holy Spirit in Puritan Faith and Experience*, Oxford: Blackwell 1946, 16–18 and notes.

38 Geoffrey F. Nuttall, *The Holy Spirit*, 17.

39 See H. More, *An Explanation of The Grand Mystery of Godliness*, London: J. Fletcher 1660, X. xiii.7, in a chapter headed, "The Authors [*sic*] Expostulation with the sincerer sort of Quakers"; Douglas Gwyn, *The Apocalypse of the Word. The Life and Message of George Fox*, Richmond, Indiana: Friends United Press 1986, xv; Geoffrey F. Nuttall, *The Holy Spirit in Puritan Faith and Experience*, 18. Dr. Nuttall reminds us that when Henry More met Fox he "felt himself, as it were, turn'd into Brass." In 1676, however, he wrote to Lady Conway that "there are some things which I hugely like in the Quakers and I wish all Christians would imitate them." The references are: R. Ward, *Life of the Learned and Pious Dr. Henry More*, London: Joseph Downing 1710, 197; M.H. Nicolson, *Conway Letters* New Haven: Yale University Press 1930, 418; letter of 10 January 1675/6. For a fuller exposition of Fox on the "seed" see Geoffrey F. Nuttall, *The Holy Spirit in Puritan Faith and Experience*, 158–59.

40 G. Fox, *Journal*, 274, 295–97.

no meaning for Fox and the early Friends till it is identifed with the revelation of God in Christ. The Light is Christ, or the Holy Spirit, the power and grace of God."[41] As to "truth," in his *Catechisme for Children* (1657) Fox's answer to the question, "What is truth?" is clear and unambiguous: "Christ, which doth enlighten every man, which cometh into the world and that is the Truth which every man is enlightened withal." This truth is not something to be assented to, but it is to be lived in. So, for example, when on one occasion a pardon was offered which would have released him from prison, Fox would not accept it; for since he had done no wrong, it would have been untruthful to allow himself to be pardoned. Again, his words to a group of soldiers, priests and preachers in Derby in 1650 were characteristic: "I told them they were not to dispute of God and Christ, but to obey him."[42] Small wonder that, according to Fox, it was "Justice Bennet of Derby that first called us Quakers because we bid them tremble at the word of God. . . ."[43]

But if Christ is the truth, he is also the light. As one Quaker scholar puts it, "Incessantly, inevitably, and unalterably George Fox identifies and defines the Light as Christ."[44] Another writes, "I find that Fox relates the light to God only twenty times while he relates it to Christ one hundred twelve times."[45] In other words, here is no mystic experience in which the self is absorbed and beyond testimony; here is no undifferentiated light; here is a profound experience of Christ construed in biblical language, and dependent upon a grasp of the historic Christ event. Fox can thus repeatedly declare that "Jesus Christ is come [not only then, but now] to teach his people himself." Moreover, far from seeking mystical retreat, Fox was impelled upon his prophetic task, taking all the consequences for Christ's sake. He writes, "Now, when the Lord God and his son, Jesus Christ, did send me forth into the world, to preach his everlasting gospel and kingdom, I was glad that I was commanded to turn people to that inward light, spirit, and grace, by which all

41 Richenda C. Scott, *Tradition and Experience*, London: George Allen & Unwin 1964, 71.

42 G. Fox, *Journal*, 51.

43 Ibid., 58.

44 T. Canby Jones, "The nature and function of the Light in the thought of George Fox," *Quaker Religious Thought* XVI nos. 1, 2, Winter 1974–75, 53. See, e.g., G. Fox, *Journal*, 33.

45 Rachel Hadley King, *George Fox and the Light Within*, Philadelphia: Friends Book Store 1940, 87 n.

might know their salvation, and their way to God; even that divine Spirit which would lead them into all Truth and which I infallibly knew would never deceive any."[46]

The Quaker writer, Harold Loukes, quotes Evelyn Underhill as regretting that "The Society of Friends has produced no great contemplative." He replies, "But Friends were not interested in contemplation, if by that is meant the mystical *via negativa* at its highest. They were concerned to be gathered up and used; and their meetings were places to be gathered in."[47] In a similar manner the Methodist Wilfred Wilkinson referred to William James's characterisation of mysticism as being marked by ineffability, noetic quality, transiency and passivity. He accepted the first two for Methodism, deemed transiency a psychological fact—"Intense things are brief"—and declared that passivity "has no place in Methodist ideas. Quietness, either in the technical or the popular sense, is not Methodism." He continues (in similar vein to Loukes on the Quakers): "Wesley guarded against the errors of subjectivism and individualism, which are the main weaknesses of Mysticism, by emphasising the social element in religion. The Class Meeting became from the earliest days of Methodism an essential part of the organization."[48] Certain it is that varied as their predilections may have been regarding silence and noise, both Quakers and Methodists, taking their respective cues from their founders, were, and remain, more than competent where the structures of Christian fellowship are concerned.

Nevertheless, Wesley's history in relation to mysticism is quite different from Fox's—indeed, as we have seen Fox hardly had a history of relations with mysticism at all: here as elsewhere he was an original. But Wesley knew the literature. In the 1720s he had read some of the works of the German Dominican mystic Johann Tauler (1300–1361), as well as a late fourteenth-century anonymous work, the *Theologia Germanica*. *The Imitation of Christ* by Thomas à Kempis (c. 1380–1471) was his favourite work, but he also found help in *The Rule and Exercise of Holy Living* (1650) and *The Rule and Exercise of Holy Dying* (1651) by Jeremy Taylor (1613–1657), and in *The Life of God in the Soul of Man* (1677), by the Scottish divine Henry Scougal (1650–1678). In addition to these, two books

46 G. Fox, *Journal*, 34–35. Cf. Revelation 14:6; Acts 26:18; John 16:13.

47 Harold Loukes, *The Quaker Contribution*, London: SCM Press 1965, 40.

48 Wilfred R. Wilkinson, *Religious Experience: The Methodist Fundamental*, London: Holborn Publishing House 1928, 157. See William James, *The Varieties of Religious Experience. A Study in Human Nature*, London: Longmans, Green 1902, 380–82.

by William Law (1686–1761), whom he knew, impressed him greatly: *On Christian Perfection* (1726) and *A Serious Call to a Devout and Holy Life* (1728). So moved was Wesley by the latter that, from 1744 he printed nineteen editions of it, all of which were distributed *gratis*.

But although Wesley retained an affection for his mystical and spiritual mentors throughout his life, he came to have serious reservations concerning mysticism itself. When he reread the *Theologia Germanica* in 1741 he wrote, "O how was it, that I could ever so admire the affected obscurity of this unscriptural writer!"[49] He criticised some of his brother's poetry as being too mystical; and he wrote, "I think the rock on which I had the nearest made shipwreck of the faith was the writings of the Mystics."[50] Yet even after his conversion experience of 1738 he was publishing abridgments of mystical works by Madame Guyon (1648–1717) and others. The only convincing explanation of this ambiguity would seem to be that when it came home to him, as it had to Luther before him, that justification was by God's free gift of grace, Wesley's determination prior to 1738 to find the assurance he longed for by the route of devotional exercises and godly living was shown to be a *cul de sac*.[51] Some writers have (perhaps unduly harshly) called it a doctrine of works, spiritual works, but works none the less.[52] We need not deny that Wesley's early spiritual discipline had value as any sincere quest of godliness must have. But not the least aspect of its value was the stimulation provided by its inability to provide the assurance he so urgently sought. From 1738 onwards Wesley judged spiritual writers, for whose sincerity he still had great respect, in the light of his profound experience of forgiveness and acceptance. He remained a voracious and eclectic reader and, as Ernest Rattenbury said,

---

49 J. Wesley, *Journal, Works* (1872), I, 347.

50 Idem, *The Letters of the Rev. John Wesley, A.M.*, ed. John Telford, London: Epworth Press 1931, I, 207.

51 This case is argued in detail by Robert G. Tuttle, *Mysticism in the Wesleyan Tradition*, Grand Rapids: Francis Asbury Press 1989. For my reservations concerning the concluding chapter see *Proceedings of the Wesley Historical Society* XLVIII pt. 3, October 1991, 103.

52 See, e.g., J. Wesley, *Journal*, I, 469–70. Cf. R.P. Heitzenrater, *The Elusive Mr. Wesley*, I, 73. Note further Albert C. Outler's assessment of Wesley's 1738 conversion experience as "the dramatic moment when he reversed the priorities between *sola fide* and holy living, never to reverse them again." See his "The place of Wesley in the Christian Tradition," in Kenneth E. Rowe, ed., *The Place of Wesley in the Christian Tradition*, Metuchen, NJ: Scarecrow Press 1976, 20. I should, however, prefer to say that the priorities were reversed for him.

> He was no more averse to getting good from a Mystic than from a Roman Catholic or even from a Unitarian, such as Firmin. But one could hardly suggest that he accepted the creeds of these men because he admired some of their writings. . . . That system of Mysticism, which has no need of a mediator, or tends to a conception of God's immanency which runs quickly into Pantheism, and is marked by fancies, dreams and speculations with little scriptural foundation, although often in itself attractive, is ultimately the foe of the plain New Testament Christianity for which John Wesley stood.[53]

IV

The experiences of Fox and Wesley impelled them into evangelism. They were at one as to the necessity of personal experience. Just as the Moravian Spangenberg had challenged Wesley, "Do you know yourself?" so George Fox challenged his hearers at Ulverston: "You will say, Christ saith this, and the apostles say this, but what canst thou say?"[54] But if Wesley sought and expected assurance of salvation, Fox challenged people to attend to the voice of the risen and returned Christ already speaking in their hearts. If Fox appealed for the recognition of the light, Wesley earnestly prayed for the coming of the fire. The content of their preaching, not to mention their preaching styles, were thus rather different.

There is a strongly apocalyptic strain in the preaching of George Fox. Christ has returned and is to be found within; the last days are here; to confront the world with the challenging word of judgment and mercy is an urgent and a solemn obligation: the day of the Lord is upon us.[55] Thus he writes in 1656 to his travelling preachers from Launceston, at about the time of his imprisonment there:

> In the power of life and wisdom, and dread of the Lord God of life, and heaven, and earth, dwell, that in the wisdom of God over all ye may be preserved, and be a terror to all the adversaries of God, and a dread, answering that of God in them all, and spreading the Truth abroad, awakening the witness, confounding deceit, gather-

---

53 J. Ernest Rattenbury, *The Conversion of the Wesleys. A Critical Study*, London: Epworth 1938, 234.

54 Margaret Fell's account of the address which resulted in her convincement in 1652. See "Testimony of Margaret Fox, concerning her late husband George Fox, etc.," in G. Fox, *Journal* (1852), II, 358. The wife of Judge Thomas Fell (1598–1658) of Swarthmore Hall, Ulverston, Margaret married George Fox in 1669. Meanwhile her home had become the centre of the Friends' mission and mutual caring.

55 G. Fox, *Journal*, 121.

> ing up out of transgression into the life, the covenant of light and peace with God. Let all nations hear the word by sound or writing. Spare no place, spare not tongue nor pen; but be obedient to the Lord God and go through the work and be valiant for the Truth upon earth; tread and trample all that is contrary under. . . .[56]

As he elsewhere put it, with reference to Matthew's narrative of Jesus's birth, "We must not have Jesus Christ, the Lord of life, put any more in the stable amongst the horses and asses, but he must now have the best chamber, the heart, and the rude, debauched spirit must be turned out."[57] Fox's was an intensely practical message, hammered out amidst exciting and occasionally harrowing experiences, and within the orbit of, though not formally expounding, the Bible and Christian doctrine. Because of this he was rebuked by some in his own time as in ours.

Thus, concerning the Bible, Fox's openings from the Lord—for example, that "every man was enlightened by the divine light of Christ"—sometimes came to him independently of Scripture, and, as he tells us, it was only "afterwards, searching the Scriptures, I found it."[58] As the Quaker scholar Douglas Gwyn explains, Fox believes that "in Christ's light he has come to know the experience of Adam, Moses, the prophets, John, and the apostles, apart from his reading of Scripture—and *beyond* it as well . . . [the] Word recapitulates *history* in personal *experience*."[59] Thus Fox speaks of seeing things "in the pure openings of the Light without the help of any man, neither did I know where to find it in the Scriptures; though afterwards, searching the Scriptures, I found it."[60] The thought of a word of God received independently of the Scriptures was too much for some of Fox's Puritan neighbours to stomach; and this not without good reason since some of the more fanatical sectaries were attributing fantastic claims to a direct word from the Lord. Thus Fox's contemporary, John Bunyan, was Puritan in the

---

56 Ibid., 263. By 1660 the Quakers had visited "Germany, America, and many other islands and places, as Florence, Mantua, Palatine, Tuscany, Italy, Rome, Turkey, Jerusalem, France, Geneva, Norway, Barbados, Bermuda, Antigua, Jamaica, Surinam, Newfoundland." See *Letters &c., of Early Friends*, ed. Abram Rawlinson, London: Harvey and Darton 1841, 292 n.

57 Ibid., 312.

58 Ibid., 33.

59 D. Gwyn, *Apocalypse of the Word*, 95. It must, however, be said that given Fox's biblical saturation, his subconscious may be responsible for the "apart from" read experiences (see the immediately following quotation). We should have been helped by examples of experiences "beyond" Scripture.

60 G. Fox, *Journal*, 33.

more orthodox sense of beginning from the Bible, regarding Quaker teaching as error, and declaring that "as the Quakers did oppose [God's] truth, so God did the more confirm me in it, by leading me into the scriptures that did wonderfully maintain it."[61]

As to doctrine, Fox's aversion to notions and systems disinclined him to speak in formal traditional terms. For this reason he has been accused of so elevating the indwelling Christ as to under-emphasise the historic saving event of the Cross and resurrection. As a Quaker writes,

> Whilst some of the [classical] plan of salvation was not denied by Friends of an earlier day, they did not think about it or preach about it. It was all covered up by their living experience of a Christ within them, a God whose presence was a daily strength. . . . They obeyed the Bible when it harmonised with the Truth they knew. They rejected it when it apparently ordained Baptism and the Supper, supported War and forbade the ministry of women. They rejected such "notions" as the Trinity, and the whole complex system of Puritan theology. . . .[62]

This does not account for the admitted reticence, however. Here Geoffrey Nuttall can help us. He suggests that Fox's emphasis upon the victorious seed of the woman, Christ, over the seed of the serpent of Genesis 3, causes him to telescope "the divine processes of creation and redemption" in such a way as "inevitably to reduce the significance for redemption of the coming of Christ and His Holy Spirit in history."[63] Part of Fox's concern was that under the Puritan system it was all too easy for Christians to think that the battle having been fought and won at the Cross, they could now, as the elect, hang up their swords. His conviction was that the battle of the Lord was still under way, and that the redeemed must engage in it. This in no way weakened his belief that one of the functions of the light was to reveal a person's plight when alienated from God, and thereby to encourage repentance and faith.[64]

The following passage from Fox's *Journal* is as revealing as it is comprehensive. It is 1653, and Fox is at Brigham, Cumberland:

---

61 John Bunyan, *Grace Abounding to the Chief of Sinners*, London: SCM Press 1955, 61.

62 John W. Graham, *The Quaker Ministry*, London: The Swarthmore Press 1925, 55.

63 Geoffrey F. Nuttall, *The Holy Spirit*, 159.

64 See, e.g., G. Fox, *A Catechisme for Children*, 1657, 23: the light "is that which lets thee see sin and thy transgression, which hath separated thee from God."

> And I brought them all to the spirit of God in themselves, by which they might know God and Christ and the Scriptures and to have heavenly fellowship in the spirit; and showed them how every one that comes into the world was enlightened by Christ the life, with which light they might see their sins and Christ their saviour, who was come to save them from their sin; with which light they might see their priest that died for them, their shepherd to feed them, and their great prophet to open for them. So with the light of Christ they might see Christ always present with them who was the author of their faith and the finisher thereof. So, opening the first covenant, I showed them the types and the substance, and bringing them to Christ the second covenant, and how they had been in the night of apostacy since the apostles' days, but now the everlasting Gospel was preached again that brought light and immortality to light, and the day of the Lord was come, and Christ was come to teach his people himself and how they might find their teacher within, when they were in their labours and in their beds.[65]

There we have many of the ingredients of a systematic theology: the persons of the Trinity are there; the universal saving light is there; humanity's sin is there, and so is Christ's saving work. The offices of Christ as prophet and priest are there, as are Christ the shepherd and Christ the teacher; and the apocalyptic note is struck. But Fox did not elaborate a system: it was not his way; to him such activity was an obstacle to the intensity of faith and the directness of proclamation. Not surprisingly therefore some, including Richard Baxter in his own day and Geoffrey Nuttall in ours, have felt that with his emphasis upon the seed, the light, the truth with Christ "he so 'telescopes' the divine process of creation and redemption as inevitably to reduce the significance for redemption of the coming of Christ and His Holy Spirit in history."[66] There is justice in this charge, though we must not overlook Fox's habit of appropriating and internalising history. In 1656 he write to Friends: "For now you know the power of God, which is the Cross of Christ, and are come to it, which crucifies you from the state that Adam and Eve were in

---

65 G. Fox, *Journal*, 155. Cf. Hebrews 12:2; II Timothy 1:10.

66 Geoffrey F. Nuttall, *The Holy Spirit in Puritan Faith and Experience*, 159. Nuttall is challenged on this and other points by Douglas Gwyn in *Apocalypse of the Word*. It may be, however, that in the interests of redressing the apocalyptic balance (a worthy aim) Gwyn protests too much. Concerning the historic Cross and related matters, Harold Loukes, speaking for Quakers, writes, "If you press us on what we mean by this kind of language, we can only say that we do not know. This is all imagery, which disappears into obscurantism when we try to analyse it. . . ." See his *The Quaker Contribution*, 95. Is an historic Cross thus adequately described?

the Fall, and so from the world. . . ."[67] There is no doubt, however, that Fox (who in any case would not have believed in making such "notions" clear) blurs the distinction between the *imago dei* and the presence of Christ by the Spirit—in other words, between natural and revealed theology. The same cannot be said of John Wesley.

Similar to George Fox in the intensity of his experience, and equally in earnest in his evangelistic mission, Wesley, as we have seen, lived in different circumstances and breathed a different intellectual air. If Fox bluntly spoke as he found, Wesley was no less to the point, but in a more carefully reasoned way. Where Fox regarded the Church of England and Nonconformity, with their hireling priests, formal worship and doctrinal "notions," as alike moribund and to be bypassed, Wesley, ever the faithful (if somewhat less than fully obedient) minister of the Church of England was primarily concerned that the dry bones should live. Indeed, his objective extended beyond the borders of his Church. The answer to the question, "What may we reasonably believe to be God's design in raising up the Preachers called Methodists?" was, "Not to form any new sect; but to reform the nation, particularly the Church; and to spread scriptural holiness over the land."[68] Despite this aim, less radical than Fox's, Wesley's mission of taking the Gospel into the fields and market places exposed him to mob violence on a number of occasions.[69]

His first venture of this kind was on 2 April 1739. He writes:

> At four in the afternoon, I submitted to be more vile, and proclaimed in the highways the glad tidings of salvation, speaking from a little eminence in a ground adjoining to the city [of Bristol] to about three thousand people The scripture on which I spoke was this (is it possible any one should be ignorant, that it is fulfilled in every true Minister of Christ?) "The Spirit of the Lord is upon me, because He hath anointed me to preach the gospel to the poor. He hath sent me to heal the broken-hearted; to preach deliverance to the captives, and recovery of sight to the blind; To set at liberty them that are bruised, to proclaim the acceptable year of the Lord."[70]

67 G. Fox, *Journal*, 283. Cf. 174.

68 See *Minutes of Several Conversations*, in Wesley's *Works*, ed. Frank Baker, XXVI, 488f.

69 For a discussion of one example of this see Alan P.F. Sell, *Dissenting Thought*, 334–36.

70 J. Wesley, *Journal*, *Works* (1872), I, 185.

It is impossible not to detect the change of key. Prior to the 1738 experience Wesley had been a preacher of correct doctrine to the point of punctiliousness; now he goes among the poor and needy with a winsomeness which finds its echo in his brother Charles's hymn, "Thy faithfulness, Lord, each moment we find," which includes the stanza:

> O let me commend my Saviour to you,
> I set to my seal that Jesus is true:
> Ye all may find favour who come at His call:
> O come to my Saviour! His grace is for all.

However it may have been with the poor and needy, the idea of free saving grace for all, and the implication that sinners have the ability to "come at His call"—all of this was fighting talk in the eyes of ardent Calvinists. Thus the evangelical Calvinist George Whitefield, the high Calvinist Baptist John Gill, and the Church of England Calvinist Augustus Montague Toplady, believing that salvation was for the predestined elect alone, were at one in denouncing Wesley's evangelical Arminianism.[71] Not indeed that Wesley the field evangelist troubled his hearers with such theological niceties, but in numerous writings, and not least in his sermons written in part for the edification of his preachers, he treated in detail the great themes of grace, justification, sanctification, perfection, and many more. But whether in his study or in the fields the heart of his message was that we are declared righteous before God by grace, to which our trust, involving repentance, love and reverence, is the response, and in natural consequence of which holy living and good works should follow. To the proclamation of this message John Wesley devoted fifty years, travelling about 225,000 miles, and preaching about fifty thousand sermons.

V

In the light of my account of the experience of these two very different men who were both impelled into evangelism, I should now like to offer some reflections on religious experience, evangelism, and the relations between them. Here, is an area in which the churches would do well to seek clarity as the third millennium for Christian witness approaches.

First, Christians do their faith a disservice if they speak as if religious experience were a mere matter of feelings. Christians have

71 See further Alan P.F. Sell, *The Great Debate*, ch. III.

sometimes been tempted in this direction by their determination to resist the view that religious faith is simply a matter of cold, rational assent to propostions deemed to be true. In the interest of God's sovereign grace and our utter inability in the matter of salvation the eighteenth-century Sandemanians came as close as any to the view that all we had to do was to give intellectual assent to the salvific arrangements God had made.[72] But this would reduce preaching to the announcement of propositions demanding assent. We do not have to imagine what Howel Harris, Wesley's Calvinistic evangelical contemporary would have thought of this. On 29 December 1746 he was in Carmarthen. He writes, "I had vast freedom of wisdom all through, and to reason with the young academicians, and to shew the danger of philosophy. . . . Was cutting to the young students that go forth to preach without knowing their own misery, or Christ."[73] Certainly Fox was at a loss until he experienced the presence of Christ, and Wesley was largely ineffectual until his heart was warmed. But it would be a mistake so to elevate experience that its connection with knowledge were severed. Julian Huxley declared that "the change in our conception of God necessitates the stressing of religious experience as such, as against belief in particular dogma, or in the efficacy of special ritual."[74] But here the wedges are driven in too sharply. For example, we cannot experience divine forgiveness if we do not believe in a God who forgives; and the religious experience of worship turns upon the belief that there is a God who is worthy of worship, and who is present and mighty to save. In a word, faith in the sense of trust (as distinct from propositional assent) incorporates knowledge; as Donald Baillie put it, "the belief and the experience *are one*. . . . [R]eligious experience simply *is faith*. And this is precisely what is forgotten by many who have spoken of faith as based on religious experience."[75] If faith is reduced to a matter of rational assent it will not permeate the whole of life; if it is reduced to feeling all claims to knowledge will be prohibited. In the words of P.T. Forsyth, "My experienced salvation is not a passing impression but a life

72 See further Alan P.F. Sell, *Dissenting Thought*, 410, 415.

73 *Howell - Harris's Visits to Pembrokeshire*, transcribed by Tom Beynon, Aberystwyth: The Cambrian News 1966, 127.

74 Julian Huxley, *Essays of a Biologist*, London: Chatto & Windus 1923, 227.

75 D.M. Baillie, *Faith in God and Its Christian Consummation* (1927), London: Faber 1964, 113. Cf. his brother John Baillie, *The Sense of the Presence of God*, London: OUP 1962, 65.

faith. It is not a subjective frame but an objective relation, and even transaction."[76]

While such an experience may fuel evangelism, as it did in the case of Fox and Wesley, it does not provide a knock-down argument by wielding which Christians can refute sceptics. Yet in modern times, and in the wake of the onslaught of Hume and Kant upon the classical arguments for the existence of God, some have sought to elaborate an argument from religious experience. Frequently associated with this is the term "feeling"—a term which flows powerfully down from the theologian Schleiermacher, who, against those who defined religion in terms of its dogmas and customs, declared that the fount of religion was a feeling of absolute dependence. In his wake came some who regarded such a feeling as self-authenticating. Among the more popular representatives of this line was the Reverend Edward Hancox, Primitive Methodist minister in the Walsall area during the nineteenth century. The local Unitarian minister, Peter Dean, reported a meeting at which Hancox spoke thus: "if anyone puzzled them as to the inspiration of the Bible, they were to act as some man who said, 'I cannot answer, but (placing his hand on his heart) the secret lies here.' Acting in this way [comments Dean], what superstition may not be held? The believer in Papal infallibility, transubstantiation, witchcraft—anything, might say—'I cannot answer it, but I feel it here.'"[77]

In our own time still more sophisticated onslaughts against the argument from religious experience have been brought—not least by Charles Martin of this University. He concludes his discussion of the point that normal testing procedures are not available when claims to religous experience are made by saying that one who insists that he has had such and such an experience is in "a perfect refuge because no one can prove him wrong, but its unassailability has been bought at the price of making no claim about the world beyond the claim about the state of his own mind."[78]

Neither is there any absolute safety in numbers. P.T. Forsyth said "Standing over my experience is the experience of the whole

---

76 P.T. Forsyth, *The Person and Place of Jesus Christ* (1909), London: Independent Press 1961, 204.

77 Quoted by Alan P.F. Sell, *Dissenting Thought*, 471. Edward Hancox was Primitive Methodist minister in Walsall in 1883. See William Leary, *Ministers & Circuits of the Primitive Methodist Church, A Directory*, Loughborough: Teamprint 1990, 91.

78 Charles Martin, "A religious way of knowing," in *New Essays in Philosophical Theology*, eds. Antony Flew and Alasdair Macintyre, London: SCM Press 1955, 86.

evangelical succession."[79] No doubt; but fifty million Frenchmen can be wrong, and the analysis of the term "shared experience" is complicated indeed. On the other hand it is quite proper to be impressed by reports of experiences presented with a fair degree of consistency by considerable numbers of people whose characters are known to be above reproach. But such people will be witnessing, making their testimony, not producing a copper-bottomed demonstration of the existence of their God. Such witnesses cannot be proved wrong, as Dr. Martin observed. Any declaration that they are in error would be no less a statement of faith than their own. As the psychologist R.H. Thouless wrote many years ago, "When the psychologist describes what he believes to be the mental laws by which such an event as conversion takes place, he in no way excludes the explanation of it which would be given by the Salvation Army—that it takes place by the Grace of God."[80]

It need hardly be added that religious experience does not confer infallibility. It was Fox's incautious words in this respect which led some of his contemporaries to charge Quakers (of all people) with Popery, and others (and sometimes the same ones) to complain that he went beyond the Scriptures. On this point Wesley was much the more balanced of the two: "Experience," he writes, "is sufficient to *confirm* a doctrine which is grounded on Scripture. Though many fancy they experience what they do not, this is no prejudice to real experience."[81] This real experience, as Wesley would have been the first to agree, cannot be at second hand; and it must continue to grow. His contemporary Howel Harris was resolved "not to speak of what we have had from the LORD, but what we have *now*, afresh from him."[82] Or as Fox's contemporary John Bunyan declared, "I preached what I felt, what I smartingly did feel."[83] With which we come full circle to evangelism.

VI

There can be no doubt that the Evangelical Revival of the second half of the eighteenth century prompted a concern for global

79 P.T. Forsyth, *The Person and Place of Jesus Christ*, 205.

80 Robert H. Thouless, *An Introduction to the Psychology of Religion*, Cambridge: CUP, 2nd edn., 1924, 9.

81 J. Wesley, *Works* (1872) V, 133.

82 Howel Harris, *Last Message and Dying Testimony*, Trevecka 1774, 8.

83 J. Bunyan, *Grace Abounding to the Chief of Sinners*, 124.

mission unequalled in modern times.[84] Many felt like Wesley that the world was their parish, and they set out to win it for Christ. Many faced great odds, not only from adverse climatic and health conditions abroad, but from conservative Calvinists at home, who felt that since God had predestined his elect for salvation, he would ensure their eternal security without any assistance from us.[85]

Today, however, as I said at the beginning of this lecture, the term "evangelism" is tarnished for many because of the antics of some evangelists. In addition, the conviction has grown since the 1960s that since the Gospel is for the whole person and not simply for some mysterious entity called the soul, we would do better to speak of "witness" or "mission"; for "evangelism" is too narrowly associated with proclamation of the Gospel with a view to the hearer's response of repentance and faith. Thus, for example, Priscilla Pope-Levison has shown that in documents published by the World Council of Churches from 1961 onwards the wider terms encouraging service of many kinds are favoured, and that on occasion the idea of calling people to repentance and to faith in Christ is almost absent.[86] She quotes from a text of 1966:

> In former times the Church was viewed as the ark, perilously afloat amidst the turbulent seas of this world; outside the safety of this vessel mankind was going down to destruction and the only salvation was to be dragged from the deep into the safety of the ecclesiastical ship. . . . In our study however we are more inclined to say that the Church is a part of the world and that thinking about the Church should always start by our defining it as a segment of the world. . . .[87]

This passage prompts two remarks. First, it is true that the Church has sometimes been viewed as an ark, but I think that from the eighteenth century onwards the record is clear that evangelicals have at least as often been pioneers of social, political, economic and educational reform. Time would fail to tell of Wilberforce, John

---

84 See D.W. Bebbington, *Evangelicalism in Modern Britain*, London: Unwin Hyman 1989, 40–42.

85 See Alan P.F. Sell, *The Great Debate*, 83–87. For a discussion of current issues relating to Christian mission see idem, *Aspects of Christian Integrity*, Calgary: University of Calgary Press 1990, and Louisville: Westminster/John Knox Press 1991, ch. V.

86 See Priscilla Pope-Levison, "Evangelism in the WCC from New Delhi to Vancouver," *Mid-Stream* XXVIII, no. 2, 1989, 159–72.

87 Ibid., 162, quoting T. Wieser, ed., *Planning for Mission*, New York: The U.S. Conference for the World Council of Churches 1966, 9.

Howard, the Quakers Elizabeth Fry, Cadbury, Huntley and Palmer, and many more. These were all in the line of George Fox with his appeals for justice and righteous social dealings,[88] with Wesley who declared that the person of catholic spirit is one whose "heart is enlarged toward all mankind."[89] Secondly, the advice that we should start by defining the Church as a segment of the world is adequate sociologically but defective theologically; for the Church comprises those called by God. Apart from this realisation we shall mistake it for one more purely human institution.

While I entirely agree that witness and mission require both words and deeds, and that if these are not in accord we are hypocrites, I suggest that we need to retain the term "evangelism" for that preaching of the Gospel which seeks a response as the Holy Spirit brings the believer's words home to others. No doubt our deeds should be consistent with our words, but if there are no words our deeds will be dumb. Moreover we need not only called and appointed evangelists like Philip of old who will herald the message, but "ordinary" Christian believers who will gossip it as those anonymous ones did to such effect in the early church.[90] Only those who have received Christ can tell of him with conviction and joy; but the substance of their message is not their experiences, but Christ's redeeming work. As Forsyth put it,

> We do not preach our impressions, or even our experience. These make but the vehicle, as it were. What we preach is something much more solid, more objective, with more stay in it; something that can suffice when our experience has ebbed until it seems to be as low as Christ's was in the great desertion and victory on the Cross. We want something that will stand by us when we cannot feel any more; we want a Cross we can cling to, not simply an objective Cross.[91]

The heart of the early apostles' message was, "We proclaim Christ—yes, Christ nailed to the Cross . . . to those who have heard his call he is the power of God and the wisdom of God."[92] So, after all our service, all our striving for social justice, all our ecological concern—

---

88 See, e.g., G. Fox, *Journal*, 37–38.

89 J. Wesley, Sermon XXXIX ib. "Catholic Spirit," *Works* (1872), V, 503. Cf. II Corinthians 6:11.

90 Acts 8:4–8; 11:19–21. The distinction between Philip's official heralding and the informal testimony of the persecuted believers is made by the two different Greek words used.

91 P.T. Forsyth, *The Work of Christ* (1910), London: Independent Press 1938, 49.

92 I Corinthians 1:23.

after all of this we need to face up to the challenge which Kierkegaard expected to have posed to him on departing this life: "Have you uttered the definite message *quite definitely*?"[93]

I conclude with five cautionary words. First, some evangelists may mislead us into thinking that genuine Christian experience is always dramatic and takes one form only. William James did much to focus attention upon the sensational when he investigated religious experience. "I have loaded the lectures with concrete examples," he writes, "and I have chosen these among the extremer expressions of the religious temperament."[94] But he knew quite well that if some—relatively few, I believe—have a Damascus road experience, the long and arduous experience of many more is of a Trans-Canada Highway kind. As to the forms of experience, if Christians stereotype these and deem certain forms only to be acceptable—as some do—then unwarrantable impositions are placed upon those amongst whom they go. Taught to expect a dramatic conversion experience, the young Joseph Parker (1830–1902), later to become minister of London's City Temple, thought that his repentance would be inadequate because his sins were not as great as those of others: "So I stood outside the gate, crying bitter tears, because I had not sinned according to the magnitude and quality of another man's transgression."[95] From stereotypical experiences flow stereotypical testimonies, as the philosopher T.E. Jessop realised when he penned these words:

> Once in saintly passion I cried with desperate grief:
> "O Lord, my heart is black with guile, of sinners I am chief!"
> Then stooped my guardian angel and whispered from behind,
> "Vanity, my little man, you're nothing of the kind!"

Or, if you prefer the same moral from the Catholic tradition, consider some words of von Hügel. He writes of Ignatius Loyola, who was born five hundred years ago this year, as follows:

> When Frederick William Faber preached the panegyric of St. Ignatius Loyola, on the occasion of the Feast of the Founder of the Jesuits . . . he spent an hour in unbroken, sympathetic, indeed

---

93 S. Kierkegaard, *Journals*, selected, trans. and ed. A. Dru, London: OUP 1959, 493. I realise, of course, that in context the message to which Kierkegaard referred was one of rebuke to the church leaders of his day. It was not "a cheerful message," and he wished that someone else could deliver it.

94 W. James, *The Varieties of Religious Experience*, v.

95 Quoted by Albert Dawson, *Joseph Parker, D.D. His Life and Ministry*, London: Partridge 1901, 22.

fervent, exposition of this saint's spirituality, and only in his last sentence did he introduce the necessary limitation and expansion: "This, then, my dear brethren, is St. Ignatius's way to heaven; and, thank God, it is not the only way!"[96]

Secondly, let us not forget that the objective in evangelism is not the salvation of individual souls who will continue in isolation from all others, but the engrafting of believers into God's servant body, the Church. God's objective is a new humanity, of which the Church, however empirically imperfect, is a sign and a foretaste.[97] From the human side, Wesley likened converts without nurture to still-born babies. Therefore as Campbell Morgan—no mean evangelist—declared, "We must hold to the very highest doctrine of the Church, or our evangelism will be weak and one-sided." He added, "The Church has largely failed in evangelism because the Church has not realized within her own borders the force of her own life."[98]

Thirdly, as any farmer knows, those who would sow seed must have some acquaintance with the soil. Where evangelism is concerned this means that individual Christians must not treat those to whom they speak as objects, but as persons with questions, doubts, fears, hopes, joys, sorrows. The message must reach the hearer or there is no communication. Where churches and their strategies are concerned there is homework to be done. What is the nature of the society they would reach? What are the opinions of its inhabitants? The Canadian churches are particularly well placed to formulate answers to such questions, for sound research has been done, notably by Reginald Bibby of the University of Lethbridge and Merlin Brinkerhoff of this University.[99] If Dr. Bibby proves that more than 90 per cent of Canadians claim a connection with a Christian group, and that the vast majority of these are not inclined to change their allegiance, Canada's churches contemplating evangelism need to pay heed. Again, the message which was addressed

---

96 F. von Hügel, *Essays and Addresses on the Philosophy of Religion. Second Series*, London: J.M. Dent 1933, 232. For an account of the varied paths by which Douglas Hyde, John Rowlands, C.S. Lewis and C.E.M. Joad came (or returned) to faith see Bernard E. Jones, "The faith-ladder," *The Expository Times* LXXII, no. 8, May 1961, 249–54.

97 See, e.g., Ephesians 2:15.

98 G. Campbell Morgan, *Evangelism*, Worthing: H.E. Walter, new edn., 1964, 26–27, 37–38.

99 See, e.g., Reginald W. Bibby, *Fragmented Gods. The Poverty and Potential of Religion in Canada*, Toronto: Irwin Publishing 1987. For an account of his Calgary-based research in connection with Merlin B. Brinkerhoff see ibid., 28–31.

to an age which readily associated anxiety with guilt and morality with the Ten Commandments literally construed will require radical modification if it is to be heard by people for whom God is but a memory, anxiety no more than a human condition, and morality only a matter of individual taste.

Fourthly, it ill behoves Christians to think that successful evangelism depends upon the use of particular methods. The charge of inventing such evangelistic "new measures" as the anxious bench, protracted meetings, the altar call has frequently been laid at the door of Charles Grandison Finney the American revivalist. However Keith Hardman has shown that most of these techniques had been used by Methodists before Finney began his missions.[100] Today the techniques and methods have multiplied, but the principle is the same: it is not the evangelist or the methods which save. We can put on the best and most lavish show possible—as the priests of Baal did of old; but apart from the gracious work of God the Holy Spirit our result will be as theirs was: "They cried still louder and, as was their custom, gashed themselves with swords and spears until the blood ran. All afternoon they raved and ranted till the hour of the regular sacrifice, but still there was no sound, no answer, no sign of attention."[101]

My last point is simply a reaffirmation of what I have just said. In evangelism the issue always lies with God. If an evangelist declares "I made fifty converts last week," he is telling a blasphemous lie. Salvation is of the Lord alone. The report of a joint consultation of representatives of the World Council of Churches and the Roman Catholic Church was much sounder: "It is the Spirit who is the primary witness to Christ, human testimony being a sharing in this witness."[102] And to what is the witness made? To Christ's reconciling work, of which Forsyth said,

> reconciliation is no aesthetic, or educational, or impressionistic affair. It is not revival. It is not a question of touching a certain number of individuals, and gathering them for salvation out of a lost mankind. It cannot be done by a magnetic temperament, a noble character, or a lofty sage. It means changing a whole race's relation to God. For good and all that could only be done from God's side; and it was done in the cross. . . . Christ did not die simply to affect men but to effect salvation, not simply to move

---

100 See Keith J. Hardman, *Charles Grandison Finney 1792–1875. Revivalist and Reformer*, Syracuse, NY: Syracuse University Press 1987, 84. Now available from Grand Rapids: Baker Book House.

101 I Kings 18:28–29.

102 Report, "Unity and Common Witness," *Study Encounter*, no. 3, 1975, 1.

> man's heart but to accomplish God's will. All we may do to reconcile men to God is but the following up of a great and final deed of God—the cross.[103]

As we do our following up of what God has done we might well have the deathbed utterances of George Fox and John Wesley in mind. To some of his Friends who came to his sick bed Fox triumphantly declared, "All is well. The Seed of God reigns over all, and over death itself."[104] As Wesley lay dying he said, "The best of all is, God is with us!"[105] May a mixture of Fox's bold confidence and Wesley's calm assurance be the portion of all who testify to God's saving grace.

103 P.T. Forsyth, *The Cruciality of the Cross* (1909), London: Independent Press 1957, 18–19.

104 As recorded by Thomas Ellwood, G. Fox, *Journal*, 760.

105 Quoted by Luke Tyerman, *The Life and Times of the Rev. John Wesley, M.A., Founder of the Methodists*, London: Hodder & Stoughton, 3rd edn., 1876, III, 654.

The Martyrs of 1593, the Church and the State

In 1996 many will be remembering the 450th anniversary of the death of Martin Luther. Although he is not the focal point of this anniversary address, some aspects of his thought will occupy us along the way. He will also, together with another poet, serve to introduce our theme. As translated by Thomas Carlyle (the bicentenary of whose birth will fall in 1995), and with reference to the diabolical enemies of God, Luther would have us sing:

> God's word, for all their craft and force,
> One moment will not linger,
> But, spite of hell, shall have its course;
> 'Tis written by His finger.
> And though they take our life,
> Goods, honour, children, wife,
> Yet is their profit small;
> These things shall vanish all:
> The city of God remaineth.

In the nineteenth century the American poet Henry Wadsworth Longfellow, whose art has been described as "an outstanding example of popular taste,"[1] struck a patriotic note in his poem "The building of the ship." He describes the building of the ship, and after many a nautical metaphor, the vessel is launched into the bosom of the sea. Then, right at the end, Longfellow thinks of another ship:

---

1 Eric Mottram on Longfellow in *The Penguin Companion to Literature III. United States and Latin American Literature*, eds. idem and Malcolm Bradbury, Harmondsworth: Penguin Books 1971, 159.

Thou, too, sail on, O Ship of State!
Sail on, O UNION, strong and great!
Humanity, with all its fears,
With all the hopes of future years,
Is hanging breathless on thy fate! . . .
In spite of rock and tempest's roar,
In spite of false lights on the shore,
Sail on, nor fear to breast the sea!
Our hearts, our hopes, are all with thee,
Our hearts, our hopes, our prayers, our tears,
Our faith triumphant o'er our fears,
Are all with thee,—are all with thee![2]

In this heartfelt expression of paganism we have the makings of civil religion, and about that I shall have something more to say. My point for the moment is that when placed side by side Luther and Longfellow clamantly pose the question, "What ought to be the relations between the city of God and the ship of state?" As the churches of the world approach Christianity's third millennium they would fail in nerve and in faith if they failed to give fresh consideration to this question. With increasing religious and cultural diversity in western lands—not least in those with officially established churches; with the dramatic political changes in the former U.S.S.R. and in eastern Europe; in view of the economic and political importance of Islamic states, and of the emergence of new nations in Africa; and in the light of the claims of aboriginal peoples in many parts of the world, the question is thrust upon us.

Where to begin? We may with some confidence take our bearings from the New Testament, for there we shall find a fundamental principle clearly enunciated, as well as encouragingly diverse applications of that principle at different times and in varying circumstances. The principle emerges from an incident which took place during Jesus's week in Jerusalem prior to the crucifixion, when those who, for a variety of reasons, were opposed to him were seeking ways of provoking him into condemning himself out of his own mouth. It is recorded, with slight variations in wording, in the Gospels of Matthew, Mark and Luke. In Matthew's version some Pharisees and Herodians come to Jesus and begin by flattering him for his honesty which, they are sure, will prompt a direct answer to their question:

> "Are we or are we not permitted to pay taxes to the Roman Emperor?" Jesus was aware of their malicious intention and said to

2 *Poems of Longfellow*, London: Kent 1880, I, 161.

> them, "You hypocrites! Why are you tryng to catch me out? Show me the money in which the tax is paid." They handed him a silver piece. Jesus asked, "Whose head is this, and whose inscription?" "Caesar's," they replied. He said to them, "Then pay Caesar what is due to Caesar, and pay God what is due to God."[3]

Under Roman rule, revenue in Palestine was raised through customs duty, a land tax, and a poll tax. Of all of these it was the poll tax which incensed many Jews of the time. The Zealots in particular, believing that Caesar's reign and God's were utterly incompatible, loathed it. (And it would not be lost on the authorities that Jesus's disciples included Simon the Zealot). The poll tax was paid in special coinage depicting Caesar's head, which Herod Philip had had struck as a means of flattering Tiberius. To strict Jews the image involved a breaking of the commandment prohibiting the making of graven images,[4] and to many Jews Caesar's head and inscription simply rubbed salt into the wound of their political subservience. If Jesus advised payment, many would angrily denounce him; if he recommended non-payment his questioners would be able to report him to the Roman authorities as one fomenting sedition. Jesus avoids the trap, and his actual reply makes it plain that Caesar is to be paid back (for that is the force of the Greek—it is not a gift, it is a debt) what is owing to him in recompense for the services of the government, and that God is to be paid back what is his. The implication is that money can be given for services provided, but worship, demanded by the Emperor, may not be given to the one whose inscription is on the coin. With reference to Jesus's reply to the Pharisees and Herodians Lord Acton wrote that it "gave to the civil power, under the protection of conscience, a sacredness it had never enjoyed, and bounds it had never acknowledged; [it was] the repudiation of absolutism and the inauguration of freedom."[5]

We must not, however, read Jesus as suggesting that the spheres of Caesar and God, though distinct, are utterly separate. On the contrary, in John's Gospel Jesus tells Pilate the Roman governor, "You would have no authority at all over me, if it had not been granted to you from above. . . ."[6] This is in harmony with the conviction twice expressed in the book of Daniel, and implicit in the

---

3 Matthew 22:17–21. Cf. Mark 12:13–17; Luke 20:19–26.

4 Exodus 20:4.

5 J.E.E. Dalberg-Acton, *The History of Freedom and Other Essays*, (1907), Freeport, NY: Books for Libraries Press 1967, 29.

6 John 19:11.

creation narratives of Genesis, that God's rule is over all.[7] Accordingly, as Oscar Cullmann wrote, "On the one hand, the State is nothing final. On the other, it has the right to demand what is necessary to its existence—but no more. Every totalitarian claim of the State is thereby disallowed."[8]

The general principle laid down by Jesus is echoed as the New Testament unfolds, but already we begin to see that its application varies according to prevailing crcumstances. Thus, for example, at a time of relative tranquillity, Paul exhorts the Roman Christians to be subject to their rulers, and to pay their taxes.[9] On the other hand, before the New Testament is closed, and at a time when Christians are on the point of being persecuted for their faith, the exiled John the Seer has his vision of an obscene woman, "'Babylon the great, the mother of whores and of every obscenity on earth.' The woman, I saw, was drunk with the blood of God's people and with the blood of those who had borne their testimony to Jesus."[10] Those in the know would without difficulty penetrate John's coded message and read "Rome" for "Babylon."

The varied applications of Jesus's principle through Christian history have not only been a response to the now kindly, now hostile faces which the state has presented to the Church. The fact is that the configurations of both Church and state undergo constant change. The visible face of the Church has been fractured to such a degree that no earthly power need much fear the return of a thirteenth-century Innocent III. The outlines of the modern nation state in all its secular glory were not laid down until the sixteenth century. In a post-Christendom age Christians may find themselves living under authorities who are content that so-called Christian values are prized and enshrined in fundamental legislation; or they may be called to witness in face of a ruling apparatus which not only does not seek the cooperation of the Church, but which seeks to stamp it out. Christians may find themselves as members of traditional nations within new territorial nations, as in many African countries.[11] In this lecture I shall use the term "state" in the general sense of the governing authorities, qualifying it by such terms as "totalitarian" and "Byzantine" when I intend to be more

7 Daniel 4:34; 7:14.

8 O. Cullmann, *The State in the New Testament*, New York: Scribners 1956, 37.

9 Romans 13.

10 Revelation 17:5–6.

11 For important elaborations of the points made thus far in this paragraph see *Church and State. Opening a New Ecumenical Discussion*, (Faith and Order Paper no. 85), Geneva: World Council of Churches 1978.

specific. It is, of course, as impossible to describe all Church-state situations as it would be impertinent to offer unsought advice as to how Christians should comport themselves *vis à vis* the authorities in their several, very different, contexts. It is possible, however, to look at some of the historical permutations through which Jesus's God-Caesar principle has passed with a view to illustrating it and underlining its permanent relevance.

I

In his valuable study, *On Religious Freedom*, Jay Newman of the University of Guelph writes that "some people may genuinely be unable to distinguish conceptually between 'church' and 'state,' and others may feel obliged for ideological or theological reasons to pretend that they cannot."[12] I suggest that the latter include those who believe that there is nothing but the state, and those who believe that there is nothing but the Church. They confer absolute power upon, and offer absolute allegiance to, whichever it is that they see. Since these are polar opposite ways of undermining Jesus's principle, I shall give them short shrift.

In 311 Constantine the Great embraced Christianity. On 27 October 312, following his celebrated vision of the flaming Cross in the sky, Rome fell to Christianity's most powerful convert, who thus became the senior Emperor. There have been many debates as to the sincerity or otherwise of Constantine's conversion, but it seems clear that he thought he owed his victory to Christ. In 313 toleration was accorded to all religious groups under the Edict of Milan, and Constantine showed special imperial favour to Christianity. The standard of living of orthodox priests went up, for example, since they were now supported from state funds. The question whether Constantine's conversion was of real benefit to the Church has received contradictory answers through the centuries. Bernard of Clairvaux (1090–1153) looked back upon the event as a landmark in the development of the papacy;[13] a modern writer suggests that "in a sense the battle was lost in 313: the battle, I mean, to be in

12 Jay Newman, *On Religious Freedom*, Ottawa: University of Ottawa Press 1991, 115.

13 Bernard of Clairvaux, *Sermones in Cantica canticorum*, Migne, PL CLXXXIII, 1862, 958–59.

the world, yet not of it. . . ."[14] A century later, and notwithstanding the formidable efforts of Bishop Ambrose of Milan, the imperial structures began to disintegrate, and Christian leaders positioned themselves to assume more and more temporal power.

For theological support they could turn to Augustine who began to write *The City of God* three years after the year of the sack of Rome by the Goths in 410; he completed the book thirteen years later. The pressing question Augustine had to address was this: "How are we to account for the strange coincidence of the rise of Christianity and the fall of the Empire?" But as his work progressed Augustine's vision grew. With the worldly powers in ruins around him he writes of an earthly city and a heavenly city: "Two loves therefore have given origin to these two cities, self-love in contempt of God unto the earthly, love of God in contempt of one's self to the heavenly."[15] It must be emphasised that Augustine does not at first intend to equate the earthly city with the state and the heavenly with the Church. Rather, in Platonic fashion, both cities are eternal realities; the earthly state is not all bad, and the visible Church is not all good. The earthly state is, however, deeply stained by sin. But there is an ambiguity in his writing which allows Augustine also to say "the Church now on earth is both the kingdom of Christ, and the kingdom of heaven."[16] Thus was spawned what became known as the Gelasian view (after Pope Gelasius, d. 492), which encouraged the medieval Popes to elevate Church above state. So it was that Hildebrand, who took the name Gregory VII and was Pope from 1073 to 1085, issued twenty-seven articles proclaiming the absolute supremacy of the Roman Church; declaring that the Roman pontiff alone may depose and reinstate bishops; that he may be judged by no one; and that he may depose Emperors. That this last claim was no piece of empty rhetoric soon became clear to the Western Emperor Henry IV, who was excommunicated on 22 February 1076. We need not at our present state of scholarship doubt Gregory's sincerity. Conditions were chaotic, civil strife abounded, and he was in quest of reform. We may how-

---

14 Geoffrey F. Nuttall, *Christian Pacifism in History*, Oxford: Basil Blackwell 1958, 5; second edn. Berkeley, CA: World Without War Council 1971. See further N.H. Baynes, "Constantine the Great and the Christian Church," *Proceedings of the British Academy* XV, 1929, 341–442; A. Alföldi, *The Conversion of Constantine and Pagan Rome*, Oxford: Clarendon Press 1948; A.H.M. Jones, *Constantine and the Conversion of Europe*, New York: Macmillan 1949. For a more adversely critical view of Constantine and Constantinianism see Alastair Kee, *Constantine Versus Christ*, London: SCM Press 1982.

15 Augustine, *The City of God*, XIV.xxviii.

16 Ibid., XX.ix.

ever regret his methods and his absolutising of churchly power. The way was now clear for Pope Innocent III (1198–1216) to declare that the Pope was lower than God but higher than any man—including Emperors. His successor Boniface VIII, in his Papal Bull *Unam Sanctam* (1302), affirmed that "The temporal sword is to be used by kings and knights, but at the bidding and by the forbearance of the priests."[17] This was to go further than Aquinas, who held that the state had its proper functions; that the ideal to strive for was harmonious relations between Church and state; that the rulers were not puppets of the Pope; but that the Church is superior to the state in that its objectives are supernatural and eternal.[18]

Concerning the extremer view that the Church is above the state P.T. Forsyth was his usual pungent self (and not quite fair to Aquinas): "From Augustine, who introduced that error into theology, to Aquinas, who authorised it, Rome has been concerned to save the State from the devil, only by organised subordination to her holy self."[19] In justice to Augustine it must be pointed out that other portions of his writings clearly support the principle which Jesus enunciated when answering the Pharisees and Herodians. But ideologists in all generations are notorious for their selective reading.

From time to time the state has usurped the place of the Church, and when this has happened Jesus's principle has been denied in the opposite direction. It happened in the East when, following the fourth-century doctrinal controversies surrounding the Nicene-Constantinopolitan Creed, the Emperor Theodosius imposed orthodoxy throughout his domain, and resolved to tolerate neither heretics nor pagans. Here we have the so-called "Byzantine" authority of state over Church. Contrasting present-day East and West on this point Gerald Bray writes,

> In the East it is the Orthodox Church which maintains the Byzantine heritage in every aspect of its life. The emperors could return tomorrow and find themselves completely at home. In the West, it is the bishops who wear the imperial purple, and the pope who reigns in splendour from the Vatican whilst the imperial palace lies in ruins on the Palatine.[20]

---

17 See further Brian Tierney, *The Crisis of Church and State 1050–1300*, Englewood Cliffs, NJ: Prentice Hall 1964.

18 See further F.C. Copleston, *Aquinas*, Harmondsworth: Penguin Books 1957, 228–34.

19 P.T. Forsyth, *The Charter of the Church*, London: Alexander and Shepheard 1896, 92.

20 Gerald Bray, "The origins of the Christian state," *Churchman* XCI, no. 1, 1985, 38.

In our own time we have witnessed two strangely contradictory things. On the one hand there have been and still are states which, on grounds of communist ideology, ride roughshod over the Church. At a time of extreme difficulty for Christians in his part of the world a significantly anonymous theologian from Eastern Europe explained that

> in a socialist state the definitions of the state and of religious life are part of an *a priori* political doctrine. The Church is subject to state legislation which has been drawn up without consultation with the Church, and which has an anti-religious character. The irony is that the Church is forced to accept the particular ideological definition of a religion on which the legislation is based, namely, that religion is a "superstructure" of a social class which is in the process of being eliminated. By its very legal description, the Church has a marginal place and role in society.[21]

During the 1980s it was my privilege to visit a number of countries in which Christians lived under precisely those conditions. I have powerful recollections of the difficulties placed in the way of pastors' children who sought a higher education; of the restrictions imposed upon Christian witness; of the demotion of Christian employees simply because they were Christian; of Christian leaders who were alleged to be fellow-travellers, but who bore pressures the like of which most of us have never experienced. But I have equally vivid—and humbling—memories of the courageous witness and resolute faith of pastors and people; of the ways in which churches, by their faithful service to the people around them without regard to religious allegiance, would earn grudging respect from communist officials and be allowed more room for manoeuvre. And I have heard more recently from some of my friends in the formerly communist eastern Europe of their fears that some of the spiritual strengths they gained under oppression may be diminished as conditions become easier and more Westernised. So I could go on: the remarkable survival of the Church in China, driven underground for so many years; the fact that under communism in Ethiopia church attendance has increased dramatically. . . .

On the other hand we have the phenomenon that the very states which seek to curtail and even obliterate the Church (and other religious expressions) themselves develop what can only be described as a civil religion. From an early age people are taught to honour the flag, to sing the Party "hymn," to observe the holidays,

21 *Church and State. Opening a New Ecumenical Discussion*, 107.

to venerate the heroes and their statues. As a Lutheran World Federation consultation reported, "Civil religion consists of a pattern of symbols, ideas and practices that legitimate the authority of civil institutions in a society. It provides a fundamental value orientation that binds a people together in common action within the public realm."[22] But the same thing can happen in societies in which there is no official repression of religion; in which there is nominal adherence by many to a religion; in which vestigial belief and concern for the religious observance of rites of passage constitute a folk religion which, in individual cases, may or may not mingle with patriotism to form a civil religion which can become a strong bulwark against the evangelistic activities of the committed Christians of the region.[23] The state in the sense of the authorities, the organs of government are, according to Jesus's principle, ordained by God and as such they are to be respected unless and until they usurp God's rights. But states in the sense of particular nations are not divinely instituted. Hence when civil religion reaches the pitch of deifying the nation you have a form of idolatry which is utterly unbliblical and potentially dangerous.[24] The fact remains that "Churches in pluralistic societies, of which there are many today, must find ways of relating with integrity to the civil religions that apparently no society lacks."[25]

So much for the usurpation of the state by the Church and of the Church by the state, neither of which enable the due recogni-

---

22 Quoted by Béla Harmati, *The Church and Civil Religion in the Nordic Countries of Europe*, Geneva: Lutheran World Federation 1984, 8.

23 For some interesting variations upon this theme see the volume at n. 21 above, especially p. 79. Susan Sundback (ibid., 39) writes of the situation in Finland: "The [national] church cannot risk pushing out those members who are already alienated from the religious part of church activity, because these are probably a majority among church members and the population as a whole." Needless to say the reference to church members who have no involvement in "the religious part of church activity" rings strangely on the ear of an English Dissenter! Indeed, there would seem to be a contradiction in terms here, not to mention a huge problem in relation to Gospel discipline. It is scant comfort to learn that of the Scandinavian countries, all of which register more than 90% of their populations as Lutheran, Finland's church attendance is the highest, with 12% of the population attending church at least once per month. See ibid., 24. Speaking of Sweden Lennart Ejerfelt makes no bones about it: "In fact this membership [of 95%] is not seen, even by the state, as an index of the real strength and influence of the Swedish Church but rather as a civil religion phenomenon." Ibid., 80.

24 See further Allen O. Miller, "The service of the state," *The Reformed and Presbyterian World* XXV, no. 6, June 1959, 261–68.

25 Roger L. Shinn in *Church and State. Opening a New Ecumenical Discussion*, 38.

tion of Jesus's principle. Let us now investigate two more hopeful possibilities and one permissible emergency response.

II

With more than a nod in the direction of a suitably selected Augustine, Martin Luther developed his doctrine of the two kingdoms. He wrote:

> God has established two kinds of government among men. The one is spiritual; it has no sword, but it has the word, by means of which men are to become good and righteous, so that with this righteousness they may attain eternal life. He administers this righteousness through the word, which he has committed to the preachers. The other kind is worldly government, which works through the sword so that those who do not want to be good and righteous to eternal life may be forced to become good and righteous in the eyes of the world. He administers this righteousness through the sword. . . . There is no human ordinance or authority in either, but each is a divine thing entirely.[26]

In stating matters as he did Luther had an eye both to the line of Popes from Gregory VII onwards who had elevated Church above state, and to the Anabaptists of his day who, with varying degrees of revolutionary zeal, were denying any connection between Church and state. It is important for us to recognise that, theologically, it was not Luther's intention to have Church and state, each with its own functions and officers, in separate compartments. Both kingdoms derived their being and authority from God, and the one was to assist the other. Thus, for example, pastors would urge their people to be loyal to the princes; the princes would ensure the protection of the Church. Unlike Calvin, however, Luther did not devise an ecclesiastical machinery which might render the theological linkage practical. Further, after the Diet of Worms (1521) he accepted the protection of his own prince of Sachsen, and during the Peasants' Revolt (1524–1526) he relied upon the princes to wreak vengeance upon the rebels. Meanwhile a number of German and Scandinavian rulers found it convenient and possibly even right to adopt the Lutheran Reform; indeed it is hard to imagine how, otherwise, Lutheranism could have spread as far and as rapidly as it did. In the following century, however, the civil arm took increasing precedence over state Lutheranism, and in the eighteenth

---

26 Luther's *Works*, eds. Robert C. Schultz and H.T. Lehmann. Philadelphia: Fortress Press 1967, XLVI, 99–100.

century pietism encouraged the Church to regard itself as increasingly separate from the state, emotionally and practically. Luther would not have approved. The Church became submissive, persuading itself that since God had inaugurated both realms, it was not for the Church to raise its voice, even if the state should begin to take on a demonic aspect—as it did. As one Lutheran theologian has written with respect to Lutheran states, "The possibility that the state itself could degenerate and become demonic was for centuries rarely considered."[27] Another, while valuing the two kingdoms theory when properly understood and practised laments the decline of the Church into political neutrality, declaring that "in practice, political neutrality always means accommodation to existing government. . . . Luther's doctrine had something quite different in view."[28]

Few outside Germany launched as blistering an attack upon the Church of that land at the outbreak of the World War I as P.T. Forsyth. State absolutism, he declares,

> has issued there in the reign of a militarism which deliberately disowns moral obligations in national interests. And this situation has neither been challenged nor repudiated with horror by the German Church. . . . It is not the Rationalism of Germany that has been so deadly to its soul, but its more than Erastianism. It is its Byzantinism that has thus severed it from the Christian conscience of the world. . . . Its witness for free thought (which is not a prime Christian issue) is sterile by its lack of witness for a free conscience (which for Christianity is not only prime but essential). It has no practical protest against the popery of Caesar. . . . If the Church lose that prophetic office to the State, it ceases, amid whatever pietism or learning, to be a Church of the living God, or an agent of His Kingdom. . . . [The German Church] is cowed and paralysed by a relation to the State which is the fatal legacy of Luther's treatment of the Princes and the exterminating dragonnade by his Protestantism on spiritual freedom in the Anabaptists. He made

27 Torleiv Austad, "Attitudes towards the state in Western theological thinking," *Themelios* XVI, no. 1, October/November 1990, 18.

28 Wolfgang Huber in *Church and State. Opening a New Ecumenical Discussion*, 117. See further Anders Nygren, "Luther's doctrine of the two kingdoms," *Christus Victor*, no. 104, March 1959, 3–10, and comments by Charles E. Raven, Geoffrey F. Nuttall, Albert D. Belden and E.L. Allen in ibid., no. 105, July 1959, 3–8. Dr. Nuttall (6) detects a lack of emphasis upon "the victory which overcomes the world by overcoming evil with good" not only in Luther's two kingdoms theory, but in his theology as a whole.

> political resignation a high virtue, which is a fatal public ethic. . . . The barrack has come to have more effect on [the German nation's] character than its Church has.[29]

Allowance for his vehemence must, I think, be made, for Forsyth had just witnessed the rape of Belgium and was writing as war raged. I have already balanced Luther's theological intentions against his political actions, and I should not wish to blame a person for not being of an age other than his or her own. Nevertheless Forsyth's horror at what can happen when the Church relinquishes its prophetic role only underscores the observations of the Lutheran theologians whom I have first been careful to quote.

It happened again in the events leading up to World War II. One of the relatively few who sought to challenge his Church's quietism was Dietrich Bonhoeffer who broadcast a denunciation of Hitler in 1933 and was thereafter a marked man. Ten years later he was arrested, and on 8 April 1945 he was hanged at Flossenberg. His last words were, "This is the end—for me the beginning of life!"[30]

The bravest and most decisive formal theological statement of this century was drawn up at Barmen, May 29–31, 1934. Here the Confessing Christians of the Lutheran, Reformed and United Churches of Germany raised their voices against the "'German Christians' of the Reich Church government" and declared:

> As Jesus Christ is God's assurance of the forgiveness of all our sins, so in the same way and with the same seriousness he is also God's mighty claim upon our whole life. . . . We reject the false doctrine, as though there were areas of our life in which we would not belong to Jesus Christ, but to other lords—areas in which we would not need justification and sanctification through him. . . .
>
> The Christian Church is the congregation of the brethren in which Jesus Christ acts presently as the Lord in Word and sacrament through the Holy Spirit. As the Church of pardoned sinners, it has to testify in the midst of a sinful world . . . that it is solely his property. . . . We reject the false doctrine, as though the Church were permitted to abandon the form of its message and order to its own pleasure or to changes in prevailing ideological and political convictions. . . .
>
> We reject the false doctrine, as though the State, over and beyond its special commission, should and could become the single and totalitarian order of human life, thus fulfilling the Church's

29 P.T. Forsyth, *Theology in Church and State*, London: Hodder & Stoughton 1915, 319, 324, 325, 327, 328.

30 Dietrich Bonhoeffer, *Letters and Papers from Prison*, London: Collins Fontana 1964, 181.

> vocation as well. We reject the false doctrine, as though the Church, over and beyond its special commission, should and could appropriate the characteristics, the tasks, and the dignity of the State, thus itself becoming an organ of the State. . . .[31]

The Barmen Declaration has ecclesiastical as well as prophetic significance. As Wolfgang Huber wrote, in Barmen's thesis on the nature of the Church we find "something which had been missing from German Protestantism since the Reformation, namely, an evangelical definition of the Church."[32] Moreover the circumstances which called forth the Declaration drew together Reformed and Lutheran theologians, whose traditions had been separated from the Reformation onwards, not least over questions of Church-state relations.[33] Prominent on the Reformed side at Barmen was Karl Barth,[34] and with the mention of his name we must retrace our steps to Calvin and his permutation of Jesus's Caesar-God principle.

---

31 *The Theological Declaration of Barmen*, 1934, reprinted in A.C. Cochrane, *Reformed Confessions of the 16th Century*, Philadelphia: Westminster Press 1966, 332–36; and in idem, *The Mystery of Peace*, Elgin, IL: Brethren Press 1986, App. I. See ibid. ch. XII for the Barmen Declaration in context. For fuller discussions see Arthur C. Cochrane, *The Church's Confession under Hitler*, Philadelphia: Westminster 1962; and John S. Conway, *The Nazi Persecution of the Churches*, New York: Basic Books 1968.

32 W. Huber in *Church and State. Opening a New Ecumenical Discussion*, 120. Huber went on immediately to say, "The translation of this definition into its own practice, constitution and relations with the state is a task which, to a large extent, still lies ahead of West German Protestantism." Four pages later he makes it clear that his own mind has not progressed beyond the collection of church taxes by the state (124). Similarly, in his report of the Consultation, *The Church and Civil Religion in the Nordic Countries of Europe*, Timothy Lull notes the obvious: "The financial dependence of the churches in all five nations on governmental revenue, much of it raised from seemingly nominal members [a new category this!], plays a part in the differing strategies for the future that are preferred" (197).

33 Traditional positions linger, however. For example, fifty years after Barmen Jens Glebe-Moller can write of Denmark: "The dominant trend in modern Danish theology, reflected in most sermons, is based on a sharp dividing line between God's kingdom and the secular realm." See ibid., 57.

34 For Barth's subsequent reflections upon Barmen see his *Fragments Grave and Gay*, London: Collins 1971, 71–81.

III

As in all his thinking, Calvin sets out from his conviction of God's sovereignty over all. Under God, magistrates—that is, the civil authorities—"have been invested with divine authority, and are wholly God's representatives. . . ."[35] Turning his back upon Augustine at this point he continues: "it has not come about by human perversity that the authority over all things on earth is in the hands of kings and other rulers, but by divine providence and holy ordinance. . . . Accordingly, no one ought to doubt that civil authority is a calling, not only holy and lawful before God, but also the most sacred and by far the most honourable of all callings in the whole life of mortal men."[36] At the same time, he regards civil law as properly imposing a restraint upon sin.[37] Setting his face against the identification of Church and state he expounds Jesus as teaching that "the office of pastor is distinct from that of prince . . . the things are so different that they cannot come together in one man."[38]

It follows from the divine institution of the state that citizens are to respect those in authority, for they are God's representatives.[39] Indeed, even unjust magistrates and wicked kings are to be obeyed here and now: God will deal with them hereafter.[40] While never condoning revolution, and ever fearful of anarchy, Calvin does have a place for passive or active resistance of evil rulers, and this on the ground that our obedience to rulers "is never to lead us away from obedience to him, to whose will the desires of all kings ought to be subject, to whose decrees all their commands ought to yield, to whose majesty their sceptres ought to be submitted. . . . The Lord, therefore, is the King of Kings, who, when he has opened his sacred mouth, must alone be heard, before and above all men; next to him we are subject to those men who are in authority over us, but only

---

35 J. Calvin, *Institute* IV.xx.4. For a fuller summary of Calvin's teaching on Church and state see Iain G. Nicol, "Church and state in the Calvinist Reformed tradition," in Ross T. Bender and Alan P.F. Sell, eds., *Baptism, Peace and the State in the Reformed and Mennonite Traditions*, Waterloo, Ont.: Wilfrid Laurier University Press 1991, ch. VI.

36 Ibid.

37 Ibid., II.vii.10.

38 Ibid., IV.xi.8.

39 Ibid., IV.xx.22.

40 Ibid., IV.xx.22–27.

in him. If they command anything against him, let it go unesteemed."[41]

Calvin's delicate balance of Church-state responsibilities could not altogether withstand the dramatic political circumstances in which the new movement found itself on leaving the walls of Geneva. As one historian has written, "Wherever sixteenth-century Calvinists found themselves in positions of political power they used the authority of the state to further reformation and enforce godliness."[42] Indeed, there is within the Reformed heritage a prominent strand of thought in which Church and state are virtually identified. The earliest major spokesman for this view is Zwingli.

Whereas Luther thought in terms of two interrelated kingdoms, Zwingli thought of the Church and society as an integrated whole, and all under the Gospel of Christ. He was prepared to think of wheat and tares within the Church, but not of the baptised and unbaptised within the state. The Church and the state had identical memberships, and since Zwingli made infant baptism a term of membership of the Church=civil society, he clearly had little patience with such Anabaptists as Conrad Grebel, who refused on biblical grounds to have his son baptised, and Felix Manz. The Word of God might for Zwingli be the foundation of the total society, but where baptism was concerned he could tolerate no other interpretations of it than his own, and he was not slow to invoke as a final authority that of the Zürich Council, which sentenced many Anabaptists to death.[43] It was not until 1710 that Anabaptists could legally be in Switzerland. It would be wrong to suggest that the Anabaptists repudiated all civil authority. They did not. On the contrary, in their Schleitheim Articles of 1527 they acknowledged that "The sword is an ordering outside the perfection of God," and that "the secular rulers are established to wield it."[44] But they

41 Ibid., IV.xx.32.

42 Michael R. Watts, *The Dissenters from the Reformation to the French Revoluton*, Oxford: Clarendon Press 1978, 31.

43 For the steps taken to heal relations between the Mennonite successors of the Anabaptists and the Reformed heirs of Zwingli see H.G. vom Berg, H. Kossen, L. Miller and L. Vischer (eds.) *Mennonites and Reformed in Dialogue*, Geneva: World Alliance of Reformed Churches and Lombard, IL: Mennonite World Conference 1986; and *Baptism, Peace and the State in the Reformed and Mennonite Traditions*.

44 *One Lord, One Church, One Hope, and One God. Mennonite Confessions of Faith*, ed. Howard John Loewen, Elkhart, IN: Institute of Mennonite Studies 1985, 80. For the ambiguities into which Mennonites have been led in their witness *vis à vis* peace and politics, and for fresh thinking on the matter see the papers by Howard John Loewen and Harry Loewen in *Baptism, Peace and the State in the*

staunchly opposed the coalescence of Church and state, and where many wished to reform the Church, they sought a restoration of the New Testament church both as regards church order and Christian ethics. Hence, for example, their advocacy of believers' baptism and their refusal to swear oaths—on which latter point, as upon their general[45] refusal to take up the sword they may be compared with the Quakers.

Much the same idea concerning the identity of Church and state flowed into England following the Elizabethan Settlement, where "the judicious" Richard Hooker explained that "with us one society is both the Church and commonwealth."[46] The people are in one aspect citizens, in another Christians; both the civic and religious leaders serve one temporal head, the monarch; and to question the Church or the civic order is to question the monarch. In this way, so the theory goes, religious uniformity is an important factor in holding the nation together, and every attempt is made to ensure that those who will not bow are broken.[47] So it was with the Anabaptists, and so it was with the English martyrs to whom we now turn as further representatives of our last permutation of Jesus's God-Caesar principle: the withdrawal on the part of Christians from society and civil life.

IV

On a number of occasions in Christian history it has been necessary for Christians to go underground—as in the Church of the catacombs, or the Church under some modern totalitarian states. For the most part such Christians have not favoured withdrawal on principle, but have been forced underground if, humanly speaking, the Church were to be spared at all; and they have normally been ardent in prayer that their distress may speedily be alleviated. About such I say no more, except to commend their faith and courage.

Reformed and Mennonite Traditions.

45 The term "general" signals the fact that the Anabaptist Andrew Fischer (c. 1480–c.1540) eventually came to believe that a Christian magistrate could rightfully use the sword. See George Huntston Williams, *The Radical Reformation*, Philadelphia: Westminster Press 1962, 414.

46 Richard Hooker, *The Works of that Learned and Judicious Divine Mr. Richard Hooker*, ed. John Keble, Oxford: OUP, 3rd. edn., 1845, VIII.i.7.

47 For the way in which this theory lives on in some of the newer African states see J. Henry Okullu in *Church and State. Opening a New Ecumenical Discussion*. 80–81.

Other groups have arisen which, whether consciously echoing one strand of Augustine or not, have believed that the world is so wicked that the only right course for Christians is to withdraw from it. They have adopted the quietist posture of living as far as possible away from the prevailing wickedness, though as with those eighteenth-century Quakers who developed a vocabulary of their own, and present day Amish, whose attitudes to technological change are ambivalent, some compromises with society have been inevitable. Some withdrawn groups become so exclusive—absolutely forbidding marriage outside their own group, for example—that they develop rigid new legalisms, for all that they might sing about free grace. About none of these do I speak, except to say that radical withdrawals on principle, when there is no physical danger, and without clearly recognised ways of showing concern for society—as in the prayer of the contemplative, for example—are difficult to square with Jesus's God-Caesar principle. It is in accordance with Scripture for Christians to strive to be in the world but not of it; but for them to seek to be neither in the world nor of it amounts to an unbiblical refusal to bear witness in the world for the sake of him who so loved the world that he gave his Son for it.[48] The minister of the Church of Scotland who informed the General Assembly of that Church that "We are not here to make the world better: we have only to pass through it on the way to glory,"[49] was a very odd son of Calvin indeed.

Rather, I am here concerned with those who, *as an emergency response*, separated themselves on principle from society because the Church had become so *identified* with the state as to be almost indistinguishable from it, and because the Church-state (for we must speak of it in hyphenated fashion) had, in their view, become corrupt. This was the position of the martyrs of 1593, to whom at last I come. John Greenwood, Henry Barrow and John Penry found themselves living in the kind of society defined and endorsed by Richard Hooker, and desired by the monarch. In order to place the martyrs in context I must say a little more concerning the political-ecclesiastical situation in England.

By the persecutions of the Roman Catholic Queen Mary a number of reforming Christians were driven into exile in Europe. Eventually, as some of them put it, "The Lord began to show mercy unto England by removing Queen Mary by death." The Protestant Elizabeth I was crowned, and many exiles returned, eager to ad-

48 John 3:16.

49 Quoted by Archibald D.B. Alexander, *Christianity and Ethics*, London: Duckworth 1931, 240.

vance the reform of the Church of England in the direction of the worship and church order they had experienced in Geneva and Frankfurt. In Geneva, for example, some 230 English exiles had formed a church organised on Calvin's model, and John Knox ministered to them. Once home, they were sadly disappointed. The Act of Supremacy of 1559 gave the Queen supreme authority in the state, and made her the temporal head of the Church. The Act of Uniformity of the same year restored the 1552 Prayer Book and made its sole use mandatory. The Queen's objective was uniformity of religion as a means to a united nation which could credibly stand against Roman Catholic Spain. The seekers of pure worship and order found much to dislike in the Prayer Book—too many Romish rites and teachings remained therein. Some sought continuing reform and were content with established episcopalianism; some, among them Thomas Cartwright, advocated an establishment but of a presbyterian kind; and some, who became known as the Separatists, did not opt into the Anglican Settlement at all. Their separated worship was illegal and underground (despite the fact that the law permitted the so-called "Strangers' Churches," where those who were not English worshipped, to be organised along Genevan lines). Among them were our martyrs.

We must understand that their "separation" was not in the first instance separation from the state or from the Church; it was separation from the world.[50] But to them the Church-state epitomised the world because of its unbiblical worship and order, because of the laxity and inefficiency of many of its clergy, and because it held within it all the baptised, however godless they might be. Over against the authorised Church they began to develop their own understanding of the Church as comprising believers gathered under the Gospel, with Christ as their only Head. In response to the growth of Separatism, and also, of course, with the Roman Catholics in view, an Act of 1582 made it treasonable to worship in any other way than according to the Prayer Book of the Church of England, and the new Archbishop, John Whitgift, had no compunction about using the secular arm, the Court of High Commission, to enforce the religious laws.

Needless to say, Whitgift was not impressed by the addresses to the Privy Council by the inhabitants of parishes up and down the land. Some of these texts make sad reading. Hear the folk of Maldon and district, Essex, whose petition of 1586 was occasioned not by lack of corn, but of spiritual food:

---

50 Cf. Romans 12:2.

> If we aske our pastors and such as are set over us to feede us, we find them crueller than the Ostrich in the wilderness, and more unkinde then the Dragons, which draw out their breasts and give sucke to their yonge.
>
> For alas the greatest number of our ministers . . . either be utterlie unfit for that office by reason of their ignorance, or all-together carelesse and unable to performe anie such dutie unto us by reason of their manifold charges and divers places thei have taken into their hands; some being nonresidents, having charges in divers shir[e]s, others being unskillfull men and ignorant, not onelie unable [to] teach but allso of an ungodlie life, such as have been popish priests, Tailours, Whelewrights, Fletchers, servingmen, and manie of them alehouse haunters, Dicers, Quarelers, Drunckards, whoremongers, and full of grosse vices. . . .[51]

Those who had John Greenwood and others like him for their pastor were much more fortunate.

A graduate of Cambridge University, John Greenwood served briefly as a Church of England incumbent in Norfolk, before resigning his benefice in 1585. The eastern counties of England, to which returning refugees and fleeing Anabaptists came, were increasingly being influenced by the Separatist spirit. Elias Thacker and John Copping had been hanged for their Separatist faith at Bury St. Edmunds in 1583, and John Greenwood was among a number who concluded that the state-Church was not the true Church of Christ. For a period he became assistant chaplain to Lord Robert Rich of Rochford, where he conducted Separatist meetings. He soon left the Established Church and went to London. There exists a list of May 1589 of "The names of sundry faythfull Christians imprisoned by the Archbishop of Canterbury and the Bishop of London for the Ghospell of our Lord Jesus Christ." Heading the list is Greenwood, imprisoned in the Fleet. The citation reads, "Having bin imprisoned by the Bishop of London thirty weeks in the Clynke for readinge a portion of Scripture on a Lorde's daye in a frynde's house, removed by hab[e]as corpus." The friend was Henry Martin, of St. Andrews in the Wardrobe, London, and Greenwood's fine, in addition to his imprisonment, was the enormous sum of 260 pounds. In May 1588 he was brought from the Clink, tried at Newgate, and then committed to the Fleet prison.[52] (It is pleasing to note that the Memorial

51 *The Seconde Parte of a Register*, ed. Albert Peel, Cambridge: CUP 1915, II, 188.

52 See *The Writings of John Greenwood 1587–1590*, ed. Leland H. Carlson, London: Allen and Unwin 1962, 312. For Greenwood see further DNB; F.J. Powicke, *Henry Barrow, Separatist (1550?–1593) and the Exiled Church of Amsterdam*, London: James Clarke 1900.

Hall, Farringdon Street, opened on 19 January 1875 in honour of the martyrs by their Congregational heirs, stood on the site of the old Fleet prison where so many Separatists had been incarcerated, and that church records were kept in the very dungeons they had once occupied).

Henry Barrow, born *circa* 1550, was about ten years older than Greenwood. He was of a well-to-do family at Shipdham, Norfolk, and graduated from Cambridge University in 1566. He spent six years of what he afterwards called his "vain and libertine youth" in London, and finally entered Gray's Inn in 1576. Whilst leading the life of a courtier he was converted. The story goes as follows:

> Walking in London one Lord's day with one of his companions, he heard a preacher very loud as they passed by the church. Upon which Mr. Barrowe said unto his consort, "Let us go in and hear what this man saith that is thus in earnest." "Tush," saith the other; "what! shall we go to hear a man talk?" But in he went and sat down. And the minister was vehement in reproving sin, and sharply applied the judgments of God against the same; and, it should seem, touched him to the quick in such things as he was guilty of, so as God set it home to his soul, and began to work for his repentance and conviction thereby, for he was so stricken as he could not be quiet, until, by conference with godly men, and further hearing of the word, with diligent reading and meditation, God brought peace to his soul and conscience, after much humiliation of heart and reformation of life. So he left the Court and retired himself to a private life, some time in the country and some time in the city, giving himself to study and reading of the Scriptures and other good works very diligently; and being missed at Court by his consorts and acquaintances, it was quickly hinted abroad that Barrowe was turned Puritan.[53]

Indeed he was, and under the influence of Greenwood, whom he somehow met, he became a Separatist. Indeed, together with Robert Browne—also of Norfolk—Barrow, with his alert legal mind, became a leading theorist of the Separatists;[54] with his sharp wit and outspoken manner he became the bane of the ecclesiastical authorities.

On hearing that Greenwood was in the Clink, Barrow went to visit him on 19 November 1587, whereupon the gaoler arrested him.

53 [John Waddington], *Congregational Martyrs*, London: Elliot Stock 1861, 66–67. For Barrow see further DNB; F.J. Powicke, *Henry Barrow*.

54 For a fuller account of the ecclesiology of Separatism and its Congregational offspring see Alan P.F. Sell, *Saints: Visible, Orderly and Catholic. The Congregational Idea of the Church*, Geneva: World Alliance of Reformed Churches and Allison Park, PA: Pickwick Publications 1986.

He was taken by boat to Lambeth Palace, and following interrogation, the Archbishop, in a characteristic action demonstrating the blurring of the distinction between Church and state, unjustifiably committed him to gaol. So began a dangerous life during which Barrow and Greenwood's writings were smuggled out of prison and printed in secret in England, or in Holland, for distribution among the Separatists. Many of these writings survive, as do accounts of the several interrogations of Barrow and Greenwood. Their general complaint against the Church-state, however, is well summarised in Barrow's *Four Principall and Waighty Causes for Separation*, which he probably wrote shortly before his arrest in 1587. The tract begins thus:

> Fower principall and waighty causes whie every on[e] that knoweth God and acknowledgeth the Lord Jesus, or seeke the salvation in him, ought spedelye without any delay to forsack those disordered and ungodlye and unholye sinagogs, and the false teacher of these tymes as they generally stand in England.
>
> 1. The fals manner of worshiping the true God. Esaias 66:17; Deuteronomy 17:1.
> 2. The profane and ungodlie people receved into and retayned in the bozom and bodie of ther churches. Esaias 65:11, 12.
> 3. The false and antichristian ministrie imposed upone ther churches. Numbers 16:21, 35.
> 4. The false and antichristian government wherewith ther churches ar ruled.[55]

So much for what Barrow and Greenwood were against. Positively, as Barrow wrote in *A Breefe Sum of Our Profession* (1587/8):

> 1. We seeke above all things the peace and protection of the most high, and the kingdome of Christ Jesus our Lord.
> 2. We seeke and fully purpose to worship God aright, as he hath commanded in his holy worde.
> 3. We seeke the fellowship and communion of his faithfull and obedient servants, and together with them to enter covenant with the Lord. And by the direction of his holy spirite to proceed to a godly, free, and right choice of ministers and other officers ordained by his to the service of his church.
> 4. We seeke to establish and obey the ordinances and lawes of our saviour Christ, left by his last will and testament to the governing and guiding of his church, without altering,

55 H. Barrow, *The Writings of Henry Barrow 1587–1590*, ed. Leland H. Carlson, London: Allen and Unwin 1962, 54.

changing, innovating, wresting, or leaving out any of them, that the Lord shall give us sight of.

5. We purpose by the assistance of the Holy Ghost in this faith and order to leade our lives. . . .[56]

Throughout their trials, Barrow and Greenwood affirmed their loyalty to the Crown, denied that they were traitors, and pledged loyalty to the true Church of Christ. Their inability to see that Church in the existing state-Church of their day, and their desire to be faithful to Scripture and to Christ, was the cause of their suffering. And not of theirs only. Soon there were some sixty Separatists distributed amongst the Bridewell, Newgate, Fleet, Clink, Wood Street and Poultry prisons, and a number of them died in the squalid conditions they had to endure.

In the autumn of 1592 Greenwood was allowed out of prison on bail. At once he began to conduct Separatist meetings together with Francis Johnson and John Penry. If Greenwood was supremely the pastor and Barrow the theorist, Penry was the evangelist. His opposition to the state-Church was fuelled by the unwillingness of that Church to provide adequately for the evangelisation of Wales—on which subject he addressed the authorities in three pungent treatises.[57]

Penry was born in 1563, probably at Cefn Brith, a farmhouse near Llangamarch, Brecknockshire.[58] He graduated in the University of Cambridge in 1584. A convinced Puritan, Penry's friends included Job Throckmorton, Squire of Haseley, Northamptonshire. Following a period at Oxford University, he married Eleanor Godley of Northampton in 1588. He had already been arrested by Whitgift in 1587, when his pamphlet, *A Treatise concerning the Aequity of an Humble Supplication*, was presented to Parliament by Throckmorton and Edward Dunn Lee. Penry became associated with Robert Waldegrave, on whose secret press the notorious *Marprelate Tracts*—lampoons of the establishment in general and of individual bishops on particular—were printed. There is no doubt that Penry used this press, but whether he was "Martin Marprelate," or but one of a

56 Ibid., 84.

57 See John Penry, *Three Treatises concerning Wales*, with an introduction by David Williams, Cardiff: University of Wales Press 1960.

58 For Penry's life see further *The Notebook of John Penry 1593*, ed. Albert Peel, London: Royal Historical Society 1944; William Pierce, *John Penry, his Life, Times and Writings*, London: Hodder & Stoughton 1923.

number of co-tractarians, has never conclusively been proved.[59] He denied the charge when it was levelled against him, and many are prepared to take his word for this, given the integrity of his character, and the fact that his known writings are in such a serious vein. Others suggest that his denial may have been based on the possibility that he alone was not "Martin," and that in his desire to protect a number of his friends he traded upon his known integrity. However that may be, the authorities began to hunt down the press with zeal. Walgedrave passed the operation to John Hodgkins, who was arrested. Penry fled the increasing danger and went to Scotland, returning to England in 1592.

It was at this point that Penry joined Barrow's group of Separatists. He had so far been a traditional Puritan, seeing further reform of the established Church; but now he saw that there was little hope of this.[60] His whereabouts were betrayed by a Marprelate victim, Anthony Anderson, Vicar of Stepney, and he was arrested on 22 March 1592/3.

Greenwood was again arrested on 5 December 1592; he and Barrow were tried in March 1593, and, on 23rd, were condemned to death. On 31 March they were taken to be executed, but were briefly reprieved. Early in the morning of 6 April, two elderly widows carrying their winding-sheets to the gallows, Barrow and Greenwood were hanged at Tyburn. In a letter addressed to a Mr. Fisher possibly in 1590 Barrow had written, "We are alwaise ready through God's grace to be offered up upon that testimony of our faith which we have made."[61] So it was.

Penry meanwhile was enduring illegal charges and a travesty of a trial. He was sentenced to death, and was hanged, aged thirty, at St. Thomas a Watering, Surrey, on 29 May 1593. He left a widow and four daughters, Deliverance, Comfort, Safety and Sure Hope, of whom the eldest was four and the youngest four months. A week before his death he had written to Lord Burleigh, "[I]f my blood were

59 While admitting that more than one hand was involved in the Marprelate Tracts, Pennar Davies regards Penry as "the life and soul of the fugitive press." See his *John Penry*, London: Independent Press 1961, 11. Donald J. McGinn, *John Penry and the Marprelate Controversy*, New Brunswick, NJ: Rutgers University Press 1966, argues in detail that Penry was Martin, but is devastatingly criticised by Leland H. Carlson, *Martin Marprelate, Gentleman. Master Job Throckmorton Laid Open in his Colors*, San Marino, CA: Huntington Library 1981, 297–307.

60 Barrow had tried to convince him of this in his substantial pamphlet, *A Brief Discoverie of the False Church* (1590). See *The Writings of Henry Barrow 1587–1590*, 426.

61 Ibid., 256.

an ocean sea, and every drop thereof were a life unto me, I would give them all, by the help of the Lord, for the maintenance of the same, my confession."[62] So he did.

The courage of the martyrs engendered such a wave of public sympathy in their favour, and the actions of the bishops provoked such horror, that Separatists were never again hanged. Imprisonment and exile remained sufficiently harsh punishments, and for many years to come there were those in England who were ready to place God above Caesar when Caesar—not least Caesar in episcopal robes—made illegitimate demands upon them.

V

As I reflect upon the changes which have been rung upon Jesus's God-Caesar principle I come to the following summary conclusions:

First, there is no justification for either the Church or the state usurping the authority of the other.

Secondly, we cannot at one and the same time uphold Jesus's principle and acquiesce in the way in which Luther's two kingdoms theory was abused so as to legitimate the divorce of Church and state (except in an administrative sense). For this is to countenance the shelving of civic responsibility by Christians, and it gags the Church's prophetic voice.

Thirdly, we should be warned by the way in which Zwingli's and Calvin's regimes could and did call upon state force to secure religious orthodoxy.

Fourthly, the attempt completely to withdraw from the world on principle cannot be justified in the light of Jesus's principle—nor, more widely, in the light of the challenge to Christian mission, except as an emergency response in particular situations. Even if complete withdrawal were theologically justifiable it would be impossible in practical terms since, for example, *legally* the Church exists by the permission of the state.

Fifthly, where Church and state are virtually identified, as in some established Church contexts, fundamental theological questions are raised. Who are the Church? Was it ever right, and is it any longer possible, to hold that the inhabitants of a nation and members of the Church in that nation are one and the same? How is the Church to be ordered, and how far should secular authorities have a hand in its ordering? May not the Church be so identified with, and secularised by, the state that its calling to stand over

62 Quoted by J. Waddington, *Congregational Martyrs*, 192.

against the state in critical judgment is rendered impossible of fulfilment?[63]

In all of these points there is food for further ecumenical thought as the churches approach a new millennium. It would be wrong to idolise specific historic applications of the God-Caesar principle, which, as we have seen, have all been made in response to particular sets of circumstances. It would be a dereliction of duty for Christians to refuse to make their contribution to whatever new governmental arrangements may be forthcoming in different times and places. Whatever the Church does in the future it is imperative that it remember one fundamental truth of its being. Although, as I have insisted, the Church may not usurp the legitimate role of the state (and *vice versa*), this does not mean that they are in all respects equal partners. The authorities come and go; the authority of the Gospel (the subject of the first lecture in this series) endures for ever. The authorities will, however, be much more likely to heed the Church's voice when that voice is uttered by a reconciled Church (the subject of the second lecture in this series), which knows that its word is of real significaance, and not by a variety of churches which behave like so many worldly corporations whose motivation and message comes from ecclesiastical power brokers or from vociferous interest groups. Above all—and here we verge upon the territory of the third lecture in this series—Christians would do well to remember that whereas we are born into this world we are reborn into the Church; and that the Gospel which is the basis of that rebirth is Good News for all—not least for the secular authorities. The psalmist's words remain true: "Happy is the nation whose God is the Lord."[64] For this reason R.W. Dale of Birmingham, the centenary of whose death will fall in 1995, declared in 1869, "If the State is to be rescued from the darkest dangers which threaten it, we must preach CHRIST—Christ not merely as the supreme revelation of God—Christ not merely as the sacrifice for human sin—Christ not merely as the Head of the Church, but Christ as the Ruler of all men, the Regenerator of nations, the Saviour of Society."[65]

In making its witness the Church must never forget that though its foundation and destiny are eternal, it is very much, and sometimes quite horrifyingly, an earthen vessel. It should be quick to

63 See further Alan P.F. Sell, *Dissenting Thought and the Life of the Churches. Studies in an English Tradition*, Lewiston, NY: Mellen Research University Press 1990, ch. XXII.

64 Psalm 33:12.

65 R.W. Dale, *Essays and Addresses*, London: Hodder & Stoughton 1899, 42.

repent of its enticement by worldly pomp and power. True it is that even the rule of the saints can be a terrifying thing—as when the soil of New England was desecrated by the blood of the Quakers under the rule of theocratic, established, Congregationalists—the heirs of Barrow, Greenwood and Penry!

Jesus's God-Caesar principle, I believe, sanctions the view that the Church is distinct from, but not absolutely separate from, the state. These two are not equal partners, for when the chips are down, Christians are to be for God. Ultimately that is the only secure place to be, for while the state depends upon public stability, the degree of which may fluctuate quite wildly—even to the state's overthrow, the Church stands upon an eternal foundation: "The city of God remaineth." This is the word which has sustained the martyrs of the ages. It is the word which both Church and state neglect at their peril.

II

Occasional Commemorative Studies

V

Through Suffering to Liberty: 1689 in the English and Vaudois Experience

On more than one occasion during the turbulent years of the seventeenth century, the Vaudois received support and encouragement from the English. When, on Palm Sunday 19 April 1655 the Duke of Savoy's commander, the Marquis di Pianezza, began to commit indiscriminate atrocities against the Vaudois in the name of Roman Catholicism, news was at once conveyed to England's Protector, Oliver Cromwell. The Vaudois spokesman, Pastor Jean Leger, sent a detailed report to his colleague, Jean-Baptiste Stouppe who, having served from 1653 as Cromwell's secret agent in France, was now back at the French Church in Threadneedle Street, London. Stouppe passed word on, and pamphlet publicity of the plight of the Vaudois was at once forthcoming on Cromwell's instruction.[1] Cromwell's secretary, the poet John Milton, composed a diplomatic letter in Latin, which was dated 25 May 1655 and addressed to the Duke of Savoy;[2] and soon Milton's more partisan

---

1 See J. P. Perrin, *Matchless Crueltie Declared at large in the ensuing History of the Waldenses . . . Published by Command of his Highness the Lord Protector*, 1655. See further, *A Looking-Glass for England . . .* ([including]) *a brief Apology on behalf of the Protestants in the Valleys of Piedmont . . .* , 1667; *A short and faithfull Account of the late Commotions in the Valleys of Piedmont . . . With some Reflections on Mr. Stouppe's collected Papers touching the same business*, 1655: Randolph Vigne, "'Avenge, O Lord, Thy slaughtered saints.' Cromwell's intervention on behalf of the Vaudois," *Proceedings of the Huguenot Society*, XXXIV 1, 1983, 10–25. Giorgio Vola, "Cromwell e i Valdesi, una vicenda non del tutto chiarita," *Bollettino della Società di Studi Valdesi*, no. 149, 1981, 11–37. For Cromwell's reaction to the news see *Calendar of State Papers, Venetian* (1930), XXX, 1655, June 5, 14, 28.

2 For the English translation see Giorgio Tourn *et al.*, *You are My Witnesses. The Waldensians Across 800 Years*, Rome: Claudiana 1989, 124–25. For Milton's less diplomatic and more personal account of the horrors see W.C. Abbott, *The Writings and Speeches of Oliver Cromwell*, Oxford: Clarendon Press 1988, 1945, III, 186–88.

sonnet, "Avenge, O Lord, Thy slaughtered saints" appeared. Not, indeed, that English assistance was all of the literary kind. Some £40,000 was collected for the Piedmontese in 1655 with, for example, the Leicestershire parishes donating amounts ranging from 3*s.* 5*d.* (Allerton) to £12 7*s.* 8*d.* (St. Martin, Leicester),[3] and Oxford University subscribing £384 "for a Brief for relief of Protestants in Savoy."[4] No doubt Cromwell was politically astute as well as altruistic: it suited him to aid the Vaudois against the French and the Savoyards; but that he set the public imagination alight on behalf of the oppressed of Piedmont cannot be denied. Moreover he anticipated the public collection for the sufferers by making a personal donation of £2,000.[5]

The English were, again, informed of the persecution and exodus of the Vaudois in 1686. A pamphlet entitled *The History of the Persecution in the Valleys of Piedmont* (1688) described the order of 31 January 1686 which prohibited the exercise of the Protestant religion; the efforts of "the monks and priests [who] have tried all the means imaginable to oblige [the Vaudois] to change their Religion;"[6] the reported deaths of more than eight thousand people—and all of this despite the history of Waldensian loyalty to the Duke of Savoy, evidence of which is appended in the form of letters from the Duke dated 5 November 1677 and 29 September 1681. In 1699, *A Short Relation of the Brave Exploits of the Vaudois* appeared; the tale of courage and suffering was reiterated, and the English were exhorted to abandon national sins in gratitude to the God who had so wonderfully blessed them by "preserving and raising up King William for our happy Deliverance from an Arbitrary Power."[7]

The "happy Deliverance" to which our anonymous author refers, the Toleration Act of 1689, is the subject of this paper. Our objective is to go behind the well-known expressions of pro-Waldensian

---

3 W. J. Payling Wright, "Collections for the Piedmontese, 1655," *Congregational Historical Society Transactions* (hereinafter CHST), XI 6, Sept. 1932, 286–88.

4 Falconer Madan, *Oxford Books. III, Oxford Literature 1651–80*, Oxford 1931, 42.

5 Robert Vaughan, *The Protectorate of Oliver Cromwell . . . in a series of letters . . .* 1839, I 192.

6 *The History of the Persecution of the Valleys of Piedmont.* Containing An Account of What hath passed in the Dissipation of the Churches and the Inhabitants of the Valleys, which happened in the year 1686, 1688, 41. Another translation of the French original in *An Account of the late persecution of the Protestants in the Valleys of Piedmont . . . in the year 1686*, Oxford 1691. Cf. S. J. Woolf, "English public opinion and the Duchy of Savoy," *English Miscellany XII*, 1961, 233–35.

7 *A Short Relation of the Brave Exploits of the Vaudois*, 1699, 19. See also, *History of the persecutions of the Reformed Churches in . . . Piedmont. From 1655 to this time*, 1699. Cf. S. J. Woolf, art. cit., 238–39.

sentiment and action, with a view to comparing the experiences of the Dissenting successors of Cromwell with those of the Vaudois; for in King William both found a saviour, and for both 1689 marked a turning-point. It is hoped that this exercise will assist in averting that "tunnel vision" which can all too easily afflict denominational history—especially, perhaps, when great anniversaries are being celebrated.

Our first task must be to offer a brief sketch of the fortunes of those who, from the time of Elizabeth I, entertained conscientious scruples concerning the drive for imposed uniformity of religion.

I

The Separatist harbingers of English Dissent included such people as Richard Fitz, whose "privie church" was meeting in London in 1567; Robert Browne (c. 1550–1633), and the martyrs Henry Barrow (c. 1550–93) and John Greenwood (d. 1593). All of these were in general agreement with the anonymous London Separatist of c. 1567, who wrote concerning Queen Elizabeth that "Our bodies, goods, and lives be at her commandment, and she shall have them as of true subjects. But the soul of man for religion is bound to none but unto God and His Holy Word."[8] On this ground, and at considerable personal risk, the Separatists stood against powers determined upon securing national unity cemented by religious uniformity. The Separatists were Puritans who sought reformation under the Word of God, and who were convinced that such reformation was not to be had under an established church of whatsoever ecclesiological complexion. Over against them stood episcopalian and presbyterian Puritans, for both of whom an established church was tolerable provided it were organised on the principles they favoured.

The opposition to separatist groups was so intense that two London churches only survived from 1600 to 1640 with an unbroken existence.[9] The attitude of James I, "let them conform

---

8 *The Seconde Parte of a Register*, ed. A. Peel, Cambridge 1915, 158. For further ecclesiological discussion and full references, see Alan P.F. Sell, *Saints: Visible, Orderly and Catholic. The Congregational Idea of the Church*, Geneva: World Alliance of Reformed Churches, and Allison Park, PA: Pickwick Publications 1986. For the general history of English Dissent to the French Revolution, see Michael R. Watts, *The Dissenters*, London: OUP 1978.

9 So A.G. Matthews in *Congregationalism Through the Centuries*, London: Independent Press 1937, 36.

themselves and that shortly, or they shall hear of it,"[10] found its way into the Canons of 1604.[11] These Canons required conformity and, by 1605, a number of Puritans had sought refuge in Holland. From these exiles came many of the *Mayflower* Pilgrims who landed at Plymouth Rock in the New World on 21 December 1620. One hundred and two persons had embarked, one died at sea, and two were born during the voyage. Of the 103 who reached land, 52 died before further compatriots arrived on the *Fortune* on 19 November 1621.[12]

James I reigned until his death in 1625, and was succeeded by Charles I. Charles strongly upheld the "Divine Right of Kings," and would brook no opposition to a unified, established church. Aided by Archbishop Laud, he ensured that others than Puritans attained high office in the Church, and that the non-submissive suffered. The House of Commons, powerfully Presbyterian in sympathy, became increasingly irked by this; the exiles returned from Holland in 1640 as matters were coming to a head, bringing important theological and other aptitudes with them (the five leading Independents at the Westminster Assembly, Thomas Goodwin, Philip Nye, William Bridge, Jeremiah Burroughes and Sidrach Simpson, had all been exiles); in 1642 Civil War broke out; and in 1649 the King was executed. From that date until 1658 Oliver Cromwell was supreme, being declared Lord Protector in 1653.

Under Cromwell life was much easier for the Independent and Baptist descendants of the Separatists, episcopacy having been abolished in the 1640s. It is possible that Cromwell would have permitted the voluntary use of the Book of Common Prayer, but he accepted contrary advice. His Triers assessed the clergymen, and were for the most part just in deposing only those who were scandalous or dangerous, whilst leaving diligent Calvinists in their posts. It has been estimated that between six and seven thousand episcopalian incumbents were ejected from their livings under Cromwell.[13]

It is, however, noteworthy that Richard Baxter, though out of sympathy with many of the church-political emphases of most of the Triers, admitted that "to give them their due, they did abundance of good to the Church. They saved many a congregation from ignorant, ungodly, drunken teachers . . . so great was the

10 William Barlow, *The Hampton Court Conference*, 1604 edn., 102.

11 *Calendar of State Papers, Domestic Series*, James I, x, 1603–1610, 175.

12 See W. Pierce, "The voyagers in the Mayflower," CHST, VIII 1, Feb. 1920, 3–15.

13 A.G. Matthews, *Walker Revised*, Oxford: Clarendon Press 1948, xiii.

benefit above the hurt which they brought to the Church, that many thousands of souls blessed God for the faithful ministers whom they let in, and grieved when the Prelatists afterward cast them out again. . . ."[14]

When considering the question of religious toleration in this period we must not overlook the turbulence of the times. The unity of the realm was a widely espoused ideal which had been handed down from the Middle Ages, and very few were inclined to accord religious liberty to Ranters, Seekers, Socinians and Papists. Robert S. Paul has clearly expressed the psychology of the matter: "intolerance was regarded as a virtue rather than as a vice, and . . . liberty of conscience was understood as an excuse for licence and immorality rather than as evidence of broadmindedness."[15] Not surprisingly, such Anglicans as Thomas Fuller, who advocated liberty of religion, were in a small minority. To their credit the Baptists, the vast majority of whose ministers remained outside even Cromwell's ecclesiastical establishment because their voluntarism would not permit them to benefit from tithes and glebe lands, had the noblest pro-toleration record.

As early as 1612 Thomas Helwys, the founder of the first Baptist church on English soil, had published *A Short Declaration on the Mistery of Iniquity*, in which he contended that "men's religion to God is betwixt God and themselves: the King shall not answere for it, neither may the King be jugd betwene God and Man. Let them be heretikes, Turcks, Jewes, or whatsoever, it apperteynes not to the earthly power to punish them in the least measure."[16] The Baptists Leonard Busher and John Murton suffered imprisonment for writing in similar vein. It was left to Roger Williams to found the first religiously free society—in Rhode Island, whither he had been banished by the Independents and Presbyterians of New England, who desired no opposition to their favoured *establishment*. The Quakers of New England suffered much, for the same reason.

As for the Independents, some of them remained outside of Cromwell's parochial arrangements on voluntarist grounds; others accepted parochial livings, or served as lecturers. It cannot be said that most of them were advocates of universal toleration at this time; on the contrary, they did not begin to become eloquent on the point until, during the Westminster Assembly, they realised that the

---

14 *The Autobiography of Richard Baxter* (the *Reliquiae Baxterianae*, 1696, abridged), ed. J.M. Lloyd Thomas, London: Dent Everyman 1931, 71; reprinted with revisions and a new introduction by N.H. Keeble, 1974.

15 Robert S. Paul, *The Assembly of the Lord*, Edinburgh: T. & T. Clark 1985, 440.

16 Thomas Helwys, *A Short Declaration on the Mistery of Iniquity*, 1612, 69.

plea for toleration was their only device against Presbyterian monopoly—and then their objective was not a toleration sufficiently elastic to include Papists, Quakers and other still more radical groups.[17] When they did begin to advocate toleration they faced the incomprehension of their New England counterparts, and took the risk of erecting a barrier between themselves and the Reformed national churches of the continent.[18]

The Presbyterians, still favouring an establishment along their own ecclesiological lines, were the most resolutely opposed to toleration. In his *Gangraena* (1646) Thomas Edwards deemed toleration "the grand design of the devil"—a conclusion at which few of his fellow-Presbyterians demurred. It is thus not surprising that, unlike the Independents and others, the Presbyterians were on the side of Royalists and Anglicans in working for the restoration of the monarchy—an objective attained in 1660 with the accession of Charles II. The protests of Milton and others had not prevailed; the episcopalians sought redress after their wilderness years, and were highly suspicious of Presbyterians and Independents alike, fearing that they were potentially rebellious groups; the Presbyterians hoped that a renewed state church would be of their complexion; many in the land were tired of Puritan theocracy; and some, as we now see with hindsight, placed too much confidence in Charles's promise in the Declaration of Breda (4 April 1660) of "a liberty to tender consciences" in "matters of religion which do not disturb the peace of the Kingdom." This Declaration begged the question, of course; and it soon became apparent that for political reasons Cromwell's policy of comprehension for all but those deemed extremists was to be replaced by a reversion to the attempt to cement political unity by means of religious conformity.

II

In justice to Charles we must note that on 4 June 1660, the month following his return, he met the Quaker Richard Hubberthorne and reaffirmed his intention of tolerating all who lived peaceably.[19] As an earnest of his good intention, on 25 October, George Fox, who had spent more than twenty weeks in gaol, was released, as were

17 R. S. Paul, op. cit., 31, 467.

18 Ibid., 103, 477.

19 R. Hubberthorne, *Works*, 1663, 268–72; G. Fox, *Journal*, ed. John L. Nickalls, London: Religious Society of Friends 1965, 393.

about seven hundred other Friends.[20] But the uprising in January 1661 of Thomas Venner and his Fifth Monarchy Men led, on 10 January, to the banning of all Anabaptist, Quaker and Fifth Monarchy meetings—Baptist and Quaker dissociation from Venner and expressions of loyalty to Charles notwithstanding.[21] Four thousand two hundred and thirty Quakers were soon in prison, John Whitehead and Isaac Pennington among them. It was not until 11 May 1664 that all were freed.[22]

Others had also begun to suffer. Following the Convention Parliament's Act of 1660 which restored sequestered ministers to their livings, many incumbents began to conform or to resign. The period between refusal to conform and resignation was uneasy for many. Thus in 1660 the Independent Thomas Jollie was arrested twice, and on the second occasion detailed in prison; he was shut out of his church at Altham, and was summoned to appear before the Bishop of Chester to explain, among other things, why he refused to use the Book of Common Prayer of the Church of England. However, "The Lord made a way of escape by taking the Prelate out of the world." When the suit was subsequently pressed, "it again pleased God that the Prelate died."[23] Jollie was eventually turned out of his chapel on 17 August 1662—the day he had himself decided to leave.[24]

The Presbyterians had meanwhile assembled at the Savoy Conference of March 1661, with a view to proposing an alternative Prayer Book and a scheme for comprehension within a modified episcopal structure. The episcopalians were not to be persuaded, however, and the attempt failed. Two months later the first of a series of Acts[25] was passed which came to be known collectively as the Clarendon Code, after Edward Hyde, Earl of Clarendon, whose

---

20 G. Fox, *Journal*, 391, 394. Cf. W.C. Braithwaite, *The Second Period of Quakerism*, [SPQ], 2nd edn., ed. H.J. Cadbury, Cambridge: CUP 1961, 477.

21 See W.T. Whitley, *A History of the British Baptists*, London: Griffin 1923, 109. So concerned were the Baptists that two General Baptist churches united with five Particular Baptist churches in London to protest against Venner's insurrection—an unusual joint stand. See G. Fox, *Journal*, 394–405.

22 See W.G. Braithwaite, SPQ, 9–13.

23 *The Notebook of the Rev. Thomas Jolly*, ed. Henry Fishwick, Manchester: The Chetham Society 1894, xvi.

24 Ibid., xviii.

25 For the terms of the Corporation Act (1661), the Uniformity Act (1662), the Five Mile Act (1665), the Second Conventicle Act (1670) and the Test Act (1673) see Henry Gee and William John Hardy, *Documents Illustrative of English Church History*, London: Macmillan 1896.

stern rule as Lord Chancellor lasted until his impeachment in 1667. Cumulatively the Clarendon Code had a considerable adverse effect upon all Nonconformists. It dashed for ever the Presbyterian hope for comprehension under a modified episcopacy, not to mention the hope for an established church on presbyterian lines.

The Corporation Act of 1661 prohibited Nonconformists from holding civil office. Aspirants to such office were required to swear an oath declaring the Solemn League and Covenant to be "an unlawful oath." This Covenant had been drawn up by Scots against Charles I's pro-Catholic leanings in 1638, and had been reaffirmed by the English Parliament in 1643. It was particularly hard for Presbyterians to contemplate reneging on an oath which they had sponsored and taken.

The Act of Uniformity of 1662 (14 Charles II, cap. 4) was the most serious of all the punitive Acts in both its short- and long-term effects. By this Act all clergy and schoolmasters were required to swear their "unfeigned assent and consent" to the entire contents of the Book of Common Prayer; ministers who had not been episcopally ordained were to be re-ordained or be ejected from their livings; and the Solemn League and Covenant was to be abjured. All of the provisions were to come into force by Bartholomew's Day, 24 August 1662. Since tithes were due shortly after that date, those who were ejected would lose not only home and future livelihood, but monies due to them for service rendered as well.

Some did not wait for the enactment of the legislation. From 1660 a number of Independent incumbents stepped down. They had already organised on congregational lines within their parishes, and they continued to minister to their gathered churches. Among these were William Bartlett of Bideford, Devonshire, Thomas Brooks of London, and John Durant of Canterbury. Some sixteen others left their posts when sequestered ministers were reinstated; and others, who had been in parochial or university lectureships, did likewise.[26]

Those ejected under the Act were confronted by the practical difficulty that many did not have a sight of the Prayer Book until within a few weeks of 24 August; but their major concerns were of principle. The differences of emphasis as between the Independents and the Presbyterians are of some significance. The Independents were against reordination as such; the Presbyterians, though not averse to a modified episcopacy, could not stomach reordination by bishops—not least because of the slur it would cast upon the

26 See R. Tudur Jones, *Congregationalism in England 1662–1962*, London: Independent Press 1962, 47–49.

ordination of the continental Reformed pastors.[27] The Independents challenged King and Parliament on the issue of prescribing a worship-book at all: this was an aspect of their broader stance concerning the Headship of Christ over his Church and the place of the Bible in church order. In addition, they objected to many of the ceremonies laid down in the Prayer Books—as did the Presbyterians, who were especially aggrieved at having to declare upon oath that they approved of things which they manifestly did not. Baxter felt this point keenly. Finally, whereas the Independents were little moved by the Solemn League and Covenant, the Presbyterians, as we have already seen, viewed the abjuration of this Covenant as the ungodly betrayal of a solemn oath. Indeed, the Independent William Hooke wrote to John Davenport of New Haven in the following terms: "Had not the Covenant pinched them, very many of them would not have stuck at submitting to the common-prayers . . . some Presbyterians are ready enough to meet the Bishop half-way, and to swallow down Liturgy, if the choke-pear of abjuration of the Covenant, or some such thing, be not added to it."[28] The Presbyterian position was consistent with the earlier statement of Edmund Calamy that if he reneged upon the Solemn League and Covenant he would be a "perjured wretch."[29]

What were the results of the Act of Uniformity? We noted earlier that the Baptists had not for the most part allowed themselves to occupy positions from which they could be ejected. Of one branch of Baptists W.T. Whitley (himself no lover of Calvinism) seemed particularly proud: "it deserves to be reiterated that not a single General Baptist ever showed such a loose hold on principles as to occupy a parish pulpit."[30]

---

27 See Joseph Hunter, *The Life of Oliver Heywood*, 1842, 136. Of the Presbyterian Philip Henry, for example, it is said that "His reasons for his nonconformity were very considerable. . . . He could by no means submit to be re-ordained; so well satisfied was he in his call to the ministry, and his solemn ordination to it, by the laying on of the hands of the presbytery, which God had graciously owned him in, that he durst not do that which looked like a renunciation of it, as null and sinful, and would be at least a tacit invalidating and condemning of all his administrations." See J.B. Williams, *The Life of Philip Henry* (1828), Edinburgh: The Banner of Truth Trust 1974, 97.

28 CSPD, Car. II, LXIX, 1662–1663, 63–64; A.G. Matthews, "A censored letter," CHST, IX 6, Sept. 1926, 262–83.

29 E. Calamy, *The Great Danger of Covenant-refusing and Covenant-breaking*, 1646, 38.

30 W.T. Whitley, "The relation of Baptists to the Ejectment," in *The Ejectment of 1662 and the Free Churches*, London: National Council of Evangelical Free Churches [1912], 86.

In this connection, however, a question mark may be placed against the name of John Skinner, who attended the General Baptist Assembly in 1689. The other seven Baptists ejected in England, who included John Tombes, Henry Jessey and Daniel Dyke, and such Welsh Baptists as Vavasor Powell and John Miles, were all of the Particular sort.[31] Among ejected ministers who subsequently became Baptists were Francis Bampfield, the leader of the Seventh-Day Baptists, and Thomas Ewins and Thomas Hardcastle, successively ministers at Broadmead Baptist Church, Bristol.[32]

The ejection between 1660–62 of some 172[33] Independent ministers, including such eminent pastors as John Flavell, and such a renowned scholar as John Owen, Dean of Christ Church and earlier Vice-Chancellor of the University of Oxford, greatly strengthened the position of those Independents who, like most Baptists, had not filled state positions.

Something over 1700 of the ejected were Presbyterians. With their often superior education they ensured that henceforth the "three denominations" (Baptist, Independent/Congregational, Presbyterian) would have a core of society's "respectable" at their heart, and that the group as a whole would, sooner or later, have to be reckoned with. Richard Baxter, Thomas Watson, Edmund Calamy, Philip Henry—these and many others were ministers of high calibre which no church could lose without weakening itself.

In all, about one fifth of the clergy of the Church of England were ejected and, according to the older historian, J.R. Green, that Church lost more than some able pastors and scholars:

> The Church of England stood from that moment isolated and alone among all the churches of the Christian world. The Reformation had severed it irretrievably from those which still clung to the

31 See Ernest A. Payne and Norman S. Moon, *Baptists and 1662*, London: Carey Kingsgate 1962, 13–15.

32 Ibid., 16–17. Payne and Moon give Paul Hobson as a Calvinist, though B.R. White cautiously notes that Hobson's "relationship to the Calvinistic Baptist community to which he had earlier belonged was by the 1660s somewhat uncertain." See his *The English Baptists of the 17th Century*, London: Baptist Historical Society 1983, 103. For the ejected see A.G. Matthews, *Calamy Revised*, London: OUP 1934, reissued 1988; A. Gordon, *Freedom After Ejection*, Manchester: Manchester U.P. 1917. For the ejected in Wales see R. Tudur Jones and B.G. Owens, *Y Cofiadur*, no. 31, August 1962.

33 Geoffrey F. Nuttall increases A.G. Matthews's figure (*Calamy Revised*, xiii, xlii) by one, adding Richard Flavell. See his *Visible Saints. The Congregational Way 1640–1660*, Oxford: Blackwell 1957, 23 n. 1; idem, "Congregational Commonwealth incumbents," CHST, XIV 3, April 1943, 155–67.

> obedience of the Papacy. By its rejection of all but episcopal orders, the Act of Uniformity severed it as irretrievably from the general body of the Protestant Churches, whether Lutheran or Reformed. And while thus cut off from all healthy religious communication with the world without, it sank into immobility within. With the expulsion of the Puritan clergy, all change, all efforts after reform, all national development, suddenly stopped.[34]

The Church of England did have its Laudian view that the State had the right and duty to order the worship of the Church reaffirmed; but the same Act which underlined that contention also, for the first time, defined Nonconformity under the law, polarised attitudes within the land, and made eventual toleration inevitable.

We may note in passing that whereas, as we saw, Cromwell's Triers for the most part turned out only scandalous ministers, the Act of Uniformity was relentless and undisciminating. Furthermore, whereas those deposed by the Triers were permitted an allowance of one fifth of their previous income, there was no such gesture in 1662.

The Act of Uniformity was by no means the last of the anti-Nonconformist enactments. The Conventicle Act of 1664 declared that if five or more persons (other than members of the same household) over the age of sixteen met for religious purposes they were liable to a fine of £5; and to transportation to a colony other than Virginia or New England for a third offence. The Five Mile Act followed in 1665. It was designed to prevent Nonconformist ministers and teachers from residing within five miles of any corporate town, or of the place where they had formerly been employed. It was the Five Mile Act which gave Presbyterians no option but to take ordinations into their own hands. As ministers left the scene of their labours others, among them George Trosse, who was ordained in 1666, were installed in their place.[35] Presbyterians were divided by the Act, however. Some fifty, including Bates and Manton, took the required oath not to disturb the peace; others, Watson and Janeway among them, refused, and were prepared to set up conventicles in defiance of the law.[36]

---

34 J.R. Green, *A Short History of the English People* (1874), London: Dent Everyman 1915, II, 589.

35 *Life* of Trosse by himself, 1714, 589.

36 CSPD, Car. II, 1671–2, 27–9; G. Lyon Turner, *Original Records of English Nonconformity*, 1911–14, III, 201–02.

The cumulative effects of the legislation so far described can readily be imagined; but we need not resort to imagination, for many accounts of the sufferings of the Nonconformists survive. Let us, then, both note a few examples from the major streams, and put matters into perspective.

III

Shortly after the passing of the Act of Uniformity Charles II announced his intention of inviting Parliament to enact legislation which would permit him to exercise discretion vis-à-vis tender consciences. In this he was thwarted by Parliament and Church alike. What, then, happened to the ejected Ministers? Richard Baxter may be our initial informant: "Hundreds of able ministers, with their wives and children, had neither house nor bread . . . some would go to church to Common Prayer, to Sacraments, and others would not. Some of them thought that it was their duty to preach publicly in the streets or fields while the people desired it, and not to cease their work through fear of men till they lay in jails or were all banished. Others thought that a continued endeavour to benefit their people privately would be more serviceable to the Church than one or two sermons and a jail. . . . Hereupon those ministers that would not cease preaching were thrust into prisons. . . . "[37]

More particularly, some Presbyterian ministers, like Jerome Littlejohn, lived "very privately, never attempting anything against the peace and quiet either of church or state."[38] Others, like Robert Collins, organised services in opposition to the established Church: he conducted worship "in time of divine service to the scandal of many." For this he was imprisoned once and fined on a number of occasions.[39] Still others—some 210 in all—sooner or later conformed,[40] and a further 50, as we saw, met the Five Mile Act's requirement of swearing not to disturb the peace. Oliver Heywood, ejected from Coley, near Halifax, was among those who both kept conventicles (at non-clashing times) and encouraged his hearers to worship at the parish church as well. He himself was "frequently present at Mr. Hoole's [his successor's] services," and on

37 R. Baxter, *Autobiography*, 175–76.

38 A. G. Matthews, *Calamy Revised*, 46, 325.

39 Ibid., 8, 125, 129.

40 Ibid., xiii, lx; R.T. Jones and B.G. Owens, art. cit.

the first Sunday of 1668 he occupied his old pulpit in Hoole's absence.[41]

As to their personal circumstances, a few, like John Owen, were able to survive without difficulty on their private estates; others, like John Howe, were supported by Puritan gentry; Henry Newcome was among those who received small donations from their former congregations;[42] some were remembered in wills; Adam Martindale was one who turned to another means of livelihood—in his case, mathematics;[43] John Angier of Devonshire was among a minority who were left alone because "the worst of men had no heart to meddle with him;"[44] but Francis Tallents's description of the ejected ministers of Shropshire applied to many: "the richest of them were brought low; and the rest into great Want and Straits: But he that feeds the Ravens has provided for them and theirs, amidst the Fewness and Poverty of their Friends, one way or another, in a wonderful manner."[45] Many lived dangerously. Joseph Oddy preached at night in a wood near Willingham—mounted on his horse lest sudden escape proved necessary;[46] the Olney Dissenters met at the conjunction of the counties of Buckinghamshire, Bedfordshire and Northamptonshire, so that when the constable of one county hove into view they could escape into another;[47] and Thomas Jollie preached from a staircase, standing behind a split door, the top portion of which would be closed to hide him if an alarm was given.[48] Such ruses notwithstanding, Jollie found himself in prison on five separate occasions.

With the oppressive legislation in place, some soon found that there was money to be made by informing against the Dissenters. Thus, in a fourteen-month period, William Thornaby, an innkeeper of Richmond, Yorkshire, and his agents, made £2,000 from seventy-nine Quaker meetings.[49] Not all informers were as successful—or

---

41 J. Hunter, *Life of Heywood*, 163, 206.

42 See his *Diary*, ed. T. Heywood, Manchester: Chetham Society 1849.

43 *The Life of Adam Martindale*, ed. R. Parkinson, Manchester: Chetham Society 1845, 175. Martindale (174) writes: "I really beleeve the Act of Uniformitie saved my life, by taking me off employment too heavie for one entering into a consumption, as I was thought to be."

44 Oliver Heywood, *Works*, 1825, I, 545.

45 E. Calamy, *An Account of the Ministers . . . who were ejected and silenced*, 1713, 573.

46 S. Palmer, *The Nonconformist's Memorial*, 1803, I, 206.

47 M. Hewett, "John Gibbs," *The Baptist Quarterly* III, 1926–7, 320.

48 T. Jollie, *Notebook*, xxl.

49 W.C. Braithwaite, SPQ, 79.

as skilful. On the first Sunday after the renewed and reinforced Conventicle Act of 1670 came into force, a London informer brought George Fox before the Lord Mayor. The unfortunate informer was found to be a Roman Catholic, and his near-lynching by the mob served to deter would-be informers in London for some years.[50] Colchester was no place for informers either. When two from Norfolk attempted to inform against the Quaker meeting there they were stoned by the mob and, on appealing to the mayor, were put in gaol for their own safety;[51] and Thomas Ellwood sent Buckinghamshire informers packing when he threatened two of them with legal action.[52] Finally, in August 1685, an informer who had successfully handed over some Quakers to the authorities became so drunk that he "abusing the mayor and others, was imprisoned."[53] So much for poetic justice.

As with informers, so with prisons: some discrimination is required. Thus, John Bunyan served his sentence in Bedford gaol from 1660 to 1672, but he was permitted to attend church meetings in 1661, 1668, 1669 and 1670; and he was called to the Bedford Congregational pastorate before his eventual release.[54] In 1664 the Altham Church Book notes the following concerning Thomas Jollie: "The Pastor was taken at Richard Ingham's and carried to Lancaster. (In prison several months). Found favour and had much liberty. Jailor kind. After some time got clear."[55] Richard Baxter, who was briefly imprisoned in 1670 for keeping a conventicle, recorded his experience thus:

> My imprisonment was at present no great suffering to me, for I had an honest jailor, who showed me all the kindness he could; I had a large room, and the liberty of walking in a fair garden; and my wife was never so cheerful a companion to me as in prison, and was very much against my seeking to be released, and she had

50 G. Fox, *Journal*, 560–66.

51 *The First Publishers of Truth*, ed. Norman Penney, London: Friends Historical Society 1907, 95. For the situation in Exeter see Allan Brockett, "The attack on Nonconformists in Exeter after the withdrawal of the Declaration of Indulgence," CHST, XVIII, 1958, 89–93.

52 *The History of the Life of Thomas Ellwood*, ed. C.G. Crump, 1900, 178–79.

53 Quoted by Craig W. Horle, *The Quakers and the English Legal System 1660–1688*, Philadelphia: University of Pennsylvania Press 1988, 200.

54 See John Brown, *John Bunyan, His Life, Times and Work* (1885), ch. VIII; W.T. Whitley, "Bunyan's imprisonment," *Transactions of the Baptist Historical Society*, VI, 1918–19, 7, 14; Joyce Godber, "The imprisonments of John Bunyan," CHST, XVI, 1949, 23–32.

55 T. Jollie, *Notebook*, 133.

> brought so many necessaries that we kept house contentedly and comfortably as at home, though in a narrower room, and I had the sight of more of my friends in a day than I had at home in half a year.[56]

Indeed, he complained that "the number of visitors by day did put me out of hope of studying, or doing anything but entertain them."[57] Later in our period, on 8 July 1685, Philip Henry wrote to his wife from prison in Chester Castle, informing her that "We are better accommodated . . . than we could have expected, though we must pay for it."[58]

On the other hand, the insanitary, disease-ridden conditions in some gaols took their toll. The Quaker Richard Hubberthorne died in Newgate in 1662, aged thirty-four; in the following year his fellow Quaker Edward Burrough died there, aged twenty eight;[59] Francis Howgill died in Appleby gaol in 1669[60] while Banbury gaol had been the scene of John Audland's death in 1663. For refusing to take the oath of allegiance, the Quaker Thomas Stordy, of Moorhouse, Cumberland, was kept in prison for twenty-four years until his death in 1684.[61]

As prison conditions varied, so did the degree of enthusiasm for law enforcement. For example, the mayor of Bristol, who had hoped to banish 400 Quakers before his term of office expired, secured 350 convictions, but managed to sentence only three—and these were subsequently put ashore on a technicality.[62] Some Wiltshire justices were Cromwellians and, as Bishop Seth Ward complained, at least fourteen Devonshire magistrates were "arrant Presbyterians."[63]

The town council of Yarmouth was in the hands of Dissenters from 1666, and by 1676 they controlled "both the civil and the military power."[64] The Lords Lieutenant of York, Lancaster and

---

56 R. Baxter, *Autobiography*, 207–08.

57 Ibid., 208.

58 P. Henry, *Life*, 158. For a series of letters written by Robert Franklin from Aylesbury gaol to his wife in 1670 see CHST, I, 1901–4, 345–52.

59 See G.R. Cragg, *Puritanism in the Period of the Great Persecution*, Cambridge, 1957, ch. IV.

60 W.C. Braithwaite, SPQ, 37.

61 See C.E. Whiting, *Studies in English Puritanism from the Restoration to the Revolution 1660–88*, 1931, 147, 149–50.

62 W.C. Braithwaite, SPQ, 46.

63 M.R. Watts, *The Dissenters*, 244.

64 CSPD, Car. II, 1667–8, 88, 145; Ibid., 1676–7, 155.

Derby were disinclined to aid episcopalians by persecuting Nonconformists and Papists; and many in the land were impressed by the self-sacrificial service rendered by ejected ministers during the Plague of 1666, and notably by Thomas Stanley of Eyam, Derbyshire.[65]

But when all the qualifications have been made the fact remains that there was colossal suffering—and by none more than the Quakers. It has been estimated that during the reign of Charles II 15,000 Quakers were fined, imprisoned or transported, and that of these 450 died.[66] The Quakers walked a hard road indeed before the plea of William Smith to the King in 1663 was granted. From Nottingham gaol Smith argued that since Quakers had received the "Light that comes from Jesus Christ, and walk in the same, they ought to have that Liberty granted them into which Christ had restored them."[67]

As for the Baptists, by the end of 1662, 289 of them were in Newgate prison, and eighteen in the Tower of London.[68] Among these was the most distinguished of all the Particular Baptist pastors, Henry Jessey. A former Trier, he had served a term in gaol in 1641 and now, twenty years on, was incarcerated once again. He died six months after his release, in September 1663.[69] For a rural General Baptist experience we may turn to Lincolnshire:

> One Radley, a gentleman of considerable property in that county, distinguished himself by his enmity against the baptists. Under the authority of the Act of Uniformity, he went with an armed force to their meeting, with a design to apprehend them: but the soldiers, struck with their innocent deportment, to the great mortification of their leader, refused to arrest them. This Radley, after doing all the mischief in his power to his pious neighbours, became a bankrupt, and died of the plague in London. His widow was reduced to great poverty, and his children thrown on the parish for support. Some

---

65 *Life of O. Heywood*, 196, 199.

66 W.C. Braithwaite, SPQ, 115. For the sufferings of Friends in one of their strongholds see Alan P.F. Sell, *Church Planting. A study of Westmorland Nonconformity*, Worthing: H.E. Walter (now Bletchley: Word Books) 1986, 31–33. See also C.W. Horle, op. cit., App. I for analysis and statistics of Quaker sufferings.

67 William Smith, *Liberty of Conscience Pleaded by several weighty Reasons on the Behalf of the People of God called Quakers. . . . With a tender Message of Love unto the King*, 1662, 6.

68 W.T. Whitley, *A Baptist Bibliography*, I, 85.

69 A.G. Matthews, *Calamy Revised*, 147, 277, 298.

of them were relieved by those very baptists whom their father had so rancorously persecuted.[70]

The pioneer hymn-writer, Benjamin Keech, suffered too. A self-taught tailor, he became pastor at the General Baptist church at Winslow, Buckinghamshire. In 1664 he was fined twenty pounds, imprisoned for two weeks, and pilloried at Aylesbury and Winslow for his anti-Prayer Book views as expressed in his *Child's Instructor: or, a New and Easy Primer.* All copies of this book were burned, but Keach rewrote it from memory and it went through several editions.[71] In the south-west Abraham Cheare, pastor of the Plymouth Calvinistic Baptists from 1650, spent most of the years from the Restoration to his death in 1668 in prison.[72] Finally, the London General Baptist layman, Francis Smith, a publisher whose books, deemed seditious, were seized, and who was imprisoned on numerous occasions, estimated that in the twenty years to 1680 he sustained "public losses and apparent damages" in excess of £1,400.[73]

Among Congregational ministerial sufferers we have already noted Thomas Jollie, but he was by no means alone. Of John Manning, Calamy wrote that "There's scarce a gaol in Suffolk which he was not sent to at some time or other;"[74] Francis Holcroft was held from 1663 to 1672 though, presumably through the good offices of his gaoler, he preached in seven Cambridge parishes in 1669.[75] John Thompson, minister at Bristol, was among the seven ejected ministers who died in prison—in his case, in 1675, owing, so his gaoler reported, to his overeating and drinking.[76] John James, minister at Flintham, Nottinghamshire, was deemed "a dangerous seducer from the Church of England," by the local Vicar. He was imprisoned for seventeen months in Nottingham, and for six years in Newark, where he remained until the Indulgence of 1672. On his release he refused to refrain from preaching; his house was entered under warrant, goods and cattle to the value of £500 were

70 Adam Taylor, *The History of the English General Baptists*, 1818, I, 197–98.

71 Thomas Crosby, *History of the Baptists*, 1738–1740, II, 186ff.

72 R.L. Greaves and R. Zaller, *Biographical Dictionary of British Radicals in the Seventeenth Century*, 1982, I, 139.

73 Adam Taylor, op. cit., 343–46.

74 E. Calamy, *An Account*, II, 649.

75 *Calamy Revised*, 272.

76 CSPD, Car. II, 1675–6, 94–95.

seized; and of his three terrified children one died within a week.[77] Laymen suffered too, and Thomas Botting of Lewes, Sussex, may represent them:

> He was listed for non-attendance [at the Parish Church] in 1663, 1665, 1670, 1676, 1699–70 and 1673–4, for refusing to have his children baptized in 1667, 1669–70 and 1673–4, for worship at a conventicle in 1673, and for being a "dissenter" in 1685. He stood surety when his nephew, John Ayers, was charged with libelling Sir Thomas Nutt, the magistrate who so zealously prosecuted hearers at Henge Lane, and in 1685 he was himself fined £20 for preaching at the house of a neighbour.[78]

As for the Presbyterian ministers, John Cole spent eight years in prison "for expounding the Scripture and praying;"[79] Richard Chantrye sought to avoid informers by going to meetings "in the twilight . . . with a Bible in his pocket and a fork on his shoulder;"[80] and, in the wake of the Conventicle Act, Adam Martindale conducted repeat services to members of his congregation subdivided into groups of the legally permitted size.[81]

We do well to observe that in addition to adverse legislation there were the mixed motives of the Anglican clergy to contend with. Some incumbents, only too eager to avenge themselves for their period of powerlessness, dealt with Quakers and others with malice—not least where the non-payment of tithes was concerned. Moreover, there was the weapon of excommunication. As B.R. White has said, "the spiritual implications of being cast out from a church which they already considered a false one would not greatly concern such people;" but there could be social and business consequences too. The Dissenters of Abingdon were among those against whom the deterrent of excommunication was invoked.[82]

In 1672 Charles II issued a Declaration of Indulgence which permitted Nonconformist ministers to take out licenses to preach. The King's action placed Dissenters on the horns of a dilemma. On the one hand, they desired freedom of worship under the law; on

77 A.R. Henderson, *History of Castle Gate Congregational Church, Nottingham, 1655–1905*, London: James Clarke 1905, 66–69.

78 Colin Brent, *"Lewes Dissenters outside the Law, 1663–86,"* Sussex Archaeological Collections, CXXIII, 1985, 198.

79 *Calamy Revised*, 125.

80 Ibid., 109.

81 *Life of A. Martindale*, 176.

82 B.R. White, *The English Baptists*, 105–06.

the other hand, they did not acknowledge the King's right to go over the head of Parliament. Furthermore, many were suspicious that the Indulgence granted to them might open the way to Roman Catholic advance in society—a suspicion shared by some Anglicans. Nevertheless 923 Presbyterian, 416 Congregational and 200 Baptist ministers took out licences.[83] The Quakers refused to do so, and their forebodings were eventually confirmed: Parliament forced the King to withdraw the Indulgence in March 1673. How the withdrawal impinged upon one Dissenting minister is clear from William Bagshawe's *Life*:

> The Declaration of Indulgence being call'd in at the Request of the Parliament, he still kept up his Meetings, tho' privately, and with great Care, prudently changing the Place almost every Lord's-Day, that he might not expose his Hearers to the Lash of the severe Laws in force against him, which by some were very rigorously put in Execution . . . towards the Close of King Charles's Reign, the Prosecution of Protestant Dissenters being renew'd with greater Violence, he was driven into Corners again. He receiv'd the News of that King's Death with a very deep Concern, and had great Fears upon his Spirit, when he saw a Popish Successor in the Throne.[84]

The Test Act of 1673, though ostensibly directed against Roman Catholic aspirations to civil and military office, encompassed the Dissenters too, and reaffirmed the provisions of the Corporation Act of 1661. From 1683 to 1689 we have the final period of persecution. It was during this period, at the beginning of 1685, that Oliver Heywood wrote:

> At this time I am under the heaviest circumstances as to my liberty of doing God service and good to souls, that ever I was in all my life. Men have broken in upon us and scattered our meetings; indicted me for a riot at the Sessions. I am bound in 100 l. to traverse and to be of good behaviour. My adversaries are watching me narrowly to find me forfeiting my bond. . . . Sometimes God helps me by prayer to roll myself on God, and then I am easy. But, oh how oft am I at a loss![85]

From 26 January to 19 December 1685 Heywood was once again in York gaol.[86] During the same period Heywood's colleague,

83 G. Lyon Turner, *Original Records*, III, 733–35.

84 John Ashe, *The Life and Character of the Reverend Mr. Bagshaw*, 1704, 6–7.

85 *Life of O. Heywood*, 328–29.

86 Ibid., 331.

Richard Frankland, was forced to remove with his Dissenting academy on no fewer than five occasions, under the provisions of the Five Mile Act.[87]

James II's Indulgence of 1687 provided a brief lull, though it was suspected by John Howe, Daniel Williams and others, for the same reasons as was that of Charles fifteen years earlier. The Quakers, too, had reservations which were proved justified:

> Howbeit, the King's aforesaid Declaration not having the Sanction of an Act of Parliament . . . we did not think our Liberty secured to us thereby, any more than it was under the Reign of His Brother, King Charles the Second, but uncertain and precarious, as it was before, when we had only that King's Specious Promises and Declarations, which lasted but a little While, and were soon made void by the Parliament and Himself, and the many Persecutors let loose upon us again, because the same Liberty granted, was not passed into a Law.[88]

When seven bishops refused to read James's Indulgence in church they were sent to the Tower. Their acquittal by the jury gave psychological impetus to the efforts by then being made to secure the succession of William of Orange. In 1688 James fled, and William set sail for England.

IV

The attempted imposition of uniformity, the efforts at comprehension and the granting of indulgences having failed, only toleration remained to be investigated. William deemed toleration to be a political and a religious necessity. As for the Dissenters, it is interesting to observe that whereas Baptists and Quakers had been in favour of toleration—the former from Helwys's *The Mistery of Iniquity* (1612), the latter from their formation in the 1640s; and whereas the state-supported Independents, prompted by Presbyterian intransigence, came around to the notion during the Westminster Assembly; following the oppressive legislation of the 1660s none were more ardent advocates of (limited) toleration than the Presbyterians. Thus, in 1672 Richard Baxter appealed to conformists to urge that those willing to profess the ancient faith, but who had conscientious scruples against the Anglican liturgy and ceremonies,

---

87 See Alan P.F. Sell, *Church Planting*, 26–28.

88 *The Christian Progress of . . . George Whitehead*, 1725, p. 629.

might be "taken in to the established Ministry, if not, yet tolerated as Lecturers under [the conformists] in such Churches, where the Ministers desire us, not taking any of their maintenance from them, but trusting God for our daily bread."[89]

From other quarters came resistance to toleration. In 1685 John Nelson adduced many arguments against it, and clinched his case by challenging "All the Dissenters in England, Scotland, and Ireland, . . . to agree, who among them are Tolerable and who are not."[90] That, he thought, would teach them how impracticable toleration was!

Despite all opposition, the Toleration Act was passed in 1689—"a curious patchwork of compromise, illogicality and good sense," as G.M. Trevelyan called it.[91] Not the least stimulus was Locke's first *Letter concerning Toleration*, written in 1685, and published first in Latin in Holland and then in English in 1689. Locke upheld the separation of Church and State, the voluntary nature of the former, and the moral impossibility of assenting to that which one did not believe. As for the Act itself, the Earl of Nottingham introduced it into the House of Lords, it passed both Houses of Parliament, and received the royal assent on 24 May 1689. To Macaulay the Act was "among those great statutes which are epochs in our constitutional history,"[92] and indeed it was. But detailed examination of its provisions lends support to Trevelyan's judgment too. The word "toleration" appears nowhere in the Act—least of all in its title: *An Act for Exempting their Majesties' Protestant subjects, dissenting from the Church of England, from the penalties of certain laws.*[93] That is to say, none of the earlier adverse legislation was repealed, but the penalties were no longer to apply to certain people on certain conditions. The people were Protestants (that is, not Roman Catholics or Jews); who subscribed to the doctrinal Articles of the Church of England (that is, not Socinians and unitarians; and some Presbyterian ministers, Edmund Calamy among them, managed to avoid subscription—an act which they opposed in principle); and who paid tithes and rates levied by the established Church. This last condition struck Quakers most adversely:

---

89 (R. Baxter), *Sacrilegious Desertion of the Holy Ministers Rebuke, and Tolerated Preaching of the Gospel Vindicated* . . . , 1672, 136–37.

90 John Nelson, *Toleration and Liberty of Conscience Considered, and Proved Impracticable* . . . , 1685, 37.

91 G.M. Trevelyan, *History of England*, 1926, 476.

92 T.B. Macaulay, *History of England*, London: Dent Everyman edn., II, 282.

93 For the Act see Gee and Hardy, op. cit., 654–64.

> Although under the early Reign of King William the Third, we had so far obtain'd Liberty by Law, as to enjoy our Religious Meetings for the Worship of God peaceably, without Molestation, or Disturbance by Informers, or other Persecutors, yet there remaining many of our Friends Prisoners, and under Prosecution by Priests and others, for Nonpayment of Tithes, and many of them detain'd in Prisons, chiefly upon Contempts, (as their Term is) for not answering upon Oath, to the Priests Bills and Plaints, &c.[94]

Ten years later we find William Penn writing to the Member of Parliament Robert Harley (then in his Whig phase), urging him "please to Remember the House that Liberty of Conscience is one of the Articles of the Originall Contract of this Revolution. . . ."[95]

The Toleration Act excused Baptists from subscribing to the final clause of Article XXVII concerning the baptism of children; and in 1696 Quakers won the right to make a solemn affirmation and declaration in lieu of taking the oath of allegiance in its accepted form.[96] Some Quakers resented this concession on the ground that while the wording would be different, the substance and intention of the affirmation were identical to that of the oath.[97]

There was good (and politically astute) sense in the Act. It gave freedom of worship to many, and at the same time imposed a penalty of £20 upon any convicted of disturbing Dissenting meetings. It drew much of the sting of the punitive legislation which seemed increasingly incongruous to many, given the manifest "respectability" of most of those against whom it was directed. But there was illogicality too. For example, there was now on the statute books an Act of Uniformity which legislated against those ministers who refused to use the official Prayer Book, and a Toleration Act which permitted certain classes upon certain conditions to break an earlier, unrepealed law.

The Toleration Act was also fragile. On a number of occasions during the following century attempts were made to enact anti-Nonconformist legislation. Thus, for example, the proposed Schism Act of 1714, which would have abolished the Dissenting academies, was kept from the statue books only because of Queen Anne's death on 1 August, the day when the Act would have become law. Many a Dissenting minister interpreted this coincidence as an unexam-

94 *The Christian Progress of . . . George Whitehead*, 636.

95 *The Papers of William Penn, III, 1685–1700*, Philadelphia: University of Pennsylvania Press 1986, 568.

96 T. Bennett, *Laws Against Nonconformity*, Grimsby 1913, 187.

97 See W.C. Braithwaite, SPQ, 181–89.

pled sign of God's providence, and the Congregationalist Thomas Bradbury was said to have preached on the text, "Go now, see to this accursed woman, and bury her, for she was a king's daughter" (II Kings 9:34).

Again, unscrupulous local authorities could still penalise Nonconformists. Perhaps the most glaring example of this is provided by the City of London which, in order to finance the building of the new Mansion House, imposed a fine of £600 upon those who refused to serve as Sheriff. With the sacramental test still in force, Nonconformists were regularly nominated for office, refused to serve, and were fined. By this means some £15,000 was raised.[98] Eventually the Dissenters took their case to the House of Lords where, in 1767, the Lord Chief Justice, Lord Mansfield delivered judgment to the effect that since the Act of Toleration "It is now no crime for a man who is within the description of that Act to say he is a Dissenter; nor is it any crime for him not to take the sacrament according to the rites of the Church of England. Nay, the crime is if he does it contrary to the dictates of his conscience."[99]

Though the bulk of the Dissenters were legally recognised in 1689, they were kept legally subservient to the Church of England for the next two centuries. In 1753 Lord Hardwicke's Marrige Act removed the right of Dissenters (except for Jews and Quakers) to marry except at a service conducted by a clergyman of the Church of England using his prescribed form of service. (The Archbishop of Canterbury could issue a special licence for marriges to take place at any convenient time and place). This legal encumbrance was not removed until 1836. It was not until the Nonconformist Relief Act of 1779 that ministers and teachers were free to teach, on condition that they declared before magistrates that "I am a Christian and a Protestant . . . and that I do receive [the Scriptures] as the rule of my doctrine and practice."[100] Until 1809 many Anglican incumbents questioned Dissenters baptism, and hence their right of burial in the parish church yard. Unitarians finally secured freedom under the law in 1813; the Conventicle and Five Mile Acts were finally repealed in 1812, the Test and Corporation Acts in 1828; and the doors of the universities of Oxford and Cambridge were opened to Dissenters in 1871, though divinity degrees were not open to them until the twentieth century.

98 T. Bennett, op. cit., 160.

99 Ibid., 169.

100 Ibid., 221–22.

V

What, in conclusion, of the legacy of the English 1689 and its likeness or unlikeness to the Piedmontese 1689?

First, having duly noted the sufferings of the pre-toleration period, we must not neglect to record the spiritual deepening which also occurred during that time. A Quaker may make the point for us: "Altho' for the Space of about Twenty Five Years, [from 1660 to 1684] we had but small Respite from some Kind of Persecution or other, notwithstanding the Liberty of Conscience so often promised and declared from the Throne, yet the TRUTH lost no Ground, but gained through all: The Persecution Time, was a Seed-Time, for the Truth and Gospel of CHRIST JESUS, which we suffered for, and the Faithful grew and multiplied."[101] This was the age of William Penn's *No Cross, No Crown* (1669), and of Bunyan's *The Pilgrims Progress* (1678/84), and such a spiritual legacy can only be valued, however much the circumstances which called it forth may be deplored. Moreover, in the immediate wake of the Toleration Act, some were alive to the rapidity with which convictions could evaporate once the heat was off—and none more so than George Fox. Eight days before he died in 1691 he:

> complained of many Demases and Cains, who embrace the present world and encumber themselves with their own businesses and neglect the Lord's and so are good for nothing; and said They that had wives should be as though they had none, and Who goeth a warfare should not entangle himself with the things of this world.[102]

Intellectually, the psychological impact of freedom under the law led in some quarters (notably Presbyterian) to a wider concern for freedom of thought. Thus, for example, in the 1740s the Presbyterian John Taylor of Norwich looked back to 1689 and waxed lyrical: "LIBERTY at the Revolution, O bright, auspicious Day! reared up her heavenly Form, and smiled upon our happy Land. . . . Men began freely to use their Understandings; the Scriptures were examined with more Attention and Care, and their true sense, setting aside human Comments, and especially the Jargon and

---

101 *The Christian Progress of . . . George Whitehead*, 631–32.

102 Quoted by W.C. Braithwaite, SPQ, p. 437.

Sophistry of School-Divinity, was sought after."[103] We should note in passing that thought could be thus free only because the requirement of Nonconformist subscription to the Anglican Articles was not enforced. Had it been enforced, the spotlight would have been turned, in an embarrassing way, upon such Anglican divines as the Arian Samuel Clarke and the Latitudinarian Hoadly, whose attachment to the Articles was, to put it mildly, less than literalistic.

Practically, the Dissenters gave themselves to the building of meeting houses. During the twenty years following the Toleration Act nearly one thousand were erected, the majority of them Presbyterian, probably followed by Baptist and Congregationalist buildings in that order.[104] Within two years of the passing of the Act the Quakers took out 230 licences.[105] The Dissenting academies, though their position was not clearly defined by the Act, nevertheless entered a more settled period, educating such eminent men as Joseph Butler and Joseph Priestley. As the century progressed some of them were to the fore where curriculum development, openness to the sciences, and hospitality to newer literature were concerned.[106]

Politically, the traditional alliance of Anglicans with Tories and of Nonconformists with Whigs was henceforth fairly firm, though with the qualification that there were political differences within each group, and that the Wesleyans, in their early days, generally sided with the Tories. Of more significance for our present purposes is the realisation of the fact that the Toleration Act made it lawful for people to be the church, without their being the state church. The fact that the inspiration here was not exclusively altruism was

---

103 J. Taylor, *A Narrative of Mr. Joseph Rawson's Case*, 2nd edn. 1742, 9. See further, Alan P.F. Sell, "Presbyterianism in England in the eighteenth century: the doctrinal dimension," in *Dissenting Thought and the Life of the Churches, Studies in an English Tradition*, Lewiston, NY: Mellen Research University Press 1990, ch. V.

104 F.J. Powicke, "English Congregationalism in its greatness and decline," in *Essays Congregational and Catholic*, ed. A. Peel, London: Congregational Union of England and Wales (1931), 301.

105 *Parliamentary Papers*, 1853, LXXVIII, 164.

106 See H. McLachlan, *English Education under the Test Acts*, Manchester: Manchester U.P. 1931; Irene Parker, *Dissenting Academies in England*, Cambridge: CUP 1914; J. W. Ashley Smith, *The Birth of Modern Education: The Contribution of the Dissenting Academics 1660–1800*, London: Independent Press 1954; Alan P.F. Sell, "Philosophy in the eighteenth-century dissenting academics of England and Wales," *History of Universities*, XI, 1992, 75–122.

not lost upon the Quakers, who saw that it also had to do with the Governments "own Safety, and the Peace of the Government and Nation where they Rule."[107]

But, as we have seen, the Nonconformists were to be tolerated, but kept in social and political subservience. We thus have the "Church *versus* Chapel" distinction enforced by law— with consequent snobbishness on the one side, and dogged self-assertiveness on the other. This distinction persists to this day— especially in the more traditionalist spheres of churchly life, though it has been considerably weakened during the past century by ecumenism, pluralism, and the increasing societal marginalisation of all the English churches, including the Established.

Theologically, perhaps the biggest long-term disadvantage of the Toleration Act was the way in which it encouraged the distortion of the congregational (including Baptist) ecclesiology. This is a subtle matter to describe, not least because of different tendencies within Congregationalism itself. As we have been, some Independents in Cromwell's day were content with religious establishements provided they were of their own kind—and so were their New England counterparts. Those Independents who were more in the line of the Separatists maintained the separation of Church and State throughout, as did the Baptists. The period of persecution threw the ecclesiological emphasis upon local autonomy at the expense of catholicity. (It also undermined the Presbyterian polity—but that is another story.)[108] That is to say, the need to survive drove local churches in upon themselves, and the adverse legislation ruled out such associations as John Owen had envisaged, even if they were desired. The freedom of the Church catholic under Christ became, after 1689, and understandably enough, transmuted into the quest of freedom from socio-political constraints. When in the second half of the eighteenth century, the Evangelical Revival brought in many "new" Congregationalists, who had a saving experience of Christ, but who were not rooted in the concept of the gathered, covenanted saints, the ecclesiology was further turned in an individualistic direction.[109] When the socio-political restrictions were finally removed, it is not surprising that, in keeping with the tendencies just described (and we cannot posit hard cause-effect relationships, or overlook the many exceptions), many came to feel that Dissent need be no more. That not all agreed with this assessment is clear

107 *The Christian Progress of . . . George Whitehead*, 632.

108 See Alan P.F. Sell, at n. 103.

109 See Alan P.F. Sell, "Confessing the faith in English Congregationalism," in *Dissenting Thought*, ch. I.

from these words of A.M. Fairbairn:

> It is perhaps harder to be a Nonconformist to-day than it has ever been in the history of England. The very decay of the disabilities from which our fathers suffered has made it harder to us than it was to them to dissent.
>
> But while it has become harder it has also become more necessary: for the need of a testimony to a Church in which Christ is supreme was never so great as now.[110]

It is the conviction of the present writer that the underlying theological questions of Dissent: "Who is a Christian?" "Who are the Church?" "How are we to honour the Headship of Christ in his Church?" and "What ought to be the relation of Church and State?" have not finally been answered and, not least because of church establishments elsewhere in the world, they merit detailed ecumenical consideration.[111] As P.T. Forsyth wrote, "mere liberty is a negative idea apart from a creative authority. And we have been doing more for liberty than for authority. . . . For in a Church of the Gospel the authority that sets free must always be prior to the freedom it makes."[112]

When we place the English Dissenters alongside the Vaudois we see that there was more than general sympathy between the one group and the other: there was a shared experience of suffering too; there was a common human saviour in the person of William of Orange. Furthermore, 1689 placed both groups in a ghetto: the Vaudois, having made their "Glorious Return" found themselves in a geographical ghetto;[113] the English Dissenters were for the next two hundred years in a socio-political ghetto. Both were involved in a societal dualism: "Catholic *versus* Reformed" in Piedmont, "Church *versus* Chapel" in England. Both have now emerged from their respective ghettos: the Waldensians, after 1860, to proclaim the Gospel which had sustained them throughout their new land of Italy; the English Dissenters to take their place in the mainstream of society—perhaps to the hurt of their distinctive witness.

---

110 W.B. Selbie, *The Life of Andrew Martin Fairbairn*, London: Hodder & Stoughton 1914, 257–58.

111 See further, Alan P.F. Sell, "Dubious Establishment? A neglected ecclesiological testimony," in *Dissenting Thought*, ch. XXII.

112 P.T. Forsyth, *Faith, Freedom and the Future* (1912), London: Independent Press 1955, 318.

113 So G. Tourn, *You Are My Witnesses*, 145–52.

Waldensians and English Dissenters are *in principle* at one with Tertullian in his address to the persecutor Scapula:

> It is a fundamental human right, a privilege of nature, that every man should worship according to his own convictions. . . . It is assuredly no part of religion to compel religion—to which free-will and not force should lead us. . . . You will render no real service to your gods by compelling us to sacrifice. For they can have no desire of offerings from the unwilling, unless they are animated by a spirit of contention, which is a thing altogether undivine.[114]

But when all that is granted, and enshrined in legislation, do Waldensians and English Dissenters *in practice* share the problem of lack of commitment and zeal when the fires of persecution, and the iniquities of oppressive laws are no more? From prison John Bunyan wrote of Christian's leading Hopeful down By-Path Meadow. It was easy on the feet, but they were soon off course for the Celestial City. The broad way (cf. Matthew 7:13) is to be avoided by all who would truly honour those whom we recall in this year of Tercentenaries; by all who would be faithful to the ever-sustaining, never-failing Gospel of the grace of God.

114 Tertullian, *Ad Scapulam*, 2.

VI

Robert Barclay (1648–1690), the Fathers and the Inward, Universal Saving Light: A Tercentenary Reappraisal

> Let the *Quakers* henceforth cease to lay any claim to the Authority of St. Augustine, or any other of the *Ancient Fathers, Greek* or *Latin*, that lived either before him, or in his time; as if they favoured this Vile Error; for no doubt St. *Augustine* better knew the mind of those holy Ancients, than any of the Quakers, or this their Apologist.[1]

Such was the stern judgment of George Keith (1638–1716). Raised a Presbyterian, Keith became a Quaker in 1664. He was Robert Barclay's mentor and friend, though ten years after Barclay's death he left the Friends and was ordained in the Church of England in 1700.[2] We shall have more to say concerning his assessment of Barclay's use of the Fathers in due course. For the moment he directs us to our task, for he prompts the questions, To what extent did Barclay draw upon the Fathers? Why, and with what degree of success, did he have recourse to them?

It is noteworthy that of Barclay's contemporary critics, Keith alone makes extensive reference to Barclay's use (or, as he thinks, abuse) of the Fathers; nor is this subject investigated in detail by recent expositors of Barclay's thought.[3] It may be suggested, as a

---

1 George Keith, *The Standard of the Quakers Examined, or An Answer to the Apology of Robert Barclay*, 1702, 240.

2 For Keith see DNB; E.W. Kirby, *George Keith, 1638–1716*, 1942; J. Philip Wragge, "The debt of Robert Barclay to George Keith," unpublished typescript, 1946; idem, *The Faith of Robert Barclay*, 1948, 21–34; John Eliot in *The Yorkshireman*, III, 1834, 4–15.

3 I have the following in mind: Eleanor P. Mather, *Barclay in Brief*, 1942; J.P. Wragge, op. cit.; Brand Blanshard, "Early thought on the Inner Light," in Howard H. Brinton (ed.), *Byways in Quaker History. A collection of historical essays by friends and colleagues of William I. Hull*, Wallingford, PA: Pendle Hill 1944; Gerardina L. Van Dalfsen, "The faith and theology of Robert Barclay," *Bul-*

reason for this neglect, that Barclay's appeal to the Fathers was, if not purely formal, at least not original—on the contrary, it was at secondhand. On this matter Keith, by now a hostile witness, "spilled the beans." Barclay, he alleges, took most of his references "at Second Hand, as I myself did the like, as touching many of them, which he had from me. . . ."[4] Keith hastens to point out that he has subsequently returned to the original sources.

What shall we make of Keith's charge? As a person of integrity, he is *prima facie* trustworthy. He admits that he had plundered Vossius and Grotius for patristic references, and that he had shared these with Barclay. By tracing Barclay's identifiable patristic quotations to their sources in the Greek and Latin, we shall show that he did not always attend to the context of the passages plundered, and that he was selective in his usage of the Fathers: he takes little account of them where they appear to oppose him. This, coupled with Keith's suggestion of a "crib list," may suggest that Barclay was unaware of contrary points. In any case, of his general indebtedness to Keith there can be no doubt, as witness the linguistic echoes of Keith's earlier works in Barclay's *Theses* of 1674.[5]

Despite the lack of originality in Barclay's appeals to patristic sources, it is our contention that the fact that he made the appeal at all is illuminating in respect of his apologetic objectives and method, and it poses a serious question to present-day Friends. Accordingly, we shall proceed to a consideration of Barclay's objectives and method in the *Apology* (Latin 1676, English 1678). We shall then investigate his actual use of the Fathers. Scattered references to patristic sources may be found throughout the *Apology*, but since the Fathers are quoted (as distinct from listed) in significant numbers in connection with the themes of inward and

---

letin of Friends Historical Association, XXXVII, no. 2, 1948, 51–62; Leif Eeg-Olofsson, *The Conception of the Inner Light in Robert Barclay's Theology*, Lund, 1954; Francis B. Hall, "The thought of Robert Barclay: An evaluation," *Quaker Religious Thought*, VII, no. 1, Spring 1965, 2–31, with replies by Maurice A. Creasey, 32–35, James Flood, 35–38, and D. Elton Trueblood, 38–43; D. Elton Trueblood, *Robert Barclay*, 1968; Donald S. Nesti, *Grace and Faith: the means to salvation. An analysis of early Quaker soteriology and sacrementality: 1650–1689*, Pittsburgh: Catholic and Quaker Studies 1975; and the following unpublished theses: George Passmore Hayes, *Robert Barclay: His Life, Works and Position in the History of Quaker Thought*, Harvard University, 1927; Maurice A. Creasey, *The Theology of Robert Barclay*, University of Leeds, 1951; James J. Flood, *A Catholic Critique of the Quaker doctrine of the Inner Light*, Pontifical Gregorian University, Rome, 1963.

4 G. Keith, *The Standard*, 230. Keith repeats his confession on p. 241.

5 See P. Wragge's tables of parallels between Barclay's *Apology*, and Keith's *Immediate Revelation* (1668, but written 1664–5), op. cit., 31–33.

immediate revelation and the universal saving light, and since these are Barclay's major doctrinal distinctives, we shall concentrate upon these matters. Finally, we shall presume to offer some kindly intentioned, albeit non-Friendly, reflections upon our findings.

I

No doubt, as W.C. Braithwaite averred, one of Barclay's motives in writing the *Apology* was domestic, so to speak: "The corporate consciousness that had come to Friends with the organization established by Fox was bound to crave for some systematic manual of Quaker principles. . . ."[6] But there was more to it than that: Barclay's purpose was political as well as "denominational." He wished to assert and defend Quaker teachings in such a way as to show the authorities that they had no need to continue persecuting so peaceable, upright and orthodox a people. In pursuing this line Barclay was also, by implication, distancing the Friends from more violent and seditious groups. As Alexander Gordon explained,

> *Apologia* is of course a vindication, yet it is clear that Barclay did not understand by this a defence in the nature of a justifying explanation, which is the meaning Dr. Newman has taught us to attach to the word, but rather a defence in the nature of a fortifying outwork or advanced guard. . . . His object was to secure for [Friends] an immunity from misrepresentation, a liberty of development, a position of acknowledged respect and weight.[7]

The benefits here mentioned were nowhere more to be desired than in Barclay's Aberdeen, where Quakers were represented as "demented, distracted, bodily possessed of the devil, practising abominations under cover of being possessed by the Spirit and as to their principles, blasphemous deniers of the true Christ, of Heaven, Hell and Angels."[8] As if this were not enough, Quakers were accused of being agents of Popery.[9]

---

6 William C. Braithwaite, *The Second Period of Quakerism*, 2nd edn., 1961, 386.

7 A. Gordon, "The marrow of Barclay," *The Theological Review*, XII, 1875, 389–90.

8 R. Barclay, *Truth Clear'd of Calumnies*, 1670, Preface.

9 E.g. by Henry More the Cambridge Platonist. See M.H. Nicolson (ed.), *Conway Letters: The correspondence of Anne, Vicountess Conway, Henry More, and their friends, 1642–84*, 1930, 416. The Aberdeen divinity students were among others who reiterated the charge—well aware that Barclay had been educated in the (Roman Catholic) Scots Theological College in Paris, of which his uncle Robert was Rector. See Barclay's vindication of the Quakers in *A True and Faithful Account*, 1675; also his *Quakerism No Popery* 1675, a reply to the accusations

A third motivation was Barclay's desire to defend God's honour, as he understood it, from Calvinism's sterner features. In this respect the *Apology* is a reply to the Westminster Shorter Catechism (1647), and Barclay's first thirteen *Theses* follow the order of the latter's questions. In this connection it is not without significance that (assuming Keith to be a reliable witness) Barclay utilised references culled from Gerard Jan Vossius (1577–1649) and Hugo Grotius (1583–1645), both of whom were Arminians who wished to distinguish their position from Pelagianism, and the former of whom argued in his *Historia de controversiis quas Pelagius ejusque reliquiae moverunt* (1618) that the doctrine of predestination was unknown in the early Church. Barclay made it quite clear that he "intended never to write of those things concerning which we do not differ from others."[10] This decision undoubtedly focused his polemics and enabled him to emphasise Quaker distinctives but, as we shall see, it had the effect of diverting attention from some of the fundamental Christian doctrines.

The fact that Barclay is fighting on more than one front influences his method. Thus, in introducing himself to "the friendly reader," he cautions that his method may appear not only deficient, but contrary to that of "the men called *divines*." He explains that, far from admiring *school-men*, he despises them, for they destroy the Christian religion. He has not sought to accommodate his work to "itching ears"—rather, "what I have written comes more from my heart than from my head." He has "followed the certain rule of the *Divine Light*, and of the *Holy Scriptures*."[11] Consistently with this, he later distinguishes between "the saving heart-knowledge, and the soaring, airy head-knowledge."[12]

On the other hand, when addressing Charles II the political motive is to the fore: "if thou wilt allow thyself so much time as to read this, thou mayest find *how consonant [Quaker] principles are both to scripture, truth, and right reason*."[13] Similarly, in the complete title of the *Apology* Barclay declares that he intends to offer "A full explanation and vindication of [Quaker] principles and doctrines, by many arguments deduced from Scripture and right

of John Menzies in his *Roma Mendax* 1675. Menzies was Professor of Divinity at Aberdeen University.

10 R. Barclay, *Truth Triumphant*, 1st edn., 1692, 732.

11 Idem, *An Apology for the True Christian Divinity as the same is held forth and preached by the people, in scorn, called Quakers, etc.*, ix. We here use the widely available 14th edn., 1886.

12 Ibid., 12.

13 Ibid., vi.

reason, and the testimonies of famous authors, both ancient and modern."

Finally, with Christians of other traditions in mind Barclay appeals to the tradition at large, and to the Fathers in particular. He piles up his authorities with a view to showing that "it was the consensus of Christian authorities that there is something better than the authority of men."[14] Not indeed that Barclay's opinion of the Fathers was particularly high. Thus, in a "Table of Chief Things" prefixed to *Truth Triumphant,* he points out that the Fathers did not always agree on points of biblical interpretation, and that they sometimes contradicted one another—and themselves. On which theme Barclay is in the line of the Reformed pastor of Paris, John Daillé, whose *A Treatise Concerning the Right Use of the Fathers, in the Decision of the Controversies that are at this Day in Religion* had been translated into English in 1651. Nevertheless he does think it worthwhile to make his appeal to the Fathers, and we shall now see how he goes about it.

II

Having affirmed, in his first Proposition, the necessity of that knowledge of God which brings life eternal, Barclay proceeds in Proposition Second to elucidate the nature of "inward and immediate revelation" (to use the *two* adjectives in the Latin text: the English gives only the latter). Divine revelation, he declares, is not subject to rational or scriptural tests; it is self-authenticating. It "is that which is evident and clear of itself, forcing, by its own evidence and clearness, the well disposed understanding to assent, irresistibly moving the same thereunto, even as the common principles of natural truths do move and incline the mind to a natural assent; as, *that the whole is greater than its part; that two contradictories can neither be both true, nor both false.*"[15] He proceeds to distinguish between literal (in the head) knowledge and spiritual (in-the-heart) knowledge. The latter alone is true knowledge of God, and it "is revealed inwardly by his own Spirit."[16] At this point Barclay produces his first batch of "testimonies of the ancients."

He first summons Augustine who, in his homily upon I John 3:18–27, declares that there is an inward teacher, Christ, and that in the absence of his inspiration and unction, "it is in vain that

14 D. Elton Trueblood, *Robert Barclay*, 134.

15 R. Barclay, *Apology*, 11.

16 Ibid., 13.

words are beaten in [or, make a noise?] from without."[17] Clement of Alexandria is next invoked for the way in which he distinguished between what anyone may say of the truth, and what the self-interpretative truth itself declares. The former derives from "exercise and discipline [learning and practice?]," the latter from "power and faith."[18] However, Clement immediately proceeds to quote John 7:17 to the effect that we come to know the truth by doing it. Barclay does not follow him here, though he may not necessarily deny the point. Even so, the impression he leaves, consistently with his other citations, is that the truth is within, whatever we do: it is not (as Clement thinks it is) acquired as we "walk the paths of righteousness." Barclay's desire to shun Pelagianism (of which heresy Clement was, of course, happily innocent), would probably have restrained him at this point had he read Clement in detail.

Tertullian is called next. In his *Liber de Virginibus Velandis* Tertullian designates the Comforter, the Spirit, the Scripture-revealing "Vicar of the Lord."[19] Jerome further assists with his conviction that a revelation is required if we are to understand the law, which is spiritual.[20] Jerome reiterates his point in more general terms later in the same letter: "in the holy scriptures one can make no progress unless one has a guide to point the way."[21] Barclay does not quote this remark, nor does he treat us to Jerome's delightful analogy drawn from Horace on poetry: "We all write poetry, whether we are taught or not."[22] "The garrulous old woman," Jerome complains, "the feeble-minded old man, the verbose sophist—all take up [the Scriptures], tear them to pieces and teach them before they have grasped their meaning."[23] Barclay does, however, quote Jerome writing to Hedibia to the effect

---

17 See Migne, PL XXXV, 2004, where the last words are: *Ubi illius inspiratio et unctio illius non est, forinsecus inaniter perstrepunt verba.* I use various standard translations and offer some renderings of my own.

18 R. Barclay, *Apology*, ibid., referring to Clement of Alexandria, *Stromateis* I.vii = Migne, PG VIII, 733–34.

19 Tertullian, *Liber de Virginibus Velandis* = Migne, PL II, 889–90.

20 Jerome to Paulinus, Bishop of Nola, Ep. LIII.4 = Migne, PL XXII, 543. The *Apology* wrongly cites Ep. CIII. In *Barclay's Apology in Modern English*, 1967, 19 n. 5, Dean Freiday mistakenly describes this letter as a "commentary on the Epistles of Paul."

21 Ibid., = Migne, PL XXII, 544.

22 Horace, Ep. II.117: *Scribimus indocti doctique poemata passim.*

23 Jerome, Ep. LIII.7 = Migne, PL XXII, 544.

that we need the Holy Spirit if we are to find our way through the "great obscurities of Paul's Romans."[24]

Barclay's fifth supportive Father is Athanasius, who rejoices that "The Saviour daily expends great effort to draw us towards religion [or, piety]."[25] With Barclay as our only guide we should not know that Athanasius's assertion falls in the context of his discussion of the implications of Christ's resurrection. His point is that, by contrast with the risen Saviour, the gods and evil spirits of those who disbelieve the resurrection of Jesus are dead. *They* cannot teach about immortality, reveal the knowledge of the Father, or inspire faith in the face of death. On the contrary, they "become dead at the appearing of Christ." No one else can achieve all of this, and hence Christ's resurrection is proved.

Gregory the Great and Cyril of Alexandria are Barclay's final witnesses on this point. Gregory argues that apart from the inward teacher, a teacher's efforts are in vain,[26] while Cyril insists that without the illumination of the Holy Spirit, we cannot know that Jesus is Lord.[27] It is noteworthy that while, on this occasion, Barclay does not violate his authors' meanings, the context of their remarks has to do with the activites of the triune God. If Keith is to be believed, Barclay may not have known this; if he did know it, it is perhaps surprising that he did not take the opportunity of adverting to it, since Quakers, especially Penn, had been accused of disbelieving in the Trinity.[28]

The question cannot but arise, "What is the relation of the inward illumination to tradition and Scripture?" As to the former, Barclay deems it an unreliable guide, citing as evidence the disagreement between Polycarp and Anicetus over the proper way of celebrating Easter.[29] In this matter, unwittingly or not, Barclay is selective in quotation. Thus, for example, when arguing that because of the errors of copyists the Bible cannot be finally authoritative, he quotes the complaint of Jerome to the wealthy Spaniard,

---

24 Jerome, Ep. CXX, question 10 (though in the *Apology* Ep. CL, question 11 is wrongly given).

25 R. Barclay, *Apology*, 14, quoting Athanasius, *De Incarnatione* XXXI = Migne, PG XXV, 149–50.

26 Gregory the Great, *XL Homilarum in Evangelia*, Hom. XXX on John 14:23–31 = Migne, PL LXXVI, 1222.

27 Cyril of Alexandria, *Thesaurus de Sancta et Consubstantiate Trinitate* = Migne, PL LXXV, 206ff.

28 A fact of which I am reminded by Dr. Geoffrey F. Nuttall.

29 R. Barclay, *Apology*, 38. The correct reference is Eusebius, *Eccles. Hist.*, V.24 = Migne, PG XX, 507.

Lucinius, that the scribes "wrote not what they found but what they understood."[30] However, Barclay is silent upon Jerome's reply in the same letter to Lucinius's query concerning fasting on the Sabbath and the daily reception of communion: "The best advice I can give you is this," writes Jerome, "Church-traditions—especially where they do not contradict the faith—are to be observed in the form in which previous generations have handed them on; and the use of one church is not to be annulled because it is contrary to that of another."[31]

Despite the perils of transcription, Barclay quotes Augustine with approval to the effect that if anything in the canonical Scriptures should seem "repugnant to truth, I shall not doubt to say, that either the volume is faulty or erroneous; that the expounder has not reached what was said; or that I have in no way understood it."[32] As to "those great heaps of commentaries" which have been written on the Scriptures, Barclay agrees with Jerome that it is harder to understand the expositions than to understand what is being expounded.[33] [A lever this for those Quakers who gloried in their *un*educated state]. Important though the Scriptures are, "they are only a declaration of the fountain, and not the fountain itself, therefore they are not to be esteemed the principal ground of all truth and knowledge, nor yet the adequate primary rule of faith and manners . . . they are and may be esteemed a secondary rule, subordinate to the Spirit. . . . Seeing then that we do therefore receive and believe the Scriptures because they proceed from the Spirit, for the very same reason is the Spirit more originally and principally the rule."[34]

None of which pleased John Brown of Wamphray. Known as "the Presbyterian David" on account of his small stature and pugilistic aptitudes, this ardent Calvinist rushed into print before the English edition of the *Apology* appeared, and produced a reply

---

30 Ibid., 56. The correct reference is Jerome, Ep. LXXI.5 to Lucinius = Migne PL XXII.671. Jerome here refers to the transcribers of his own writings, explaining that although he had ordered corrections to be made, he had been so occupied with passing pilgrims that some errors had no doubt gone uncorrected.

31 Jerome to Lucinius, Ep. LXXI.6 = Migne, PL XXII.672. Cf. Augustine to Jerome, Migne, PL XXXIII.281.14, from which Barclay next quotes a different point.

32 R. Barclay, *Apology*, 57, quoting Augustine's letter to Jerome, Migne, XXXIII.277.3.

33 Ibid., 59. The correct reference is Jerome's letter to Cyprian, Ep. CXL.1 = Migne, PL XXII.1166.

34 Ibid., 46.

which was longer than the text to which it was an answer.[35] He is especially opposed to Barclay's understanding of the immediacy of revelation. To him, revelation is *via* the Scriptures, and he considers that Barclay's position necessarily demotes the Bible. He claims the Fathers (and others) whom Barclay cites as belonging to his own camp, and throws down his challenge thus:

> can he produce any of the Fathers, or of our Reformers, maintaining such Inward and Immediate Revelations of the Spirit, as the *Quakers*, with their predecessors, the *Enthusiasts*, do assert now to be necessary, and do pretend to? If he is so well acquainted with the writings of the Fathers, as by these his citations, he would have us beleeve, he hath done wisely for himself, but not very honestly, in concealing what several of the same Fathers, and Others, write expressly against such high Pretenders, as the *Quakers* now are, and in whose footsteps they, in many things, now tread. . . .[36]

Brown proceeds to catalogue a list of patristic and later sources against imposters such as Valentinus and enthusiasts such as the Montanists, and here he is on firm ground. He takes Barclay's point that spiritual illumination is essential, denying only that it is immediate. But, alas, "it is usual with this sort of men, to speak . . . after an high and loftie manner, as if they were alwayes ravished in an ecstasy; for as they alwayes have the Spirit in their mouth, so they use a strange idiome, that such as hear them are at the first amazed; and this they affect of purpose to deceive their hearers, and raise in them an admiration of them and their Opinions."[37]

No doubt Barclay's emphasis upon inward and immediate revelation was in part prompted by his realisation that literalistic biblical interpretation is a game that more than one can play. It could, as he was well aware, lead to Socinian reductionism. As to Brown, his hackles were raised in part by Barclay's assertion of the universality of the light *qua Christ*, and by Barclay's repudiation of the doctrine of predestination. To this aspect of the matter we now turn.

35 For John Brown (1610?–1679) see DNB.

36 J. Brown, *Quakerisme the Path-Way to Paganisme . . . an examination of the Theses and Apologie of R. Barclay, etc.*, 1678, 21.

37 Ibid., 23.

III

Although in Proposition IV Barclay has taken sin and humanity's resulting estrangement from God with full seriousness, in Propositions V and VI he contends against the "horrible and blasphemous" doctrine of reprobation, and in favour of his view that Christ's redemption is universal in scope, and that everyone is a recipient of saving and spiritual light.

Barclay refers, without quoting, to Augustine in support of his view that until the Pelagian heresy broke upon the world, the doctrine of reprobation, which is "contrary to the scripture's testimony, and to the tenor of the gospel" was passed over "with a profound silence."[38] This, declares Brown in his rejoinder, is simply, "the old saying of the *Arminians*." In fact, he continues, the doctrine of reprobation is to be found in the Scriptures, though it is true that before Pelagianism, "that Enemy of the grace of God arose, the Church had no occasion to debate such questions. . . ."[39] Brown further notes that Augustine does cite Ambrose, Gregory of Nazianzus and Cyprian as agreeing with him. But his most telling point against Barclay is the *tu quoque*: "Is this mans Religion grounded upon the authority of men? And will he beleeve no more, than what the Fathers said in the first foure ages? Let him follow what cisterns he pleaseth, we will satisfie ourselves with the Word, as ther ground of our Faith. . . ."[40] In other words, on Barclay's own principles concerning the primacy of inward, immediate revelation, he should not make so much of an appeal to patristic silence.

Barclay proceeds to produce a further catalogue of quotations from the Fathers by way of underscoring his point that while "there is not one scripture, that I know of, which affirms, *Christ not to die for all*, there are divers that positively assert, *He did*." Furthermore, "all the *fathers*, so called," of the first four centuries "boldly held forth the gospel of Christ, and efficacy of his death; inviting and entreating the *heathens* to come and be partakers of the benefits of it . . . not telling them that God had predestinated any of them to damnation, or had made salvation impossible to them, by withhold-

---

38 R. Barclay, *Apology*, 78.

39 J. Brown, *Quakerisme*, 145.

40 Ibid., 145–46. For John Owen and Richard Baxter on this point see Geoffrey F. Nuttall, *Visible Saints. The Congregational Way 1640–1660*, Oxford: Blackwell 1957, 59 and n. 2.

ing power and grace, necessary from them."[41] Barclay's case thus is that the universal call of the Gospel is meaningless if the reprobation of any is predestined. He turns to Augustine for support, which he presents thus: "The blood of Christ is of so great worth, that it is of no less value than the whole world."[42] The reference is indeed to Augustine's *Enarrationes in Psalmos* XCV.5, but Barclay has telescoped his words, which are as follows:

> The blood of Christ was the price. What is equal to this? What, but the whole world? What but all nations? They are very ungrateful for their price, or very proud, who say the price is so small that it bought the Africans only; or that they are so great, as that it was given for them alone. Let them not exult, let them not be proud: He gave what He gave for the whole world.[43]

This, of course, is a long way from the claim that all will actually be saved, but Brown took Barclay as intending this. Barclay, he loftily replied, "bewrayeth much impudence, seeing it is sufficiently known to all, that are aquainted with [Augustine's] writings, that he was of a far other opinion."[44] Brown lists a dozen passages from Augustine in support of his view that Barclay is quoting selectively, among them one from *De Trinitate* in which Augustine declares that the devil cannot draw to himself "anyone of those whom Christ . . . had redeemed by pouring out his blood without being obliged to do so; but that they belonging to the grace of Christ, foreknown, predestined, and chosen before the foundation of the world, should die only insofar as Christ Himself died for us, by the death of the flesh only, not of the spirit."[45] It cannot be said that Barclay positively asserts that all will be saved in the section under review, but his use of the Fathers when they are emphasising the universal call of the Gospel, and his relative shunning of them when they are proclaiming predestination, makes Brown's anxiety intelligible.

Prosper of Aquitaine is next in line. Barclay quotes accurately the first sentence of Prosper's *Responsiones ad Capitula Gallorum*, and then adds other material:

---

41 R. Barclay, *Apology*, 88.

42 Ibid.

43 Augustine, *Enarrationes in Psalmos*, XCV.5. The reason for the telescoping is that Grotius copied incorrectly from Vossius, Keith made the best sense he could of the mangled Latin, and passed the result to Barclay. See A. Gordon, "The Marrow of Barclay," 403 n.3.

44 J. Brown, *Quakerisme*, 211.

45 Augustine, *De Trinitate* XIII.15 = Migne, PL XLII.1029.

> the Redeemer of the world gave his blood for the world, and the world would not be redeemed because the darkness did not receive the light. He that saith, the Saviour was not crucified for the redemption of the whole world, looks not to the virtue of the sacrament, but to the part of infidels, since the blood of our Lord Jesus Christ is the price of the whole world; from which redemption they are strangers, who either delighting in their captivity would not be redeemed, or after they were redeemed returned to the same servitude.[46]

In context, however, Prosper is not advocating a universal light which actually saves all—as Brown was quick to point out.[47] Not indeed that Barclay says he did—he is still concerned with the universal call of the Gospel. But he certainly makes no reference to Prosper's "inconvenient" point in the same passage to the effect that "though it is right to say that the Saviour was crucified for the redemption of the entire world, because He truly took our human nature and because all men were lost in the first man, yet it may also be said that He was crucified only for those who were to profit by His death."[48] Prosper does make much of the fact that salvation is not limited to the Jews, but he also, in the same passage from which Barclay quotes, declares that "no man attains eternal life without the sacrament of baptism"—a complicating ecclesiological point on which Barclay is silent. A similar silence is detectable in Barclay's immediately following, and seriously garbled, quotation from Prosper. In his version, Barclay refers to Christ, "whose death was so bestowed upon mankind, that it belonged to the redemption of such who were not to be regenerated."[49] Prosper has nothing like this. On the contrary, he writes, "[Christ's] death did not act on all of humanity in such a way that even those who would never be reborn in baptism would share in the redemption, but so that the mystery accomplished once and for all in the person of Christ should be renewed in each and every man by the sacrament of baptism which he is to receive once also."[50] As before, Barclay makes no reference to the necessity of the sacrament of baptism. His third quotation, from Prosper's *De Vocatione Omnium Gentium (The Call*

46 R. Barclay, *Apology*, 88.

47 J. Brown, *Quakerisme*, 211.

48 Prosper of Aquitaine, *Pro Augustino Responsiones as Capitula Gallorum*, IX = Migne PL LI.165–6.

49 R. Barclay, *Apology*, 88.

50 Prosper of Aquitaine, *Pro Augustino Responsiones as Capitula Objectionum Vincentianarum*, I = Migne, PL LI.177–9.

of All Nations) is correctly given (though wrongly placed in chapter 6). Prosper's emphasis here is upon the fact that people of all nations are called, and that the grace of Christ cannot be confined within Roman territorial boundaries.[51]

Barclay proceeds to cite John Chrysostom once and Ambrose twice, to the effect that if the light is not received, it is not because it is unavailable, but because it has been spurned.[52] Barclay omits from his second quotation from Ambrose the telling words, "Those who perish, therefore, perish through their own fault, while the saved are freed by the judgment of Christ, who wishes all men to be saved and to come to the recognition of truth." As before, Brown cites John Chrysostom and Ambrose against Barclay, as if Barclay were claiming that the Fathers teach that all will in fact be saved.

Barclay takes an important step further when he affirms

> *That God, in and by this Light and Seed* [that is, by the inward Christ], *invites, calls, exhorts, and strives with every man, in order to save him;* which, as it is received and not resisted, works the salvation of *all*, even those who are ignorant of the death and sufferings of Christ, and of Adam's fall, both by bringing them to a sense of their own *misery* , and to be sharers in the sufferings of Christ inwardly, and by making them partakers of his resurrection, in becoming holy, pure, and righteous, and recovered out of their sins.[53]

Clearly, the patristic emphasis upon baptism and the Church is far from his mind at this point. He does not invoke the Fathers here, and hence Keith's rebuke, in which he refers to the divines just named as if Barclay attributed the point now made to them, is unjust.[54]

It must be emphasised that to Barclay the light, the seed, is, or contains, *Christ*. Barclay is not advocating the presence of a natural light, or of a general principle of illumination in all human beings as such. Indeed, he can speak of the light in strongly trinitarian terms. He says that the light which enlightens everyone is

---

51 Idem, *De Vocatione Omnium Gentium*, II.16 = Migne, PL LI.702.

52 R. Barclay, *Apology*, 88–89, citing John Chrysostom, *Homiliae LXXXVIII in Joannem*, Hom. VIII on John 1:9 = Migne, PL LIX.641. Ambrose, *Expositione psalmum CXVIII*, Sermon VIII = Migne, PL XV.1318.57, and idem, *De Cain et Abel*, Lib. II, III.11 = Migne, PL XIV.346.

53 R. Barclay, *Apology*, 93.

54 G. Keith, *The Standard*, 230.

> *not the proper essence and nature of God precisely taken, which is not divisible into parts and measures*, as being a *most pure, simple being, void of all composition or division*, and therefore can neither be resisted, hurt, wounded, crucified, or slain by all the efforts and strength of men; *but we understand a spiritual, heavenly, and invisible principle, in which God, as Father, Son, and Spirit dwells;* a measure of which divine and glorious life *is in all men as a seed*, which of its own nature draws, invites, and inclines to God; and this we call *vehiculum Dei*, or the *spiritual body of Christ, the flesh and blood of Christ, which came down from heaven*, of which all the saints do feed, and are thereby nourished unto eternal life . . . but we are far from ever having said *that Christ is thus formed in all men*, Or *in the wicked*.[55]

Negatively, he continues, the light is not our natural conscience or reason, both of which are liable to corruption.[56]

---

55 R. Barclay, *Apology*, 96–97, 100.

56 Ibid., 102; cf. 351. This is the most interesting *philosophical* contention in the whole of the *Apology*. Barclay's denigration of reason in the cause of his light, and his differentiation of the latter from the former, placed him at odds with his Cambridge Platonist critic, John Norris, who found Barclay's *Vehiculum Dei* "gross" and "material," given that, in his own opinion, there is "no medium between God and the creature." (See his *Two Treatises Concerning the Divine Light*, 1692, the second of which is addressed to Barclay). The pressing of the Platonist way of asserting the matter/spirit dualism cannot but threaten a doctrine of Incarnation; but that doctrine is likewise threatened by Barclay's view—if the seed is utterly apart from conscience and reason. (Cf. Brand Blanshard in the chapter cited at n. 3 above; and for a contemporary Quaker advocate of dualism see D. Elton Trueblood, art. cit. n. 3 above). As to the degree of affinity between the Cambridge Platonists and the Quakers, Geoffrey F. Nuttall has written, "In actual fact there is . . . an utter difference of spiritual climate between the rationalist Cambridge men's *logos* theology and the theology of the Holy Spirit which the untutored Quakers worked out in their own experience." (See Geoffrey F. Nuttall, *The Holy Spirit in Puritan Faith and Experience*, 1946, 18). On the other hand, Melvin B. Endy, Jr. thinks that "Even Nuttall was misled here," because "The Spiritualists" conviction that the inward Christ provided them with a direct knowledge of divine realities was similar in certain ways to the rationalists' conviction that the structure of the human mind was congruent with, if not a replica of, the structure of the divine mind, and both epistemological principles were used to put forward the belief that true knowledge of God was universal.' (See his "The interpretation of Quakerism: Rufus Jones and his critics," *Quaker History*, LXX, Spring 1981, 20). To us it appears that Mr. Endy is misled in not distinguishing the psychological-charismatic import of the position he is attacking from his own epistemological concerns. However the matters here broached are finally to be resolved, there is *prima facie* evidence that when Quakers have misconstrued Barclay's "light" as "natural light," and when Platonists have contented themselves with immaterialism, fundamentals of the Christian Gospel have been at risk.

Against the suggestion that, by denying predestination and asserting the free offer of the Gospel, Barclay has embraced Pelagianism, Barclay reiterates his view that the creature is called not to *resist* grace—in other words, passivity is what he has in mind. At which point he enlists the aid of Cyril of Alexandria: "Let not the world accuse the word of God, and his eternal light, but his own weakness; for the sun enlightens, but the creature rejects the grace that is given unto it. . . ."[57] Two further barrages of patristic quotations (some garbled) are presented in support of belief in the universal light. The first comprises references to Clement of Alexandria, Justin Martyr and Prosper of Aquitaine;[58] the second, to Lactantius (citing Cicero), Justin Martyr, Clement of Alexandria and Augustine.[59]

We have already noted Barclay's view that, provided they did not resist it, even those who had not heard of Christ could be saved by the universal light. The reference to Justin just noted strongly reinforces this point, for Justin declares that Socrates, Heraclitus, and others who lived according to the light, were Christians.[60] No doubt in Justin and others the Logos can signify both God's eternal reason and his outgoing Word,[61] but the question of the relation of the former to the latter remains. Barclay, as we have seen, does not intend to denigrate the Scriptures; rather, he holds that apart from divine illumination their meaning will not come home to us. So far, so good: the difficulty is with the converse. If *knowledge* of Christ's saving act is not necessary for salvation, how far is the act itself necessary—will not the inward universal light suffice by itself? George Keith certainly thought that Barclay was tending towards an affirmative answer at this point, and he has a number of polemical pages in which he turns Barclay's sources against him by claiming that the Fathers cited did not intend to suggest that any could be saved apart from the historic act of God in Christ, to which the Scriptures testify. The Christian cannot but construe the inward

---

57 Ibid., 115.

58 Ibid., 120–22. The readily identifiable quotations are to be found in Clement of Alexandria, *Stromateis*, II.6 = Migne, PG VIII.961–2; idem, *Cohortatio ad Gentes* XI = Migne, PG VIII.227–38; idem, *Paedagogus* I.3 = Migne, PG VIII.257–8.

59 R. Barclay, *Apology*, 134–37, citing Lactantius, *Divinarum Institutionum* VI.8 = Migne, PL IV.660–1; Justin, *I Apology*, LXI; Augustine, *De Civitate Dei* XVIII.47 = Migne, PL XLI.609; idem, *Confessionum* XI (wrongly given as II) 9 = Migne, PL XXXII.813–4.

60 Ibid., 135.

61 Cf. Maurice Wiles, *The Christian Fathers*, London: Hodder & Stroughton 1966, 27.

divine light very differently from the heathen.[62] Keith concludes that when it serves their purpose, the Quakers "magnifie the Fathers;" when it does not, they "slight them, and prefer their own writings to them."[63] He even invokes the Quaker Thomas Ellwood, who had charged Keith with "supposing Friends Books to have been written with no better Guidance nor clear sight than theirs, who lived and wrote in those dark Times."[64] Keith clearly felt that patristic darkness would have served Friends better than Quakerish light.

IV

What are we to make of our sometimes agonised pursuit of Barclay's patristic sources? We have seen ample proof that he is not always accurate in quotation or referencing; and that he selects what suits his case (or relies on his "crib list" for it), whilst neglecting contrary opinions expressed by the Fathers whom he cites. Brown and Keith were by no means entirely unprovoked in giving their counter examples. Barclay, as we saw, did not take too lofty a view of his patristic and other authorities but, and this leads us to our first concluding reflection, he did think it appropriate to draw upon the heritage of Christian testimony.

Three hundred years after Barclay's death, where do Friends stand on this point? This is by no means only an "in-house" Quaker matter. It is of some ecumenical importance, and that is why an outsider is impertinent enough to raise it. Not, indeed, that voices within the Friends are altogether silent on the subject. For example, the contemporary Friend Alastair Heron has recently expressed his conviction that "we must look more closely at the fact of our Christian heritage, and what it means to Friends today."[65]

Friends seriously intent upon addressing this matter will find a perusal of Barclay very revealing. For in Barclay we have one who, of set purpose, did not set out to elaborate upon those doctrines held by all Christians in common. Rather, he wished to emphasise Quaker distinctives in such a way as to show that they were not

62 G. Keith, *The Standard*, 240–48, 276–77. For the "historic act" see further Geoffrey F. Nuttall, *The Holy Spirit in Puritan Faith and Experience*, 159, and the cited reference to H.G. Wood, "William Penn's *Christian Quaker*," in H.H. Brinton (ed.), *Children of Light*, New York, 1938, 23.

63 Ibid., 346.

64 Ibid.

65 Alastair Heron, *Speaking to Our Condition: A Ministry to Friends*, Canadian Quaker Pamphlets, 30, Argenta, BC: Argenta Friends Press, 1989, 5.

hostile to the public authorities, or to the generally received tradition. Thus, while he makes a number of references to the Trinity and to the Atonement,[66] he does not elaborate upon these, or refer them unproblematically to the inward, universal light. To put it otherwise, while he wishes to counter what he regards as Calvinism's predestinarian slighting of God's justice, he is so convinced of humanity's total depravity that he knows that the forgiveness of sins is by the sacrifice of Christ alone. Yet the universal light, which shines upon those who have never heard of Christ, and can save them provided they do not resist it, cannot but divert the gaze from the historic Cross and raise the question of the relation of the universal light to a particular Calvary.

My second concluding reflection may be encapsulated in the question, "How do contemporary Friends stand on the relation of the inward Christ to the outward?" Barclay's lack of definition at this point opened the way for some later Friends, under the influence of Enlightenment rationalism, or under that of post-Hegelian immanentism, to sit loose to the historic events, and to focus upon the inward light, now construed not Christologically, but as a natural possession of all people. The Cambridge Platonist Henry More went too far in saying that the Quakers excluded "the external Christ from the business of Religion" in favour of the "internal Christ,"[67] but it is not difficult to see how the balance of Barclay's material could tempt others in this direction. Later Quakers have taken the point,[68] none more bluntly than D. Elton Trueblood:

> There are many things wrong with "that of God in every man" as an effort to state the essence of Quaker faith and life. One is that it makes no reference to Christ. This, of course, is one of the reasons for its popularity in our generation, for there are some who do not want to face the fact of the Christ-centredness of the Quaker commitment. They want an eclectic system which they think is superior to a faith centred in Christ. . . . We do not need to be very astute to see that this is really a disguised humanism. . . . It is partly because of the intellectual vigour of Robert Barclay that Quakerism is not tied to such a position.[69]

---

66 We have quoted him on the Trinity; for the Atonement see *Apology*, 143–44, 159.

67 Henry More, *Divine Dialogues*, 2nd edn., 1713, 565.

68 E.g. Edward Grubb, *The Historic and the Inward Christ*, 1914, 51; Maurice A. Creasey, "Comment" on F.B. Hall's paper (see n. 3 above), 34–35; P. Wragge, op. cit., 43, 46; D. Elton Trueblood, *Robert Barclay*, 127; M.A. Creasey, review of L. Eeg-Olofsson, op. cit., in *Journal of Theological Studies* N.S. V, 1954, 288; H.G. Wood, review of ibid., *Theology* LVII 1954, 351.

69 D. Elton Trueblood, "Comment" on F.B. Hall's paper (see n. 3 above), 40–41.

Francis B. Hall's rueful comment is similarly motivated: "Most Quakers accept the universalism of Barclay and of the early Friends, but some are happy to drop entirely the particularity."[70]

My own conclusion is that Robert Barclay did not draw *enough* on the Fathers. They could have helped him—and perhaps later Friends—on the questions: What was done for our redemption? Who alone could do it? How is the Christian understanding of redemption to be expressed in trinitarian terms? As it is, there is some justification for Alexander Gordon's judgment:

> No doubt [Barclay's] theology is of the *solus Pater supremus* type. It would not be fair towards Barclay's own estimate of his position, or we should on this ground characterize his Confession as in its essence Unitarian; not that this would be true, in the sense of identifying it with any extant school of Unitarian faith; but the reason is mainly this, that no existing Unitarian school is strong enough to take up and assimilate Scripture so completely and *ex animo* as Barclay does.[71]

This suggests a somewhat cheekier way of posing my question: "How happy are contemporary Quakers to be endorsed, on doctrinal points, by a distinguished Unitarian?"

May it be that Friends and others need to return to the heritage of Christian testimony in order to recover emphases which Barclay did not dwell upon because they were common currency? If so, our reason for doing so will be that the currency has subsequently been devalued.

70 Francis. B. Hall, ibid., 19.

71 A. Gordon, "The Great Laird of Urie," *The Theological Review* XI, 1874, 545–46.

VII

The Message of the Erskines for Today

The campus of Erskine College and Seminary reverberates to such family names as Pressly and Grier. But the name I focus on today is "Erskine." This name is not only on your notepaper and buildings; it is at the heart of the testimony of the Associate Reformed Presbyterian Church; for from the Secession Church of Ebenezer and Ralph Erskine and their friends there flowed one of the two strands (the other being that of the Covenanters or Reformed Presbyterians) which, in 1782, entwined to form the Associate Reformed Presbyterian Church in America.

My title, "The Message of the Erskines for Today" implies that I think that they do have a word to say to us. I am well aware that history is not simply a repository of illustrations to be plundered when the pressing concerns of a subsequent period need to be illuminated. On the other hand, if we believe that God acts in history, and that the events of our lives—not least of our churchly lives—are all part of the theatre of his providence and grace—then instruction and guidance from the past are not in principle impossible to acquire. My reflections on the Erskines and their times lead me to suggest that they pose two challenges to us, and also that in their story a warning is implicit. The challenges are to proclaim the good news of the free grace of God; and to honour Christ's Headship of his Church. The implicit warning is to beware of that sectarian spirit which by elevating "new circumcisions" (Galatians 1) denies the very grace we proclaim and divides those whom *Christ* has accepted.

Before turning directly to the challenges and the warning we shall do well to locate the Erskines in history. Ebenezer and Ralph Erskine were sons of the Reverend Henry Erskine (1624–96),[1] Pres-

1 Henry, Ebenezer and Ralph Erskine are in DNB.

byterian minister at Cornhill, Northumberland, who was one of nearly two thousand ministers ejected under the Act of Uniformity of 1662. Ebenezer was born at Dryburgh on 22 June 1680; Ralph at Monilaws, Northumberland, on 15 March 1685. Ebenezer became minister at Portmoak in 1703, and remained there for twenty-eight years until, in 1731, he removed to Stirling, where he died on 2 June 1754. Ralph Erskine was ordained to the second charge at Dunfermline on 7 August 1711, and remained there until his death on 6 October 1752. The Erskines were both men of faith and earnest contenders for the faith; and in the eighteenth century to contend for the faith was to become embroiled in controversy.

I

The Erskines first come to our attention as controversialists in connection with the question of the free offer of the gospel. Here they took the side of those who became known as the Marrowmen.[2] *The Marrow of Modern Divinity* was published in 1646 by one "E.F.," over whose identity debate has raged.[3] A collection of generally received High Calvinist teachings, it provoked little comment at the time.

---

2 For the Marrow Controversy, see John MacLeod, *Scottish Theology in Relation to Church History since the Reformation*, Edinburgh: Free Church of Scotland 1945, reprinted by The Banner of Truth Trust, 1974; James Walker, *The Theology and Theologians of Scotland*, Edinburgh: T. & T. Clark 1872; John McKerrow, *History of the Secession Church*, Edinburgh: Fullerton 1848; Henry F. Henderson, *The Religious Controversies of Scotland*, Edinburgh: T. & T. Clark 1905; Donald MacLean, *Aspects of Scottish Church History*, Edinburgh: T. & T. Clark 1927, J.H.S. Burleigh, *A Church History of Scotland*, London: OUP 1960, 288-91, David C. Lachman, *The Marrow Controvercy, 1718–1723*, Edinburgh: Rutherford House, 1988. For a brief account of Boston (also in DNB), see D.J. Innes, "Thomas Boston of Ettrick," in *Faith and Good Conscience*, London: Puritan and Reformed Studies Conference 1963, 32-46. For the text itself see C.G. McCrie (ed.), *The Marrow of Modern Divinity*, Glasgow, 1902. The classic account of Boston is George D. Low (ed.), *A General Account of my life by Thomas Boston*, London: Hodder & Stoughton 1908. See also Stewart Mechie, "The Theological Climate in Early Eighteenth Century Scotland," in Duncan Shaw (ed.), *Reformation and Revolution*, Edinburgh: The Saint Andrew Press 1967. Boston had sat under the ministry of Henry Erskine. See G.D. Low, op. cit. 6-7, 37. I take the remainder of this paragraph and the next thee paragraphs from my book *The Great Debate: Calvinism, Arminianism and Salvation*, Worthing: H.E. Walter (now Bletchley: Word Books) 1982, Grand Rapids: Baker Book House 1983.

3 Some have attributed the work to Edward Fisher (fl. 1627-56) of Oxford, for whom see DNB. Others have ascribed the work to an illiterate barber. In the Dedication to John Warner, Lord Mayor of London, the author describes himself as a "poore inhabitant" of that city.

The story of Thomas Boston's discovery in 1700 of two books in the home of one of his parishioners at Simprin has often been told.[4] One book, by Saltmarsh, did not appeal to him; but the second, *The Marrow*, moved him greatly. In the first part of it Evangelista, a true minister of the gospel, demolishes the arguments of Nomista the legalist, and Antinomista, the antinomian. In the second part Evangelista expounds the decalogue, pithily expressing the orthodox Reformed position on the law of works and the law of Christ thus: "Both these laws agree in saying, Do this. But here is the difference. The one saith, Do this and live; and the other saith, Live and do this. The one saith Do this for life; and the other saith Do this from life."[5] It is not surprising that James Hervey (1714–58), the English Calvinistic Methodist, could describe *The Marrow* as "a book designed to guard equally against Antinomian licentiousness and legal bondage."[6] But the Scottish Church had meanwhile judged differently.

The occasion of the controversy was the so-called "Auchterarder Creed." As a bulwark against Arminianism the presbytery of Auchterarder composed the following affirmation to be confessed by candidates for license: "I believe that it is not sound and orthodox to teach that we must forsake sin in order to our coming to Christ, and instating us in covenant with God." This was, of course, a clumsily worded attempt to exclude works-righteousness, but it was open to an antinomian interpretation. One candidate refused to subscribe, was not licensed, and appealed to the General Assembly of 1717. The Assembly repudiated the presbytery's statement, reversed its (strictly improper) action, and authorized the licensing of the candidate in question. Boston was among those who attacked the Assembly's action, and in conversation with John Drummond of Crieff, he testified to the aid *The Marrow* had given him years earlier on the disputed issue. Drummond mentioned the matter to James Webster of Edinburgh, and he to James Hog of Carnock (1658?–1734), at whose behest the book was republished in 1718. The ensuing controversy was debated at the Assembly of 1720, Principal James Hadow (1670?–1747) being a leading opponent of *The Marrow*.[7] He favoured the High Calvinist position, but on this occasion he was joined by the more moderate Baxterian types. As Macleod says of Hadow, "He laid his lance in rest and had a bout of

4 E.g. in his *Memoirs*, Edinburgh, 1899.

5 Quoted by D.J. Innes, art. cit., 42.

6 Quoted by H.F. Henderson, op.cit., 24.

7 James Hadow and James Hog are in DNB.

tilting at windmills."[8] He found what he took to be a number of antinomian statements in *The Marrow*, including one to the effect that the believer is not subject to the divine law as a rule of life, and another which suggested that holy living is not essential to salvation. The book was further criticized by the High Calvinists for teaching that Christ had effected a universal atonement. In this connection the Assembly took exception to the phase which asserted that Christ's death was "the deed of gift and grant to mankind lost." Of course Boston and the Marrowmen were ardent defenders of particular redemption. They merely wished to urge that the warrant to believe is common to all, and that the believer may derive assurance from the evidence of the Spirit's working in him: "Say then, I beseech you, with a firm faith, the righteousness of Jesus Christ belongs to all that believe; but I believe; and therefore it belongs to me."[9]

Undeterred, the Assembly condemned the book. Subsequently Boston and eleven others, including Ebenezer and Ralph Erskine, presented a representation against the Assembly's Act, but on 28 May 1722 the Assembly reiterated its earlier decision, albeit in slightly modified form.[10] With hindsight the historian Walker duly appreciated the importance of the Marrowmen for the Church's mission: "Boston and the Marrowmen, first of all among our divines, entered fully into the missionary spirit of the Bible; were able to see that Calvinist doctrine was not inconsistent with world-conquering aspirations and efforts."[11]

It is not difficult to find numerous examples of those in the Calvinistic line who have advocated the free offer of the gospel. Thus Zanchius, Calvin's younger contemporary, exhorts his readers to emulate Christ and the apostles "who all . . . took every opportunity of preaching to sinners and enforced their ministry with proper rebukes, invitations and exhortations as occasion required."[12] Again, the first chapter of the Second Helvetic Confession (1566), prepared by Heinrich Bullinger (1504–75), contains a classic state-

8 J. MacLeod, op. cit., 144.

9 *The Marrow*, 114.

10 It is interesting to note that in the concurrent debate over the liberal views of Professor Simson, Hadow and his supporters and the Marrowmen found themselves on the *same* side.

11 J. Walker, op. cit., 60.

12 J. Zanchius, *Absolute Predestination*, Grand Rapids: Sovereign Grace Publications 1971, 87. For this paragraph see my *Theology in Turmoil. The roots, causes and significance of the conservative-liberal debate in modern theology*, Grand Rapids: Baker Book House 1986, 138.

ment of the duty of freely offering the gospel, and of the distinction between the preacher's external call to all hearers and the Holy Spirit's internal call to the elect. "Beloved," cried Tobias Crisp to his seventeenth-century flock, "will you starve in a cook's shop, as they say? Is there such plenty in Christ, and will you perish for hunger?"[13] Robert Traill expounded the free offer in masterly fashion.[14] John Mason appealed to sinners, "Come as you are; come poor, come needy, come naked. . . . His heart is free; His arms are open, 'tis His joy and His crown to receive you;"[15] In the nineteenth century Horatius Bonar reminded his hearers that "the Gospel is not, 'Christ died for the elect;' neither is it 'Christ died for all.' But it is 'Christ died for sinners.'"[16] Finally, in our own time, Professor John Murray and others have defended the free offer of the gospel.[17]

This was the line in which the Erskines stood. Said Ebenezer, "It is my desire in every place to send forth the savour of that Name which is as ointment poured forth; and I look upon it as my crown, my glory, and my joy, when He helps me in any measure to commend Him unto souls."[18] Or again, "Oh invite others to come to the Tree of Life and to see that His fruit is good, pleasant, profitable and plenteous. Tell the hungry what excellent fruit is here; tell the weary what glorious rest is here; tell the diseased souls what healing leaves are here. Let your resentment run against those who would hew down the Tree of Life."[19] Ralph Erskine concurred—in equally pictorial terms: "There are many pipes—full of water for refreshing, full of wine for cheering, full of milk for nourishing souls. And we are come to set the pipe to your mouth: 'Ho, everyone that thirsteth, come to the waters.' Here is a pipe for every mouth, by which you may draw Christ to your heart, though He be in heaven, and you on earth."[20]

The Erskines, then, protested against a hyper-Calvinism which would limit the gospel offer to the elect. Consistently with this they

---

13 T. Crisp, *Christ's Pre-eminence*, reprinted Sheffield: Zoar Publications, c. 1974, 13–14.

14 R. Traill, *Works*, Edinburgh: The Banner of Truth Trust 1975, I, sermon II.

15 J. Mason, *Mason's Sayings*, reprinted Sheffield: Zoar Publications, c. 1974, 14.

16 H. Bonar, "God's will, man's will and free will," Wilmington: Sovereign Grace Publications 1972, 30.

17 J. Murray, *Collected Writings of John Murray*, Edinburgh: The Banner of Truth Trust 1976, I, Ch. XVII.

18 Quoted by A. R. MacEwen, *The Erskines*, Edinburgh 1900, 39.

19 Quoted ibid., 60.

20 Quoted ibid., 44.

set their faces against that introspective self-examination which was designed to reassure the believer of elect status but which, in fact, only served to divert the gaze from Christ and the mind from the objectivity of the ground of faith. As Ralph Erskine wrote to John Wesley: "The true spirit of God within a believer leads him to a dependence upon Christ *without* him, and not upon a Christ *within* him, not upon any created or communicated graces, gifts, experiences, tears, sorrows, joys, frowns, feelings, or whatever else. . . . He must be brought off from confidence in, or dependence upon frames, enlargements, influences and attainments, to a solid life of faith, upon the grounds that are unchangeable."[21] In a word, the heart of the gospel, and the message of the Erskines, is grounded in the finished work of Christ.

Hence the challenge to us: what is at the heart of our message? What do we preach? We are called to proclaim the inexhaustible riches of God's grace; to declare that in Christ God has visited and redeemed his people; to announce that by his cross and resurrection God in Christ has won the victory over all that could keep us from him—sin and the grave are vanquished—and all because of God's free and overflowing grace, and not because of our merit or status. Is this what we are preaching? Are we working out the implications of this for life in today's threatened and dangerous world? Or is it not true that some preachers are enmeshed in the gospel of success, where "success" is construed materialistically and quite unbiblically? How dare we tell people that if they will only believe they will be blessed with *material* success? Conversely, how dare we tell them that if they suffer a loss of income it is necessarily because their faith is weak? Again, are not some preaching on apocalypticism which feeds on whipped-up fear of some enemy superpower? Are not others still preaching off the headlines, or according to the latest fads and fashions? Are not some still psychologizing the message of the gospel into a spiritual potion which will make you *feel better*? The Erskines knew what the message was. Do we? They proclaimed the message indiscriminately to all. Do we? That is their first challenge to us today.

II

The second challenge is closely related to the first. Because of their clear grasp of the heart of the gospel, the Erskines could not bear to see the intrusion into pulpits of ministers who did not believe or

21 Quoted ibid., 123.

preach it. From their point of view the enemy in eighteenth-century Scotland was Moderatism, and the patronage system was that by which unevangelical ministers could be placed over congregations. It is a complicated question, and we must proceed step by step.

First, what exactly was Moderatism? It is not easy to say, for there were degrees of both Evangelicalism and Moderatism; and some ministers were now inclined in one direction, now in another. With hindsight we may certainly agree with Friedhelm Voges that the two parties were more akin in apologetic and exegetical method, and in dogmatic and political views, than has commonly been supposed.[22] But in the heat of battle the lines were sometimes drawn quite sharply. Thus we may characterize Moderatism in general terms as an unevangelical attitude of mind on the part of some ministers which, as the eighteenth century progressed, became associated in some cases with a libertarian, social-climbing style of life. To understand the situation we have to go back to the Revolution Settlement of 1680, which abolished episcopacy in Scotland and reinstated the survivors of the four hundred episcopalian ministers who had been expelled from their livings in 1662. The 1690 General Assembly of the Scottish Church was the first for thirty-seven years. In his message to the Assembly King William enjoined a "calm and peaceable procedure" upon all, and declared that "Moderation is what religion enjoins, neighbouring Churches expect of you, and we recommend to you." After turbulent seventeenth-century years some former exiles were only too pleased to enjoy security and a quiet life; and some former episcopalian clergy made the transition from their erstwhile church order to Presbyterianism so smoothly that the conclusion can only be that doctrine was not their most pressing concern. Not all were happy with the Revolution Settlement. The Cameronians continued their protest in favour of the Covenants of 1638 and 1643, and made their disappointment at the passing over of these Covenants in the Revolution Settlement plain. Their societies continued to meet, and in 1706 the Rev. John Macmillan of Balmaghie became their first minister. In 1743 they constituted themselves as the Reformed Presbyterian Church—the other parent strand in the heritage of the Associate Reformed Presbyterian Church.

Despite the Cameronian protest most Scots were content with the position expressed in *A Seasonable Admonition* (1698), which emphasized that

---

22 See F. Voges "Moderate and Evangelical thinking in the later eighteenth century: differences and shared attitudes," *Records of Scottish Church History Society* XXII pt. 2, 1985, 141-157.

> We do believe and own, that Jesus Christ is the only Head and King of His Church; and that He hath instituted in His Church, officers and ordinances, order and government, and not left it to the will of man, magistrate, or church, to alter at their pleasure. And we believe that this government is neither prelatical nor congregational, but presbyterian, which now, through the mercy of God, is established among us; and we believe we have a better foundation for this our Church government than the inclination of the people or the laws of men.[23]

The Moderate-Evangelical conflict was a function of the Scottish Church's post-1690 comprehensiveness. The satirist's words no doubt applied to some Moderates:

> I do believe in stone and lime
> a manse of large dimensions,
> Broad acres for a glebe and farm;
> that is my church extension.
> My folk may perish if they like—
> Christ's name I rarely mention;
> I take the stipend due by right
> to men of good intention.[24]

Moderatism took root in an intellectual soil fertilized by the alleged unorthodoxy of Professor John Simson of Glasgow, whose views were described by a hostile critic as "a hotch-potch or bagful of Arrian, Arminian, Socinian, Pelagian, old condemn'd damnable errors."[25] The scepticism of David Hume gave impetus to later versions of Moderatism.

The Moderatism of the middle years of the eighteenth century was wittily characterized by John Witherspoon (1723–94), whose book of 1753 entitled *Ecclesiastical Characteristics, or the Arcana of Church Polity, being an attempt to open up the Mystery of Moderation* was in its fifth edition by 1763. Witherspoon writes:

> All ecclesiastical persons of whatever rank, whether Principals of Colleges, Professors of Divinity, Ministers, or even Probationers, that are suspected of heresy, are to be esteemed men of great genius, vast learning and uncommon worth; and are by all means to be supported and protected.

---

23 *A Seasonable Admonition*, 1698, 5.

24 Quoted by G. N. M. Collins, *Whose Faith Follow*, Edinburgh: Free Church of Scotland 1943, 26.

25 Patrick Walker, *Six Saints of the Covenant*, London: Hodder & Stoughton, 1901, I, 149.

> When any man is charged with loose practices or tendencies to immorality he is to be screened and protected as much as possible; especially if the faults laid to his charge be "good-humoured vices."
>
> It is a necessary part of the character of a Moderate man never to speak of the Confession of Faith but with a sneer; to give sly hints that he does not thoroughly believe it; and to make the word orthodoxy a term of contempt and reproach.
>
> A good preacher must not only have all the above and subsequent principles of moderation in him, as the source of everything that is good, but must, over and above, have the following special marks and signs of a talent for preaching.
>
> 1. His subjects must be confined to social duties. 2. He must recommend them only from rational considerations, viz.: the beauty and comely proportions of virtue and its advantages in the present life without any regard to a future state of more extended self-interest. 3. His authorities must be drawn from heathen writers, none, or as few as possible, from Scripture. 4. He must be very unacceptable to the common people.
>
> A minister must endeavour to catch as much of the air and manner of a fine gentlemen as possibly he can.[26]

Of Moderate preaching Thomas Chalmers said in the nineteenth century that "A Moderate sermon is like a winter's day, short and clear and cold. The brevity is good; the clarity is better; the coldness is fatal. Moonlight preaching ripens no harvest."[27]

It takes no great insight to grasp that the Erskines were appalled by Moderatism and especially by Moderate preaching. It was at the opposite pole from the warmly evangelical stance of the Marrowmen. Their concern was heightened by the reintroduction of patronage in the Scottish Church, for this permitted wealthy patrons to intrude Moderate ministers upon congregations which did not call them and did not desire their services.

The storm which eventually led to the Secession of 1733 was a long time brewing. King William died in 1702. During the reign of his successor Queen Anne the Act uniting Scotland with England was passed 1707. The Act of Union guaranteed the continuance of

---

26 Quoted by J. MacLeod, op. cit., 205-206. For a description of Moderate preaching see James Hamilton's life of his father, Hamilton of Strathblane, quoted by David Scott, *Annals and Statistics of the Original Secession Church*, Edinburgh (1886), 13-14.

27 Quoted by Hugh Watt, *Thomas Chalmers and the Disruption*, Edinburgh: Nelson 1943, 6. Hume and Simson are in DNB. Though suspended from his teaching post in 1729, Simson was not deposed from the ministry. In 1729 Francis Hutcheson became Professor of Moral Philosophy at Glasgow. His deistic stance and his empiricist ethics did not endear him to the Evangelicals. Hutcheson is in DNB.

Presbyterian order in Scotland. The Jacobites were, however, still bent upon restoring the Stewart line to the throne and they joined forces with the episcopalian high churchmen in the Scottish Church, and with the Tories, to engineer conflict between the Scottish Church and the Government. Thus in 1712 they secured the reintroduction of Patronage, which had been abolished at the Revolution Settlement of 1690. The Act was not strictly enforced until 1729, when under pressure from patrons and with the connivance of Moderates, the General Assembly of the Church restored powers to the patrons. In the following year the Assembly removed the right of minorities formally to dissent from the imposition of a minister upon them. The last straw was the Act concerning the Planting of Vacant Churches (1731). Henceforth pastoral vacancies were to be filled solely by the heritors and elders. Many heritors were episcopalians; some were virtual unbelievers, and the people's right of call was completely removed from them. The parishes of Balfron, Kinross, West-Linton and Bristo Street, Edinburgh, were filled according to the new arrangements and over the heads of people.

The Secession of 1733 thus came about because of a zeal for the Gospel which could not bear to see unevangelical ministers intruded upon congregations which did not want them by Assembly legislation which removed the right of call from the people's representatives, and by giving power to patrons—however worthy—deprived Christ of the headship in his Church. In the words of Ebenezer Erskine to his Stirling congregation:

> Is it so that the government is laid upon His shoulders? Then see the nullity of all acts, laws and constitutions, that do not bear the stamp of Christ, and that are not consistent with the laws and orders He has left for the government of His Church. They cannot miss to be null, because Zion's King never touched them with His sceptre, and there is no church authority but what is derived from Him . . .[28]

On 10 October 1732 Erskine followed up his charge in the sermon delivered as Moderator of the Synod of Perth and Stirling on the text "The stone which the builders rejected, the same is made the headstone of the corner":

> God's promise of guidance is given not to heritors or patrons, but to the Church, the body of Christ. As it is a natural privilege of every house or society of men to make the choice of its own

28 Quoted by A. R. MacEwan, *The Erskines*, 67.

servants or officers, so it is the privilege of the house of God in a particular manner.[29]

At the Assembly of 1733 Ebenezer Erskine, James Fisher of Kinclaven, William Wilson of Perth and Alexander Moncrieff of Abernethy were first suspended and then, in 1740, deposed from the ministry. Known as the Seceders, they consistently protested that they had not broken from the Church of Scotland, but only from the currently prevailing party in the Established Church. On 15 December 1737 Ralph Erskine "gained clearness" on the matter and joined the Seceders, as did Thomas Mair.

How do the Erskines' challenge us today—over and above their challenge to us to proclaim the evangel? The settlement of our ministers is not governed by alien legislation. We have no patrons who have usurped the rights of the people. Undeniably our *circumstances* are very different from those obtaining in eighteenth-century Scotland. But is not the challenge of the Erskines on the principle of honouring Christ's sole headship of the Church still worthy of consideration? And is not that principle still open to abuse—even, or perhaps especially, by ourselves?

I sometimes think that one of the worst things we have done is to persuade ourselves that our church order is democratic. If by democracy we mean "one person, one vote" and rule by the majority, then it is quite anachronistic to suppose that our forebears espoused any such notion. At their best they sought to be Christocratic: they wished Christ to rule in his Church; and in their decision-taking their quest was for *unanimity* in him. How do we measure up to this ideal? Is Christ's rule never impeded by our church-politicking? Do not some congregations so exalt their pastors as to put them in a position which only Christ should occupy—and do not some ministers rather enjoy such treatment? Do not some elders think that they have been called to run the affairs of the Church as *they* think best?

Associated with the Erskines' concern that the sole headship of Christ be honoured in his Church was a deep consciousness of the sanctity of the relation between pastor and people. That relation was so sacred that it could be created only by Christ himself. The people in calling a pastor were supposed to be calling Christ's man. Is that what we think we are doing when we call a pastor today? I have seen weighty dossiers compiled by vacant charges. The ingredients they *desire* in a minister are all listed. But do they always call the minister they *need*? In some quarters the corporate model

29 Quoted ibid., 71.

seems to prevail to such an extent that the profound distinction between the calling of a pastor and the hiring of staff is all but obliterated.[30]

And what of the ministers themselves? John Robinson, the pastor to the Pilgrims, wrote this:

> The bond between the minister, and people is the most strait, and near religious bond that may be, and therefore not to be entered but with mutual consent, any more than the civil bond of marriage between the husband, and wife.
>
> It makes much, both for the provocation of the minister unto all diligence and faithfulness: and also for his comfort in all the trials, and temptations which befall him in his ministry, when he considereth how the people unto whom he ministereth, have committed that most rich treasure of their souls, in the Lord, yea, I may say, of their very faith and joy, to be helped forward unto salvation, to his care, and charge, by their free and voluntary choice of him.[31]

Is this how ministers of today feel? Or is it not true that if the corporate model has overtaken some churches, the career model has become uppermost in the minds of some ministers? Have not some almost scorned the pastorate as being beneath their specialist skills—as if the pastoring of old and young, sick and well, godly and downright awkward is not a very particular kind of specialism? Do not some ministers regard one pastorate as merely a launching pad to the next—bigger and "better," (whatever that means) of course? Have not some ministers come to think of themselves as managers rather than as physicians of souls? I think I would jump out of my skin if I were visited at my sick-bed by a Senior Executive Pastor!

William Bagshawe (1628–1702), England's "Apostle of the Peak"—that hilly district of Derbyshire—had a high view of the relationship between pastor and people. "When ministers think," he wrote, "of the preciousness of one soul, and their being charged with many, and the account to be given of them, may not every one of them cry out with St. Paul: "Who is sufficient for these things?"[32]

---

30 See further, Alan P.F. Sell, *Aspects of Christian Integrity*, Calgary: University of Calgary Press 1990 and Louisville: Westminister/John Knox Press 1991, ch. VI.

31 *The Works of John Robinson*, London: John Snow 1851, II, 396–97.

32 John M. Brentall, *William Bagshawe, The Apostle of the Peak*, London: The Banner of Truth Trust 1970, 112. Bagshawe is in DNB. For Fawcett, next to be mentioned, see DNB and John Julian, *Dictionary of Hymnology*.

Or, again, higher up the same range of hills is the village of Wainsgate, near Hebden Bridge, Yorkshire. This was the scene of the ministry of the Baptist pastor John Fawcett (1740–1817). In 1772 he was called to Carter Lane, London, to succeed Dr. John Gill. The call was accepted, the farewell services held, the pastor's possessions packed on wagons. But the tears and pleadings of the Wainsgate Christians prevailed. The Fawcetts moved back into the manse and the ministry continued. It is said, though there is no hard evidence for the statement, that Fawcett composed one of his most famous hymns following this incident. It is certainly not hard to believe that that experience led to one of the strongest expressions of the relationship of pastor and people ever written:

> Blest be the tie that binds
> Our hearts in Jesus's love,
> The fellowship of Christian minds
> Is like to that above.

The Erskines challenge both churches and ministers to ponder deeply the sanctity of their mutual responsibilities, and to reflect carefully upon the nature of the calling of Christian ministers.

III

The Erskines challenge us concerning the gospel we preach and the ministry we offer. But there is a shadow side to the story of the Secession, and it holds a warning to us all. In their Testimony the Seceders strongly denied that they were motivated by the sectarian spirit; yet we cannot but notice that sectarian attitudes crept in both during and after their lifetime. I offer two pieces of evidence.

Consider, first, the case of George Whitefield the pioneer Calvinistic evangelical of the eighteenth century. On Sunday 22 July 1739 Whitefield recorded in his diary the receipt of a letter from Ralph Erskine.[33] There was thus initiated a correspondence between Whitefield and both Erskines, which led to Whitefield's first visit to Scotland in 1741. On 10 April Ralph Erskine had written to ask Whitefield to associate only with the Associate Presbytery: to do otherwise would unduly comfort the Seceders' opponents.[34] Whitefield could not agree. On 16 May he replied to Ebenezer

33 *George Whitefield's Journals*, London: The Banner of Truth Trust 1960, 312. Whitefield is in DNB.

34 For the text see Luke Tyerman, *The Life of the Rev. George Whitefield*, London: 1890, I, 504-505.

Erskine "I come only as an occasional preacher, to preach the simple gospel, to all who are willing to hear me, of whatever denomination."[35] On 5 August 1741 Whitefield met the Associate Presbytery in Dunfermline, on 8 August he wrote his report of the proceedings to Mr. Noble of New York—an account confirmed by Ebenezer Erskine himself.[36] Whitefield wrote:

> My dear Brother,—"The Associate Presbytery" are so confined that they will not so much as hear me preach, unless I will join with them. . . . They . . . set me right about the matter of church government, and the Solemn League and Covenant. I replied, they might save themselves that trouble, for I had no scruples about it; and that settling church government, and preaching about the Solemn League and Covenant, was not my plan. . . . The answer was, that I was not desired to subscribe immediately to the Solemn Luge and Covenant, but to preach only for them until I had further light. I asked, why only for them? Mr. Ralph Erskine said, "They were the Lord's people." I then asked whether there were no Lord's people but themselves, and, supposing all others were the devil's people, they certainly had more need to be preached to. . . . The consequence of all this was an open breach.[37]

According to Ebenezer Erskine's biography, "From that time [the Associate Presbytery] not only disavowed all connection with [Whitefield], but preached against him publicly, and even went so far as to stigmatize him as an agent of the devil."[38] In 1742 the Seceder Adam Gib, who had been present at the Dunfermline meeting, published seventy-five close pages under the title *A Warning against countenancing the Ministrations of Mr. George Whitefield. . . . Together with an Appendix . . . wherein are shewn, that Mr. Whitefield is no Minister of Jesus Christ; that his call and coming to Scotland are scandalous; that his whole doctrine is, and his success must be, diabolical; so that people ought to avoid him, from duty to God, to the Church, to themselves, to their fellow-men, to posterity and to him.*

Two years later the Associate Presbytery published an official tract of 138 pages in which it listed Scotland's sins. In the course of this lament they declared that "The sins and provocations of this land are further increased by the kind reception that many, both

35 *Letters of George Whitefield* (1734-1742), Edinburgh: The Banner of Truth Trust 1976, 262.

36 Quoted by L. Tyerman, op. cit., 510-511.

37 *Letters*, 307-309.

38 Quoted by L. Tyerman, op. cit., 511.

ministers and people, have given Mr. George Whitefield, a professed member and priest of the superstitious Church of England; and by the great entertainment that has been given to *latitudinarian tenets*, as propagated by him and others; whereby any particular form of church government is denied to be of divine institution.[39]

What are we to make of the Whitefield episode? For his part Whitefield was not of the dissenting kind, and questions of church order were not much in his mind. His way of honouring his *and the Erskines'* convictions concerning the free offer of the gospel was to preach indiscriminately wherever he could get a hearing. Indeed, in his letter to Mr. Noble from which I quoted he declared that "if the Pope himself would lend me his pulpit, I would gladly proclaim the righteousness of Jesus Christ therein."[40] Moreover, he knew that many good evangelicals remained within the state Church. On the other hand we can understand something of the feelings of the Seceders. They had lost their livings and counted the cost of their principles. They had experienced a disorderly church government which was threatening the sure preaching of the Word. Moreover, modern psychology has given us the theory which explains what they actually experienced: the need on the part of those who separate on principle to distance themselves from their parent perceived as erring.

The fact remains, however, that although Whitefield could write in his Journal in 1751, "I have met and shaken hands with Mr. Ralph Erskine. Oh when will God's people learn war no more!" the immediate Seceder reaction to him was inherently sectarian. It was as if they were elevating a particular church order and particular understanding of Church-state relations into a term of Christian fellowship. They were invoking a "new circumcision." Not indeed that they were alone in doing this. When Howel Harris, one of Wales's pioneer Calvinistic methodists, visited Rees Davies of Llanboidy, Pembrokeshire, on 10 March 1740, he "Heard dreadful things . . . of the Anabaptists. . . . On receiving some to communion last time at Rhydwilym near here, they asked the young ones if they thought all were damned that were out of their persuasion, they said they thought they were damned. Rees Davies heard one of them to preach on Romans 8:1, that one sort of those that were out

---

39 Act of the Associate Presbytery for renewing the National Covenant of Scotland, 23 December 1743.

40 *Letters*, 308.

of Christ were those that maintained infant baptism and so were damned."[41] Those were heady sectarian days.

Now what happens when those of a sectarian spirit have separated themselves from those deemed to be unfaithful? E. J. Carnell's dictum concerning twentieth-century fundamentalists often applies: "When there are no modernists from which to withdraw, fundamentalists compensate by withdrawing from one another."[42] That, sadly, is what the Seceders did. It is a complicated story, and I cannot pursue it in detail now. Suffice it to say that before the Erskines died The Breach had occurred. The issue was the Burgess Oath which was required to be taken in some towns. Burghers were required to "confess and allow the true religion presently professed within this realm and authorized by the laws thereof." In 1745 Adam Gib (he of the pungent pen in whom, perhaps, integrity had a decided tilt towards pigheadedness) and Alexander Moncrieff petitioned the Secession Synod to rule that this oath was inconsistent with the Secession testimony because it implied endorsement of the corrupt Established Church. Others, including the Erskines, denied this and held that in taking the oath burghers were only vowing to uphold the true Protestant religion as the law allowed. Eventually, after much wrangling, in 1747 the Breach occurred. Gib and Moncrieff led the General Association Synod, commonly known as the Antiburgher Synod. They slandered their opponents, excommunicated Ralph Erskine in 1749 and Ebenezer in 1750. They declared that the Erskines should be "holden by the faithful as heathen men and publicans."[43]

It still happens. Before we condemn the eighteenth-century Scots too harshly let us note that in the last thirty years fifty new Presbyterian *denominations* have been formed in South Korea. Let us also recall that the Presbyterianism of the United States continues in some disarray. If it were fiction we might smile. But, I wonder? One of the most devastating characterizations of sectarianism I have read is in Garrison Keillor's *Lake Woebegon Days*. Listen to Keillor's description of the Brethren in his mythical Minnesota village:

> We were "exclusive" Brethren, a branch that believed in keeping itself pure of false doctrine by avoiding association with the

41 *Howell Harris's Visits to Pembrokeshire*, transcribed from Harris's diaries by Tom Beynon, Aberystwyth: The Cambrian Press News 1966, 24.

42 E. J. Carnell, *The Case for Orthodox Theology*, London: Marshall, Morgan and Scott 1961, 117.

43 Adam Gib (1714-88) and Alexander Moncrieff (1695-1781) are in DNB.

> impure. . . . Once having tasted the pleasure of being correct and defending True Doctrine, they kept right on and broke up at every opportunity, until, by the time I came along, there were dozens of tiny Brethren groups, none of which were speaking to any of the others. . . .
>
> Mr. Johnson's sermon was against women's slacks . . . but Mr. Cox, though he was hardly pro-slacks, felt Mr. Johnson failed to emphasize grace as having superseded the law, and when Mr. Johnson said, "An abomination to God under the law is still an abomination to God under grace," Mr. Cox smelt the burning rubber of Error and stood up and marched.[44]

Have we never encountered such a spirit? Of course truth matters: but let us pause before declaring that we have it all. Of course church order matters, but let us beware of elevating secondary things into terms of Christian fellowship. In the seventeenth-century Richard Baxter, the Reformed pastor *par excellence*, wisely advised his contemporaries not to "make a larger creed and more necessaries than God hath done."[45]

The crucial thing is the relation of truth to love. God has called us in Christ—it is all of his free grace. But what did Garrison Keillor's grandpa say about the Johnson Brethren? "Anytime they want to come to us and admit their mistake, we're perfectly happy to sit and listen to them and then come to a decision about accepting them back."[46] There you have the heart of sectarianism: we alone have the truth, and we will accept you only when you see it in our way. As Baxter's contemporary, John Howe, saw long ago, "without all controversy the main inlet of all the distractions, confusions and divisions of the Christian world, hath been by adding other conditions of Church communion than Christ hath done.[47]

The Erskines challenge us to preach free grace to all who will hear, but they and their friends on occasion come near to sectarianism of a "Pelagian" kind. They challenge us to accord the crown rights to the Redeemer in his Church and to have a high view of the calling of the ministry. And they—who were children on their day just as we are of ours—warn us who have been accepted in Christ to think twice before adopting a sectarian posture and elevating non-essentials into terms of Christian communion.

---

44 Garrison Keillor, *Lake Wobegon Days*, New York: Penguin Books 1986, 130-132.

45 R. Baxter, *The Reformed Pastor*, London: S.C.M. Press 1956, 101.

46 G. Keillor, op. cit., 133.

47 In Howe's reply to Bishop Stillingfleet's "Sermon of Schism," *Works*, H. Rogers (ed.), 1873, V, 232 ff. Howe (1630-1705) is in DNB.

Ralph Erskine's last words were "I shall be for ever a debtor to free grace. Victory, victory, victory."[48] A good note on which to leave this life. And would we not all do well to make Ebenezer Erskine's personal covenant our own?

> Lord, if I have done iniquity, I am resolved through Thy grace to do so no more. I flee for shelter to the blood of Jesus and His everlasting righteousness; for this is pleasing unto Thee. I offer myself up, soul and body, unto God the Father, Son and Holy Ghost. I offer myself unto Christ the Lord, as an object proper for all his offices to be exercised upon. I choose Him as my prophet, for instruction, illumination and direction. I embrace Him as my great Priest, to be washed and justified by His blood and righteousness. I embrace Him as my King, to reign and rule within me. I take a whole Christ, with all His laws, and all His crosses and afflictions. I except against none of them. I will live to Him; I will die to Him; I will quit with all I have in the world for His cause and truth.[49]

48 Quoted by A. R. MacEwen, *The Erskines*, 143.

49 Ibid., 33.

VIII

Revival and Secession in Early Nineteenth-Century Geneva: The British Connection

While we cannot stay to demonstrate the point here, it is generally agreed that as the eighteenth century progressed, the Genevan Protestant Church became increasingly rationalistic in its theology, and quiescent rather than evangelistic in its manner. As A.M. Fairbairn put it, in the wake of Bayle's critical scepticism "Geneva became the school of what was called Socinianism, and D'Alembert rallied its pastors on the success with which they had sifted religion clear of mysteries, while Rousseau in his impassioned way denounced them as so double-minded and faithless that they would neither affirm Christ to be mere man nor affirm him to be God."[1] In 1805 the Genevan Church authorities declared that pastors need no longer sign a uniform confession of faith—an action which was variously construed as favouring freedom of thought, departing from the old paths, and making for peace within the Church. Such tranquillity as was secured by this means was rudely shattered by three secessions during the early decades of the nineteenth century. These secessions, for which the ground had to some extent been prepared by Moravians and pietists, led, respectively, to the formation of l'Église du Bourg-de-Four (1817), whose most prominent members were Emile Guers, Henri Pyt, Ami Bost, Henri-Louis Empaytaz and Felix Neff; the group which met at Caesar Malan's Église du Témoignage (1818); and the Société Évangélique (1831), which numbered Louis Gaussen and Merle d'Aubigné among its leaders.[2] The issues were complex. They included the desire of some to proclaim what they deemed to be evangelical truth consis-

1 A.M. Fairbairn, "The Westminster Confession of Faith and Scotch Theology," *The Contemporary Review* XXI, December 1872–May 1873, 77.

2 See Olivier Fatio, "Quelle Réformation? Les Commemorations Genevoises de la Réformation à travers les siècles," *Revue de Theologie et de Philosophie*, CXIII 1986/II, 116. Cf. Jean Heyer, *L'Église de Genève*, 1909, 119–20.

tent with the Bible and the classical Reformed confessions; the concern of others to maintain peace and harmony in the national church; the alarm of some at what they regarded as the spiritual decadence of the national church; the conviction of others that good order must be preserved in that church; the attachment of some to "the faith once delivered to the saints"; the openness of others to new ways of thought and fresh modes of expression.

As if all of this were not enough, there was the gratitude of the evangelicals for the support of like-minded Christians from other lands, and the annoyance of Genevan ecclesiastical officials at what they construed as the untoward meddling of outsiders in their affairs. Not least among the "meddlers" were the Britons, Robert Haldane, Henry Drummond and John Pye Smith. We shall examine their contribution to Genevan affairs, especially in relation to the Caesar Malan episode; and we shall review the position of Professor Jean-Jacques-Caton Chenevière and his English ally, Robert Bakewell.[3] The entire episode will underline the fact that when, within the Church, the concern for Gospel truth and fidelity to the confessional tradition clashes with, rather than encompasses, the concern for church discipline and unity, secession and impaired witness are the almost inevitable consequences.

I

Of the importance of Robert Haldane for the Genevan revival there can be no doubt. It would, however, be a mistake to suppose that he was the first to light the tinder. As his own biographer acknowledges,

> For several years before Mr. Haldane was so unexpectedly conducted to [Geneva], through no wisdom or foresight of his own, some smoking embers had been collected, and some sparks of light already kindled amidst the gloom of its spiritual apostacy. Even as early as 1810, MM. Empeytaz, Bost, and a few other youthful but

3 Whereas my emphasis in this paper is upon the activities of, and the responses to, the British "meddlers," that of Timothy Stunt is upon the impact of the Genevan revival upon British evangelicals at large. See his "Geneva and British evangelicals in the early nineteenth century," *Journal of Ecclesiastical History*, XXXII, no. 1, January 1981. I have not been able to consult R.P. Evans, *The Contribution made by Foreigners to the French Protestant Réveil, 1815–1850*, unpublished doctoral thesis, University of Manchester, 1971.

> earnest inquirers after truth, had become impatient of the wretched food supplied by their spiritual pastors, and instituted a reunion, called "*La Société des Amis.*"[4]

This meeting had ceased to exist by 1814, some of its keener members having joined the Moravians. In 1813 Henri Empeytaz became chaplain in the sympathetic Baroness Kruedener's house, "but her own views were indistinct, flickering, and, in some respects, visionary."[5] Early in 1816 an English or Welsh Calvinistic Methodist artisan, Richard Wilcox, had godly, and apparently homespun, conversation with former members of the Société des Amis on the ruins of the convent of Rive, but he left the city in January 1817, shortly after Haldane's arrival at the end of the preceding year.[6]

In order to place Haldane in context we must examine the Scottish intellectual climate from 1750 onwards. On the one hand, there was the continuing influence of Scottish Moderatism; on the other, an upsurge of Evangelicalism. This, at least, is how it appeared to partisans on both sides. But, as so often happens, the two parties shared overlapping interests, and there were differences of view within each. Thus, the exegetical and apologetic methods of the Moderates and Evangelicals were similar, as were many of their dogmatic and political views.[7] Whereas some among the early eighteenth-century Moderates adopted "advanced"—that is, Arian—views, later Moderates were in some cases influenced by Humean scepticism. Finding the older supernaturalism increasingly suspect, some Moderates put their trust in the natural goodness of humanity, and dispensed with the doctrine of total depravity. In still other cases "Moderatism" came to be used as a pejorative term descriptive of those ministers who adopted a social-climbing life-style.[8]

Evangelicalism was not an entirely homogeneous phenomenon either. If such Evangelicals as the Erskines were perturbed by the

4 Alexander Haldane, *Memoirs of the Lives of R. Haldane of Airthrey, and of his Brother, J. A. Haldane*, London, 1852, 423; reprinted Edinburgh: The Banner of Truth Trust 1991.

5 Ibid., 424. Described as a Russian mystic, Barbara Juliana von Kruedener (1764–1824) was converted at Riga in 1804. She travelled in northern Switzerland between 1816 and 1818, winning souls, in her manner, for the kingdom of heaven. So G. Krüger in *The New Schaff-Herzog Encyclopedia of Religious Knowledge*, Grand Rapids: Baker Book House 1959, VI, 383–84.

6 Ibid., 424–26.

7 See F. Voges, "Moderate and Evangelical thinking in the later eighteenth century: differences and shared attitudes," *Records of Scottish Church History Society*, XXII, pt. 2, 1986, 141–57.

8 See further ch. VII above.

desire of the English Calvinist Whitefield to proclaim the Gospel to all who would hear him in Scotland, and not merely to their own family of Seceders,[9] others later in the century were fired by missionary zeal, and wished to broadcast the message far and wide. Prominent examples of the latter type were Robert Haldane (1764–1851) and his brother James (1768–1851).[10]

Their father having died in 1768 and their mother in 1774, the Haldane brothers were raised by their grandmother, Lady Lundie, and their uncles. They were educated at Dundee grammar school and at Edinburgh high school. Robert proceeded to Edinburgh University, where he remained only a short time before, in 1780, he went to sea under his uncle, Captain (later Viscount) Duncan. He saw service against the French, who had intervened in the American War of Independence, and with the peace of 1783 he left the navy. For a while he studied in Gosport with David Bogue, a nonconformist evangelical Calvinist, and then spent a further two years at Edinburgh University. Following a "grand tour" in 1785, he lived on his inherited estate at Airthrey for the next ten years.

Having noted the religious climate in Scotland, we should now recall that the industrial revolution was well under way during the Haldanes' youth; workers were migrating from rural areas to the growing towns; Thomas Paine's *The Rights of Man* found its way even into Gaelic; by 1783 church attendance was considerably lower than it had been twenty years earlier; the aristocratic pretensions of some of the Moderate ministers aroused resentment; and many responded favourably to the outbreak, if not always to the final results of, the French Revolution. Indeed, Robert Haldane, who declared that he was "aroused from the sleep of spiritual death by the excitement of the French Revolution,"[11] went so far as to write:

---

9 See ibid.

10 For the Haldanes see DNB; Alexander Haldane, op. cit. For the Haldanes as the inspiration (though not the architects—that honour belongs to Greville Ewing) of Scottish Congregationalism, see James Ross, *A History of Congregational Independency in Scotland*, Glasgow: James MacLehose 1900, chs. V–X; Harry Escott, *A History of Scottish Congregationalism*, Glasgow: The Congregational Union of Scotland 1960, chs. VI–VIII. It is interesting to note that whereas, over against established Anglicanism, the *raison d'être* of English Congregationalism was ecclesiological, Scotland's Congregationalism was acquired following home missionary zeal in face of an established Church deemed to be asleep. For English Congregationalism see Alan P.F. Sell, *Saints: Visible, Orderly and Catholic. The Congregational Idea of the Church*, Geneva: World Alliance of Reformed Churches and Allison Park, PA: Pickwick Publications 1986.

11 A. Haldane, op. cit., 74.

> A scene of melioration and improvement in the affairs of mankind, seemed to open itself to my mind, which, I trusted, would speedily take place in the world; such as the abolition of slavery, of war, and of many other miseries, that mankind was exposed to, and which appeared to me wholly to result from the false principles upon which the ancient governments had been constructed.[12]

But if revolutionary tendencies stirred Haldane, it was not until 1795 that, as he said, he "obtained the consolations of the Gospel," and was overtaken by evangelistic fervour. With his brother James he was among the first subscribers to the London Missionary Society (1795).[13] Robert Haldane gave considerable financial support to the Society for the Propagation of the Gospel at Home (1798), which encouraged Sunday Schools, circulated tracts, established devotional libraries, and covered the expenses of ministers willing to preach in the unchurched districts around their parishes. The members of this Society established a chain of Tabernacles—preaching houses—of which the earliest was Edinburgh's Circus Tabernacle, in which the first sermon was delivered by the English evangelical Rowland Hill.[14] The evangelical Anglican Charles Simeon was among other English preachers invited to Scotland.[15]

At first some of the Scottish parish ministers were involved in Haldane's endeavours, but in May 1799 the General Assembly of the Church of Scotland prohibited ministers of the Kirk from employing, or "holding ministerial communion with" those who were not qualified to hold a living in the Church of Scotland (Haldane never sought ordination). Few things had done more to provoke the opposition of the Kirk than the increase of Sunday Schools and the encouragement of lay preaching, both of which were deemed by some to foster sedition. The Established Church was not alone in opposing Haldane and his colleagues. Though born out of zeal for evangelical doctrine, ideas concerning good church order took

---

12 R. Haldane, *Address to the Public, Concerning Political Opinions, etc.*, Edinburgh, 1800, 4.

13 For this Society see C. Silvester Horne, *The Story of the L.M.S. 1795–1895*, London: London Missionary Society 1895; Richard Lovett, *History of the London Missionary Society*, London: London Missionary Society, 2 vols., 1899; Norman Goodall, *A History of the London Missionary Society 1895–1945*, London: OUP 1954.

14 For Rowland Hill (1744–1833) see DNB.

15 For Charles Simeon (1759–1836) see DNB.

precedence in the General Associate (Antiburgher) Synod (1788), which, in 1796 and 1798, prohibited cooperation on the part of its ministers with unauthorised persons.[16]

On 16 June 1798 Haldane left his estate at Airthrey, which he had sold in order to finance his Christian activities. In January 1799 he resigned his membership in the Church of Scotland in favour of Congregationalism, which in Scotland (certain independent antecedents notwithstanding) was the product of the Evangelical Revival, and anti-Moderate in tendency. Among other projects, he opened a ministerial training college in 1799, through which nearly three hundred students passed prior to the closure of the institution in 1808. The closure resulted from the withdrawal of Haldane's financial support: in that year he had adopted Baptist views, while retaining his ardent evangelical Calvinism.[17]

II

Robert Haldane, now a Baptist, arrived in Geneva at the end of 1816. The revolutionary war was over, and the opportunity of travel was seized upon by increasing numbers of Britons. Haldane's motives were clear:

> For many years I had cherished the idea of going to France, with the view of doing something to promote the knowledge of the Gospel in a country in which I had been three times before as a traveller. Accordingly, when the return of peace rendered my design practicable, I went to the Continent. Being, however, unacquainted with a single individual there, and therefore unable to arrange any particular plan of action, I feared that my object might prove abortive; and, in consequence, when asked, before I left Scotland, how long I expected to be absent, I replied, "Possibly only six

16 See John McKerrow, *History of the Secession Church*, Edinburgh: A. Fullarton 1847, 384, 393–94. H. Escott, op. cit., 72, follows others in declaring that "The Cameronians at Glasgow in 1796 excommunicated some of their members for attending a sermon which a minister of the Church of Scotland had preached on behalf of the Glasgow Missionary Society." This is represented as indicating an un-missionary attitude. But what is here misconstrued as opposition to mission was in fact consistent with the continuing protest of the Covenanters against the existing constitution of the Scottish Church. See Matthew Hutchison, *The Reformed Presbyterian Church in Scotland*, Paisley: J. and R. Parlane 1893, 248–50.

17 See Ralph F.G. Calder, "Robert Haldane's theological seminary," *Congregational Historical Society Transactions* XIII, no. 1, September 1937, 59–63 and 53.

> weeks." The Lord, however, was pleased to open a wide and effectual door, leading me in a way that I knew not, and my residence abroad continued about three years.[18]

Haldane had no planned itinerary. He passed through Paris, finding the city lost in "Egyptian darkness," and affording no scope for his ministry. Mr. Hillhouse of the American Embassy there advised him as to possible contacts in Montauban and Geneva: "He told me that at Geneva there were only two individuals to whom I could have access, the one (M. Moulinié) a pastor, in advanced years, the other not a pastor (M. Galland), but what is termed a minister, and that nearly the whole of the other pastors were Arians or Socinians."[19]

Haldane proceeded to Geneva, where he received a kind welcome from Moulinié, and then moved on to Berne, where he remained for eight days, conversing from ten in the morning until ten at night with Galland, who had by now moved to that city. He next moved on to Basle, where he met Empeytaz and Baroness Kruedener, and then returned to Geneva. Moulinié, who had offered to show Mrs. Haldane some of the local sights, was prevented by sickness from doing so, and sent a young divinity student in his place. So it was that Haldane made contact with the Genevan students.

The escort, M. James, brought a friend, Charles Rieu, to meet Haldane on the following day, and Haldane records their meeting thus:

> I questioned them respecting their personal hope of salvation, and the foundation of that hope. Had they been trained in the schools of Socrates or Plato, and enjoyed no other means of instruction, they could scarcely have been more ignorant of the doctrines of the Gospel. They had, in fact, learned much more of the opinions of the heathen philosophers, than of the doctrines of the Saviour and his Apostles. To the Bible and its contents their studies had never been directed. After some conversation, they became convinced of their ignorance of the Scriptures, and of the way of salvation, and exceedingly desirous of information. I therefore postponed my departure from Geneva.[20]

---

18 Quoted in A. Haldane, op. cit., 416.

19 Ibid., 417. These terms were used, sometimes with less than full accuracy, to characterise those whose Christology was subordinationist.

20 Ibid., 419.

During Haldane's visit to Berne, Galland had given him the name of Françoise S.R.L.Gaussen (1790–1863), pastor at Satigny, who was to become one of the founders of the Evangelical Society, and a professor at the theological school eventually established in rivalry to that of the national Church. The two met, and Gaussen later recalled that Haldane's "visit to Geneva was blessed to us all." He further noted, "I visited him only occasionally, but I make bold to number myself with those who cherish his memory with the fondest and most affectionate gratitude."[21] Others had more regular contact with Haldane. On 6 February 1817 he began to expound Romans to those who came to his rooms and, in the words of Henri Pyt who was present, "Never, we venture to say, since the days of Francis Turretine, and Benedict Pictet, of holy and happy memory,—never had any doctor expounded the whole counsel of God with such purity, force, and fulness—*never since that period had so bright a luminary shone in the city of Calvin.*"[22]

To Frederic Monod (1794–1863), later a founder of l'Union des Églises Évangéliques de France, Haldane was

> that blessed man, whom, under God, I call with a loving and grateful heart my spiritual father. . . . Though students of theology, true theology was one of the things of which we knew the least. God's holy Word was to us *terra ignota*, whilst Unitarianism, with all its chilling influence, and all its soul-destroying appendages, was the only doctrine taught to us by our Professors. . . . During the four years I attended the theological teachers of Geneva, I did not, as part of my studies, read one single chapter of the World of God, except a few Psalms and chapters, exclusively with a view to learning Hebrew, and that I did not receive one single lesson of exegesis of the Old or New Testaments.[23]

In the words of J.H. Merle d'Aubigné (1794–1872), founder (in 1832) and professor of church history at the Evangelical Faculty,

> When I and M. Monod attended the University of Geneva, there was a Professor of Divinity who confined himself to lecturing on the immortality of the soul, the existence of God, and similar topics. As to the Trinity, he did not believe in it. Instead of the Bible, he gave us quotations from Seneca and Plato. . . . I afterwards met Mr. Haldane. . . . I was astonished to hear of men being corrupt by nature. . . . If Geneva gave something to Scotland at the time of the

21 Ibid., 420.

22 Quoted ibid., 427.

23 Quoted ibid., 429–30.

> Reformation,—if she communicated light to John Knox, Geneva has received something from Scotland in return, in the blessed exertions of Robert Haldane.[24]

Similar sentiments were expressed by the President of the Evangelical Society at a meeting in June 1852: "Geneva remembers with gratitude that it was France that sent her Farel, Calvin, and Theodore Beza, nor is she ashamed to trace the origin of the present revival to a pious Scotsman, Robert Haldane."[25]

Haldane continued his exposition of Romans until the summer of 1818 (with a break in Montauban, where he arranged for the printing of two editions of the Bible in French), and his lectures were published in French in the following year—the year of his return to Scotland. In all, some twenty-five students had learned from him.

III

Two days prior to Haldane's departure, and without any collusion whatsoever, Henry Drummond (1786–1860) arrived in Geneva.[26] Born into a banking family, he had been educated at Harrow and Christ Church, Oxford, though he left the latter without taking a degree. He joined the family bank, made a tour of Russia in 1807, and became a Member of Parliament in 1810. By 1817 he was "satiated with the empty frivolities of the fashionable world." He closed down his hunting stables, sold his mansion, set out for the Holy Land, but arrived in Geneva.

Whereas F. Monod could write of Haldane that "not a shadow of sectarianism was mixed up with" his teaching,[27] the same eirenic spirit did not animate Drummond. On the contrary: he used his wealth not only to promote revival in Geneva, but to circulate Martin's version of the Bible in opposition to the version adopted by the "Arian" pastors; and he had no qualms about encouraging evangelicals to secede from the national Church. Professor Chenevière and others visited him at Sechêron on behalf of the Venerable Company of Pastors, but to no avail. Drummond wrote a letter to

24 Quoted ibid., 431. The Evangelical Faculty was conducted under the auspices of the Société Évangélique de Genève (founded in 1831). F.S.R.L. Gaussen (1790–1863), C.L. Pronier (1831–1873) and Caesar Malan (for whom see below) were among others who taught there.

25 Quoted ibid.

26 For Drummond see DNB; A. Haldane, op. cit.

27 Quoted in A. Haldane, op. cit., 454.

the Pastors, in which, in the words of Gaussen, he "displayed the same brilliant talent and many courage which he has since evinced in his exposure of Cardinal Wiseman and the Jesuits."[28] The ensuing controversy was such that Drummond was summoned before the Council of State, and shortly left Sechêron for the villa Campagne Pictet—safe on French soil. Here, on 21 September 1817 the Lord's Supper was celebrated by Caesar Malan (1787–1864). Malan was another of Haldane's hearers, though as a pastor already he had visited Haldane independently of the theological students. This was the first "separated" observance of the sacrament by members of the national Church. Encouraged by Drummond, the evangelicals decided to secede on the same day.

We need follow Drummond's career no further. Suffice it to say that among his endeavours on returning to Britain were the establishment of the Chair of Political Economy at Oxford in 1825, and his enthusiastic support of Edward Irving's Catholic Apostolic Church. The latter was based at Drummond's mansion, Albury Park, Surrey. He became successively an apostle, and then an angel for Scotland.[29]

IV

It is now time briefly to introduce Caesar Malan, around whose head so much of the ecclesiastical storm broke. The Malan family originated in Piedmont, and reached Geneva via France in 1714. Caesar Malan was born in 1787, educated at the College of Geneva and, following a short sojourn in Marseilles where his objective was a career in business, he returned to the Theological Faculty in Geneva in order to train for the ministry. He was appointed a teacher at the College in 1809, and ordained in 1810. As he afterwards wrote, "During my four years' study of theology, and especially during the two last, I frequently preached, sometimes in the rural parishes of Geneva, sometimes in the neighbouring countries. At that time, I was utterly ignorant of gospel grace, and though my character as a young man was upright, even to severity, no thought had ever entered my mind of any other salvation than that of my

28 Quoted ibid., 458.

29 For this strangely catholic-cum-charismatic group see A.L. Drummond, *Edward Irving and His Circle*, London: James Clarke 1937; H.C. Whitley, *Blinded Eagle*, London: SCM 1955; C.G. Strachan, *The Pentecostal Theology of Edward Irving*, London: Darton, Longman and Todd 1973.

own work and deservings."[30] On these points his theological course utterly failed to help him. Indeed, "I should fail to find a single instance in which instruction was given me on the divinity of our Saviour, man's fallen nature, or the doctrine of justification by faith."[31]

1816 was, for Malan, the "year of deliverance." Following Bible study with Herr de Sach, a visitor from Berlin, and Wendt, the Lutheran pastor in Geneva, he came to a knowledge of the way of salvation. Malan thus had his theology in order before Haldane came upon the scene—a point which is sometimes overlooked. Nevertheless, something remained to be added. In Malan's own words: "I was in the faith, though I had not the assurance of salvation. That blessing I experienced while Mr. Haldane, whom I love as a father, instructed me in the way of the Lord more perfectly. This was at the commencement of the year 1817, a period in which I made the acquaintance also of Dr. Mason, and of the Rev. Mr. Bruen of New York, with whom I read and meditated over the Word of God."[32]

In his *Conventicle of Rolle* (London, 1865, from the French of 1821) Malan, in the character of "Genevan Minister" answers the question, "Who was it that led you to the knowledge of the truth?" as follows: "It was the respectable Robert Haldane of Scotland. [He] came to reside some months at Geneva . . . he was a man of retired and unassuming habits, and not forward to make himself known or listened to."[33] (There is a tinge of hagiography in the last phrases here. As we shall see, Haldane was well able to rise to the defence of the Gospel).

Malan's preaching took on a new tone. On Christmas Day 1816, and again in January 1817, he preached in a country church on justification by faith. On 15 March he brought the message to Geneva. It deeply offended the formally religious. His parents deserted him; his wife was distressed; but Haldane rejoiced: "Thank God, the Gospel has again been preached in Geneva."[34] To Chenevière

---

30 César Malan (the Younger), *The Life, Labours and Writings of Caesar Malan*, London: Nisbet 1868, 24.

31 Ibid., 25, quoting C. Malan, *Procès du Methodisme*, 18.

32 Ibid., 45. The Mason here referred to is John Mitchell Mason (1770–1829), of the American Bible Society.

33 C. Malan, *Conventicle of Rolle*, 1865, 111. The French version (p. 62) specifies Haldane as a "Christian of the Presbyterian church of Scotland." As we have seen, Haldane had by now passed from the Church of Scotland, through Congregationalism, to a Baptist position.

34 *Life* of Malan, 55. Cf. A. Haldane, op. cit., 449.

Haldane wrote,

> this doctrine of salvation, possessed of such incomparable energy, and, when carried home to the heart by Divine influence, accompanied with such signal effects; this doctrine, which had for so long a period been unknown in the pulpits of Geneva, and which formed such a contrast to what was then held forth in its Arian, Semi-Arian, Pelagian, Arminian, insipid nothingness, could not be borne among you.[35]

Nor could it. Chenevière visited Malan on behalf of the Venerable Company of Pastors to urge him "to change his doctrine on account of the mischief that might ensue from preaching that good works were not required as the procuring cause of salvation."[36] Malan could not oblige, and thus all city pulpits, and many in the surrounding countryside, were closed to him.

It must in fairness be said that Malan did not set out to be a seceder. For this he was complimented by Bruen in a letter to Mason of 7 November 1817, and in letters of 1821 and 1823 to himself from David Bogue, one of the founders of the London Missionary Society.[37] On the other hand, like John Wesley before him, Malan had already acted in such a way as to displease the establishment. Where Wesley had encouraged field preaching, lay preaching, and had ordained Thomas Coke—actions which could not but distress many in the Church of England—Malan had publicly criticised the national Church of his day, and had conducted an extra-parochial communion service.

The defence of Malan and his colleagues was that the majority of the Genevan pastors were false shepherds, who had exchanged the doctrinal heritage of Geneva for a mess of Arian pottage. Matters were little helped by the evangelical recollection of Jean LeR. d'Alembert's article on Geneva in Diderot's *Encyclopédie*, in which the controversial disciple of Bacon and Locke declared that "many of the pastors of Geneva have no other religion but a perfect Socinianism." This was too sweeping a statement, but to the ears of such an evangelical as Haldane such a sentiment would remind him of the Moderates at home—and with them he had little doctrinal sympathy.

When, on 3 May 1817 the Venerable Company enacted a Regulation prohibiting undue emphasis upon the divinity of Christ,

35 A. Haldane, op. cit., 450.

36 *Life* of Malan, 55.

37 See ibid., 56 n.; 124–26. For David Bogue (1750–1825) see DNB.

original sin, effectual calling, and predestination, the fears of the evangelical party were confirmed. They construed the Regulation to mean that while the Genevan Church was not prepared to deny the specified doctrines, little prominence was to be given to them. For his part, Malan was eager to recall his Church to its confessional roots, and to proclaim the doctrines of grace in an unrestricted way.

In 1819 *Sermons, translated from the French of Caesar Malan, Minister of the Gospel at Geneva. . . . To which is prefixed A Sketch of the Religious Discussion which have lately been taking place at Geneva,* was published in London. The *Sketch* contains the following charges:

> Many faithful servants of Christ are suffering. . . . Some have been deprived of their means of subsistence for no other cause, than that they cannot conscientiously adopt these unscriptural opinions, and will not abjure the divinity of our Lord and Saviour. . . . The Bible, originally in use, has been withdrawn from the church, and another edition, favouring different doctrines, has been substituted. The general confession of the French reformed churches has been revoked. The catechism of Calvin has been changed for one on the Socinian system, which is now generally taught. M. Vernet's *System of Theology,* which affirms that our blessed Lord was a mere man, is the standard work of divinity in the university.'[38]

In the following year, *Documents relative to the Deposition of The Rev. C. Malan, from his Office in the College of Geneva,* was published in Gloucester. Once again, the Preface is blunt, pro-Malan, and opposed to the official stance of the Genevan Church. Of Malan we read that

> His opponents may triumph on account of their great majority in the Church of Geneva; but they should know, that the Churches of Great Britain, after the most deliberate investigation and severest trials of the doctrinal questions now agitated in that city, are entirely decided against them; as also are the greater part of those who are separated from our established communions. [Malan] must be contemplated as the defender of the Christian Faith in a fallen Church.[39]

Among the reasons offered for the declension are the following: a reaction against the excessive discipline of Calvinistic forebears;

38 *Sermons*, iii–v.

39 *Documents*, v.

the progression from Arianism, through Arminianism to the present "Christianised Deism"; the baneful influence of Voltaire and Rousseau; the tranquillity of Geneva, which has not required the defence of the Faith. It is affirmed (somewhat against the evidence as we have presented it) that Malan does not play the role of accuser. The Venerable Company is faulted for neither admitting nor denying the doctrinal charges laid before it; and it is regretted that the Venerable Company has "been careful to remove from their Church everything which might disturb a Socinian peace; their translation of the Bible, Liturgy, and Catechisms have been systematically reduced to the level of that view of Christianity."[40] English readers are informed that Malan has so many hearers that a chapel is to be built for them (the Chapelle du Témoinage was built in 1820), and the Preface ends with a pious hope: "The time, let it be trusted, is not far distant, when neighbouring places of worship shall be consecrated anew to the service of the same Lord, and M. Malan's congregation be distinguished only, as having been the first to return to THE FAITH."[41]

V

Having had his fill of British meddlers, Chenevière at last took up his pen. In October 1823 he wrote the first of a series of articles under the title, *A Summary of the Theological Controversies which of late Years have agitated the City of Geneva.* The articles were published between January and March 1824—significantly in *The Monthly Repository*, the organ of British Unitarianism.

Chenevière begins in wounded fashion:[42] Geneva, once held in high esteem as a beacon of light amidst Roman gloom, is now under attack—not from Jews or pagans, but from "a sect amongst the Reformed." Peace having come to Europe, Geneva "was fixed on by a zealous sect" as "the central point whence its missionaries should go forth to propagate Methodism on the Continent." Pastors have been abused, and the sectaries have been sustained in their efforts by financial donations. The tumult has erupted, according to Chenevière, "because the people of Geneva have not consented, and will not consent, to become Methodists."

He proceeds to chronicle the disturbances which have hurt the peace of the Church. He refers to the presence of some Moravians,

---

40 Ibid., xi.

41 Ibid., xii.

42 J.J.C. Chenevière, *The Monthly Repository* XIX, 1824, 1–2.

holders of "exclusive opinions," who had been left undisturbed by the Church; he mentions Empeytaz and Baroness Kruedener; and he quotes the Consistory regulations, adopted on 24 December 1813 for the guidance of theological students:

> 1st. Any student who, after being dehorted by the pastors from attending a religious meeting not established by the Consistory, persists in frequenting it, cannot be ordained to the ministry in our Church.
>
> 2ndly. The following expression shall be inserted in the formulary of ordination: "You promise to abstain from all sectarianism, and to avoid whatever would be the occasion of schism, or interrupt the unity of the Church."[43]

Empeytaz was not to be checked, however, and soon published his *Considerations on the Divinity of Jesus Christ*, in which he charged the Genevan pastors with theological error. A French Abbé Labouderie published a "scurrilous" sequel to this work, and Chenevière comments: "Every member of a reformed church who attacks the reformed clergy may reckon on the support of the Romish priests."[44]

Chenevière proceeds to introduce Haldane and Drummond in these terms:

> A Scotchman, Mr. Haldane, a rigid Calvinist, whose theological principles are to be found in print, especially in his Commentary on the Epistle to the Romans, in which those who have the courage to undertake the task may judge of his doctrines;—Mr. Haldane invited to his house some students and ministers, occupied their minds with the mysterious points of the Christian religion, and inoculated them with his own exclusive and intolerant spirit. He insisted so strongly on the contempt with which reason, proud reason, ought to be regarded, that one of his hearers in going out of his house once cried out, "Yes, I see plainly that in the affairs of religion, reason ought to be trodden under foot!" Mr. Haldane waged war so indiscreetly against good works, that they were spoken of with disdain in the discourses of his adherents, and in the pamphlets circulated to perpetuate his influence after his departure. . . . Scarcely had this champion ceased his warfare when he was succeeded by another, of less skill but greater impetuosity—Mr. Henry Drummond. The latter kept no terms; he openly urged those who united with him to secede from the Genevan

43 Ibid., 2–3.

44 Ibid., 3.

> Church. . . .[45] [Chenevière next turns to the Regulations on 3 May 1817. He explains, in terms which a confessional Calvinist might well find less than full-blooded, that] Each one of the pastors confessed that Jesus was a Divine Being, that all men were sinners, that the grace of God was necessary for salvation, that man was free, and that there was no limit to the Divine knowledge. They all confessed likewise, that, from the origin of Christianity no one had been able to comprehend the manner in which the Son had proceeded from the Father; the imputation of Adam's sin to his posterity; the way in which God influences the human mind; and the means of reconciling the prescience of the Almighty with the undeniable liberty of man. All were, at the same time, equally convinced of the necessity of banishing these disputed topics from the Christian pulpit; of giving importance not to the words but to the spirit of the gospel; of loving and cherishing peace. In this temper, and with the consent of all parties, was drawn up the regulation of the 3rd of May, 1817. . . .[46]

Under the Regulation students for the ministry were required to make the following pledge:

> We promise, as long as we reside and preach in the Canton of Geneva, to abstain from discussing, either in whole discourses or in parts of our discources the subjoined topics:- 1st. The manner in which the Divine Nature is united to the person of Jesus Christ. 2dly. Original Sin. 3rdly. The operation of Grace, or Effectual Calling. 4thly. Predestination. We engage also not to oppose in our public discourses the sentiments of any minister on these subjects. Lastly, we promise that if we should be led to mention these topics, we will do so without expatiating on our own views, or departing more than is unavoidable from the words of the Holy Scriptures.[47]

The Regulation, declares Chenevière, achieved its objective of securing the peace of the Church, though it was represented by the Church's enemies as being tyrannous.

Chenevière next cites thirteen attacks by the disaffected upon Genevan pastors, and quotes testimonies of esteem for, and confidence in, the pastors from the Council of State, from hundreds of citizens, from many theological students, and from other Swiss churches. He then turns to Malan, whom he presents as one whose

---

45 Ibid., 4.

46 Ibid., 5.

47 Ibid. The last promise here probably means both that students were declining scholastic doctrinal speculation, and that they were undertaking not to wax unduly "enthusiastic" concerning the "doctrines of grace."

motto might well be, *Malo videri quam esse.* He alludes to money received by Malan [an unsupported charge subsequently denied by Malan and others], and to the persecutions he claims to have suffered, drily remarking that "This sort of martyrdom is more easy and more pleasant than that of primitive times."[48] He presents his case against Malan in terms of church discipline: Malan refuses to conform to the Regulation of 1817. There follows a detailed account of the steps taken by the Consistory to bring Malan around to its own views. The nub of the matter, as expressed by the Consistory to the Council of State was this:

> Although several doctrinal points taught by M. Malan are not contained in the Sacred Writings; although the doctrine, in particular, of the influences of the Spirit on the minds of individuals . . . is attended with incalculable danger . . . yet it is not of this we complain. . . . We took no cognizance of M. Malan until we were compelled to do it by the offensiveness of his conduct, and by the fears and remonstrances of numerous members of our Church, and until we found the pastoral authority, with which you have entrusted us, questioned, and by a natural consequence the very existence of our Church endangered.[49]

The displeasure of the Council and the Consistory was made clear to Malan. When formally questioned Malan's replies were deemed to be inadequate, for though couched positively, they hid denials. To give one example:

> Do you retract everything in your discourses, either public or private, which has led to the idea that you make a distinction amongst our pastors, of such as are evangelical, and of such as are not evangelical?
>
> Answer. *Yes.*, I retract the distinction, if I have made it otherwise than the word of God makes and commands me to make it. . . .[50]

The result was that Malan was regarded henceforth as "degraded from his office, and deprived of the ecclesiastical character, conferred on him by the National Church of Geneva."[51]

In his concluding instalment, Chenevière offers a critique of what he calls "Methodism." From the references to Whitefield, and

48 Ibid., 65.

49 Ibid., 69.

50 Ibid., 73.

51 Ibid., 75.

to the predilection of the "Methodists" for the doctrine of election, it seems that he has evangelical Calvinistic Methodism in mind, rather than the evangelical Arminianism of the Wesleys.[52] The "Methodists," he complains, emphasise a few selected truths at the expense of the full range of Christian doctrine, and play down the importance of good works. Further, "Even the women, in this sect, lose the reserve and modesty which are their natural characteristics; instead of keeping at home and serving as examples of private virtues, witnessed only by God and their little circle of friends, like the peacock spreading its admired plumage, they go about attracting attention, in what they call doing the work of the Lord, or revealing his counsel. . . . [Furthermore], girls of 13 or 14 years of age lecture their pastors, and unblushingly accuse them of not being Christians. . . ."[53] The "Methodists" favour a "Jewish" observance of the Sabbath and, in all respects, where true Christianity unites, "Methodism" divides: "Who then can wonder that the pastors of Geneva should strive to preserve their flock from this leprosy, or to cure those who have been infected?"[54]

Chenevière admits that in 1805, "for reasons which this is not the place to set forth,"[55] the Genevan Church ceased to require all pastors to sign a uniform confession of faith. Nevertheless,

> There is not one of the pastors of the Church of Geneva who does not affectionately confess Jesus Christ as his Saviour, his Mediator, his Intercessor. There is not one who does not say with the apostle, *Neither is there salvation in any other; for there is no other name under heaven given among men whereby we must be saved;* who does not say, it is by Jesus Christ that we are justified. . . . There is not any Genevan pastor who does not *honour* the Son as the raiser of the dead and the judge of all the children of men; there is not one who does not know it to be his duty . . . to obey his precepts, and to make his name known and loved on earth; and to glorify by his words and actions the God of holiness and mercy.[56]

---

52 For this distinction see further, Alan P.F. Sell, *The Great Debate. Calvinism, Arminianism and Salvation*, Worthing: H.E. Walter (now Bletchley: Word Books) 1982, Grand Rapids: Baker Book House 1983, ch. III.

53 *The Monthly Repository*, 131.

54 Ibid., 132.

55 Ibid., 134.

56 Ibid.

VI

It was only to be expected that Chenevière's *Summary* would provoke responses. One of the first came from Dr. John Pye Smith (1774–1851), tutor at Homerton [Dissenting] College.[57] Displaying commendable journalistic balance, the editor of *The Monthly Repository* not only published the extensive reply of the evangelical Calvinist, but also permitted its republication as a separate pamphlet, which also incorporates Pye Smith's rejoinder to Robert Bakewell's defence of Chenevière. Before examining Pye Smith's text we shall do well to place him i . his intellectual context.

On 17 December 1695, the "Happy Union" between Presbyterians and Congregationalists having broken down, the Congregational Fund Board was established.[58] Its purpose was to lend financial support to ministerial students. As a matter of policy, assistance was afforded only to those who had already received a classical education. Those dissatisfied with this rubric founded the King's Head Society in 1730.[59] Its objective was to provide a full six years of education, of which the first two would be classical. The Society was, moreover, strongly of the evangelical Calvinist persuasion, and students were soon required to subscribe to ten articles in that vein. First published in 1732, the articles were reissued until 1805. In the latter year Pye Smith was ordained, and became theological tutor at Homerton, the Academy founded by the King's Head Society in 1730.

---

57 For Pye Smith see DNB; John Medway, *Memoirs of the Life and Writings of John Pye Smith, DD.,LL.D.*, 1853; *Congregational Year Book*, 1851, 233; Geoffrey F. Nuttall, *New College, London and Its Library*, London: Dr. Williams's Trust 1977, 9–13, 52–55. For Homerton Academy (later College) see H. McLachlan, *English Education Under the Test Acts*, Manchester: Manchester University Press 1931, 175–88; *Congregational Magazine*, 1825, 133, 187; Irene Parker, *Dissenting Academies in England*, Cambridge: CUP 1914; T. H. Simms, *Homerton College 1695–1978. From Dissenting Academy to Approved Society in the University of Cambridge*, Cambridge: Trustees of Homerton College 1979. In 1850 Homerton united with Coward and Highbury (formerly Hoxton) Colleges to form New College, London. New College, which had united with Hackney College in 1924, closed in 1977.

58 See *Congregational Historical Society Transactions*, V, 134–48.

59 For the King's Head Society see the New College, London, MSS, at Dr. Williams's Library, London.

Trained at Rotherham under the evangelical Calvinist Edward Williams,[60] Pye Smith had already served Homerton as teacher of logic, rhetoric, mathematics, science, Hebrew and Greek. That he was in thorough accord with the evangelical Calvinism which his institution had been founded to preserve and promote is clear from his *Scripture Testimony to the Messiah* (2 vols., 1818–21)—a defence of the doctrine of the Trinity. That he was in the van of those who sought to accommodate biblical theology to modern scientific developments may be seen in his *Relation between the Holy Scriptures and some parts of Geological Science* (1839).[61]

We can thus see that behind Pye Smith's defence of Malan there lies a shared theology, and a deep concern to oppose the advance of Unitarianism. Arian and unitarian thought had in the eighteenth century made considerable inroads into English trinitarian Presbyterianism; some Congregationalists had likewise succumbed,[62] as had many of the General (that is, rationalistic Arminian) Baptists.[63] Unitarianism itself had been legalised in 1813.

Pye Smith was further motivated, *qua* Dissenter, by despair over national church establishments which failed to proclaim the Gospel with zeal, and which stood in the way of those who do. Thus, in the first letter of his *Vindication* he declares that Chenevière "has made an extremely uncandid and unjust attack upon persons, whom I regard as deserving the esteem of all the friends of liberty and religion: and he has committed a heinous aggression against the dearest right and most imperative duty of mankind, the open pro-

60 For Edward Williams (1750–1813) see DNB; W.T. Owen, *Edward Williams, D.D. His Life, Thought and Influence*, Cardiff: University of Wales Press 1963. For Williams and Rotherham Academy see W.T. Owen, op. cit., Ch. VI; H. McLachlan, *English Education*, 199–208; Kenneth W. Wadsworth, *Yorkshire United Independent College*, London: Independent Press 1954, Ch. VII.

61 For this matter see further, Alan P.F. Sell, *Theology in Turmoil. The Roots, Course and Significance of the Conservative-Liberal Debate in Modern Theology*, Grand Rapids: Baker Book House 1986, ch. III.

62 See Alan P.F. Sell, "Presbyterianism in eighteenth-century England: the doctrinal dimension," in *Dissenting Thought and the Life of the Churches. Studies in an English Tradition*, Lewiston, NY: Mellen Research University Press 1990, ch. V. For a detailed account of the views characteristically held by the Presbyterian Arians see idem, "A little friendly light: the candour of Bourn, Taylor and Towgood," ibid., ch. VII.

63 See William Turner, "Unitarian General Baptists," in *Unitarianism Exhibited in its Actual Condition*, ed. J.R. Beard, London: Simpkin Marshall 1846; Ian Sellers, "The Old General Baptists, 1811–1915," *The Baptist Quarterly*, XXIV, no. 1, January 1971, 30–41.

fession and peaceable practice of religious conviction."[64] Furthermore, while Chenevière and his colleagues plainly dislike evangelical views, they are evasive concerning their own opinions:

> Why do they use language capable of a variety of interpretations? Why do they use language calculatred to mislead and deceive: as when M.C. says, "Each one of the Pastors confessed that Jesus was a Divine Being"? They know well that, had they the integrity and the honour to speak out, one would say, "I am an Arian of the old school"; another, "I incline most to the sentiments of the Polish Socinians"; another, "I rather attach myself to those of the modern English Unitarians"; a fourth, "I adopt the system of the German Antisupernaturalists"; and, last of all, not a few would have to confess, "I have never taken the pains to make up my mind upon any religious doctrines or opinions whatsoever."[65]

At the heart of the problem is "a fundamentally wrong view of the proper ground of authority in religion, an attachment to the established system from civil and political motives, the idea of religion as consisting of a certain routine of outward actions, and the regarding of the Christian ministry as a genteel and agreeable profession for youths of a studious turn and a love for letters, apart from a supreme deference to its particular nature and proper qualifications."[66] Standing upon the principle of religious liberty, Pye Smith announces his thesis thus:

> *That by the letter and spirit of the act for abolishing subscription, any and every Genevese minister had, and ever has,* THE SAME RIGHT *to retain or revive, and to defend and propagate, the old faith of their own Church, which any other Genevese minister had or has to deny and oppose it.*[67]

Accordingly, it ill behoves the Venerable Company to "persecute" those who preach the classical Reformed doctrines. Pye Smith admits that Malan has flouted ecclesiastical authority, but contends that this was the appropriate response to the perverse exercise of such authority.

Pye Smith finds no evidence that the evangelicals are disturbers of the peace, and he repudiates Chenevière's suggestion that people have been paid to leave the national Church. Chenevière's charges

64 John Pye Smith, *A Vindication of those Citizens of Geneva, etc.*, 1825, 1.

65 Ibid., 2–3.

66 Ibid., 4.

67 Ibid., 5; cf. ibid., 42.

against "Methodist" excesses are so unspecific that no reply can be made; but his representation of the doctrines he despises are so faulty that, if he had read the works of those whom he accuses, "he can be no more than a foul and base calumniator."[68] Moreover, as far as Pye Smith knows, none of the Britons who visited Geneva were either Calvinistic or Arminian Methodists.

A running charge in Pye Smith's *Vindication* is that moral decline has followed doctrinal declension in Geneva. This was the point on which he was subsequently challenged by Robert Bakewell, a geologist, who was probably one of the Quaker Bakewells of Nottingham. He had lived in Geneva during the winters of 1820 and 1822. Bakewell adduced evidence—including Servetus—to show that morality under Calvinism left something to be desired, and that the reputations of other Reformed cities—Rotterdam with its 500 *spiel-houses*, for example, were not untarnished.[69] Bakewell suspected that Pye Smith's main objective was to attack the English Unitarians *via* Chenevière. There is, however, one point at which Bakewell has to dissent from Chenevière. Chenevière "speaks of M. Malan, as if he considered him censurable for continuing to conduct religious worship in his own chapel, in defiance of what he styles the civil and religious authority. Surely when M.M. had entirely separated himself from the Genevese Church, he was, or ought to be, at liberty to worship according to the dictates of his conscience; and, in fact, notwithstanding this censure, he was left at perfect liberty so to do."[70]

Pye Smith replied to Bakewell, noting in particular that Bakewell had been unable to refute his main charge, namely, that Malan and his colleagues have the right to preach the doctrines they believe. He further reminded Bakewell that he, too, had condemned intolerant Calvinism, and he repudiated the accusation that his main objective was to attack English Unitarians.[71]

In the course of his *Vindication*, Pye Smith rises to the defence of Empeytaz and Haldane. Of the latter, against Chenevière, he writes, "There are few persons who are more addicted to *cool reasoning*, or who have more correct views or more consistent practice on the subject, I will not say of *toleration*, but of the entire rights of *religious liberty*. . . . As to Mr. Haldane's 'waging war against good works,' I have no hesitation in saying, that the assertion is another

68 Ibid., 15.

69 For Bakewell's letters see *The Monthly Repository*, XIX, 1824, 513–19, 593–98, 661–68, 739–44. For Bakewell (1768–1843) see DNB.

70 Ibid, 664.

71 J. Pye Smith, *Vindication*, 46–72; cf. *The Monthly Repository*, vol. cit.

instance of unprincipled calumny."[72] On Henry Drummond, Pye Smith writes, "Not having the honour of knowing this gentleman, and having received no precise information of his transactions at Geneva, I presume not to say much. . . . Perhaps he was unguarded in some respect or other. . . . At all events I must have better testimony than that of this accuser, before I can entertain a feeling of disrespect towards him."[73]

Pye Smith concludes on a peak of emotion, calling capital letters to his aid: "I appeal to any man who has but a moderate acquaintance with the rights of human nature, whether the treatment of M. Malan by the Ecclesiastical power has been any other than a constant course of INJUSTICE, CRUELTY, and TYRANNY."[74]

Chenevière offered a brief reply to Pye Smith, in which he defended himself against specific, relatively minor, charges, and reasserted his main point thus: "[Malan and his friends] preach doctrines opposed to the letter and the spirit of the gospel; they have sown division in families . . . they tend by their doctrines to throw ridicule on Christianity, the gift of God. . . . Let them overwhelm me with insults, let them paint me under false colours, still I will bless God that the enemies of the Reformation cannot make out a better story against its defenders."[75]

Three further replies to Chenevière must be noted. The first is that of Robert Haldane. In a long letter published in 1824 he levelled his charges thus: "You have entirely abandoned the principles of your church at the Reformation, and your complaint now is of the revival of *Calvinism*, the very doctrine that was then taught . . . the manner in which M. Malan has been treated has moved the earth. Yet his great crime amounts to this, that, instead of 'speaking smooth things, and prophesying deceits,' he has, like the prophets of old, lifted up his voice to show the people their transgressions and their sins."[76] Haldane proceeds to answer the charges levelled against himself. He refers to his Bible studies on Romans, to the scriptural ignorance of the theological students; he rebuts the charge of exclusiveness, denies that he diparages reason and, arguing from Romans and elsewhere, makes it clear that he does not oppose good works as the fruit of faith. He challenges the

72 Ibid., 21–22.

73 Ibid., 27–28.

74 Ibid., 45.

75 *The Monthly Repository*, XIX, 1824, 593.

76 *Letter from Robert Haldane, Esq. to M.J.J. Chenevière, Pastor and Professor of Divinity at Geneva, etc.*, Edinburgh, 1824, 3, 18.

articles of May 1817 on the ground that by their prohibitions they undercut the Gospel, and faults Chenevière for describing Malan and himself as "Methodists." He concludes in sepulchral tones: "Your city in former times was highly favoured with the Gospel, which laid the foundation of all its prosperity. But the honourable distinction is lost; and on its churches, in which the Gospel was once so purely preached, is now written *I-chabod*, for the glory is departed from them."[77]

The second reply is that of Malan himself:

> I remember, my dear Chenevière (for *dear* I must still call you), that one of the last things you said to me, five or six years ago, was that nothing could interrupt our entire mutual unreserve, or render it possible for us to condemn or abuse each other as enemies. I believe I have adhered to this sentiment. . . . I am compelled to draw a distinction between my old friend and the theological teacher. In this last capacity I cannot hold any intercourse with you, nor even acknowledge you. . . . I have been most unwilling to raise my voice against you. . . . The nature of your written sentiments . . . will provoke against you and against the Church in which you are an authorised theological teacher, a unanimity, not indeed of attack, but of rejection on the part of all those who reverence the Bible. . . . But there are more important considerations still in reserve. The safety of your own soul, dear Chenevière, is a matter more intensely solemn, and demanding even greater interest and anxiety. . . . What I intensely desire, is that He Who has called me by His grace to the knowledge of Himself, would incline your heart to listen to and accept the good tidings of that salvation which is "from Him, by Him, and for Him."[78]

It remains only to add that at a meeting of nearly one hundred Protestant Ministers of the Three Denominations (that is, Presbyterian, Congregational and Baptist), held in Red Cross Street Library, London, on 3 May 1825, a statement in support of religious liberty, and of the Genevan evangelicals, was unanimously adopted.[79] The Chairman on that day was John Pye Smith.

---

77 Ibid., 140.

78 *Life* of Malan, 194–98.

79 See *Les Ministres Protestans Non Conformistes des Trois Dénominations*, Dr Williams's Library, NCP.B.40. For the English version see J. Medway, *Life* of Pye Smith, 271–73. For this body see Geoffrey F. Nuttall, *The General Body of the Three Denominations. A Historical Sketch*, privately printed for The General Body of the Three Denominations, London, 1955, repr. 1962.

VII

How shall we adjudicate this complicated matter?

In the first place, it is impossible not to feel a certain sympathy with Chenevière. His objective of a Church at peace was *prima facie* laudable. Just as the Scottish Moderates and English Arians feared a return to the sectarian strife of the seventeenth century, so Chenevière and his colleagues sought a tranquil life. Moreover, we can understand Chenevière's reluctance to give Rome scope for attacking and ridiculing the national Church; and we can appreciate why he would have regarded the British visitors of whom we have spoken as unwelcome irritants. Indeed, a close reading of the texts suggests something verging upon paranoia on his part—as when he walked in the vicinity of Haldane's rooms, "chafing with indignation at [his students'] disregard of his wishes, frowning on them as they entered Mr. Haldane's door, and noting down their names."[80]

All the evidence suggests, however, that Chenevière goes too far in calling Haldane an agitator. He did not deny the importance of good works as flowing from faith, and at no time did he advocate or encourage secession from the national Church. The latter cannot be said of Henry Drummond, whose spirit seems to have been open and generous, albeit pugilistic and eccentric. Of him Thomas Carlyle declared that he was "a singular mixture of all things—of the saint, the wit, the philosopher—swimming, if I mistake not, in an element of dandyism."[81] Again, a biographer of Edward Irving, the founder of the Catholic Apostolic Church, says of Drummond that "The egotism of this religious enthusiast, with wealth, power and wit and yet no responsibility, outweighed commonsense."[82] He later asks, "Was [Drummond] in fact Irving's evil genius?"[83] Certainly Chenevière's indignation against Drummond was more justifiable than his invective against Haldane.

As for Malan, he was in breach of ecclesiastical discipline but, as Pye Smith so clearly argued, Chenevière nowhere showed why it was theologically wrong, morally objectionable, or unlawful for Genevan pastors to enjoy the liberty to preach Calvinism if they wished when, since the abolition of confessional subscription, they

80 A. Haldane, op. cit., 429.

81 Quoted in J.A. Froude, *Thomas Carlyle*, London: Longmans 1909, II, 181.

82 H.C. Whitley, *Blinded Eagle*, 22–23.

83 Ibid., 41.

could preach Arianism and Socinianism with impunity. At the same time, there is a smugly self-righteous air about some of Malan's utterances: to say that one hopes for the salvation of a theological professor is an unkind cut! This impression is reinforced by the fact that when Philip Schaff, the distinguished historian, and one of the pioneers of the World Alliance of Reformed Churches, visited Geneva, Malan branded him an heretic and a Pelagian on account of his alleged weakness on double predestination.[84]

But with the mention of doctrine we come to the heart of the matter. It cannot be denied that here Chenevière was evasive. Haldane rightly noted in a letter to Cheneviere of 3 May 1817 that where doctrinal dispute is in hand, it will not do to say "Jesus was a divine being," or that "all men are sinners,"[85] without specifying whether Jesus was a divine being who differs from us in degree or in kind, and whether we have, as it happens, become sinners, or whether we were "born in sin." Furthermore, even allowing for the fact that theological students seldom consider that they have been adequately trained, the testimony we have cited as to the sparse handling of classical Christian doctrines by Chenevière and his colleagues at the Academy cannot be discounted.

In 1835, ten years after the episode with which we have been dealing, Geneva celebrated the tercentenary of its Reformation. Chenevière was the leading national churchman, and he represented the Reformation as conducing to the "emancipation of thought."[86] Malan was still outside of the establishment, and was still among its severest critics. To him, what was being celebrated in 1835 was the "deformation of Geneva."[87]

The British were in Geneva for the tercentenary celebrations, and one of them made a formal address in the course of which he said,

> I very much regret that a larger number of my countrymen has not come to express their affinity and their joy on this solemn occasion. However, I wish to explain that the English do not lack attachment to the same principles which we are avowing here. In particular, the Dissenting denomination of which I am a member, that is to

84 See George Shriver, *Philip Schaff: Christian Scholar and Ecumenical Prophet*, Macon, GA: Mercer University Press 1987, 11.

85 R. Haldane, *Letter* to Chenevière, 1824, 141–43.

86 J.J.C. Chenevière, *Jubilé de la Réformation de Genève. Août 1835. Liturgies et Sermons*, Geneva, 1835, 131.

87 C. Malan, *Le Vrai Jubilé. Dialogue entre deux Genevois, l'un de la veille roche; l'autre de goût moderne*, Geneva, 1835, 18.

> say, the English Presbyterians, have been noted for this since almost the beginning of the last century; they have rejected confessions of faith, and it is worthy of remark that our Chandler, Benson, Towgood, James Peirce and others, who are well known here and in France and Germany, were publishing their treatises for the defence of these principles at precisely the same time as your Jean-Alphonse Turretin and many Genevans were writing their fine and excellent works. There, Gentlemen, is the common bond between yourselves and us. The Anglican Church also contains a large number of people who are, like the Dissenters, devoted to religious liberty. Even in the Scottish church, although her [confessional] symbols are narrow, one finds some ministers and some professors . . . who are at one with us concerning the supreme authority of the Holy Scriptures, as rule of faith and conscience, with the principle which necessarily follows, the obligation of free examination and the right of individual judgment. . . . [He comments on the debt which England owes to Geneva, and continues:] In my opinion, we have need of your help at this time as we did formerly. My constant wish is that the Dissenters follow the example of the Church of Geneva, not only in respect of freedom of worship, the exercise of individual judgment and sincerity of spirit, of justice and harmony, but also in respect of the means which she has adopted for the instruction of ministers and youth, and for wise and salutary discipline.

This speaker was no Haldane, Drummond or Pye Smith. The principal British greetings on the occasion of the tercentenary of the Genevan Reformation were conveyed by James Yates, who used "Presbyterian" in an historic sense, and who was in fact a distinguished (albeit unordained) *Unitarian* minister.[88] No doubt the Genevan evangelicals felt that their case was proven.

* * * * *

I dedicate this paper to my friend and former colleague, Dr. Edmond Perret, sometime General Secretary of the World Alliance of Reformed Churches, and Genevan pastor.

88 For Yates's speech see *Jubilé de la Réformation de Genève. Août 1835. Historique et Conférences*, Geneva, 1835, 190–92. For James Yates (1789–1871) see DNB. I am grateful to my colleague, Dr. G. W. Campbell of the Department of French, Italian and Spanish of the University of Calgary, for checking my translation of this quotation.

IX

The Pembrokeshire Congregational Magazine

One hundred and fifty years ago, in July 1837, the first issue of *The Pembrokeshire Congregational Magazine* was published. As far as can be ascertained its editor was the Revd. John Bulmer (1784–1857)[1] who, after training under Edward Williams at Rotherham, ministered at Albany, Haverfordwest from 1813 to 1840. Measuring 8" × 4.5" the *Magazine* was printed and published by William Perkins (fl. 1837–1880) of Market Street, Haverfordwest.[2] The last number appeared in June 1839.

The declared motives in launching the *Magazine* are interesting. There is no articulated Christian motive; rather, "If we have a spark of patriotism in our bosoms, we must desire to see a Literary Publication, the product of our own country."[3] Such a publication will foster the spirit of reading in the rising generation, "break the slumbers" of the local populace, and provide an outlet for Welsh authors against whom the *Evangelical* and *Congregational Magazines* are normally barred. As if this were not enough, "The relics of Druidism and Popery will be destroyed."[4] The *Magazine* was in its day "the only periodical, in any language, printed in Pembrokeshire,

---

1 For Bulmer see *The Dictionary of Welsh Biography*, 1959. The Pembrokeshire Library, Haverfordwest, holds the complete run of the *Magazine* with the exception of the August 1837 number. The National Library of Wales, Aberystwyth, has the issues of July 1837 and May 1839. I am grateful to Mr. Clive Hughes of the Record Office, Haverfordwest, and to Mrs. Beti Jones of the National Library for information supplied.

2 See Ifano Jones, *A History of Printing and Printers in Wales to 1810*, Cardiff 1925, 127, 131 and n. 1.

3 PCM I, 54.

4 Ibid., I, 56.

and, as far as I know, the only English one printed in Wales."[5] What were its contents?

A number of articles are devoted to extolling the congregational order. The primitive churches were congregational and independent and, *pace* the Bishop of St. David's, they were not gathered by human authority. As to polity:

> We are *Independents*, and think our independency worth preserving. It is chiefly valuable, because it leaves us at liberty to do *what our duty seems to require*; and because, *when we are disposed to do what is good and useful*, there is no one to *hinder*, or *forbid* us. Our churches have the power to *exercise their own judgment*, to *choose their own pastors*, and to *manage their own affairs*, by their own officers.[6]

Moreover, the churches comprise saints:

> We consider the act of joining a particular church of Christ, as being, eminently, a public profession of godliness, and dread the idea of persons professing what they have not; nor do we see how any can discharge the duty of church-members, or answer the important purposes of church-communion, without being *decidedly religious*.[7]

True saints are not isolationist, they know that they are "members of the *universal church of Christ*."[8] Certainly Congregationalists ought to co-operate with one another—and the twenty-fifth anniversary of the Congregational Union of Scotland, at which Dr. Ralph Wardlaw spoke on the consistency of the Congregational Union with scriptural principles was fully reported.[9]

The fullest published "Address on the Nature of a Gospel Church" was that delivered by the Revd. T. Harries of Pembroke at the settlement of the Revd. J. J. Braine at Tenby:

> Oh happy society!—glorious type of heaven! Christ its head, and governor, his word its rule, love its bond of union, the Holy Spirit its inhabitant, guide, and comforter, joy and peace for its solace

---

5 Ibid., I, 188.

6 Ibid., I, 9.

7 Ibid.

8 Ibid., I, 10.

9 Ibid., I, 93.

> under all trials,—all its wealth, gifts, and graces, its common property,—the glory of God its highest ambition![10]

Harries intends his hearers to understand that a Gospel church is:

> Founded on a revelation of the divine will; that the will of God must be declared in order to collect men into public assemblies for divine worship; that divine truth must be believed, to render our worship acceptable to God; that it must be professed, in order to our admission to church fellowship, and attendance on the ordinance of the Lord's supper; and that it is maintained by the appointment of suitable officers in the church, namely pastors and deacons.[11]

Such a church has spiritual liberty: "Voluntariness is the air it must breathe."[12]

In the second volume of the *Magazine* "J. B." defended infant baptism and enumerated its obligations: there is a sense in which we "come into him *by baptism*. But those who oppose our practice, make it necessary that a person should be *in Christ before he is baptized*." The propriety of believers' baptism is granted "if such believers were *not baptized in their infancy*, or if they are *proselytes from the Jews, or the Heathen*. . . ." Baptism "is a *seal*, or *confirming sign*, of the covenant of grace, as to its reality, and the possibility of your partaking of its advantages in God's appointed way. It assures you that Jehovah is willing to be your God; that he has provided for your salvation according to the gospel. . . ."[13] Nor did the author hesitate to urge eschatological motives upon the young *vis à vis* the kind of life which their baptism into Christ requires: "During the twenty-six years of my ministry in one place, I have now had the pleasure of devoting to God, in the solemn ordinance of baptism, no less than eighty-eight infants, who seemed as likely as children generally are, to continue their pilgrimage here below; of these, how many are now among the dead! Perhaps nearly half the number! [Hence] remember your Creator in the days of your youth."[14]

From time to time the *Magazine* refers to the practice of ministry. At the Scottish Congregational Union Assembly Dr. Russell said,

10 Ibid., I, 210.

11 I, 211–12.

12 Ibid., I, 212.

13 Ibid., II, 10–13.

14 Ibid., II, 15–16.

> It is important not only that a minister should be free from entanglements in worldly concerns, but also that his mind should be thoroughly cultivated and richly stored with useful knowledge . . . we live in an age of excitement and enquiry. . . . Let not the preachers of the gospel be behind their age. Let them strive to keep pace with the rising tide, and adapt themselves to the varying circumstances of those around them.[15]

For their part, the ministers at Llanelli Assembly resolved to establish an academy at Brecon—an earlier proposal for such an institution at Newtown having been thwarted by the London Congregational Fund Board on 21 March 1836.[16]

That at least some ministers were concerned for sound doctrine is confirmed by N. Harries's (Merlin's Bridge) tale of the Welsh pastor who routed a Socinian on the Trinity. The pastor utilized the illustration of fire, which is *all* fire, *and* heat, *and* light, and concluded: "If this can be discovered in a foundry, in a created element, doubtless it may exist in Eternity, in that which is uncreated, and full of glory." "Silent and mortified," says Harries, "the objector retired to ponder on the simple means employed to convince him of his folly and conceit."[17] Some victories were more easily won a century and a half ago.

An indication of the non-doctrinal challenges faced by ministers is given in "The state of religion and morals in Pembroke":

> It is much to be lamented that, in the streets of towns and villages, even in Wales, so many strollers and loiterers should be found on a Sabbath day, employing themselves either in making rude remarks on those who are going to or returning from places of religious worship, or otherwise conducting themselves in an improper and disgraceful manner . . . we observe in our streets, not only adults, but youths of both sexes, boys and girls, and almost infants, indulging in riot and noise, altogether careless of the sanctity of the time which they thus abuse, disturbing those who are desirous of quiet and peace.
>
> If it be asked, What is to be done to correct this increasing evil? I would say, Visit the Sunday Schools of Pembroke, and then decide whether *they* do not deserve attention?[18]

---

15 Ibid., I, 93.

16 Ibid., I, 194–96. But T. Stephens, *Album Aberhonddu*, Merthyr Tydfil 1898, 106, states that the Academy at Brecon opened on 20 February 1839, having moved there from Newtown.

17 Ibid., I, 137.

18 Ibid., I, 232–33.

In articles of a pastoral nature the duty of prayer is enjoined, as is the practice of family religion. Detailed guidance is offered by "J. G." of St. David's "On choosing partners for life":

> Be determined . . . not to take anyone who is not possessed of those qualifications which are indispensably necessary for your happiness. . . . Seek a partner similar to yourself;—similar in age, in education, in habits of life, and in taste. . . . Seek a person of prudence. Prudence will make up for many defects. . . . Avoid the haughty, domineering types (man or woman), the sordid worldling, the spendthrift, and the sullen of temper. . . . Regard should be had to the pecuniary circumstances of the person. . . . If you are desirous of being both comfortable and useful, *seek a person that feareth the Lord*. . . . Lastly, make a point of earnestly seeking direction of the Lord in this weighty concern. . . . Before I conclude, I would add, as a caution, See to it that you do not act treacherously in this affair.[19]

Among other items in the *Magazine* are obituaries—including that of J. L. Morgan of Forge, Langan, a student at Homerton College who died on 5 May 1835, aged eighteen; verse; a series of anecdotes of Rowland Hill; accounts of such Dissenting worthies as Samuel Jones and Richard Morgan; extracts from Justin Martyr and Tertullian; a serial "History of the Church and Congregation of Protestant Dissenters assembling at The Green Meeting, Haverfordwest"; and news items. From these last we note that the Pembrokeshire and Haverfordwest Auxiliary Bible Society sold 180 Bibles and 305 New Testaments during the year ended 5 July 1938; the sum of £62 4s. 1d. was received. The Pembrokeshire and Haverfordwest Sunday School Union reported 51 schools in membership, 3,835 scholars and 691 teachers. In 1836 the London Missionary Society received £516 4s. 4d. from Pembrokeshire, the Church Missionary Society £284 3s. 5d., the Baptist Missions £250 2s. 2d., the Wesleyan Missions £217 13s. 7d., and the Moravian Missions £62 12s. 8d. A total of £30 2s. 0d. was collected by the Pembrokeshire Congregational Itinerant Society for the support of Richard Morris. The Community felt sorry that the sum was not larger.

Book reviews comprise the last major category of contributions, and among these are notices of two hymn books. The first is *The Congregational Hymn Book: a Supplement to Dr. Watts's Psalms and Hymns. Compiled by direction of the Congregational Union of England and Wales* (1836):

19 Ibid., I, 235–36.

> Now, we confess that, from its earliest movements, we have viewed the Congregational Union with some little jealousy, lest, in time, it should induce our churches to abandon the primitive platform, rob them of their independency, and form them into a new body. . . . We confess, also, that our fears and jealousies have been somewhat increased by this "Congregational Hymn Book," and the means employed to secure its adoption, which have presented to us the appearance of an *Act of Uniformity*. . . . We would therefore recommend those of our Ministers, who feel that they can provide a superior hymn-book for the use of their own congregations, to employ their talents for that purpose. . . . The selection and arrangement . . . of suitable hymns for congregational use, seems more properly to belong to those who have the care and direction of divine service. . . . There are many good hymns in it . . . but the greater part of them are, in our opinion, unfit for [congregational worship] . . . we have, under the name of *Hymns* (which ought, as the term signifies, to be addressed to God) a number of essays in rhyme, declarations of faith and experience, exhortations to saints and sinners, together with frequent addresses to heaven, earth, and the human soul, which are all, in our opinion, improper in acts of worship. . . . We cannot praise the *arrangement* of this hymn-book. The plan is too complicated, and too much like the outlines of a Body of Divinity.

Some hymns, however, "have our unqualified approbation," and no. 123 is printed "partly because it is a Pembrokeshire hymn, and partly because it is suitable for our pages."[20]

The other hymnal reviewed is John Campbell's *The Comprehensive Hymn Book* (1837). With its twelve parts and one hundred and eleven sections "This very superior hymn-book is, in our opinion, too *Comprehensive*." The threefold division is preferred, "presenting us with suitable hymns for the introductory parts of divine service, and such as are to be sung before and after sermon." Among the best hymns in the book are three from Pembrokeshire (where else?), and these are quoted in the review.[21]

Not even the considerable variety of material provided could secure the survival of the *Magazine*. A letter to readers in the eighth number of the first volume contained the following lament:

> The worthy Editor has neither lot nor portion in the [*Magazine*], only in common with others, save the trouble of superintending it, without recompense . . . and I am sorry to say, that almost the whole task of supplying it with materials, is left to him alone—a

---

20 Ibid., I, 11–14.

21 Ibid., 213–17.

> sad reflection on neighbouring ministers, and other literary persons. . . .[22]

The work could not be sustained, and the preface to the bound version of volume II, dated 28 May 1839, explains that:

> Such was the diminished circulation of our little work . . . that the Editor was recommended to discontinue it in September last. . . . We exceedingly regret the want of such a Congregational Union, in the English parts of our County, as might possess a *fund* to meet the contingent *general expenses* of the Denomination . . . one of which should be the certain support of a *Pembrokeshire Congregational Magazine.*[23]

The South Wales English Congregational Union was not formed until 1899. By the time the South Wales Congregational Church Aid Society was established in 1860 John Bulmer was dead. Twenty years earlier he had left Wales for the English pastorates of Rugeley, Bristol, Newbury, and Langmore and Ruxton. The scarce copies of *The Pembrokeshire Congregational Magazine* are a not unimportant part of his elusive literary legacy.

22 Ibid., I, 187.

23 Ibid., II, Preface, iii–iv.

X

In the Wake of the Enlightenment: The Adjustments of James Martineau and Alexander Campbell Fraser

It may well be that, as some Biblical scholars advise us, prophecy is more a matter of forthtelling than of foretelling; but foretellers are ever with us. Thus, according to Dr. Bebbington,

> At the beginning of 1863 *The Record* announced that "the good sense of LOCKE, the analogies of BUTLER, and the 'Common Sense' of REID, will preserve us from the vagaries of Prussian or German Rationalists. . . ."[1]

No nineteenth-century scholar worked more assiduously to harvest the choicest philosophical fruits of the British Enlightenment, and to issue warnings concerning encroaching absolutism than Alexander Campbell Fraser (1819–1914).[2] Not, indeed, that Fraser was

---

1 D.W. Bebbington, *Evangelicalism in Modern Britain. A History from the 1730s to the 1980s*, London: Unwin Hyman 1989, 143, quoting *The Record*, 2 January 1863, 2.

2 For Fraser see DNB; A.S. Pringle-Pattison's memorial notice in *Proceedings of the British Academy*, VI, 1913–14; idem, "Alexander Campbell Fraser 1819–1914," *Mind*, NS XXIV, July 1915, 289–325; J.M. Barrie, *An Edinburgh Eleven*, 3rd edn., 1896, ch. VI. This last is a collection of sketches first published in *The British Weekly* in 1888. In a letter of 9 January 1921 Barrie reminded W. Robertson Nicoll that Dr. W.G. Grace had tossed Barrie's volume aside "on discovering that none of my eleven could bowl." See T.H. Darlow, *William Robertson Nicoll, Life and Letters*, London: Hodder & Stoughton 1925, 299. DNB describes Barrie's book as "a skit on his professors"—but skits, though humorous, can be revealing too: "I see [Fraser] rising in a daze from his chair and putting his hands through his hair. 'Do I exist' he said, thoughtfully, 'strictly so-called?' . . . It is no wonder that the students who do not go to the bottom during their first month of metaphysics begin to give themselves airs, strictly so-called." Op. cit., 58, 59. I shall later refer to the contrast between Fraser's patient probing for answers which he genuinely sought, and the articulation by Edward Caird and his pupil Henry Jones of the vision from which they set out. Cf. n. 90 below.

uninfluenced by the thought of his day; but his philosophical position was undergirded by an epistemology which owed more to Berkeley and Reid than to any others, and he sought to adjust both earlier and subsequent thought to this. Such a task could not be accomplished overnight. On the contrary, as Fraser wrote, "The perfection of philosophical opinion, and any well-grounded assurance of certainty in these high matters, are the results only of cautious, long-continued, and patient reflection."[3] Despite his efforts, however, Fraser lived to see his work eclipsed and *The Record*'s prophecy unfulfilled. By the end of the nineteenth century large tracts of British philosophy had been overtaken by an absolute idealism which could rejoice that "The unity is as real as the differences, and the differences as ideal as the unity."[4] But with this testimony of Henry Jones against the philosophy of James Martineau (1805–1900)[5] we come to the second of our two authors,

---

3 A.C. Fraser, *Essays in Philosophy*, Edinburgh 1856, iv.

4 Henry Jones, *The Philosophy of Martineau in Relation to the Idealism of the Present Day*, London: Macmillan 1905, 27. For the development of British philosophy of religion from the heyday of idealism onwards see Alan P.F. Sell, *The Philosophy of Religion 1875–1980*, London: Croom Helm and New York: Routledge 1988.

5 For Martineau see DNB; J. Julian, *Dictionary of Hymnology;* James Drummond and C.B. Upton, *The Life and Letters of James Martineau*, 2 vols., London: Nisbet 1902; A.W. Jackson, *James Martineau. A Biography and Study*, London: Longmans, Green 1900; J. Estlin Carpenter, *James Martineau, Theologian and Teacher*, London: Green 1905; James Martineau, *Biographical Memoranda* . . . at Manchester College, Oxford; S.H. Mellone, "James Martineau as an ethical teacher," *International Journal of Ethics*, X, October 1899–July 1900, 380–86; P.T. Forsyth, "Dr. Martineau," *The London Quarterly Review*, XCIII, 1900, 214–50; A. Caldecott, *The Philosophy of Religion in England and America*, London: Methuen 1901, 343–53; John Watson, "James Martineau: A saint of theism," *The Hibbert Journal*, I, 1902–3, 253–71; A.M. Fairbairn, "James Martineau," *The Contemporary Review*, LXXXIII, 1903, 1–10; Alexander H. Craufurd, *Recollections of James Martineau*, Edinburgh, 1903; C.B. Upton, *Dr. Martineau's Philosophy: A Survey*, London: Nisbet 1905; A.S. Pringle-Pattison, "Martineau's Philosophy," in idem, *The Philosophical Radicals and Other Essays*, Edinburgh: Blackwood 1907, 78–107; John Dickie, *Fifty Years of British Theology*, Edinburgh: T. & T. Clark 1937, ch. II; Horton Davies, *Worship and Theology in England. From Newman to Martineau, 1850–1900*, Princeton: Princeton University Press 1962, 271–75; A series of studies in *The Hibbert Journal* LXI, 1963; H.L. Short in C.G. Bolam *et al.*, *The English Presbyterians*, London: Allen & Unwin 1968; J.B. Scheewind, *Sidgwick's Ethics and Victorian Moral Philosophy*, Oxford: Clarendon Press 1977; Ralph Waller, "James Martineau: The development of his religious thought," in *Truth, Liberty and Religion. Essays celebrating two hundred years of Manchester College*, ed. Barbara Smith, Oxford: Manchester College 1986; and the following unpublished doctoral theses: G. McCulloh, *The Theism of James Martineau*, U. Edinburgh

and to another prophecy.

Concerning Martineau, John Watson wrote in 1902: "No one can anticipate what the readers of fifty years hence may think of the writers whom we counted masters; but one may suggest with fair grounds of reason that the critic of 1950, as he examines the department of religion in the nineteenth century, will give a foremost place to the names of Newman and Martineau."[6] With Newman we are not here concerned, but as for Martineau, we may now report that he was receiving little attention *circa* 1950. B.M.G. Reardon accords him four pages in *From Coleridge to Gore* (1971),[7] while Alasdair Heron can write on *A Century of Protestant Theology* (1980)—a work which justifiably reaches back to the Enlightenment—without mentioning Martineau at all. As for those who have written on twentieth-century Christian thought, neither John Macquarrie (*Twentieth Century Religious Thought*, 1963, etc.) nor the present writer (*The Philosophy of Religion 1875–1980*, 1988) have seen reason to refer to Martineau. As Ralph Waller has said, "It would be difficult to escape the impression that Martineau's influence on the twentieth century has been negligible."[8]

What, then, is our justification for returning now to Martineau and Fraser (for, like Martineau, Fraser has not regularly been invoked in the philosophical discussions of this century)? Simply this: that these two nonagenarians lived through most of a century in which it proved necessary both to harvest the results of the Enlightenment and to apply those results to a rapidly changing world of thought. In the new intellectual climate Deism was no longer the "enemy," and debate restricted entirely to the field of Christian doctrine[9] would have entailed the shelving of the apologetic task made urgent by current materialism, naturalism, agnosticism and pantheism. Against all of these Martineau and Fraser set their faces, and nowhere were their adjustments more agonising (and in Martineau's case more ambiguous) than in

1938; R. Waller, *James Martineau: His emergence as a Theologian, his Christology, and his Doctrine of the Church*, U. London 1986.

6 J. Watson, art. at n. 5 above, 253.

7 Subsequently republished under the title, *Religious Thought in the Victorian Age*, London: Longmans 1980.

8 R. Waller in *Truth, Liberty and Religion*, 259.

9 There was, of course, a good deal of nineteenth-century discussion of Christian doctrine—and Martineau contributed significantly to it. Here, however, we must concentrate upon themes on which both Martineau and Fraser wrote. Undeniably, Martineau's writings cover a much wider range—philosophical, theological, pastoral, homiletic, ecclesiastical, political—than do Fraser's.

respect of the last. By the time (largely in their retirement years) they felt ready to publish their philosophical summations absolute idealism was a philosophical force in Britain. They both charged absolutism with pantheising tendencies, and in face of it they sharpened their eighteenth-century philosophical tools.

Their philosophical progress was interestingly different. During the course of his career Fraser worked patiently through the major British philosophers of the eighteenth century (with sidelong glances at Leibniz, Spinoza and others) in the order of Berkeley, Locke and Reid. Hume provided an ever-present challenge. It was only following his retirement from the Chair of Logic and Metaphysics at the University of Edinburgh at the age of seventy-two that Fraser's appointment as Gifford Lecturer elicited from him his *Philosophy of Theism* (1896). In this work he finally drew the strands of his world view together.

Martineau, on the other hand, reached his main conclusions much earlier in life, but the exigencies of his teaching and public duties gave him no leisure to offer his major works to the public until he was in sight of his retirement from the Principalship of Manchester College, Oxford, in 1885. Whereas Fraser's thought matured to its conclusion towards the end of his long life, Martineau's major works, on publication, seemed even to the friendliest of critics, to bear the marks of the debates of fifty years earlier.[10] Since truth is not determined by weight of numbers, or by accordance with prevailing philosophical fashion, this does not, of course, render Martineau's contribution worthless.

Martineau and Fraser were led, by somewhat different routes, to espouse ethical theism. Their accents are not identical, however. We shall find that while neither failed to grasp "the fundamental facts of moral experience."[11] Fraser's emphasis is more epistemological, Martineau's more psychological. Where Fraser asks, "What can we know (that is, what can our minds encompass)?" Martineau's question is, "What is the ground of our moral experience?"

We shall first discover how Martineau and Fraser adjusted themselves to their Enlightenment inheritance, and then see how they used it in their own time. As we proceed we shall be greatly assisted by the accounts of their philosophical pilgrimages which have come down to us from their own hands.

---

10 See, e.g., J.E. Carpenter, *James Martineau*, 550; P.T. Forsyth, art. cit. at n. 5 above, 226; A.S. Pringle-Pattison, *The Philosophical Radicals*, 80; J.H. Muirhead, *Reflections by a Journeyman in Philosophy*, London: Allen & Unwin 1942, 67.

11 The phrase is J.E. Carpenter's, see op. cit., 546.

I

"It is with deliberate conviction that I profess adherence to the English psychological method, and build all my hope for philosophy on accurate self-knowledge."[12] Thus Martineau in his address at the beginning of the 1854 session of Manchester New College, London. But this "deliberate conviction" was that of one who had served a protracted period of seeking and questioning, as a result of which he repudiated the philosophical tradition in which he had been nurtured.

In his Preface to *Types of Ethical Theory*, dated 1 January 1885, Martineau explains that he had brought to "moral and metaphysical speculations" a scientific background and a training in civil engineering. He was thus predisposed towards empiricism and necessarianism, and he "served out successive terms of willing captivity to Locke and Hartley, to Collins, Edwards and Priestley, to Bentham and James Mill." When his allegiance to this tradition was threatened by the "dogmatism and acrid humours" of Bentham and Mill, personal contact with John Stuart Mill drew him back.[13] In the philosophical discussion groups which Martineau conducted during the early years of his Liverpool pastorate (1832–40) he was content to expound James Mill's *Analysis of the Phenomena of the Human Mind* (1829) and the views of Thomas Brown—especially those concerning cause and effect, concepts which Brown cashed in associationist terms.

But a change of direction was pending. Negatively, and owing to its exaltation of actions above motives, Bentham's *Deontology*, which Martineau reviewed in *The Monthly Repository*, fuelled his conviction that disinterested affections have a worth which eudaemonianism may not be permitted to deny. On this matter Martineau was at one with Carlyle, whom he held in high esteem; and he reiterated his opinion in *The Rationale of Religious Enquiry* (1836). Positively, he came increasingly under the influence of his favourite poets, Wordsworth and Coleridge; and his affection for F.D. Maurice was deep.[14] Martineau could also learn from Newman, and he was

12 James Martineau, "A plea for philosophical studies," in his *Essays Philosophical and Theological*, 1869, 424.

13 James Martineau, *Types of Ethical Theory*, [1885], 3rd edn. 1891, viii–ix.

14 See *Life and Letters*, I, 452; J.E. Carpenter, *James Martineau*, 438. See also Jeremy Goring's illuminating Essex Hall Lecture for 1987, *Where to Belong Religiously: Martineau, Maurice and the Unitarian Dilemma*, London: Unitarian Publications 1987. Interestingly, Coleridge, Maurice and Martineau were all raised in

later to place the erstwhile Anglican in the company of Coleridge and Carlyle (with generous accompanying references to Maurice), speaking of them all thus: "when they are interpreted by their inner spirit, rather than by their outward relations, one thought will be found secreted at the heart of all—the perennial Indwelling of God in Man and in the Universe . . . however threatening the mists from which [this idea] has to clear itself, it is the dawn of a truth. . . . To them, and not to the noisy devotees and pharisees of party, do we look for the faith of the future."[15] Again, from Channing Martineau was learning of the God within, in respect of whom Biblical literalism and external theistic "evidences" were alike redundant.[16] As Carpenter has it: "Listen to the proclamation of the Christian's duty—'To set up within our mind an ideal of perfected goodness, the very image of Christ, to aim at expressing its beauty in the life, and, in spite of failure, to renew the faithful effort day by day, to feel a fresh penitence at every fall, and rise again saddened but not defeated,' and you detect the devotional idiom, not of the follower of Priestley, but of the student of Channing."[17] Above all, as his Liverpool lecture on "The Christian view of moral evil" makes plain, Martineau could not square necessarianism with the idea of a *holy* God who could not be implicated in evil.

Appointed to teach at Manchester New College, Manchester in 1840, Martineau found that

---

Unitarianism, Martineau alone remaining there—but in his own way. In 1850 Fraser, then on a visit to London, found a "sympathetic friend" in F.D. Maurice: "I found in him a larger humanity than in the abstract theology and ecclesiastical polemic of Scotland." See his *Biographia Philosophica*, Edinburgh: Blackwood 1904, 140–41. Fraser eventually left the Free for the Episcopal Church.

15 James Martineau, "Personal influences on our present theology: Newman—Coleridge—Carlyle," [*National Review*, October 1856], in *Essays Philosophical and Theological*, 404–05. The sermon quoted, "Christian self-reverence" (John 12:24, 25), was delivered in Liverpool in 1835 and London in 1870.

16 See Geoffrey Rowell, *Hell and the Victorians*, Oxford: Clarendon Press 1974, 52–53. Were I concerned with the total scope of Martineau's thought, and not only with his philosophy, I should have to note his critique of that "priestly" religion of external rites to which his inwardness led him, and in which connection he learned from Joseph Blanco White, who arrived in Liverpool from Dublin in 1835. See R. Waller, *Truth, Liberty and Religion*, 240–42. For Martineau on Channing see his "William Ellery Channing: Memoir and Papers," [*Prospective Review*, August 1848, and *Westminster Review*, 1849], *Essays, Reviews and Addresses*, 1890, I, 81–148.

17 J.E. Carpenter, *James Martineau*, 174, quoting Martineau's *National Duties and other Sermons*, 1835, 261.

> the more I scrutinised the physical science assumptions, which I had carried as axioms into philosophy, the less could I rest in them as ultimate and valid for all thought. Above all, I had to concede to the self-conscious mind itself, both as knowing and as willing, an autonomous function distinct from each and all the phenomena known and changes willed,—a self-identity, as unlike as possible to any growing aggregate of miscellaneous and dissimilar experiences. Visiting me first as mere suspicions, these ideas insensibly loosened the set attitude of my convictions, before I became distinctly conscious of a gradual veering in the direction of my thought: the same text-books were still in use, though doubtless with more frequent comments of dissent; but in effect, I was educating myself out of a school into which I supposed that I was educating others. . . .
>
> It was the irresistible pleading of the moral consciousness which first drove me to rebel against the limits of the merely scientific conception. . . . The secret misgivings which I had always felt at either discarding or perverting the terms which constitute the vocabulary of character,—"responsibility," "guilt," "merit," "duty,"—came to a head, and insisted upon speaking out and being heard. . . .[18]

In his *Biographical Memoranda* Martineau further explains that

> The change of view was very inconvenient to me. Almost everything I had written became worthless in my eyes: the familiar text-books could no longer be used in that capacity in my private classes: and every subject had to be melted down again in my own mind, and be recast in other moulds. For all this however there was ample compensation, in the sense of inward deliverance which I seemed to gain from artificial system into natural speech. It was an escape from a logical cage into the open air.[19]

In a word, Martineau had concluded that "ought" takes precedence over "is," that voluntary moral causation is ineluctable, and that therefore determinism was untenable. As he later expressed it in the course of an exposition of Coleridge's thought:

> It is precisely in the *freedom of the will* that a person is distinguished from a thing, and becomes a possible subject of moral law. And so it is in the recognition of a good other than the sentient, of an authority transcending all personal preference, of a right over us and our whole cargo of "happiness," actual and potential, that the sense of Duty and the conditions of morality

18 James Martineau, *Types of Ethical Theory*, I, xi, xii–xiii.

19 Idem, *Biographical Memoranda*, 19.

> begin. Hence Edwards and the necessarians, Priestley and the materialists, Paley and the Epicureans, depict a universe from which all moral qualities and beings, divine or human, are excluded: and whether reasoning down from God as absolute *Sovereign*, or up from man as simply *sentient*, miss whatever is august and holy in its life.[20]

Martineau's change of direction did not escape the attention of J.S. Mill. Acknowledging receipt of Martineau's course syllabus and introductory lecture, Mill wondered, "Are not your general metaphysical opinions a shade or two more German than they used to be?"[21]

The conclusions to which Martineau had been led were soon to be undergirded by Maine de Biran, Royer-Collard, Jouffroy and Cousin—especially by Cousin's critique of Locke. Further support was to come from some German philosophers. Martineau relates that a fifteen-month period of leave (1848–9) was spent under the guidance of the German Aristotelian scholar Trendelenberg, under whom Martineau experienced "a new intellectual birth."[22] In particular, he found such a new understanding of self-consciousness as "lifted the darkness from the pages of Kant and even Hegel," and came to see than, as with morality, so with cosmology:

> never again could I say that phenomena, in their clusters and chains, were all, or find myself in a universe with no categories but the like and unlike, the synchronous and successive. The possible also *is*, whether it happens or not; and its categories of the right, the beautiful, the necessarily true, may have their contents defined and held ready for realisation, whatever centuries lapse ere they appear. To do this is the work, not of objective science, but of self-reflection.
>
> By this division of labour, the whole group of natural sciences is left absolutely free to legitimate development, without the possibility of collision with Ethics.[23]

---

20 Idem, "Personal influences on our present theology," 372–73.

21 Mill to Martineau, 21 May 1841; quoted by C.B. Upton, *Dr. Martineau's Philosophy*, 23.

22 James Martineau, *Types of Ethical Theory*, I, xiii.

23 Ibid., xiv. It is interesting to note that Upton (op. cit., 161) finds it "somewhat remarkable" that there is no clear evidence that Martineau's intellectual conversion owed anything to the Scottish intuitionists, Reid and Stewart. But on p. 25 he mentions Martineau's affinity with Royer-Collard and Jouffroy, who had introduced the Scots to French students. Perhaps, therefore, Martineau was influenced by the Scottish school at one remove. It certainly seems too much to say, with James Lindsay, that Martineau "set out from Reid and Hamilton." In

But if the German experience lifted the darkness from Kant's pages, Martineau was not blinded by the light. In his College lectures he declared that

> We solve no mystery . . . by plunging into the *idealism*, to which, as Jacobi has conclusively shown, Kant's doctrine of the pure subjectivity of space and time inevitably leads; hence, while we admit that they are objects of *a priori* knowledge given us through the subjective action of our own perceptive faculty, we must retain them as objects of real and not imaginary knowledge,—the infinite, uncreated, eternal data which constitute the negative conditions of all being and all phaenomena.[24]

This, as we shall see, is to veer in the direction of Berkeley as interpreted by Fraser. But it was the ethical deficiency of the Germans which most disturbed Martineau:

> It is my sad persuasion that the direction taken by *all* recent German philosophy, though comprising nominally opposite schools, is quite irreconcilable not only with Christianity, but with all forms of religion which place men under a Personal God and a proper Law of Duty. Their theories have been developed just as they would have been if the principles of action and the moral sentiments had for the last half-century been absolutely *scored out* of human nature, and men had been made up entirely of the ingredients requisite for the dialectician, the naturalist, and the artist.[25]

It is possible that this harsh judgment, which seems unjust to Kant's exaltation of the moral, was, as J.H. Muirhead suggests, prompted by the fact that Trendelenberg had "entirely missed the deeper significance of Kant's teaching. No wonder, that instead of following the clue that Kant had put into the hands of his successors, Fichte, Schelling and Hegel, Martineau was fain to fall back on a form of intuitionalism, resembling that of Jacobi, which at the time was the other alternative to the reigning empiricism. . . ."[26] It is also possible, however, that Muirhead is somewhat unjust to

---

Donald Macmillan, *The Life of Robert Flint*, London: Hodder & Stoughton 1914, 357. C.B. Upton (op. cit., 16–17) finds it "somewhat remarkable that there is no clear evidence" of Martineau's being influenced by his Unitarian forebear, Richard Price.

24 Quoted by C.B. Upton, *Dr. Martineau's Philosophy*, 30.

25 Martineau to J.H. Thom, 25 February 1849; quoted by C.B. Upton, op. cit., 77.

26 J.H. Muirhead, *Reflections by a Journeyman in Philosophy*, 66.

Martineau, who was seeking to find his philosophical feet in an intellectual climate among the ingredients of which was an agnosticism which had taken off (however one-sidedly) from *Kant's* epistemology. Moreover, were not idealists on all hands flirting with pantheism? This, at least, was Martineau's conviction. So it was that he attempted to steer a middle course between empiricism and Deism on the one hand, and idealism and pantheism on the other: "Against Pantheism he never ceased to protest on behalf of individual liberty; and against empiricism, whether starting from the side of mind, like that of the Mills, or of society and history, like that of Comte, he waged unceasing war on behalf of the permanent realities which underlie all appearances, and supply the imperishable ideas of space and time, of substance and cause, the soul and God."[27] We shall examine some of Martineau's particular proposals in due course, but meanwhile we must turn to Fraser in order to see how he gradually developed the position in which he finally rested.

II

Whereas Martineau, having come quite early to his intense conviction of the ineradicability of the voluntary will as causative, proceeded to employ his discovery as a criterion by which to measure alternative theories which came his way, the impression which Fraser gives is of one who proceeded much more cautiously. His epistemological *question* is never far from his mind, and for many years he devoted himself to textual criticism. Only then did he feel able to adumbrate his *via media*, which is that between omniscience and nescience. To follow this path requires the frank recognition of the limitations of the human mind; we are summoned to the "final venture" of faith—faith conceived as a properly *rational* response to the ultimate mystery by which we are confronted. Where Martineau's criterion shows him which theories will not do, Fraser's question prompts him to plough the eighteenth-century philosophical soil (especially the British soil), with a view to discovering what harvest it may yield.

"In 1836," writes Fraser of his student days, "philosophy was at a lower ebb in Scotland than at any time since the advent of Francis Hutcheson from Ireland to Glasgow, rather more than a century before. . . ."[28] Thomas Brown, Dugald Stewart and James Mackin-

---

27 J. E. Carpenter, *James Martineau*, 548.

28 A.C. Fraser, *Biographia Philosophica: A Retrospect*, 46.

tosh were dead; Hamilton's star had not yet arisen—neither had those of Schopenhauer and Comte in Europe. There, "Hegel was lately dead," though he and the currently lively Cousin and Schelling "were all unknown in the Scottish universities."[29]

In this vacuum Fraser, puzzled by the concepts of "cause" and "power," turned to Brown's *Inquiry into the Relation of Cause and Effect* for guidance. Brown's *quasi*-positivistic solution provided temporary relief (as it had for Martineau), "But by degrees the prospect clouded. . . . How am I justified by reason, when I believe that a series in the universe *is* inexorably constant [as Brown declared it could be]?"[30] From this perplexity a reading of Hume's *Treatise of Human Nature* did nothing whatever to deliver him! On the contrary, total scepticism threatened. "In this uncertainty," he continues, "I adopted [Descartes's] method for not remaining paralysed in action, although pure reason only admitted doubt. Like him I thought I could not do better than follow meantime the opinions of those among whom I lived; and prefer, among their discordant opinions, the most moderate, as probably the best, since extremes are commonly erroneous."[31]

Further light dawned as, in the summer of 1838, Fraser "increased [his] acquaintance with Berkeley, and was introduced to Coleridge, besides listening to echoes of Kant. Berkeley helped to make living mind instead of dead matter prominent."[32] But Coleridge's *Aids to Reflection* was crucial in dislodging Brown's mechanical view of causation from Fraser's mind and, influenced by John Wilson's lectures on moral philosophy, he became convinced of "an originating cause, as essentially efficient and teleological, exemplified only in acts of intending Will."[33] The similarity between Fraser's philosophical conversion and Martineau's—and of both as centring in ethical considerations—is clear. Significantly, during his theological course under Thomas Chalmers, to whom Jonathan Edwards was "the prince of modern theologians," Fraser was repelled by the "wholly necessitated universe of Edwards [which] seemed to resolve the wicked volitions of persons into necessitated sequences, thus making an evil act an effect for which the apparent agent could not be responsible."[34]

29 Ibid., 47.

30 Ibid., 50.

31 Ibid., 52.

32 Ibid., 53.

33 Ibid., 54.

34 Ibid., 68.

During the winter of 1838–9 Fraser, now a graduate, was in close contact with William Hamilton—"I owe more to Hamilton than to any other intellectual influence. He moved us all to think out questions for ourselves."[35] By the end of the winter, "the world of the senses had receded; the world of living mind appeared to reduce it to subordinate reality. Causes independent of physical nature began to take precedence of the caused causes that depend mechanically upon certain antecedent phenomena. A dualism [of the starry heaven above and the moral law within], partly suggested by Kant, was now coming dimly into view."[36] This dualism prompted his reflection upon our common sense as "a reservoir which holds for us in a latent state the *rationale* upon which human action and knowledge at last depend, and which it is the work of the philosopher to interpret."[37] Fraser also found that "Butler's reverential submission to reality was always refreshing."[38] As enlightenment gradually dawned, Fraser heard, but was not overcome by, Chalmers's advice that those disinclined to study German philosophy should not "suspend for it their ordinary readings. Their very ignorance of German idealism, the very confinement of their mental philosophy to the doctrines and metaphysics of the Scottish school, are guarantees in themselves against the deleterious influence of these outlandish speculations."[39] Over against Chalmers's "inductive science of mental phenomena in man" Fraser increasingly placed "the divine rationale of the universe, which Berkeley alone among British metaphysicians approached, and which German philosophers were labouring to articulate."[40]

From 1843 onwards Fraser increasingly felt the force of J.S. Mill's *System of Logic*: "My old questions about the *trustworthiness* of any interpretations of the appearances with which we come into contact in sense again became urgent."[41] Accordingly, he returned to Aristotle, and to Locke's epistemology, "supplemented and corrected by Kant. My inclination was to an English manner of treatment, so far as it keeps firm hold of what is given in concrete experience, under conditions of place and time, and refuses to pursue a unity that is possible for men only in a world of abstractions. I seemed to

35 Ibid., 58.

36 Ibid., 59.

37 Ibid., 60.

38 Ibid., 65.

39 Ibid., 74.

40 Ibid., 133.

41 Ibid., 137.

find that in philosophy things must *at last* be 'left abrupt,' as Bacon puts it."[42] This is a statement of the very greatest importance for the understanding of Fraser: Bacon's abruptness becomes for him the entry-point for *rationally grounded* faith.

The advent of Hegelianism in Britain sharpened some of Fraser's questions, and he came to express his *via media* thus:

> On the one hand there was scientific Naturalism, with its dogmatic assumption of progressive and regressive evolution as final synthesis,—all beyond this, the darkness of the Unknowable. On the other side was the new gnostic Idealism, bound by its profession to eliminate all mysteries, and at last to reach infinite science of Reality. . . .
>
> I found myself on a *Via Media*, repelled alike from an agnostic science wholly ignorant of God, and from a gnostic science which implied Omniscience.[43]

His way forward, prompted by Locke, Kant and Hegel, was through his own interpretation of Berkeley:

> I expanded Berkeley's divine language of vision into a universal sense-symbolism, and our moral consciousness of our own free agency into perfect moral agency at the heart of the Whole. Implicates of pure reason, which with Kant make human reason possible, led to implicates of moral reason, which presuppose the universe of reality to be morally constituted reality, although by us incompletely interpretable. I gradually came to think of this theistic faith, not as an infinite conclusion empirically founded in finite facts, but as the necessary presupposition of all human conclusions about anything.[44]

En route to this conclusion Fraser had become convinced that Hume was the true heir of Locke, and that although Berkeley had often been treated as a sceptic who placed no reliance upon sensation, he was in fact a spiritual *realist*. This interpretation is developed in Fraser's edition of Berkeley's *Works* (1871)—an undertaking which greatly enlarged Fraser's reputation; in his *Berkeley* (1881); in various articles, and in his last book, *Berkeley and Spiritual Realism* (1908). His view was confirmed as he sandwiched

---

42 Ibid., 138.

43 Ibid., 184, 186. This theme is frequently reiterated; see, e.g., A.C. Fraser, *Berkeley*, Edinburgh: Blackwood 1881, 232–34, and *Thomas Reid*, Edinburgh: Oliphant 1898, 155.

44 Ibid., 188–89.

his *Encyclopaedia Britannica* article on Locke (1890), his book *Locke* (1891), and his edition of Locke's *Essay* (1894) between his Berkeleian writings; and was further vindicated by his study of *Thomas Reid* (1898).

We may, in summary, say that as Fraser looked back on the period of the Enlightenment, he found that *the* philosophical problem was posed by Locke's epistemology; and that if the scepticism of Hume and later agnosticism on the one hand, and the "gnosticism" of the absolute idealists on the other were to be avoided, recourse must be had to Berkeley and Reid, both suitably adjusted by Kant and Coleridge.[45] Only so would epistemology be humble—indeed, human. Only so would morality be preserved and due account be taken of the fact of mystery. So convinced was Fraser of this that at times he can sound almost pessimistic: "The only conviction which the student of the history of human speculation can regard as necessary is the conviction of our hopeless ignorance of all the mysteries of existence. Truth, like the Deity, is hid in darkness. It is not that we are unable to divine the mysteries of the soul and God; the simplest phenomenon of common sense defies our wit."[46] Not surprisingly, "It is . . . evident that the perfect philosophy must recognise and include a body of first principles, resting on faith, by which all knowledge of things divine and human must be regulated."[47] At the conclusion of his book on Locke Fraser once again reasserted his *via media*:

> One seems to hear three conflicting voices in the course of [the preceding two] centuries. The response to the philosophic question made by one of them is—that "nothing can be known because nothing may be presupposed, except indeed the mechanical presuppositions of natural science." An opposite philosophical utterance comes from another quarter: "The universe may be seen through and through, and its secret is revealed in the light of the

---

45 I do not overlook the fact that Fraser judged Reid guilty of misinterpreting Berkeley's system: "He misconceived its whole purport. He misrepresented its every tenet. He imported into it a monstrous chimaera, which made it a chaos of contradictions; and while Berkeley was in reality to be identified with Plato, with Cudworth, and with Clarke, identified him with Gassendi, Hobbes, and Condillac." See his "Berkeley's idealism," *The North British Review* XXXIV no. LXVIII, May 1861, 456. Fraser's point is that Reid is mistaken in holding that philosophers from Plato to Hume believe that the object of perception is some image present to the mind (463). In fact, while Berkeley does describe ideas as "real beings" he means that we cannot "separate, even in thought, any of our ideas from *perception*" (467).

46 Ibid., 480.

47 A.C. Fraser, "Life and philosophy of Leibnitz," *Essays in Philosophy*, 34.

> Divine Reason that is immanent in it." These two voices are apt to overbear the third, which pleads that man may see enough to justify the faith that he is living and moving and having his being in a universe in which Nature is in harmony with, yet subordinate to, the ethical and spiritual Order with which his higher faculties connect him; and that the more his latent faith or inspiration is made to respond, by reflection and by the facts of history, the more clearly each man can see the little that is intellectually visible at the human point of insight, and the more wisely and religiously he can direct his life.[48]

III

Having now observed the adjustments of Martineau and Fraser to their intellectual inheritance we must compare and contrast their findings on specific themes to which they both devoted attention. We shall first reaffirm the major points of comparison between them: they both understand reality as spiritual; they regard human beings *qua* intellectual and moral agents as holding the clue to the meaning of existence; and they are both ethical theists.

As we saw, Martineau's repugnance for Priestley's necessarianism was inspired by his consciousness of moral freedom. This led him to draw a clear distinction between mechanical causation and moral agency. Characteristically, he was prepared to find what common ground he could with the position to which he was in general opposed: "The libertarian, in refusing to surrender a free personal power, does not dispute the influence of either the immediate 'motives' of the 'formed character,' to which exclusively the necessarian attributes the action. . . . It is perfectly possible for a free mind to behave as it would if it were not free: and there is no small portion of human life in which it may legitimately do so"—as in habitual acts and "*Single-motivated* acts, which are dictated by some uncontested want."[49] Despite such concessions, Martineau stoutly maintained his distinction and, consistently with it, he denied the possibility of explaining ethical values in non-ethical categories. On this basis he dissociated himself from the hedonism of Hobbes, Bentham and Bain; the moral sense views of Shaftesbury and Hutcheson; and, although he ended close to the intellectual intuitionism of Cudworth, Clarke and Price, his favoured "ideo-psychological" approach, heralded by Butler and the Scottish

48 A.C. Fraser, *Locke*, Edinburgh: Blackwood 1891, 296.

49 James Martineau, *A Study of Religion*, Oxford: Clarendon Press, 2nd edn., 1900, II, 243–44.

common sense philosophers and their Paris disciples, "who have declined to betray their science to the physiologist on the one hand, and the ontologist on the other,"[50] enabled him to emphasise the conscience, and to regard moral judgments as the articulation "of what is given to us ready-made."[51]

It is crucially important that we note Martineau's resistance to subjectivism at this point. He will learn from Kant's emphasis upon the sense of obligation under which we stand, but he construes this after the manner of a spiritual realist. The moral law is not self-proposed; it is proposed to us by One who stands higher than ourselves, to whom we are "immediately introduced."[52] We need to know that the "gleaming ideal is the everlasting Real . . . the abiding presence and persuasion of the Soul of souls."[53] This "dual relation" is essential. Duty "cannot belong to a soul *in vacuo*, but must be for ever a disconsolate and wandering illusion, till it rests with Him to whom the allegiance is due."[54] Apart from this duality we have no freedom, and are back to pantheism in either its necessarian or absolutist form.

With the capital "H" we arrive at Martineau's theism. He declares that "Ethics must either perfect themselves in religion, or disintegrate themselves into Hedonism; and . . . there is an inevitable gravitation in all anti-theological thinkers to the 'greatest happiness' doctrine."[55] As he elsewhere wrote, bringing causation and morality together, "Faith in the Infinite God seems to have a twofold root; viz., in the Axioms, or first truths, of Reason, and, distinctively, in the necessary idea of *Causation*, which supplies the *dynamical* element of Theism; and in the Intuitions of *Conscience*, which constrain us to know that our moral life is a Trust, susceptible of sympathy with the Divine life or of alienation from it. This supplies the faith in a *Holy* as well as a Causal God."[56] The most succinct statement of the matter occurs in Martineau's opening lecture of the 1878 session of Manchester New College, London: "Devout faith is a belief of *real Being* on the strength of *what ought*

50 James Martineau, *Types of Ethical Theory*, I, 20.

51 Idem, *A Study of Religion*, II, 6.

52 Ibid., II, 27.

53 Ibid., I, 12.

54 Ibid., II, 27.

55 Ibid., I, 24.

56 Letter of 1857 to J.J. Thom, quoted by C.B. Upton, *Dr. Martineau's Philosophy*, 38.

to be."[57] As S.H. Mellone rightly pointed out, for Martineau our knowledge of God is not so much an inference from the moral consciousness as a "deeper insight into what the moral consciousness verily is."[58] As Martineau's definition has it, "The word of conscience is the voice of God."[59] We should not, however, have done justice to Martineau if we did not note his important caveat:

> We have said, that in the Conscience and Moral Affections we have our *only* revealers of God. Let it be understood that we mean our

---

57 James Martineau, *Ideal Substitutes for God*, 1878, 13.

58 Quoted by S.D.F. Salmond in his review of S.H. Mellone, *Leaders of Religious Thought in the Nineteenth Century* (1902) in *The Critical Review*, XIII, 1903, 69.

59 James Martineau, *The Seat of Authority in Religion*, London: Longmans 1890, 71. Cf. *Types of Ethical Theory*, II, 104–05. It was partly because Martineau thus appeared to make morality captive to theism (and hence impossible for atheists); partly because he too readily assumed that his own sensitive conscience was typical of all consciences; and partly because of his emphasis upon an hierarchy of motives to the (almost complete) exclusion of teleological considerations, that Martineau found himself at odds with Henry Sidgwick's utilitarianism. Martineau, however, fully realised that since moral evaluations entailed comparisons, the resulting judgments would vary in accordance with the societal and personal position of the judge. See *Types of Ethical Theory*, II, 74–77. He even granted (though Widgery questions his psychology here) that "the computation [of pleasure and pain] is already more or less involved in the preference of this or that spring of action; for in proportion as the springs of action are self-conscious, they contemplate their own effects, and judgment upon them is included in our judgment of the disposition." Ibid., 275. Further, in a letter to G. Lyon Turner of 27 February 1886 Martineau wrote: "Consequences once foreseen and contemplated become *intentions*, and are transposed into the *springs*: for, being consequences to *some one* for 'better or worse,' they touch the affections, which insist on being heard and having their voice in the decision of the Will." Quoted by J.E. Carpenter, *James Martineau*, 563–64. A.G. Widgery writes: "in discussing conflicts between impulses, Martineau, says Sidgwick, implicity appealed to the canon of consequences. On his part, Martineau might have urged that the idea of a scale of values could also be applied to consequences, and that Sidgwick's Utilitarian principle is unsatisfactory as a basis for moral decision between alternative sets of consequences." See Widgery's chapter in H. Sidgwick, *Outlines of the History of Ethics*, [1886], London: Macmillan 1949, 304. But Martineau did urge this: "Throughout his criticism Professor Sidgwick has lost sight of the place which I expressly reserve for his utilitarian *canon of consequences*, and has argued as if I proposed to work out a *code of morals* from intuitive data. He does not notice the fact that I only give *priority* to the *canon of obligation proper*, and contend that consequences to the general happiness can carry no obligation, *unless the altruistic affections are in their nature invested with authority over impulses that conflict with them*; so that we must go to the scale of impulses before we proceed to the reckoning of consequences." *Types of Ethical Theory*, II, 300. See further H. Sidgwick, *The Methods of Ethics*, London: Macmillan 1874; C.B. Upton, *Dr. Martineau's Philosophy*, *passim*; J.B. Schneewind, *Sidgwick's Ethics and Victorian Moral Philosophy*, ch. VIII.

> only *internal* revealers of Him; . . . We mean to state that, without this faculty, the bare intellect, the mere scientific and reasoning power, could make no way towards the knowledge of divine realities. . . . But we do *not* mean to state that the Moral Sense can stand alone, dispense with all outward instruction, and supply a man with a natural religion ready made. Nor do we mean that the every-day experiences of man, and the ordinary providences of God, are enough, without special revelation, to lead us to heavenly truth. And we are therefore prepared to advance another step, and to say, that, while regarding the human consciousness as the only inward revealer of God, we have FAITH in CHRIST as *his perfect and transcendent outward revelation*. We conceive that Jesus of Nazareth lived and died, not to *persuade* the Father, not to *appease* the Father, not to make a sanguinary *purchase* from the Father, but simply to '*show* us the Father.'[60]

With Martineau's general conclusion as to the reality of the world *qua* spiritual, and of the viability of ethical theism, Fraser is in complete accord. However, he reaches his conclusion in his own way. Unlike Martineau, Fraser does not treat us to an extended analysis of conscience; he is less psychological in approach. He does not, for example, seek to classify motives as Martineau does, nor does he work his way in detail through alternative ethical theories. His interests are, as we have seen, governed by the epistemological question. Where Martineau stakes his all on conscience (albeit conscience as influenced and supported from elsewhere), Fraser declares that "It is to the necessary implicates of consciousness in man, not to phenomena presented to the senses, that we should look for the true key, at least the best key within man's reach."[61]

We shall do well to summarise Fraser's position as found in its maturest form in *Philosophy of Theism*. He here finds that we are under the obligation of presupposing a cosmic order that is eternally trustworthy and divine. Otherwise the cosmos would not be "even physically interpretable."[62] Again, "The trustworthiness of my original nature, and the interpretability of universal nature, *presuppose* the constant action of the morally perfect Power at the heart of the Whole."[63] Not indeed that we can fully penetrate the mystery which lies at the heart of all things. There is a proper

---

60 James Martineau, *Studies of Christianity*, London: Longmans 1879, 192–93.

61 A.C. Fraser, *Philosophy of Theism*, 141.

62 Ibid., 139.

63 Ibid., 176.

agnosticism—not least a Christian one. The latter is quite different in kind from Hamilton's Kantian modification to the effect that we do not have infinite knowledge.[64]

At the heart of the cosmos stands the human being. We are supernatural in that we are self-determining causes. Furthermore, we are conscious of a supreme Power. But this Power is not sheer force: it is moral through and through; and this we conclude from the goodness which we ourselves pursue, and from the consciousness of moral obligation in which we live:

> If scientific faith is *baseless* confidence that the world will not in the end put to *intellectual* confusion those who rely on the universality of its natural order, religious faith not only gives its basis to this physical faith, but is the *absolute* assurance that the Supreme Power will not put to permanent *moral* confusion those who strive to realise the true ideal of man, assured that the universe it eternally working for good to those who thus live. God represented in the Ideal Man is, for man, the revelation of perfect goodness on the throne of the universe.[65]

As between atheism (excluded by the *reductio ad absurdum* of total nescience), and pantheism (whose *reductio ad absurdum* is its implicit human omniscience), "Theistic faith gave the reasonable conviction that is found under a knowledge that must be ultimately incomplete. *In tenebris semper* might be the formula of Atheism; *In Luce Divina* that of Pantheism; *In tenebris Lux* was the intermediate formula of Theistic Philosophy."[66]

Let us pause for a moment in order to relate what Fraser is doing to his seventeenth- and eighteenth-century philosophical inheritance. James Seth concluded that whereas "Martineau's philosophy is simply a revised version of the Natural Realism and the Natural Theology of the earlier Scottish philosophers, Fraser's is a moral idealism, a new philosophy of theism which has shaped for itself a *via media* between the deism of the eighteenth century and the pantheism of the nineteenth."[67] Seth here underestimates

64 Hence, for example, Fraser's objection to Ferrier's claim that our necessary knowledge is absolute. See his *Essays in Philosophy*, 321 f.

65 A.C. Fraser, *Philosophy of Theism*, 152–53.

66 Idem, *Biographia Philosophica*, 322. Cf. his "Introductory Lecture of Logic and Metaphysics" in *Inauguration of the New College, Edinburgh*, Edinburgh 1851, 171–72; and his paper on "Philosophical development," *Mind*, no. 57, January 1890, 9–10.

67 J. Seth, *English Philosophers and Schools of Philosophy*, London: Dent 1912, 310.

Martineau, as we shall see; he correctly notes Fraser's middle course, but what interests us at the moment is his description of Fraser's theism as "new." James Lindsay bluntly disagreed with this description: Fraser's "philosophy of theism, which Professor Seth calls 'new,' is an amalgam of Locke, Berkeley and Coleridge."[68] It is more than that, as we have seen; but it is not new in the sense of absolutely novel—no philosophy is. Rather, what Fraser does is to extract from the philosophical heritage those insights which he finds most valuable, and to construct a position over against the materialism, agnosticism, pantheism and absolutism of his day. These were his foes, where Butler's was Deism, and Reid's, Humean scepticism. In all of this his supreme guide was Berkeley conceived as a spiritual realist, and seasoned with Reid's common sense.

The question of Fraser's use of his sources has raised eyebrows in certain quarters. Thus his pupil Pringle-Pattison felt that Fraser minimised

> the empiricism and nominalism in which [Berkeley's] theory had its starting point and which had their inexorable consequences in Hume. And when he suggests the practical agreement of Berkeley and Reid as "immediate" Realists in common opposition to the hypothetical or mediate Realism—the representative perception—of the majority of philosophers, he can easily be shown to ignore the ultimately more important speculative difference between the two positions; for "the ideal theory" of the representationists—the doctrine that we immediately know only our own states—is the very foundation of Berkeley's immaterialism. Naturally Fraser was not ignorant of points like these. . . .[69]

Indeed he was not. But he did feel that Berkeley's thought

> becomes, when we pursue it further than he did, a sublime intuition of the phenomenal realities of sense, inorganic and organic, as established media for the intellectual education of finite spirits by means of physical sciences; for intercourse between individual moral agents; and for a revelation of the Eternal Spirit, in whom the merely phenomenal things of sense, and moral agents too, have their being. It includes the fundamental faith that the universe exists for an eternal moral purpose, so that our experience in it, with the conditions of thought and belief presupposed in the experience, must be practically trustworthy and reasonable.[70]

---

68 J. Lindsay in *The Life of Robert Flint*, 358.

69 A.S. Pringle-Pattison, "Alexander Campbell Fraser," 311.

70 A.C. Fraser, *Berkeley*, Edinburgh: Blackwood 1881, 223–24.

Among the weaknesses of Berkeley was his failure to "extract from the phenomena of perception the evidence of a substance different in kind from the self-conscious spirit which perceives them."[71] At this point Reid came to the rescue. But if Reid corrects Berkeley, he must in turn be corrected by him: "the philosophy of Common Sense, as represented by Reid, did not rise to the conciliation of the natural order of the material with the originative freedom of the spiritual world, in which operating law in outward nature is recognised as immediate divine agency, or a part of a revelation of perfectly reasonable Will in and through a universe of things and persons."[72]

We have said enough to show how, by their own routes, which converged at certain points, both Martineau and Fraser were led to propound ethical theism. There are differences of emphasis—and of temperament, of course. Martineau did not make so much of that proper agnosticism before ultimate mystery as did Fraser, but on many points they were at one—not least as regards their common foes.

The question of how far Martineau *differed* from Fraser is much harder to answer, and to this elusive matter we now turn.

IV

James Seth will introduce us to the problems which confront us. He writes: "Martineau . . . follows much more closely than Fraser the traditional lines of the Scottish School . . . Fraser, on the other hand, has been too profoundly influenced by that 'ideal theory' which was the *bête noir* of Reid to attach much importance to the independent reality of the material world."[73] The questions are, "Does Martineau follow the natural realism/dualism of the Scottish School more closely than Fraser?" "Is it true that Fraser is adversely affected by idealism in the way Seth suggests?"

We have already reviewed evidence enough to give us pause in face of Seth's strong disjunction. To say that Martineau is much more the realist and Fraser more the idealist is to overlook the blurred edges in *both* authors; it is to take insufficiently seriously their claim to be philosophers of the *via media*. Let us proceed step by step.

71 Idem, "Life and philosophy of Leibnitz," 49.

72 Idem, *Thomas Reid*, 125.

73 J. Seth, *English Philosophers and Schools of Philosophy*, 309–10.

Does Martineau follow the Scottish School more closely than Fraser? In the first place we must note that the later phase of the common sense philosophy, to which both Martineau and Fraser had to adjust, was that represented by Hamilton. Hamilton had published his paper on "The philosophy of the unconditioned" in the *Edinburgh Review*, 1829. He here welcomed Victor Cousin's endorsement of his own inherited natural realism but, under Kantian inspiration, he denied Cousin's conclusion that knowledge of the absolute was open to us.

Positively, Martineau wishes to retain the realism and the dualism, and deny the agnosticism. Hence his rhetorical question in his essay on "Sir William Hamilton's philosophy": "Because God can be contemplated only, like other objects of thought, as differenced from our subjective selves, is it needful to say, that he is merely phaenomenal to us and not cognizable in his reality?"[74] Elsewhere he put the point in the indicative: "The act of Perception gives us simultaneous knowledge of a subject and an object, with perfect equipoise of reason for affirming the reality of the one and of the other."[75] Yet again, "That our cognitive faculties should be constituted in accordance with *things as they are* is no more surprising than that the instinct of animals should adapt their actions to things *as they are to be;* and much less surprising than would be a constitution of them conformable to *things as they are not*."[76] In a word, "So long as knowledge is a relation, and an antithetic relation, between knower and known, it cannot dispense with equal faith in both."[77]

Negatively, Martineau wishes to counter not only the subjectivism of Kantian idealism, but the pantheism which in later life he felt that ascendant absolutism could scarcely avoid. Indeed, the inspiration of his protest against pantheism was identical with that against necessarianism. At the point of violating moral freedom, and of making God appear to be the author of sin, the opposites were one. By 1876 Martineau waxed as lyrical as he was apocalyptic:

> Take away all objective seat from your inward vision, turn it from a perception into a phantom, let it hang in the air and never have been; and though it may raise a sigh, and pour a plaintive music

74 James Martineau, *Essays, Reviews and Addresses*, III, 481.

75 Idem, "Morell's History of Modern Philosophy," *The Prospective Review*, 1846, 562.

76 Idem, *A Study of Religion*, I, 75.

77 Letter of Martineau to the Rev. J.H. Allen, 29 January 1884; quoted by J.E. Carpenter, *James Martineau*, 552.

> over life, it can inspire no worship and nerve no will. There is a wave of heathen Pantheism sweeping over our time which threatens to obliterate the consciousness of this truth, and to leave us only the phrases of ancient piety with the life washed out, the empty ghosts of the saint's prayer and the martyr's cry.[78]

In face of all pantheising immanentisms, which would lose the individual—and God, and deprive us of the Other with whom, supremely in morality, we have to do, Martineau protested,

> You do not so much as touch the threshold of religion, so long as you are detained by the phantoms of your thought: the very gate of entrance to it . . . is the discovery that your gleaming ideal is the everlasting Real, no transient brush of a fancied angel wing, but the abiding presence of the Soul of souls: short of this there is no object given you, and you have not even reached the specified point of "*admiration.*" Within the limits of pure sincerity, no one can *worship* either a nature beneath him or an idea within him.[79]

At the same time, Martineau asserted that the immediacy of the divine entails immanence; but it is the immanence of the transcendent One. The pantheist, however, can make no room for the transcendence, and thus "The opposition . . . lies between *All-immanency* and *Some-transcendency.*"[80] Martineau summed up his conviction on the matter thus:

> The whole external universe, then (external, I mean, to self-conscious beings), we unreservedly surrender to the Indwelling Will, of which it is the organised expression. . . . But the very same principle which establishes a *Unity* of all external causality makes it antithetic to the internal, and establishes a *Duality* between our own and that which is other than ours: so that, were not our personal power known to us *as one*, the cosmical power would not be guaranteed to us as *the other.*[81]

The realist claim that the one must always be over against the

---

78 John James Tayler, *A Retrospect of the Religious Life in England; or, The Church, Puritanism and Free Enquiry*, 2nd edn., reissued with an introduction by Martineau, London 1876, 42.

79 James Martineau, *A Study of Religion*, I, 12–13.

80 Ibid., II, 142. See A.W. Jackson, *James Martineau*, 353 and n. for Edward Caird's charge (subsequently withdrawn) that Martineau was among those who held that "a God immanent in the world is no God at all." The reference is to the first and second editions of Caird's *The Evolution of Religion*, II, 8.

81 Ibid., II, 166.

other lands Martineau in difficulties and ambiguities where God is concerned. The general thrust of his writing is that space and matter exist eternally with God, though in one place[82] he appears to deny eternity to matter. In his last major work he opens the door once again to matter as eternal.[83] The theologian H.R. Mackintosh found this way of making God's existence dependent upon an eternal duality unsatisfactory, yet he agreed with Martineau "in regarding a personal self-expression or object as necessary for the Divine Spirit." His remedy was "to resort to the great New Testament conception of the unbeginning Word, in whom is given the resonance of life vital to either love or knowledge in perfect form, yet not separate from God as we from other selves."[84]

The introduction of this theological note brings matters to a head, for as a number of writers have noted, Martineau does not seem to include in his philosophical writings all he needs in his worship. C.B. Upton suggests that there is an epistemological block at work here. Martineau's declaration, already quoted, that we know God in the way we know other objects (that is, by inference) militates against the immediacy which Martineau claims in his religious faith, and which creeps into his philosophical writings—above all when the concept of worship is in his mind.[85] Upton quotes two sentences in support of his view: "in the very constitution of the human soul there is provision for an immediate apprehension of God."[86] And, "All that we believe without us, we first feel within us; and it is the one sufficient proof of the grandeur and awfulness of our nature, that we have faith in God; for no merely finite thing can

82 Ibid., I, 381ff.

83 Idem, *The Seat of Authority in Religion*, 32–33.

84 H.R. Mackintosh, *The Doctrine of the Person of Christ*, Edinburgh: T. & T. Clark, 2nd edn., 1913, 521.

85 See C.B. Upton, *Dr. Martineau's Philosophy*, 103, 219, 225. We need not, however, attribute this lapse, as Upton does, to lingering Deism. With Carpenter, op. cit., 52n., we find that "Dr. Martineau was never a Deist." A.S. Pringle-Pattison was another who found Deism in Martineau. See his *The Idea of God in the Light of Recent Philosophy*, 2nd edn. revised, New York: Oxford University Press 1920, 36–37; 257–58. C.C.J. Webb demurred in his *Divine Personality and Human Life*, London: Allen & Unwin 1920, 124 and n. See further A.W. Jackson, *James Martineau*, 401–22. From the other side, some Christian absolutists did not seem able to contain their entire Gospel within their philosophy—despite absolutism's propensity for mopping everything up. This, at least, was our verdict upon John Caird. See Alan P.F. Sell, *Defending and Declaring the Faith*, Exeter: The Paternoster Press and Colorado Springs: Helmers & Howard 1987, ch. IV.

86 James Martineau, *The Seat of Authority in Religion*, 651.

possibly believe the infinite."[87] To Upton's evidence we may add this: "all religion must be *revealed*, if by that word we mean, '*directly given by divine communication*,' as opposed to mediate discovery of our own."[88] Is the solution to the matter to be found in Pringle-Pattison's word, "the transcendence which must be retained, and which is intelligible, refers to a distinction of value or of quality, not to the ontological separateness of one being from another"?[89] Martineau seems sometimes inclined to believe this, sometimes not—especially in his philosophical writings, where he needs to wield dualism over against pantheism. It is impossible to believe that he would ever have yielded to the blandishments of Henry Jones, who so zealously preached the absolute idealism he had learned from Edward Caird. In his discussion of Martineau's philosophy Jones correctly diagnoses Martineau's motive, and pounds out his own remedy:

> the real source of the opposition of Dr. Martineau to the theory of the Absolute Idealists . . . comes primarily, not from the desire to sever man from Nature and God, but from the conviction that *not to sever them* is to merge man into them and to lose him within them. . . . The fallacy rests on the belief that the *distinction* between the self and the world is the same thing as the *separation* of them. . . . But to the Idealist who sets forth from experience, that is, from a self related to a not-self, the unity in difference is given; for that *is* experience.[90]

---

87 Idem, *Endeavours after the Christian Life*, London: Longmans, 10th impression, 1900, 1.

88 Idem, "Personal influences on our present theology," *Essays Philosophical and Theological*, 373.

89 A.S. Pringle-Pattison, *The Idea of God*, 255.

90 Henry Jones, *The Philosophy of Martineau*, 23, 31. Cf. idem, "Divine immanence," *The Hibbert Journal*, V no. 4, July 1907, 758. I use the term "preaching" advisedly of H. Jones. The contrast between Fraser's agonised questions (cf. n. 2 above), and his careful treading of his *via media*, and Edward Caird's manner of propagating his philosophical faith could not be greater; and Jones learned from Caird (though with Welsh oratory and a delight in controversy thrown in). Caird felt no need to wrestle with the past in the way Fraser did; he simply utilised what was convenient to his *evolutionary* method. As Jones wrote of him, "Session after session passed and no allusion, near or remote, was made to the 'Scottish School' of Common Sense. . . . No Scottish name later than that of David Hume passed his lips. . . . He went on his way stating the truth as he knew it, trusting its defence to itself." See H. Jones and J.H. Muirhead, *The Life and Philosophy of Edward Caird*, Glasgow: Maclehose 1921, 67, 68. For his part, Fraser held that the questions of philosophy were perennial, and that the discipline, unlike the physical sciences, was not subject to progress. See A.C. Fraser, *Rational Philosophy in History and Science*, 1858, 41–42, 47.

This, however, is further than Martineau's *philosophical method* would take him.

Although he goes too far, we can at least understand why A. Caldecott should think that Martineau is doubly misleading in calling his approach ethical theism, (*a*) because of the methodological importance of causation in his scheme; and (*b*) because an inadequately acknowledged mystical-intuitionism hovers throughout his writings. This last surfaces preeminently in his references to the Soul of souls, to reverence, to a religious sense distinct from other senses whereby we are aware of the transcendent.[91] In all of this the debt to Channing is clear.[92]

It would therefore seem that when Martineau is taken whole his position is not so different from that of Fraser, and hence Seth's assertion that he is closer to (natural) realism than Fraser, though understandable, is misleading. Indeed, there is almost some excuse for Henry Jones's too easily reached proselytising conclusion—even if the attendant lyricism seems somewhat cloying in these hard-nosed times:

> Burdened with our doubts, baffled by our own reasonings, stumbling all to frequently over our own simplest thoughts, climbing the Hill Difficulty, creeping from fact to fact, as on our hands and knees, those of us who have embraced divine philosophy will prize most highly of all those moments when Religion takes us by the hand and plants us in a purer air where we can see, though from afar, the Golden Gates of the City of God. And in this respect at least, the contrast of the two philosophies [that is, his own and Martineau's], nay of all the errant searchings of man after truth, melt into a greater harmony.[93]

We now turn to James Seth's claim that for his part Fraser was too influenced by idealism to attach much importance to the question of the independent reality of the world. We may subdivide matters thus: Was Fraser unduly influenced by idealism? Did he in consequence sit loose to the independent reality of the world?

---

91 Alfred Caldecott, *The Philosophy of Religion in England and America*, 347–49. Cf., e.g., J. Martineau, *Types of Ethical Theory*, II, 221ff.

92 See R. Waller, *Truth, Liberty and Religion*, 243–44. It is worth recalling that in adopting the stance he did, Martineau was setting his face against fellow-Unitarians who remained committed to Locke's epistemology. See, e.g., R.V. Holt, *The Unitarian Contribution to Social Progress in England*, London: Lindsey Press, 2nd rev. edn., 1952, 343.

93 H. Jones, *The Philosophy of Martineau*, 37.

Our understanding is that, some of his language notwithstanding, Fraser was never finally entangled in the web of idealism in any of its forms. This emerges in numerous of his writings. Thus, for example, he can applaud Locke, who set out to "clip the wings of Idealistic omniscience, which, by help of verbal abstractions, concealed from itself its own failure to eliminate all mystery, and to substitute perfect rational insight for faith and presumptions of probability,"[94] whilst at the same time declaring that "An experience that *ends* in sense and empirical generalisation must end incoherently and must contain the seeds of nescience. . . ."[95] As we have seen, however, Fraser stoutly kept idealism at bay by walking his *via media* between nescience and "gnostic" omniscience. In fact it was precisely his resistance to monism that prompted his opposition to Ferrier's attempted demonstration that the data of common sense can be construed into clear and more intelligible forms. Indeed, Fraser went so far as to brand this rationalistic (as distinct from intuitionist) version of common sense theory "a kind of Scottish Hegelianism."[96]

None of which is to deny that Fraser has a place in his thought for the divine immanence—that concept so ardently promoted by neo-Hegelians over against the discredited Deism of the eighteenth century.[97] Thus in his last work on Berkeley Fraser can conclude: "If Nature is practically trustworthy, and fit to be scientifically reasoned about, the Omnipotent Spirit immanent in it must be perfectly good and design the goodness of all. This is final faith."[98] That is precisely the point: it is faith, not sight; and Fraser never ceased to think that the Hegelians overreached themselves:

> the Hegelian seems to claim, as attainable philosophy, an intuition of the rational articulation of the universe of things and persons in

94 A.C. Fraser, "Philosophical development,' *Mind*, XV, 1890, 12.

95 Ibid., 14.

96 Idem, "Ferrier's theory of knowing and being," *Essays in Philosophy*, 1856, 312. In his *Scottish Philosophy, the Old and the New*, 1856, Ferrier strongly resented this charge. See further A.C. Fraser, "The philosophical life of Professor Ferrier," *Macmillan's Magazine*, no. 99, January 1868. It would seem that Ferrier's "German speculations" lost him the Chair of Logic and Metaphysics at Edinburgh—to Fraser. See further, G.E. Davie, *The Democratic Intellect: Scotland and her Universities in the Nineteenth Century Edinburgh*, Edinburgh: Edinburgh University Press 1961, 293–303.

97 See further, Alan P.F. Sell, *Theology in Turmoil. The roots, course and significance of the conservative-liberal debate in modern theology*, Grand Rapids: Baker Book House 1986, ch. I.

98 A.C. Fraser, *Berkeley and Spiritual Realism*, London: Constable 1908, 84.

> the unity of the creative thought. This, if really attained, would eliminate mystery from our physical and moral experience, and convert philosophy into absolute science. If it has fulfilled its purpose it has translated all faith into rationalised thought. But I cannot find that this all-comprehensive system really tallies with the experience which it is bound to formulate adequately, and also to explain; or that it has yet got so far as to solve even so clamant a difficulty as the existence within the universe of immoral agents and moral evil. We ask for intellectual relief for moral difficulties, and we are offered "the organisation of thought." We look for bread and we find a stone.[99]

At this point C.B. Upton found Fraser and Martineau at one.[100]

Fraser could never swallow the "gnostic" evaporation of all mystery. To him faith, construed as a rationally grounded response in face of ultimate mystery could never be redundant, given humanity's limitations and God's greatness. Moreover, the complex of issues denominated "the problem of evil" could not be evaded by such idealistically inspired notions as that evil is but a stage on the way to good; on the contrary, evil *ought not* to exist.[101] Fraser's pupil, Pringle-Pattison, was fully justified in writing, "The definite declinature of the Absolutist or "gnostic" solution is perhaps from first to last the most outstanding characteristic of Fraser's thought.'[102] This despite Fraser's speculation that between "Hegelian speculation humanised" and his own position there may possibly be no final divergence.[103] After all, "The issue of a true philosophy is to disclose the horizon of mysteries by which the power of philosophising is bounded."[104]

Whereas Martineau the philosopher wields dualism against idealism whilst Martineau the seer is more open to absolutist blandishments, Fraser never ceases to oppose to idealism his own philosophy which ends not with the solution of all mysteries (even in principle), but with Baconian abruptness. We cannot therefore say that Fraser was unduly influenced by idealism—as we have seen, he even interpreted Berkeley as a spiritual realist, leaving much of the latter's immaterialism, or psychological idealism, on one side, and invoking Reid by way of compensation.

---

99 Idem, *Berkeley*, 228–29.

100 C.B. Upton, *Dr. Martineau's Philosophy*, xxxv.

101 A.C. Fraser, *Philosophy of Theism*, 253.

102 A.S. Pringle-Pattison, "Alexander Campbell Fraser," 300.

103 Ibid., 324–25.

104 A.C. Fraser, "Introductory Lecture on Logic and Metaphysics," 179.

Neither, secondly, can we endorse Seth's view that, because of the influence upon him of idealism, Fraser was little concerned by the question of the independent reality of the world. The point is made, for example, in Fraser's critique of Ferrier. Ferrier's system will permit us only to say of any existent that it must be combined with consciousness; it cannot demonstrate that x exists.[105] He declares that the twofold question, "Why do I believe in sensible things, or permanent syntheses of phenomena contributed by the senses; and in a plurality of finite egos, as distinguished from the Absolute Ego," is neither answered nor raised by Ferrier. He thus leaves us with two propositions: "Being cannot be meaningless," and "Its essence must be conscious," which are but "the step into philosophy."[106]

It is true, as Pringle-Pattison pointed out, that Fraser was not concerned to defend natural realism as such;[107] he set out with his epistemological questions, and proceeded *via* morality to theism; but it cannot be denied that he arrived at a spiritual *realism* in which the focus was very much upon the material phenomena of the world. To the end Fraser construed Berkeley as one who, "in the spirit of Bacon and English philosophy, kept hold of the concrete and ever-changing universe, in its experienced relation to human life and to God."[108] But he ever opted for final faith rather than final synthesis.

V

Thus ends our account of the ways in which two long-lived nineteenth-century philosophers adjusted themselves to the philosophy of the two centuries which preceded them, and to the idealism which was coming into vogue from the 1860s onwards. Much more might be said concerning their arguments and their conclusions. Both have been charged with minimising the importance of the social dimension of life and religion. Martineau's "conscience," and his classification of motives have severely been criticised, as has Fraser's utilisation of Berkeley's thought. The question has been raised whether either can deal adequately with evil and sin without making more of the atonement. But into these matters we cannot now delve.

---

105 Idem, "The philosophical life of Professor Ferrier," 202.

106 Ibid., 204–05.

107 A.S. Pringle-Pattison, "Alexander Campbell Fraser," 295.

108 A.C. Fraser, *Biographia Philosophica*, 154.

Rather, as we approach the centenary of Martineau's death and the opening of a new millennium, let us be respectively challenged and inspired by our two theists. Fraser writes: "an account of the idea and conviction we have concerning God must involve a theologian in an investigation of certain alleged first principles of knowledge, or else he must assume these metaphysical elements of theology without any examination at all."[109] It is difficult to suppress the feeling that a number of present-day theologians are deaf to—even innocent of—this challenge. Martineau prays: "Awaken us to feel how great a thing it is to live at the end of so many ages, heirs to the thoughts of the wise, the labours of the good, the prayers of the devout."[110] One of the ways of expressing gratitude for one's inheritance is to use it well.[111]

---

109 Idem, "Introductory Lecture on Logic and Metaphysics," 177.

110 James Martineau, *Home Prayers*, London: Longmans 1891, 6.

111 But that, of course, presupposes that we know what it is. In order to resist the temptation of suggesting that too few are nowadays being adequately grounded in this regard I shall, with *quasi*-Baconian abruptness, stop!

XI

J.H.A. Bomberger (1817–1890) versus J.W. Nevin: A Centenary Reappraisal

The former English poet laureate, John Betjeman, declared that "History must not be written with bias, and both sides must be given, even if there is only one side."[1] Where Mercersburg is concerned we shall do well not to take my whimsical fellow-countryman too seriously. There is more than one side to the Mercersburg story, and both parties to the historic debate had points in their favour. I shall attempt to demonstrate this by reference to the not-always-elevated and sometimes-quite-boring dispute between J.W. Nevin and J.H.A. Bomberger, the centenary of whose death falls this year. Generously ignoring their common abuse of the noble term "Puritan," I shall attempt an impartial reappraisal of the issues at stake. My motives are more than commemorative, more than antiquarian. I shall suggest that for all the blessings flowing down from Mercersburg (and I shall specify these), Bomberger rightly utters cautionary words in relation to three major doctrines. I shall further suggest that the Bomberger–Nevin debate throws into relief the crucial issue of authority. This question, which was not fully discussed at the time, remains before all the churches, and not least before the Reformed, to this day. There is thus much more to the Bomberger–Nevin episode than fuddy-duddy reaction on the one hand and liturgical fuss-pottery on the other. The very polarities of the debate challenge us to distinguish between irreconcilable contradictions, and those paradoxes of faith to which we must cling with all the tenacity we can muster.

1 John Betjeman, *First and Last Loves* (1952), London: Century 1987, 5.

I

John Henry Augustus Bomberger was born at Lancaster, Pennsylvania, on 13 January 1817, to George H. and Marry Hoffmeier Bomberger.[2] Following schooling in York and Mercersburg, Bomberger became the first graduate of Marshall College (to which status Mercersburg School had been elevated in 1836) in 1837. During his year at Mercersburg Seminary (1837–8) Bomberger studied under Frederick A. Rauch, the Professor of Biblical Literature who, on the resignation of Lewis Meyer, had inherited the entire syllabus and had charge of the only student.[3] With such a staff-student ratio it is just as well that Bomberger "ever held in grateful memory the instruction of this Christian scholar, and counted him the first real

2 For Bomberger see *The New Schaff-Herzog Encyclopedia of Religious Knowledge*, Grand Rapids: Baker Book House 1956, II, 220; *Bomberger Memorial Discourse, Delivered in Trinity Reformed Church of Waynesboro', Franklin Co., Pa., by the Pastor, Rev. F.F. Bahner, A.M., on Sunday, September 14, 1890*. Various authors, *The Rev J.H.A. Bomberger, Doctor of Divinity, Doctor of Laws 1917–1890*, Philadelphia: Publication and Sunday School Board of the Reformed Church in the United States 1917; *Ursinus College Bulletin*, VII, Memorial Number 1890, no. 1; *Ursinus College Commencement Herald*, 25 June 1891, 53–56; J.H.A. Bomberger, *Five Years' Ministry in Race Street . . . Philadelphia . . . [with] An Ecclesiastical Appendix*, Philadelphia, 1860; Grant E. Harrity, *The Events Leading to the Foundation of Ursinus College*, unpublished B.D. thesis, Evangelical and Reformed Theological Seminary, PA, 1949; [Typescript] *Extracts from the Diary of Rev. Albert R. Thompson, Student [at Ursinus College] from 1874 to 1879*, prepared by Rev. Arthur P. Thompson (son), Saxton, PA, 1954; Gerald H. Hinkle, *The Theology of the Ursinus Movement: Its Origin and Influence on the German Reformed Church*, unpublished doctoral thesis, Yale University, 1964; idem, "Professor without portfolio," *Ursinus College Bulletin*, November 1964, 5–8; Calvin D. Yost, *Ursinus College, A History of its First Hundred Years*, Collegeville, PA: Ursinus College 1985. I am grateful to Mrs. Florence M. Bricker, the former archivist of the Evangelical and Reformed Historical Society and of the United Church of Christ at Lancaster Theological Seminary for her assistance; and to the Social Sciences and Humanities Research Council of Canada for funding a research trip to Lancaster. Thanks are due to Dr. John B. Payne of Lancaster Theological Seminary, for some stimulating observations upon the first version of this paper. I dedicate this work to President Richard P. Richter of Ursinus College, as an expression of friendship and esteem, and in appreciation of my having been awarded the College's Honorary D.D. on Sunday 15 May 1988.

3 See George Warren Richards, *History of the Theological Seminary of the Evangelical and Reformed Church at Lancaster, Pennsylvania*, Lancaster: Theological Seminary of the Evangelical and Reformed Church 1952, 198.

teacher whose tuition he had enjoyed."[4] In 1854 (prior to the dispute which will concern us) Franklin and Marshall College honoured Bomberger with its Doctorate of Divinity.

The Synod of Lancaster licensed Bomberger in October 1838; he accepted a call to Lewiston (a three-point charge) and removed there the following month. He was ordained on 27 December 1838. He preached three or four times each Sunday in English and German, and augmented his stipend, which was only about half the sum he had been led to expect, by assuming responsibility for the classical school in the town. He proceeded to Waynesboro with its four congregations in July 1840. Whilst there he promoted "protracted meetings" of the revivalist kind—this, be it noted, during the period of his support for Nevin, and Nevin's publication of *The Anxious Bench* (1843), that pungent attack upon the "new measures" which were widely, if not altogether accurately, supposed to have originated with C.G. Finney.[5] There followed seven years at Easton, from April 1845, and then in August 1852 Bomberger began his ministry at Race Street Church, Philadelphia.

The church at Race Street had passed through troubled times, and numbers were depleted. Bomberger's predecessor, Joseph F. Berg, a determined opponent of Nevin, Schaff and the Mercersburg Theology, had just transferred his allegiance to the Dutch Reformed Church and assumed a teaching post at Rutgers College.[6] Under Bomberger's leadership the tide was turned, and eventually three branch churches were formed, of which one survived for only three or four years. In Philadelphia, writes Hinkle, Bomberger

> was thrust into the bustling, spirited atmosphere of America's great voluntary society movement. In short order he was an officer at the local, state, and national levels in the American Bible Society and the American Sunday School Union, as well as a spokesman for abolition, temperance, and several other causes. Ministerial associates in Philadelphia also schooled Bomberger in the typical anti-

4 Anon., *Ursinus College Bulletin* VII, 1890, no. 1, 21.

5 See further Charles Yrigoyen Jr., "John Williamson Nevin's *The Anxious Bench* and Evangelical Piety," *The New Mercersburg Review* I, Autumn 1985, 3–19. See also Keith J. Hardman's admirable work, *Charles Grandison Finney 1792–1875, Revivalist and Reformer*, Syracuse: Syracuse University Press 1987; reprinted Grand Rapids: Baker Book House 1990.

6 Among other Mercersburg opponents who defected were John Craig Guldin, who went to New York under Dutch Reformed and Presbyterian auspices as a missioner to German immigrants; and Jacob Heffenstein, who became a New School Presbyterian. See G.H. Hinkle, *The Theology of the Ursinus Movement*, 71–76.

> catholic bias of evangelical Protestantism, a bias which in Bomberger's case nurtured his growing suspicions that the Mercersburg theologians were less Protestant than the denomination might wish them to be.
>
> Slowly, but unceasingly, his heart was won over to largely non-credal, non-liturgical, and ultra-activistic concerns of this order. Yet at the same time Nevin and his associates at Mercersburg were becoming increasingly critical of such evangelical interests.[7]

It would seem that Hinkle here overstates the case, and two important caveats must be entered. First, Bomberger and his people did not lend their voices to the loud-mouthed anti-Romanism which was then in vogue in some circles. On the contrary, he writes, "Because we would not join in the violent anti-popery tirades of the day, we were accused of cherishing a latent affection for Rome."[8] Secondly, Bomberger's participation in evangelistic enterprises was, like everything he did, considered. Thus, he wrote to Edwin M. Long concerning the latter's tent meetings in Philadelphia:

> so far as my observation went, the operations of the Tent in this city were conducted in a manner which seemed carefully to avoid all collision with the ordinary means of grace employed by the various churches in its neighbourhood. Indeed, it was not until after I had fully understood that all occasions of evil in this respect would be scrupulously guarded against, that I consented to participate in the movement. It was a rule carefully observed, I believe, always to consult pastors and churches in whose vicinity the Tent was pitched, in regard to the time of its services.[9]

Again, eight years later the now staunch opponent of Mercersburg could nevertheless note with regret that from the early decades of the nineteenth century

> great and in some respects radical changes were introduced [into the worship of the German Reformed Church]. By a combination of causes which it is unnecessary to enumerate, excepting that the so-called "New Measures" were among the most prominent and active of them, some of her most distinctive principles and usages were set aside, and made wholly to disappear from some portions of the Church. To some degree the tone of fundamental doctrines was lowered. In many congregations the leading Festivals were

---

7 G.H. Hinkle, "Professor without portfolio," 7.

8 J.H.A. Bomberger, *Five Years' Ministry*, 14.

9 Idem, "Introductory Remarks" to Edwin M. Long, *The Union Tabernacle; or, Movable Tent-Church*, Philadelphia 1859, 23.

> neglected or despised. For the earnest catechetical instruction of youth, and such as sought admission to full communicant membership, other means were substituted—strange and uncongenial. In a word, whilst she still retained the ancient name, the Church had, in districts where these innovations prevailed, lost well nigh all resemblance of form and features, as well as of inner life, to that founded by our fathers.[10]

These are not the words of one innocent of liturgical and credal concerns.

In 1870 Bomberger became the first President of Ursinus College and its Theological Department. He served concurrently as pastor of St. Luke's, Trappe, until 1883. The College was supported by, and identified with, the so-called "low Church" party. It was scarcely necessary to read between the lines of Bomberger's inaugural Presidential address: "Here, then, we stand today solemnly committed to the momentous task of educating young men and youth, truly and thoroughly, intellectually, morally, religiously (and are not these essentially one), and all in harmony with the pure principles of Evangelical Christianity."[11] In offering theological instruction Bomberger had the support of the Philadelphia Classis, but he had not been officially appointed as a theological teacher by the Church.[12] Such churchly sanction was required by a Synod decision of 1820, and this resolution was duly invoked against Ursinus College at the Martinsburg, West Virginia, Synod of October 1872.[13] Matters were finally resolved in Bomberger's favour at the General Synod of Fort Wayne (1875).

Bomberger was active in numerous other ways. Prior to launching Ursinus College he had published two volumes of a condensed translation of Herzog's *Realencyclopadie* (1856–60); a revised translation of Kurtz's *Text-Book of Church History* (1860); and a number of pamphlets which will directly concern us. In 1868 he founded *The Reformed Church Monthly*, the principal anti-Mercersburg organ within the German Reformed Church; it continued until 1877. The

---

10 J.H.A. Bomberger, *The Revised Liturgy. A History and Criticism of the Ritualistic Movement in the German Reformed Church*, Philadelphia, 1867, 15–16.

11 Quoted by C.D. Yost, *Ursinus College*, 13.

12 In 1868 Bomberger had withdrawn his name from the list of those under consideration for appointment at Mercersburg Seminary as Professor of Didactic and Practical Theology in succession to the late Henry Harbaugh. See G.W. Richards, *History of the Theological Seminary*, 351.

13 See H.M.J. Klein, *The History of the Eastern Synod of the Reformed church in the United States*, Lancaster: Eastern Synod, 1943, 260–61; cf. C.D. Yost, *Ursinus College*, 24–25.

following year, under the presidency of Bomberger, the Synod at Easton endorsed the idea of a Peace Commission to heal the division over liturgical matters within the Church.[14] Bomberger ardently served the cause of peace, and two generations of churchly strife ended without a major permanent secession's having taken place (an unusual Reformed circumstance indeed!) For many years Bomberger presided over the Board of Home Missions; and his wider influence was felt in the fledgling World Presbyterian Alliance (1875), whose Second General Council he addressed on "Regeneration" in 1880.[15] At the Fifth General Council the now deceased Bomberger was recalled as "an early friend of the Alliance, and an earnest worker for Bohemia."[16]

Bomberger's first wife, Marion Elizabeth Huston of Mercersburg, died *circa* 1855. His second wife, Julia Aymer Wright, whom he married in 1863, died in 1888. Bomberger himself died, leaving eight children, on 19 August 1890. He was buried in the graveyard of Trinity Reformed Church, Collegeville, Pennsylvania. Characteristically, "It was the earnest desire of our lamented President, expressed in his last will, that the details of his funeral should 'be decently simple, in harmony with the devout and plain usages of the Reformed Church of his fathers.'"[17]

II

> One of the most painful positions in which it is possible for a man to be placed, is to find himself arrayed in open and decided antagonism against those in whose fellowship he once found sincere pleasure, and with whose real or supposed views he once thought himself in happy agreement.[18]

Bomberger's words, written in 1867 in the heat of the liturgical controversy, precisely describe his predicament. He *had* been a staunch supporter of Nevin in earlier years. Thus, when Berg, through the Philadelphia Classis, pressed for a heresy trial of the Mercersburg professors, Bomberger rose in their defence at the

---

14 See H.M.J. Klein, op. cit., 267.

15 See *Proceedings of the Second General Council of the Presbyterian Alliance*, Philadelphia 1880, 543–53.

16 *Proceedings of the Fifth General Council*, London 1892, 27.

17 *Ursinus College Bulletin* VII, 1890, no. 1, 2.

18 J.H.A. Bomberger, *Reformed Not Ritualistic: A Reply to Dr. Nevin's "Vindication,"* 1867, 5.

Synod of 1845,[19] which marked the beginning of a period of controversy within the German Reformed Church which was to last for more than thirty years. The flames were fanned by the liturgical question which occupied seventeen years from the appointment of a liturgical committee by the Hagerstown Synod of 1848.

It is not necessary here to chronicle the liturgical controversy. This has been exhaustively done by Jack Martin Maxwell.[20] Our purpose will be served if we note Bomberger's enthusiastic support of Nevin during the early years of the liturgical committee's life, and if we specify the causes of the breach which followed.

In his article of 1853 entitled, "Dr. Nevin and his antagonists," Bomberger declared of Nevin that "Few men, occupying a similar position, have encountered so much misrepresentation in the prosecution of their work. And we know of no one, whose words and warnings, from the first utterance of his protest against the pernicious extravagances of the Anxious Bench system, to his latest reprehension of Leahey-itical, anti-popery harangues, have been so diligently caught up and improved, and who has yet at the same time been so unsparingly denounced for uttering those words and warnings."[21] More specifically, Bomberger set out to undermine the position of Berg and his supporters:

> If Dr. Nevin has indeed revived Eutychianism, charged our Lord Jesus Christ with being a sinner, denied the divine authority of the Scriptures, rejected the Reformed doctrine of the atonement and justification, plead [sic] for purgatory, and prayers for and to the dead, advocated the worship of the Virgin Mary, taught the crassest transubstantiation, reviled Protestantism, and made common cause with Popery as far as this could be done by him in the existing premises, then the German Reformed Church, which has all the while not only looked calmly on, but refused to listen to the alarm-cry raised by two or three watchmen within her walls, and repeated with magnified force by thrice as many more without, must either be most irretrievably astute, or most perversely set upon ruining herself, and doing mischief to others. And this precisely is what some of those professedly concerned for her peace and prosperity fear and prophesy. For ourselves we feel assured

19 See G.W. Richards, *History of the Theological Seminary*, 255; H.M.J. Klein, *History of the Eastern Synod*, 205.

20 See J.M. Maxwell, *Worship and Reformed Theology. The Liturgical Lessons of Mercersburg*, Pittsburgh: The Pickwick Press 1976. For the Mercersburg movement at large see J.H. Nichols, *The Mercersburg Theology*, New York: OUP 1966.

21 J.H.A. Bomberger, "Dr. Nevin and his antagonists," *The Mercersburg Review*, V, January 1853, 91.

> that their fears are gratuitous, and that their dire prognostications will prove most happily delusive.[22]

In the second part of his article Bomberger trundles out his *tu quoque:* Nevin's "real *proton pseudos,* the actual 'head and front of his offending,' we suspect rather to be this, that he has forced out incontrovertible evidence of the defection of many of the self-constituted leaders of modern Protestantism, from the doctrines of the very standards by which they hoped to condemn him. . . ."[23] Nevin's opponents have succumbed to the rationalism and laxity of what Bomberger (like Nevin) brands New England "Puritanism." Certainly, *"Dr. Nevin cannot be convicted of treachery to the true Church, nor the German Reformed Church of infidelity to her history, her character, and her profession, in having refused to condemn him."*[24]

Consistently with this, Bomberger had already made it clear, in his 1850 article on "The Old Palatinate Liturgy," that he was not opposed to liturgical usage and revision as such. On the contrary, he answered the objections of those who were against liturgies.[25] He was a tireless worker on the liturgical committee from the outset. But from 1861 he became increasingly uneasy with the Mercersburg stance as a whole. By 1866 his words in his oration at Samuel Helfenstein's funeral could have been spoken of himself: "Differing both from those who at first violently and unqualifiedly opposed the [Mercersburg] system, and from those who, regarding it as an honest and legitimate effort to revive a sense for the true doctrines of the Church, and her traditional usages, for a time favored it, [Helfenstein] seemed to discern, amidst all the good it might contain, dangerous elements of evil and of mischief."[26] By 1867 Bomberger had come to believe that "the German Reformed Church has been solicited to sanction and introduce what amounts to a complete repudiation of many of her most distinctive customs and fundamental doctrines, and to substitute in their place usages and dogmas obviously at variance with her traditions and her creeds. Considered in its relative bearings, this movement involves

---

22 Ibid., 96.

23 Ibid., April 1853, 145.

24 Ibid., 180, italics original.

25 See J.H.A. Bomberger, "The Old Palatinate Liturgy of 1563," *The Mercersburg Review*, II, 1850, 81–96, 265–87.

26 Idem, *A Funeral Discourse, delivered in St. Peter's German Reformed Church, North Wales, PA, October 22d, 1866, on the occasion of the death of the Rev. Sauel Helfenstein, D.D.*, Philadelphia, 1866, 21.

a liturgical and doctrinal revolution, the influence and effects of whose success cannot be measured or described."[27] In the following year Bomberger launched *The Reformed Church Monthly*, and among his "First Words" to his readers were the following:

> The conflicts of the sixteenth century seem about to be renewed. Errors, so like those then exposed and routed that they can scarcely be distinguished from them, are rearing their heads again, and with greater boldness than ever. Ridicule, sarcasm, reproaches, similar to those heaped upon the principles of the Reformation,—upon the cardinal doctrines of justification by faith and the Holy Scriptures as the only final rule of faith and practice,—are hurled at those blessed principles and doctrines now. Indeed, the parallel between the leading points in controversy, and the kind of weapons used by the foes of the holy cause, is most striking and instructive. This is done, too, by men professing the faith of the Church whose principles they thus assail, and whose foundations they seem to be laboring to undermine. Nay, in some instances, like the case of Dr. Pusey and his leading disciples in England, they cling to high positions in the communion they seek to subvert, and use the influence of their positions for the more successful prosecution of their schemes.[28]

Here we have the spirit and the techniques of those who set out to guard the ark: the invocation of (selected) saints of old; the foretelling in violent language of dire assaults about to fall upon the saints of today; the invocation of the bogeyman—in this case, Pusey: and this despite Nevin's opposition to Anglo-Catholicism on the ground that its understanding of history was deficient. In subsequent articles Bomberger accused the Mercersburg theologians of seeking to refashion the Reformed Church according to their own lights because they are dissatisfied with "her doctrinal standard, her constitutional order, and her traditional usages."[29] By 1873 he was agreeing with G. Dering Wolff, a Roman Catholic writer in *The Catholic Standard*, that "what he says of the inward and outward Romish affinities of Nevinism is true."[30] This last remark was made in connection with the defection of the Rev. Edward O. Forney to Rome; but Bomberger was equally willing to invoke the departure of two "rather prominent" Mercersburg ministers to the Presbyterian

27 Idem, *The Revised Liturgy. A History and Criticism of the Ritualistic Movement in the German Reformed Church*, Philadelphia, 1867, 6–7.

28 Idem, *The Reformed Church Monthly*, I no. 1, January 1868, 3.

29 Idem, "The liturgical controversy," ibid., I, 1868, 60–61.

30 Idem, "Nevinism a feeder for Rome," idem, IV, 1873, 409.

Church. From the fact that they went over to a *less* liturgical church than the German Reformed, he drew the inference that they thought that Mercersburg was getting out of hand.[31] What was written by Bomberger of Ursinus College's stance well encapsulates the position to which he was led:

> Whoever prefer that young men or youth should be trained under influences which tend Rome-ward, or which are calculated to awaken doubts and dislikes of Evangelical Protestantism, had better not send them or advise them to come to Ursinus College. The whole spirit, life and teaching of the College, are strongly set against all sorts of Popery, Puseyism, and deadening Ritualism; and the more so because they are positively, and by the deepest convictions, thrown in favor and support of that primitive Apostolic Christianity which never did, and never can *coexist with* Romanism, Ritualism, or any of their deceptive imitations. With any such things Ursinus College has no sympathy or affinity.[32]

In 1867 Bomberger published his pamphlet, *Reformed Not Ritualistic,* in reply to Nevin's *Vindication of the Revised Liturgy* of the same year. Also in 1867 there appeared *Prayers and Hymns for Sunday Schools*. The Prefatory Note, written by Bomberger, begins with a sentence most notable for its negative implication: "The Prayers and Hymns herewith offered for use in Sunday-Schools, were prepared, selected and arranged with special reference to what are believed to be the wants and desires of Reformed Churches." Next, Bomberger enlisted the aid of the German theological heavyweight, I.A. Dorner, whose articles in *The Reformed Church Monthly* were reprinted under the title, *The Liturgical Conflict in the Reformed Church of North America* (1868). Nevin took ample space for his reply in *The Mercersburg Review,* and his response was also published in pamphlet form: *Answer to Professor Dorner* (1868).

Why did Bomberger's attitude towards Mercersburg change? We may well set our consideration of this question within the wider context of the churchly debate within the German Reformed Church. J.M. Maxwell specifies ten causes of the liturgical controversy:[33]

1. The denomination wrongly supposed that liturgical unity entailed liturgical uniformity.

---

31 Idem, "Mercersburg transitions," ibid., VIII, 1875, 527–30. The defectors were J.S. Foulk and Joshua Riale.

32 Idem, "A historical sketch," ibid., V, 1872, 30.

33 See J.M. Maxwell, *Worship and Reformed Theology*, 345–51.

2–6. Synodical procedural difficulties (which need not detain us here).
7. Poor communications between the Western and Eastern branches of the Church.
8. External—especially Dutch Reformed—criticisms of Mercersburg.
9. Unresolved personal conflicts.
10. The failure of the Mercersburg leaders to give Bomberger a hearing following his initial questioning of the Provisional Liturgy in 1861.

Maxwell considers that the two final reasons are the decisive ones.

It seems to me that Maxwell has accurately enumerated what, in Aristotelian terms, might be called the proximate causes of strife. In Bomberger's case, however, *as it eventually turned out*, the remote cause was theological. If he changed his stance vis-à-vis Mercersburg—and he did—it was because he *finally* became convinced that on vital doctrinal matters Nevin had first changed. The liturgy was the occasion of the controversy, but the deepest cause *came to be* theological. (The words just italicised indicate an enigma on which I shall comment shortly.) It is not difficult to extract from Bomberger's writings examples of his dissatisfaction with some of the content of the proposed new liturgy. But he became convinced that the content was doctrinally inspired—by the notion of baptismal regeneration, for example. Again, he objected to the proposed responses in the interest of free worship—and it must be admitted that Nevin had been needlessly provocative concerning the alleged deficiencies of free prayer.[34] Bomberger further felt that the minister was being interposed between the believers and God where both prayers and sacraments were concerned. Moreover, he feared the "rigid enforcement" of liturgical practice which would contradict the past position of the German Reformed Church.[35]

It is important that we underline the fact that Bomberger was no free-wheeler where liturgy was concerned, and he strongly upheld the place of catechetics. Indeed, it was his conviction of the educative power of liturgies as such which inspired his protest on particular points: "With such proofs before us of the *educational power* of liturgies, it would not be easy to overrate the doctrinal significance of the ritualistic movement, into which the desire and effort of our Church to provide herself with an order of worship suitable to her historical character and spiritual wants, have been

34 See J.W. Nevin, *The Liturgical Question*, Philadelphia, 1862, 1–11.

35 See, for example, J.H.A. Bomberger, *Reformed Not Ritualistic*, 95–115, for Bomberger's adverse points.

turned."[36] Far more important to Bomberger than what believers were being asked to *do* in the proposed liturgy, was what they were being encouraged to *believe.* Mixing eulogy, sentiment and fact, one of the Bomberger memorial writers gets to the point thus:

> On its surface, the conflict concerned the nature and extent of fixed forms and ceremonies in religious worship; inwardly, this battle of intellect was one in which many of the distinctive historical customs and vital doctrines and beliefs of the German Reformed Church were skilfully attacked and valiantly defended. The irritating source from which the controversy sprang was the question of the formation and adoption by the denomination in general of a new and improved Liturgy or order of worship . . . But the deep and controlling cause . . . is found in the well-defined efforts made through the period . . . by a number of master minds under a distinguished leader, to infuse into the entire church certain theological ideas with which they themselves had become strongly and sincerely identified, but which were earnestly held by our departed President and others to be totally at variance with the true principles of the German Reformed government and belief. Here is found the influence which stirred so profoundly our beloved chief and moved him to strive through many trying years so persistently and well. His motives in the struggle were the impulses of a heart to which the unsullied faith of the fathers was dearer far than life; and if in the course of events he occasionally went to extremes, he erred alone from an over-weening love for this blessed heritage to which he had consecrated his all.[37]

Howard Hageman has written that the remarkable thing about the Mercersburg liturgy was that "it was the first liturgy in the Reformed Church to articulate a theology."[38] As far as Bomberger was concerned this was precisely the trouble: the theology articulated was bad theology.

Before turning to the theological crux of the matter I ought to justify the view expressed above that Bomberger's change of opinion concerning Mercersburg followed Nevin's general doctrinal shift. James I. Good wrote, "It must be acknowledged that Dr. Bomberger changed his views between 1853 and 1860, but this only directs attention to the far more remarkable changes of theological position on the part of his principal antagonist, Dr. Nevin. The latter was first a Presbyterian, then he inclined to Catholicism, and toward the

36 Ibid., 64. Nevin also was persuaded of the educational power of liturgies; see, for example, his *The Liturgical Question*, 11 ff.

37 *Ursinus College Bulletin*, VII, no. 1, 1890, 24–25.

38 Howard G. Hageman, *Pulpit and Table*, Richmond: John Knox Press 1962, 92.

end of his life he leaned to Swedenborgianism."[39] Few were more adept than Bomberger at quoting his opponents against themselves. Thus, on the question of theological foundations Bomberger places side by side some utterances of Nevin which are separated by twenty years. In the period 1840–47 Nevin had written, "The more we can be brought to commune familiarly and freely with the spirit of the Reformation . . . the better it is likely to be with us in all respects, at the present time. . . . Let us have progress, by all means; but let it be progress upwards, within the sphere of the original life of the Church itself . . . not progress outwards, by which the life of the past, together with its form, is renounced." In 1862–3 he writes, "The Provisional Liturgy has not professed at all to be of one order, simply with the Liturgical practice of the German Reformed Church in the 16th century . . . it was constructed throughout on another theory altogether . . . it makes common cause with the liturgies of the ancient Church. . . . It is a question of very material change in our church practice, if not in our church life."[40]

Again, ever ready to wield a *tu quoque*, Bomberger relates Nevin's *The Anxious Bench* to the alleged liturgical legalism of Mercersburg in these terms: "Is the hard yoke of the bondage of formalism which . . . is being prepared for our necks, less to be deprecated and denounced, than the fetters of fanaticism? Was it right to warn against the fiery furnace, and shall it be wrong to warn against the lion's den?"[41]

When noting Maxwell's accurately enumerated proximate causes of the Bomberger–Nevin dispute, I suggest that the underlying cause, *as it eventually turned out, came to be* theological. These careful words signal a puzzle which it is by no means easy to solve. The question which has been posed to me by Dr. John B. Payne is, "Why did Bomberger delay so long in opposing Nevin's theology?" It is undoubtedly the case that by the time Bomberger *defended* Nevin in 1853, Nevin had already articulated his "catholic" views: his very words of the 1840s, which Bomberger used against him, indicate this. Yet thirteen years later Bomberger was earnestly defending Nevin. Bomberger's change of view regarding Mercersburg did follow Nevin's doctrinal change, but why was Bomberger still defending Nevin so long after the latter's terminus had been reached? Far from

39 James I. Good in *The Rev. J.H.A. Bomberger*, 259; cf. C.D. Yost, *Ursinus College*, 2. While discussing Bomberger's in some detail, G.H. Hinkle does not allow sufficiently for *Nevin's* doctrinal change. See his *The Theology of the Ursinus Movement*, 207.

40 J.H.A. Bomberger, *Reformed Not Ritualistic*, 27.

41 Idem, *The Revised Liturgy*, 1867, 8; cf. idem, *Reformed Not Ritualistic*, 145.

aiding us at this point, Good does not even advert to the difficulty. The simplest explanation is that Bomberger only gradually became aware of the (to him) adverse implications of Nevin's position. This would seem to be borne out by his expression of the pain he felt on making the discovery. A more cynical suggestion would be that Bomberger, fuelled by personal animosity, dressed his ire in theological clothes so that it would appear more "respectable." But this would entail that his expression of pain was insincere, and I find no evidence of this. May it not also be that, for the sake of peace in the church, Bomberger delayed his opposition for as long as he could in the hope that mutual consultation would remedy matters? As Maxwell explains, there was no such consultation.

However these things may be, the fact remains that three theological concerns in particular fuelled Bomberger's protest: the christological, the pneumatological and the ecclesiological. To these we must turn, for on these matters Bomberger has a word for the theological and ecumenical discussions of our own time.

III

The Bomberger of 1853 had written, "Whatever else might give offence or excite suspicion, no cause, assuredly, could be found for taking exception to the Christology of the Mercersburg school."[42] By 1867, however, we find him saying of the Mercersburg theology that

> Its distinctive peculiarity may be discovered in the almost exclusive prominence which it gives to the *incarnation* of the Lord Jesus Christ . . . the great purpose of the incarnation of the Son of God, was to furnish a substantial basis of a new organic order of life; so that our human nature, which is corrupt and depraved by virtue of its relation to the first Adam, may have a vivifying portion of the real personal life of Christ infused into it, and thus be regenerated, justified and saved. . . . All else pertaining to Him,—His humiliation, passion, death, burial, is but incidental and accessory. By virtue of this "mysterious constitution of His person,"—not by virtue of His atoning passion and death, He penetrates the Church with His own real, substantial personal life, so that it is but the continual reproduction and perpetual remanifestation of His incarnation. . . .[43]

42 Idem, "Dr. Nevin and his antagonists," 164.

43 Idem, *Reformed Not Ritualistic*, 127.

What is supremely at risk, according to Bomberger, is the doctrine of the atonement. He never ceased to point out that Paul gloried in the Cross, not in the Incarnation. Not, indeed, that he undervalued the birth, life and ministry of Christ,[44] but he staunchly held that our mystical union with Christ was not our automatic birthright, but the gift of God's atoning grace through the regenerating work of the Holy Spirit; and hence that the Church is the community of the redeemed, not in some immanentist sense the continuation or extension of the Incarnation.

The development of Nevin's ideas was not, of course, simply a perverse reaction against older German Reformed positions. Both he and Bomberger were responding, in opposite ways, to a climate of thought customarily labelled "Romantic," and Nevin's response was fertilised by his deep appreciation of the incarnational emphasis of the Eastern Fathers. As we might expect, the Romantic thrust was multi-directional. In general Romanticism stood for the inward drive; human experience—even emotion—came to the fore over against the cerebralism of rationalism and necessarianism. This finds subtle expression in Goethe, Schleiermacher and Coleridge, and reaches bowdlerised form in Henley's poem, "Invictus," that Victorian gem which includes the immoral (no misprint) lines: 'I am the captain of my fate / I am the master of my soul,' which Robert Mackintosh once sardonically described as "a truly elegant expression of paganism."[45]

In the same general direction there flowed down from Hegel and his heirs a strongly immanentist thrust which finally drove bankrupt deism from the stage. Where deism (which was, however, no one thing) had tended to remove God from the created order and the human soul, immanentism restored him to both.[46] Again, it is not without significance for Mercersburg theology that Philip Schaff met F.D. Maurice in England, and became attached to his brand of Romantic theology.

The greatest risks which Romantic theology in all its forms runs are those of losing its moorings in the historic Christ event, of ideal-

44 G.H. Hinkle is thus almost correct in saying of Bomberger that "at no time did he endorse a strictly atonement-centred Christology." It would be more accurate to say that Bomberger's christology was centred in the atonement, but not exclusively concerned with the atonement. See G.H. Hinkle, *The Theology of the Ursinus Movement*, 216.

45 See Alan P.F. Sell, *Robert Mackintosh, Theologian of Integrity*, Bern: Peter Lang 1977, 34.

46 See further, Alan P.F. Sell, *Theology in Turmoil: The Roots, Course and Significance of the Conservative-Liberal Debate in Modern Theology*, Grand Rapids: Baker Book House 1986, ch. I.

ising Christ off the stage of history, and of succumbing to pantheising tendencies. Not surprisingly, Howard Hageman wrote of the Mercersburg theology that "the historical and the theological began to mean less and less as the demands of the psychological and the aesthetic loomed larger."[47]

The immanentist thrust, together with the revival of classics and thence of patristics at Oxford under Benjamin Jowett in the middle of the nineteenth century, gave impetus to an incarnationalism that was in part a reaction against soteriology gone legalistic and externally transactional. As the same Jowett complained, "God is represented as angry with us for what we never did; He is ready to inflict disproportionate punishment on us for what we are; He is satisfied by the sufferings of His Son in our stead."[48] Like Maurice in England, Nevin was in justifiable reaction against such crudity; and just as Maurice found himself accused of having gone too far by the Scottish theologian R.S. Candlish, so Bomberger rose up against Nevin.[49] Needless to say, both Candlish and Bomberger denied that they were guilty of soteriological crudity.

Against this background we may now view the christological, pneumatological and ecclesiological points of friction between Bomberger and Nevin. Though three, they are one, for all are facets of Nevin's incarnationalism. These themes are not randomly selected; they are roughly those which Nevin himself identified when characterising the Mercersburg theology: "In the first place, it is Christological, or more properly perhaps Christocentric; in the second place, it moves in the bosom of the Apostles' Creed; in the third place, it is Objective and Historical, involving thus the idea of the Church as a perennial article of faith."[50]

Bomberger sets out what he calls "The Great Contrast" thus:

47 H.G. Hageman, *Pulpit and Table*, 81. We should not, however, forget Nevin's opposition to the purely emotional, which he trenchantly denounced when rebuking Finneyism. See further, James H. Nichols, *Romanticism in American Theology: Nevin and Schaff at Mercersburg*, Chicago: University of Chicago Press 1961.

48 B. Jowett, "On atonement and satisfaction," quoted by B.M.G. Reardon, *Religious Thought in the Victorian Age*, London: Longmans 1971, 332.

49 See further, Alan P.F. Sell, *Aspects of Christian Integrity*, Calgary: University of Calgary Press 1990, and Louisville: Westminster/John Knox Press 1991, ch. II.

50 J.W. Nevin, *Vindication of the Revised Liturgy*, 1867, in *Catholic and Reformed. Selected Theological Writings of John Williamson Nevin*, eds. Charles Yrigoyen, Jr., and George M. (*sic*) Bricker, Pittsburgh: The Pickwick Press 1978, 365.

The Nature of the Incarnation

Reformed theology teaches . . . that the Eternal Son . . . voluntarily and graciously took into union with His divine nature a perfect individual human nature . . . whilst the union between these two natures was mysteriously close, . . . there was no fusion of the two. . . .

Mercersburg teaches that the Incarnation was an "organic conjunction" of the Godhead with the *human race;* that in this conjunction it took human nature into such union with itself, as to form a third nature or life, which Mercersburg calls theanthropic. . . . Hence, the Mercersburg theory confuses the two natures of Christ, and involves itself in a pantheistic view of God and humanity.

The Purpose of the Incarnation

Reformed theology teaches, that the Word became flesh in order to redeem lost man from the punishment of sin, by Christ enduring that punishment, in His Human nature, in man's stead; and to restore man to the favor of God, and to newness of life, through the Holy Spirit.

Mercersburg maintains the Word became flesh, *not* so much to make atonement for the sin of the world, by offering Himself as an expiatory sacrifice, *but* that by joining Himself to the race, He might infuse into mankind the very substance of His own divine-human or theanthropic life. . . . It is *not* by being the Lamb of God, sacrificially offered to take away the sin of the world, that He saves men, but by entering organically into the life of the race, and perpetuating the Incarnation literally, and, in substance, in the Church. . . .

The Church

According to Reformed theology, the Church is so far the body of Christ as it is made up of all, in all ages, who are gathered, defended and preserved by Christ, through the Spirit, out of the whole human race, and who, by the Spirit, agree in regard to all things essential to the true faith.

Mercersburg affirms, that the Church visible *is* literally and substantially Christ—the perpetuation of His very theanthropic life. . . .[51]

51 J.H.A. Bomberger, "The great contrast," *The Reformed Church Monthly*, IV, 1871, 367–69; cf. idem, ibid., VIII 1875, 126–35 on "Mercersburg errors."

Such is Bomberger's account of his own theology in relation to that which he is convinced underlies the liturgical controversy—with all that that entails concerning the theology of the sacraments and of the ministry. In brief, the substance of the theanthropic life is sacramentally conveyed, and ministers receive "some special character" in ordination which permits them to administer sacraments and declare absolution.

It may be that in opposing Mercersburg to the Reformed theology in the way he does, Bomberger is unduly disjunctive. Perhaps we do not have two monolithic blocs with no blurred edges, as he implies. It is certainly the case that he overstates his case. Nevin, for example, denied that we enjoy an hypostatic union with God:

> There is but one Incarnation (*one* Mediator between God and man, the *Man* Christ Jesus), but he is of such constitution, carrying our universal nature in his person, that all men may be joined with God also through him, by receiving into themselves the power of his life. This implies in their case no hypostatical union with Deity, no new theanthropy in the sense of Christ's person, but just the reverse; since the only medium of union with the Godhead is Christ's manhood, as something that must necessarily intervene between the Divine Word and all other men.[52]

Bomberger might still object, however, that atonement is not said to be necessary to any of this.

Nevin is, however, right (and Calvinistic, to boot) in wishing not to focus exclusively upon the atonement, but rather "to embrace at once the whole Christ and all His benefits."[53] Bomberger concurs. But there is no smoke without fire, and it is not difficult to draw from Nevin's writings passages which provoke the kind of charges levelled by Bomberger (and Bomberger was skilled in the art of selection). Thus, for example: "The mediation of Christ, we say, holds primarily and fundamentally in the constitution of his person. His Incarnation is not to be regarded as a device *in order* to his mediation, the needful preliminary and condition of this merely as an independent and separate work; it is itself the Mediatorial Fact, in all its height and depth, and length and breadth. . . ."[54] If this

52 J.W. Nevin, "Wilberforce on the Incarnation," *The Mercersburg Review*, II 1850, quoted by J.H. Nichols in *The Mercersburg Theology*, 87.

53 Idem, *Answer to Professor Dorner*, 41.

54 Idem, "Wilberforce on the Incarnation," in J.H. Nichols, op. cit., 79. At this point, and in passing, it is interesting to recall another of this year's centenaries: that of the death of John Henry Newman. His incarnational theology was described by the Unitarian James Martineau thus: "The one grand gift of the Gospel to the

mode of expression appears to minimise the once-for-all atoning act in the historic Cross, it is not difficult to find passages in Nevin's writings which clearly affirm that act. Thus, of the Mercersburg theology he writes, "No theology has insisted more earnestly on the great cardinal truths of the Trinity, the Eternal Generation, the Divinity of the Son, the Incarnation, the Mediatorial Work and Reign of Christ [but note the absence of reference to the Spirit's regenerating work]."[55] Again, he declares that "The historical character of the Gospel, objectively considered, meets us, first of all, in the Person and Work of Christ Himself, as they are exhibited to us in the Creed."[56] On the other hand, in a private letter to Henry Harbaugh—that is, in a non-polemical context in which he could express himself non-defensively—Nevin writes: "Christ saves the world, not ultimately by what he teaches *or by what he does*, but by what he *is* in the constitution of his own person."[57] This would seem once again to minimise the historical atoning act. Yet two pages later Nevin says, "The distinguishing character of the Mercersburg Theology . . . is its Christological interest, its way of looking at all things through the Person of the *crucified and risen* Saviour."[58] Finally, in his closing sentence, Nevin *omits* the atoning act from his list of truths emphasised by Mercersburg: "all stress is laid on the Person of Christ, on his resurrection from the dead, on the sending of the Holy Ghost, and on his presence and working through all time in the Church which is his body, the fulness of Him that filleth all."[59] At the very least, we may say that there is an oscillation here sufficient to justify the concern of Nevin's critics.

While Nevin strongly denied that his christocentrism left no room for the believer's faith,[60] it does appear that on occasion he played down the Holy Spirit's regenerating work (except in connec-

---

human mind is that, by the Incarnation, it has determined the *personality* of God, and His relations of *character and affection* towards man. *This*, and not what is called the 'doctrine of the Cross,' is the specialty and living kernel of the Gospel." See his *Essays, Philosophical and Theological*, 1866, 360. What a trick Bomberger missed here—a Roman Catholic and a Unitarian who might have been used to trump Nevin!

55 J.W. Nevin, *Theological Vindication of the New Liturgy* in *Catholic and Reformed*, 370.

56 Ibid., 377.

57 J.W. Nevin, "Letter to Dr. Henry Harbaugh," in *Catholic and Reformed*, 408. We have italicised the quoted phrase.

58 Ibid., 410; our italics.

59 Ibid., 411.

60 J.W. Nevin, *Answer to Professor Dorner*, 37.

tion with baptism, where Bomberger held him to err[61]), conversion, and the *resulting* union with Christ. For Nevin,

> The atonement as a foreign work, could not be made to reach us in the way of a true salvation. Only as it may be considered *immanent* in our nature itself, can it be imputed to us as ours, and so become available in us for its own ends. And this is its character in truth. It holds in humanity, as a work wrought out by it in Christ. When Christ died and rose, humanity died and rose at the same time in his person; not figuratively, but truly; just as it had fallen in the person of Adam.[62]

It would seem that at this point Nevin fails adequately to guard his position against an interpretation which he would not have wished to endorse. His words suggest what we might call an immanentist-automaticism concerning salvation: because of Christ's incarnation, life and victory the whole of humanity is saved. This would exclude the human response of faith; and since the latter has correctly been understood as *enabled*, the Spirit's work in what used to be called "the application of redemption" would be redundant. It is not without significance that when Bomberger addressed the World Presbyterian Alliance he should have taken "Regeneration" as his theme and thundered: "Christ is *not* our life in any pantheistic sense. Nay, the mystical union established between the regenerated soul and him is not even a hypostatical union of their two natures [and, as we saw, Nevin denied that it was this]. Man is not deified by regeneration. In it men become Christians, but are not made Christs."[63] The associated peril is that the Church comes to be regarded as the continuation or extension of the Incarnation, rather than as the result of the Spirit's regenerating work.

---

61 Though Nevin has his answer to this. He holds that the grace communicated by baptism is not saving grace, but that it becomes such when it meets with the recipient's *faith*. See further, John B. Payne, "Nevin and the sacrament of baptism," *The New Mercersburg Review*, II, Autumn 1986, 35.

62 Idem, *The Mystical Presence*, 163. Bomberger described this work as "a queer sort of mystico-metaphysical nondescript (at least so far as the latter half of it is concerned) . . . a book which may have been expected to revolutionize the theological world, but which, after a few revolutions on its own axis, seems to have rolled into oblivion." See "Mercersburg transitions," *The Reformed Church Monthly*, VIII 1875, 528–29.

63 See *Proceedings of the Second General Council*, II, 1880, 552. It is interesting to compare his remarks here with those in his earlier tract, *Infant Salvation in its relation to Infant Depravity, Infant Regeneration and Infant Baptism*, Philadelphia, 1859, especially 30–39, where he maintains the necessity of infant regeneration, as distinct from infant conversion, as necessary to the salvation of infants.

In justice to Bomberger we should note that Nevin could be quite as disjunctive as he. Thus he writes:

> Where the idea of the Church has come to make itself felt . . . as involving the conjunction of the supernatural and the natural continuously in one and the same abiding economy of grace, its sacraments cannot possibly be regarded as outward signs only of what they represent. They become, for faith, seals also of the actual realities themselves, which they exhibit; mysteries, in which the visible and the invisible are bound together by the power of the Holy Ghost (not physically or locally, as vain talkers will forever have it), in such sort, that the presence of the one is, in truth, the presence of the other.'[64]

But it was quite open to Bomberger and others to query the ecclesiology here without landing in a memorialist view of the sacraments.

As for overstatement of the case, here too Bomberger was not alone. He at least had given Nevin no cause to give vent to the following invective:

> The Gospel of the Creed is, throughout, Christological, concentrates itself in Christ, throws itself, in full, upon the Incarnation, and sees in the objective movement of this Mystery of Godliness . . . the whole process of grace and salvation on to the resurrection of the dead and the life everlasting; while this other scheme, which we now call, for distinction's sake, the Gospel of Puritanism, substitutes for all this a construction of Christianity that is purely subjective, centering in the human mind, and that gives us then notions for facts. . . .[65]

One way of putting the Bomberger/Nevin contrast was expressed by a memorial writer thus: "[Bomberger's] religious thinking may be said to have approached, more or less closely, to the rationalistic type, in a good sense, characteristic of the English and American Puritan divines, rather than to have partook of the mystical character so common in the Evangelical theologians of Germany of the last forty or fifty years. His doctrinal system was intensely Pauline, and he had little sympathy with that type of theological dogma and life which may be denominated Johannean."[66] The same writer

64 J.W. Nevin, *Theological Vindication of the New Liturgy*, 380–81.

65 Ibid., 386.

66 F.F. Bahner, *Bomberger Memorial Discourse*, 2–3. While we should not overlook Nevin's indebtedness to Paul's "Christ-mysticism," the line from John to the Eastern Fathers is especially clear.

was able to imagine Bomberger, Nevin and others singing these words in their "high station in glory": "Here, hand in hand, firm-linked at last, / And, heart to heart, enfolded all, / We smile upon the trouble past, / And wonder why we strove at all."[67] Let us hope so!

IV

Much has been written and, no doubt, much remains to be written, in praise of Mercersburg theology. As I seek to adjust myself to it I find that I am grateful for Mercersburg's re-emphasis, in the face of sectarianisms of all kinds, upon the catholicity of the Church; and for its reminder to the Reformed that the heritage of the Christian ages is theirs, and that it is foolish to hop from the New Testament to the Reformation as if nothing of importance had happened in between. The Mercersburg witness to the inescapability of the Church for believers, and on the Church's nature as an organism (provided that slippery term be carefully construed), is entirely appropriate. I welcome Mercersburg's concern that the sacraments be given their rightful place in worship, though I wish that the Mercersburg theologians had had more to say on the relation of Word and sacrament. Above all, I endorse the implication that the first word of the Gospel is grace, not sin, and the concomitant refusal to endorse any doctrinal caricatures which would suggest that the wrathful Father punishes the innocent Son.

On the other hand, some of the points which Bomberger made stand as warning beacons. Before summarising these let me remind you that I have been attempting to evaluate a dispute, and that the literature with which I have been principally concerned has been of the polemical sort. Polemicists frequently emphasise the alleged errors, and play down the strengths, of their opponents. Thus, if we recall that the agreed text underlying the theology of both Nevin and Bomberger is the Heidelberg Catechism, and in relation to *some* of the words we have quoted from Nevin, we cannot say that he had *no* place for the Cross and the Spirit. But in the polemical literature, and when underlining what he thinks has been overlooked by the Reformed, or when haranguing the more gruesome understanding of the atonement and of conversion which sectaries all around him were peddling, he does say things which warrant the checks and balances proposed by Bomberger.

67 Ibid., 7.

Thus on christology: of course Nevin was right when he said that "The Saviour must come into the world before He could die in the world."[68] That is a truism. Furthermore, Christ can only do what he does because he is who he is—that is another truism. But, against some of Nevin's unguarded assertions, which might appear (against his actual beliefs) to endorse immanentist-automaticism in the matter of salvation, and against theosophies whether old-time or New Age, we must maintain the centrality of the once-for-all, historic, Cross-Resurrection event, and agree with James Denney that "the rationale of the Incarnation is in the atonement."[69] If we forget this we are on the way to a reduced, idealised christology.

On the Holy Spirit, our Reformed ecclesiology, whether Reformed, Presbyterian or Congregational, has, however ambivalently at times, understood that there is a distinction of eternal significance between those who are in Christ and those who are not.[70] By opposing in the name of the Spirit's work a Christ-mysticism which entails the union in the Incarnation of Christ with the whole of humanity, Bomberger challenges us at a fundamental point in our ecclesiology. If much Reformed theology has had too little regard to the old creation, may not Mercersburg play down the novelty of the new? As to the Mercersburg conviction that the Church is an extension of the Incarnation—and again in the interests of the Spirit's work—I side with P.T. Forsyth, who declared, "That which owes itself to a rebirth cannot be the prolongation of the ever sinless."[71] This is not at all to deny that the risen Christ is with his people, that they abide in him, that they are called to be about his business in the world. But it is to recognise that the empirical Church is an earthen vessel.

---

68 J.W. Nevin, *Answer to Professor Dorner*, 69.

69 James Denney, *The Christian Doctrine of Reconciliation*, London: Hodder & Stoughton 1917, 65. See further Alan P.F. Sell, *Aspects of Christian Integrity*, ch. II, where the authors of *The Myth of God Incarnate* (1977) are gently rebuked from this point of view. For an account of Denney's main thrust see Alan P.F. Sell, *Defending and Declaring the Faith: Some Scottish Examples 1860–1920*, Exeter: The Paternoster Press, and Colorado Springs: Helmers & Howard 1987, ch. IX.

70 Calvin was not the least among the ambivalent on this matter. He oscillated between a "both–and" and an "either–or" ecclesiology. See Iain G. Nicol, "Church and state in the Reformed tradition," in *Baptism, Peace and the State in the Reformed and Mennonite Traditions*, eds. Ross T. Bender and Alan P.F. Sell, Waterloo, Ont: Wilfrid Laurier University Press 1991.

71 P.T. Forsyth, *The Church and the Sacraments* [1917], London: Independent Press 1947, 83.

So much for the major doctrinal cruces on which other anthropological and sacramental points turn. For all the "sound and fury" (and both terms are in order) of the Bomberger *versus* Nevin debate, there is one vital matter which was not treated in sufficient depth. The point at issue continues to perplex theologians to this day—or, if it does not, it ought to.

At one level the question is "What are the criteria for evaluating doctrinal change?" It is perhaps surprising that this issue was not more directly faced—though no doubt matters liturgical and constitutional were sufficiently exhausting. Even so, the nineteenth century *was* the century during which evolutionary thought came to the fore, and the evolutionary theme was invoked not only in the interests of incarnationalism, but also with reference to the development of doctrine (does not this year also mark the centenary of Newman's death?)[72] The question of the *Church's* development through history did occupy Nevin greatly,[73] so much so that Bomberger chided the Mercersburg theologians with "developing the faith of the Reformed church out of its proper house and home."[74] But the second-order question concerning the criteria for evaluating doctrinal change was not discussed in detail by Bomberger and Nevin, though each independently and in his own way adverted to Scripture and tradition. In mitigation it must be said that Reformed theology as a whole had not produced, and still has not produced, a clearly articulated doctrine of the development of doctrine. Perhaps prior to the rise of modern biblical criticism it did not need to. I am certainly not advocating the introduction into our thought at this late date of the slippery term "development." "Development" is sometimes taken as entailing the judgement, for which there is no justification, that in doctrinal matters later statements are necessarily preferable to earlier ones. I should rather speak of doctrinal change (which can be and is multi-directional) and then seek criteria by which to assess it.

Bomberger thought that Nevin was wrong in being guided so much by the early Church and not (as he thought) by the Bible. Nevin thought that his opponents were bogged down in the Reformation. Nevin's criterion for doctrinal propriety was the Apostles' Creed: "As there is but one method of the objective movement of the Gospel in Christ Himself, so there can be only one method for the

---

72 For the evolutionary motif, see Alan P.F. Sell, *Theology in Turmoil*, ch. III.

73 See, for example, his article on "Early Christianity" reprinted in *Catholic and Reformed*.

74 J.H.A. Bomberger, "What they mean by development," *The Reformed Church Monthly*, VI, 1873, 524.

apprehension of it on the part of believers. That method we have in the Apostles' Creed. . . ."[75] To which Bomberger responded, "We most cordially accept of Dr. Nevin's rule. . . . The spirits must be tried. Only he and we differ as to the standard. He says, the fourth century; we say, the first. He says, by patristic authority; we say, by Apostolic authority. He says, by the *Creed* in the third and fourth century sense; we say, by the *Creed* as explained in our Heidelberg Catechism, which gives, in all essentials, the true Gospel sense."[76] We should not infer from this that Bomberger has no place for creeds and confessions; but they must be judged against Scripture as the "ultimate and supreme rule of faith,"[77] and this not least because they "may be mixed with human infirmities, and are open to formal development and exhibition. . . ."[78]

Here is the point at which, rising above the liturgical question as such, the issue might more deeply have been joined. For creeds and confessions are called forth by historical circumstances. They are in the first instance acts of confess*ing* on the part of those who devise them. Thus, the Apostles' Creed, countering Docetism as it does, emphasises the key historical moments of Jesus's life. But it does not specify the work of the Holy Spirit and, as Forsyth said, "The doctrine of Redemption is signally absent from the creeds, yet the Church has a more direct connection with Redemption than with Incarnation."[79]

But if creeds and confessions are to a degree occasional, and if they require human evaluations for their construction and subsequent interpretation, have we not nowadays come to perceive that exactly the same may be said of the Scriptures, which are already tradition? Does this mean that neither of the time-honoured *loci* of authority, Scripture and Tradition, are trustworthy? No, it simply means that these witnesses to the *Gospel* have to be judged in the light of that Gospel which is brought home to believers in every generation by the Holy Spirit. Upheld by the same Spirit, though able to resist him, believers live more or less faithfully and interpret more or less accurately. This Gospel of the Father's grace finds its fullest expression in the Son's Cross-Resurrection victory, the

75 J.W. Nevin, "Theological vindication of the new liturgy," in *Catholic and Reformed*, 372.

76 J.H.A. Bomberger, *Reformed Not Ritualistic*, 94.

77 Idem, "Mercersburg and Reformed theology contrasted," *The Reformed Church Monthly*, VI, 1871, 182.

78 Albert R. Thompson, "The Lectures of Dr. John H.A. Bomberger," II, 9; Lancaster Theological Seminary Archives.

79 P.T. Forsyth, *The Church and the Sacraments*, 83.

import of which is made alive in each successive generation in the lives of those who are called by the Spirit through the Word to be the Church. Discerning *that* Spirit is ever the task of the Church. It is a corporate task in which all believers should share, and if polity forbids, then polity must be reformed. In undertaking this task the Church listens *for* the Spirit and *to* the witness of the Christian ages, viewing all in the light of the primary witness, the Bible. Such discerning is both our praise and our response to God the Holy Trinity.

If the Bomberger-Nevin episode challenges us as to how our churches can be Gospel-grounded centres of discernment of the Spirit it will have served us well, and we shall be on the way—not to infallible pronouncements—but to faithful witness in our time.

XII

Harley College and its Congregational Alumni

Devotees of *The Congregational Year Book* will have observed that between 1881 and 1968 there are references to fifty-one ministers and missionaries who were trained at Harley College from its foundation in 1878 to its closure in 1915. The *Year Books* yield no further information on Harley College (and standard Congregational histories are silent upon it), though earlier ones provide the clue that prior to "Harley College" it was known as "Harley House," and that its first name was "Guinness's Training Institute." We are thus in the world of the Guinness dynasty, the branches of which concerned themselves variously, one might say, with Bible, banking and beer.[1] My primary concern is with Henry Grattan Guinness.[2]

Grattan Guinness's father was Captain John Grattan Guinness (1783–1850), whose ill health prompted his retirement from the service of the East India Company. Captain Guinness's first wife was Susanna Hutton. Her father, a Dublin Alderman, was an ardent supporter of evangelicalism in Ireland. His second wife was Jane Lucretia, the widow of Captain J.N. D'Esterre. In February 1815 Parnell had denounced "the beggarly corporation of Dublin," of

1 See Michele Guinness, *The Guinness Legend*, London: Hodder & Stoughton 1990.

2 For H. Grattan Guinness see in addition to the above, DNB; *Who Was Who 1879–1916*; Henry Boylan, *A Dictionary of Irish Biography*, Dublin: Gill and Macmillan 1978; William Urwick, *Sketch of Life and Ministry* prefixed to *Sermons by the Rev. H. Grattan Guinness*, Dublin: John Robinson 1859. *In Memoriam. H. Grattan Guinness, D.D., F.R.A.S.*, a special number of *Regions Beyond* (i.e., XXXI, nos. 1, 2, January–February 1911). I am most grateful to Mr. Geoffrey Larcombe, the former Director of the Regions Beyond Missionary Union, for granting me access to the records of the Union, which were packed in readiness for their transferral to the missionary archive at the University of Edinburgh; and to the staff of Latin Link, which body has assumed some of the work formerly done by the RBMU.

which D'Esterre was a member, and the latter challenged Parnell to a duel—and lost. Parnell resolved never to duel again, and provided a pension for Jane Lucretia. Her father was the violinist, Wilhelm Cramer; her grandfather, the flautist Jacob Cramer, and her half-brother the pianist Johann Baptist Cramer.[3] Grattan Guinness, born on 11 August 1835 at Montpelier House, near Dun Laoghaire, was her eldest son.

John and Jane were members of York Street chapel, Dublin. The chapel had been built by the Countess of Huntingdon's Connexion in 1808, and since 1826 William Urwick (1791–1868) had been minister there. Urwick writes, "Soon after [Grattan's] birth [his parents] brought their infant son and dedicated him to the Lord in baptism, before the congregation, as a child to be brought up in Christian discipleship."[4] The family subsequently lived at Edinburgh, Clifton and Cheltenham. Grattan was educated in private schools. Never robust in health as a child, a period of sickness when he was eleven years of age frightened him, and drove him to seek solace in Christ. From that time onwards he counted himself a Christian. He began medical studies at about the age of sixteen, but could not tolerate the mental strain. By way of a complete change he sailed for Mexico, and thoroughly enjoyed the life at sea. On his return he acceded to the wishes of his friends, and took up farming in the west of Ireland; but when he learned from his younger brother, Robert Wyndham,[5] of his sixteen-month voyage around the world, and in particular of the impression made upon Wyndham by the Christian chief mate, Peek, Grattan, now maturely committed to Christ, wanted nothing more than to join his brother on Peek's next voyage. Peek, by now a captain, was in the process of engaging crew members. Among those who enlisted were Wyndham and Grattan Guinness. They sailed from London, but Grattan became almost immediately ill, and was put ashore at Hartlepool. He returned to Ireland and stayed with a friend in County Tipperary. His condition improved, and soon he was evangelising the Roman Catholics of the

---

3 The DNB article on "Guinness, Henry Grattan" states that Jane's father was William (*sic*), but, incorrectly, that her grandfather was Johann Baptist Cramer. We follow M. Guinness, op. cit., 21; DNB, "Cramer, Wilhelm," *The Oxford Companion to Music*, ed. Percy A. Scholes, London: OUP 1955, and the editor in *The New Oxford Companion to Music*, ed. Denis Arnold, Oxford: OUP 1983. Arnold does not, however, mention Jacob.

4 W. Urwick, *Sketch*, vi. For Urwick see DNB.

5 Subsequently the Reverend Robert Wyndham Guinness (1837–1919), of Rathdrum. Jane Lucretia's other son was the Reverend Frederick William Guinness (1839–1885), of Cheadle, Cheshire.

area, and being denounced from the altar by the priests for so doing. His life was threatened, but he was spared.

At about this time he received a letter from his mother in which she enquired whether he had ever thought of becoming a Christian minister. Grattan gave the matter careful consideration, and applied to New College, London, whose principal was John Harris.[6] He was accepted for training, and in the months preceding his enrollment as a probationer in January 1856, he occupied himself in evangelistic labours among the poor of Cheltenham, and preached his first open-air sermon on Psalm 30:5, "Weeping may endure for a night, but joy cometh in the morning." On his reception as a full member of New College, Grattan Guinness dutifully attended lectures, but spent every spare moment distributing tracts, and visiting such places as the St. Pancras Workhouse and the St. John's Wood Barracks. During his first summer vacation in Cheltenham he continued his evangelistic work, attracted the favourable attention of the press, and did not return to college until a third of the ensuing session had passed. The principal took a lenient view of this, and Guinness began to make up for lost time. But invitations to preach so inundated him that the choice between fulfilling engagements and completing his college course had to be made. He passed the examinations at the end of his second session, and then in June 1857 left New College to become a full-time evangelist, declining a unanimous call to the prestigious Moorfields Tabernacle, which pulpit he had supplied for three months whilst a student. In the following month he was ordained an evangelist at a service held in the Tablernacle. On his departure from New College, Urwick comments, "Let no other young man . . . hastily do as Mr. Guinness did advisedly. His circumstances were peculiar. . . ."[7]

Grattan Guinness undertook preaching tours of England, Wales and Scotland, and was for a short time in France. In February 1858 he spent two weeks based at York Street, Dublin, at Urwick's invitation, though also preaching in the Music Hall and elsewhere. Fellows and Professors of Trinity College sat under him, as did clergy of all denominations, the Lord Lieutenant, and numerous others of all social classes. On his front page, the editor of *The Daily Express* mused upon the phenomenon thus:

6 For John Harris (1803–1856) see *Congregational Year Book*, 1858, 207–09. From a letter of 1882 we learn that Grattan Guinness sent some books to his old College. See New College, London, MS 188/60, at Dr. Williams's Library, London.

7 W. Urwick, *Sketch*, xiii.

> Why do people of all classes, from the highest officers of State, and the highest dignitaries of the Law, down, throng so eagerly to hear the young minister whose case has suggested these remarks? Why is the large chapel where he officiates crowded an hour before the time? Is it because he is a youth; because his hair is dark, his face pale, and his voice musical? Is it because he bears the honoured name of Guinness, and his mother was the widow of Mr. D'Esterre . . . ? Is it because there is something about him eccentric, extravagant, spasmodic? Does he present a cunning exhibition of oratorical fireworks, a dazzling stage effect, or theatrical contrivances to get up a galvanic "revival"? No, it is nothing of this kind. . . . It is simply the preaching of the Gospel. . . . Mr. Guinness's case is worth studying, as showing how vast is the power of the gospel when its saving truths go forth to the people through an intellect that comprehends, and a heart that feels them. . . . Mr. Guinness has been hailed by all denominations.[8]

From Dublin Grattan Guinness itinerated throughout Ireland, and of his welcome in every place Urwick declared, "Altogether, nothing to compare with it has been known in Ireland within living memory. An announcement that he was to preach, was enough to put the population on the move."[9]

Urwick characterised Grattan Guinness's preaching as earnest, fluent, biblical, pictorial, direct. It was not perfect: "Zealously loyal as he is to the Truth, a bystander would say that in going forth to prostrate a Goliath who defies it, he does not always choose the best stones he might find in the brook, or take the best aim with his sling."[10] But he speaks to the people, not before them; his youth leaves time for any necessary improvements to follow; and he continues humble, and unspoiled by success. As to his theology:

> If he proved himself to be certainly not an Arminian, he proved himself to be, as certainly, not an Antinomian; for while he affirmed what I understand by "Election," though not "Reprobation"—Election *personal* as well as *national*. . . . he proclaimed salvation in Christ as commensurate with the wants of all—free for the appropriation of all—binding on the reception of all—to whom the testimony of it comes. His pleading with sinners to turn and live, kept pace with his teaching the necessity of the Spirit's influ-

---

8 *The Daily Express*, Monday, 15 February 1858; quoted by W. Urwick, *Sketch*, xx–xxi n.

9 Ibid., xxii–xxiii.

10 Ibid., xxviii–xxix.

> ence to render the truth effectual, and with his asserting redemption to be throughout of grace—of grace Divine.[11]

Grattan Guinness was in England during the summer of 1859. At Reading he preached for two hours on the text, "Ye must be born again," a sermon which was instrumental in the conversion of F. Beedel, who became a well-known Baptist minister in Australia.[12] Then it was back to Ireland at the height of the Ulster Revival. In August he preached in the open air to at least 15,000 people in Belfast; 6,000 heard him in Coleraine.[13] Dr. James Morgan, of Fisherwick Place, Belfast, who heard three out of Grattan Guinness's four Belfast addresses, afterwards compared him with Spurgeon, who came the the city a few months later: "There was a great contrast between them. Mr. Spurgeon was gay, lively and humourous; Mr. Guinness was solemn and earnest, and very reserved. Mr. Spurgeon is by far the abler man, yet were there a poll tomorrow in Belfast for the two, it would be in favour of Mr. Guinness."[14]

From November 1859 to May 1860 Grattan Guinness was in America, and on 1 August he was found in Bristol, where he preached to 1,800 people in the Broadmead Rooms. He married his first wife, Fanny Fitzgerald (1831–1898)[15] on 2 October 1860 and, with her, spent the next twelve years in extensive journeyings. They visited Canada in 1861, and Egypt and Palestine in 1862. Following a brief pastorate in Liverpool, they returned to Ireland where, in 1865 Grattan Guinness opened at training school for evangelists and missionaries at 31 Bagot Street, Dublin. This proved to be a

---

11 Ibid., xxv.

12 See F. Beedel, *Memorials of the Lord's Loving Kindness*, Sydney, 1905, 7.

13 See *The Freeman*, 10 August 1859, and J.W. Massie, *Revivals in Ireland*, London: John Snow 1860, II, 74. See further, J. Weir, *Irish Revivals. The Ulster Awakening*, London: Arthur Hall, Virtue 1860. The standard history of the revival is J. Edwin Orr, *The Second Evangelical Awakening in Britain*, London: Marshall, Morgan and Scott 1949, and from this we cull the details in this paragraph. Grattan Guinness does not appear in the index to John Kent, *Holding the Fort. Studies in Victorian Revivalism*, London: Epworth Press 1978; he is, however, mentioned in D.W. Bebbington's more broadly-based study of *Evangelicalism in Modern Britain. A History from the 1730s to the 1980s*, London: Unwin Hyman 1989, Grand Rapids: Baker Book House 1992.

14 James Morgan, *Recollections of My Life and Times*, Belfast: W. Mullan 1874, 314; quoted by W.Y. Fullerton, *C.H. Spurgeon. A Biography*, London: Williams and Norgate 1934, 115.

15 See further, *"Enter Thou." Pages from the Life Story of Fanny E. Guinness*, being *Regions Beyond*, January–February 1899.

forerunner of Harley College. In the following year he took charge of the Merrion Hall Mission, and it was at a Bible study meeting there that Thomas Barnardo dedicated himself to Christian service. In 1867 the family removed to Bath, and from that year until 1872 Grattan Guinness was frequently in France. In 1873 they settled in London, which became Grattan Guinness's base until he returned to Bath two years before his death on 21 June 1910. Meanwhile, following Fanny's death, he had married Grace Hurditch on 7 July 1903, and by her he had two sons. Of these one became the Reverend Paul Grattan Guinness. Of Grattan Guinness's children by Fanny, Dr. Harry Grattan Guinness (1861–1915)[16] assumed responsibility for Harley College and the Guinness missions activity (known as The Regions Beyond Missionary Union from January 1899) in 1886;[17] Mary Geraldine married Dr. James Hudson Taylor of the China Inland Mission,[18] and Lucy Evangeline[19] married Dr. Karl Kumm of the Sudan United Mission.[20]

I

Both Henry Grattan Guinness and Thomas Barnardo had intended to become overseas missionaries, the former under Captain Gardiner in Terra del Fuego, the latter as a medical missionary in China; but the needs of "darkest England" prevailed, and they both dedicated themselves to the preparation of evangelists for the home front and missionaries for the foreign. Accordingly, Grattan Guinness established the East London Institute for Home and Foreign Missions in 1873, with Barnardo as co-Director. Their motivation was threefold: their evangelistic zeal; Hudson Taylor's

16 See C.W. Mackintosh, *Dr. Harry Guinness. The Life Story of Henry Grattan Guinness, M.D., F.R.G.S.*, London: The Regions Beyond Missionary Union 1916.

17 For the RBMU see, in addition to other sources noted, Kenneth Holmes, *The Cloud Moves*, London: The Regions Beyond Missionary Union, rev. edn., 1974.

18 See F. H. and M. G. Taylor, *Hudson Taylor in Early Years. The Growth of a Soul*, London: Morgan 1911; idd. *Hudson Taylor and the China Inland Mission. The Growth of a Work of God*, London: Morgan & Scott 1918; idd., *Hudson Taylor's Spiritual Secret*, London: China Inland Mission 1932; M. Broomhall, *Hudson Taylor,The Man Who Believed God*, London: China Inland Mission 1936; Frank Houghton, *The Fire Burns On*, London: China Inland Mission/Overseas Missionary Fellowship 1965; Leslie T. Lyall, *A Passion for the Impossible. The China Inland Mission 1865–1965*, London: Hodder & Stoughton 1965.

19 H. Grattan Guinness published a memoir of Lucy: *Lucy Guinness Kumm. Her Life Story*, London: Morgan & Scott 1907.

20 See further J.L. Maxwell, *Half a Century of Grace: A Jubilee History of the Sudan United Mission*, London: Sudan United Mission [1953].

presentation of the dire need of missionaries in China; and "their study of Scripture and especially of prophecy, which had convinced them not only of the Divine purpose that Christ should be *preached to every creature*, but also that His Coming must be near, and that *the time was short*."[21] For eighteen years the Institute's secretary was Fanny Guinness, who also wrote books in collaboration with her husband and in her own right, prepared annual reports of the Institute's work, was secretary of the Congo Mission, and editor of *Regions Beyond* from its inception in 1878 until her death twenty years later—a responsibility then assumed by Lucy for a further eight years.

The Institute acquired the house at 29, Stepney Green, and Fanny's first annual report begins thus:

> It is an ancient brick house, very old-fashioned inside and very shabby outside, and, by force of contrast it looks shabbier now than it did when we took it a year ago; for its neighbours on either hand have modernized themselves, and abolished the dark walls and high iron gates that enclosed them. But 29 still stands behind the barricade of brick and iron work, which, in the days when Stepney Green was a stylish country suburb of London, gave a mansion-like dignity to the residence.[22]

She proceeds to note that there is comfortable, but not luxurious, accommodation for eighteen to twenty persons: "[W]e provide beds, not to soothe the restlessness of the slothful, but only to give rest to the weary, and two feet six is enough for that."[23] The house is to be a home where Christian young men "may prepare for Missionary labour, by actually attempting it among the godless masses of the East-end of London. . . ."[24] It is not for the wealthy, and its objective is not the production of scholars: "We want rank and file in the Mission army as well as officers."[25]

The house having been obtained, Grattan Guinness announced its availability at meetings he addressed in Birmingham, Sheffield, Liverpool, Manchester, Preston, Kendal, Kilmarnock, Edinburgh, Alloa, Newcastle, Sunderland, Darlington, Bury and elsewhere. Thirty-two were selected from the hundred who volunteered:

---

21 C.W. Mackintosh, *Dr. Harry Guinness*, 12.

22 By an Hon. Sec. [i.e., Fanny Guinness] *29, Stepney Green; or, Our First Year*, London: S.W. Partridge [1874], 1.

23 Ibid., 2.

24 Ibid., 3.

25 Ibid., 4.

> As to religious association, some were Church of England, some Presbyterian, some Independent, some Baptist, some Wesleyan, and two were Brethren.
>
> Two were French, one a Russian, one a Hindoo, one a Syrian, several Scotch and Irish, while there were Englishmen from Newcastle, Sunderland, Liverpool, Manchester, Bury, Sheffield, and London.[26]

The curriculum was governed by what missionaries needed to know: geography, navigation, botany, the rudiments of medicine, mechanics, cookery, gardening, world, biblical and Church history, the story of modern missions, and grammar. Above all the missionary must know the Bible as a whole, and its doctrines in their variety and harmony.

The Institute day began with the ringing of a bell at six. Family worship followed at seven-thirty. Since no servants were employed, students had to undertake household chores. Breakfast was at eight. At nine classes began. The tutor, Mr. W. Penn, F.R.A.S., taught from four to six hours daily; Grattan Guinness and Mr. Grant, a missionary from Singapore, conducted theological and biblical classes; Mr. Carruthers, F.R.S. gave occasional lectures on science, and Barnardo on general subjects. Students also attended courses on Christian evidences and other subjects by James Culross, Thain Davidson, and others. Following lunch at one-thirty, the first part of the afternoon was devoted to the learning and practise of trades, the second to house-to-house visitation. Tea followed at six, and then on four days per week all students were despatched to preach either in the open air, or in a mission hall. At nine-thirty the company reassembled in the Institute for evening devotions. The work was entirely financed by donors, 220 of whom, in the first year, contributed £1,569. "God," wrote Fanny, "is testing us all continually . . . by the presence of 800 MILLIONS OF HEATHEN IN THE WORLD. It is a tremendous test! so real! so practical!"[27]

By the second year of operations, 1874, 29 Stepney Green had become too small for the growing work. It was retained as a dormitory, and Harley House, two miles to the east, was taken as the Institute's main centre, though it too had at once to be enlarged, a new wing being opened in December 1875. Barnardo's work likewise had expanded to such an extent that he was unable to continue as a Director. Accordingly, the Guinness's came to reside at Harley

26 Ibid., 8. Cf. *"Enter Thou,"* 33.

27 Ibid., 20. For the accounts for the first year of operation see ibid., 25–28.

House.[28] In the following year Cliff House, Calver, Derbyshire, the home of the late J.H. Hulme, a staunch Congregationalist and former Recorder of Salford, became available rent-free for ten years through the good offices of Mrs. Hulme, who had paid a visit to Harley House and been impressed by the Institute's work.[29] Renamed Hulme Cliff College in honour of its former owner, it became the Institute's country training branch, and was also made available during the summer for Christian holidays. Mr. Dening of Bath became the first tutor there.[30] In 1879 Harley College was built in the grounds of Harley House, and in 1884 a training centre for deaconesses, Doric Lodge, was opened. A mission centre at Berger Hall, and Bromley Hall for missionary nurses were among other parts of the Guinness enterprise. Meanwhile the overseas missions proceeded apace.[31]

II

We have seen that from the outset Harley's student body was inter-denominational, and the same may be said of its directors and teachers. Early "referees" of the Institute included Barnardo, the Baptist James C. Culross,[32] the evangelist Dwight L. Moody of Chicago, C.H. Spurgeon, Hudson Taylor, Lords Farnham and

---

28 See [Fanny Guinness], *Harley House, Bow, E. Or, Our Second Year at the East End Training Institute*, London: S.W. Partridge [1875], 5, 8.

29 The property was built *circa* 1790. Hulme, whose first wife was a daughter of the first owner, Mr. Gordon, inherited it. His second wife was an aunt of the distinguished Congregational minister, Robert Forman Horton. On leaving Lyndhurst Road church Horton made his home with her (she was now the wife of the Revd. David Robertson). Although she loved her nephew, she never read Horton's books on the Bible. She nevertheless denounced them on the ground of their infidelity (she being an upholder of plenary inspiration), and branded him a Unitarian. See Albert Peel and J.A.R. Marriott, *Robert Forman Horton*, London: Allen & Unwin 1937, 160–62.

30 See [Fanny Guinness], *Hulme Cliff College, Curbar; or, The Story of the Third Year of the East End Training Institute*, London: S.W. Partridge [1876].

31 For accounts of the institutions associated with the East London Institute see *These Thirty Years*, London: Harley House, Bow: RBMU 1903; *"Not Unto Us." A Record of 21 Years' Missionary Service*, London: Harley House, Bow: RBMU 1908. The latter records the first twenty-one years' life of the RBMU, which was so named in 1887, when Harry Guinness assumed the Directorship of the Institute.

32 Following pastorates at Stirling, Highbury Hill, London, and Adelaide Place, Glasgow, Culross became Principal of Bristol Baptist College, 1883–1896. See *Baptist Union Handbook*, 1900, 209; Norman Moon, *Education for Ministry. Bristol Baptist College 1679–1979*, Bristol: Bristol Baptist College 1979, *passim*.

Radstock, and a number of others less exalted. The earliest extant minute book lists the following as members of the Council: Archibald G. Brown, W. Cuff, W. Fuller Gooch and F.B. Meyer (Baptist ministers); G.H.C. MacGregor (Presbyterian); E.W. Moore (Methodist); G. Campbell Morgan (Congregationalist); W. Darlow Sarjeant (Wesleyan)[33]; W.H. Griffith Thomas (Church of England); together with Grattan and Harry Guinness.[34] In June 1908 the Council was re-formed thus: J. Cuming-Brown, Henry Oakley, and Frederick Chambers Spurr (Baptists); W.H. Condy; D. F. Mackenzie; Alfred Jabez Palmer (Congregationalist); together with Dr. Milne, the Institute's medical referee, Principal Forbes Jackson and staff.[35] Among later members of the Council were J. Stuart Holden (Church of England); Robert Wright Hay (Baptist); J. Gregory Mantle (Wesleyan); J. Horace Johnston[36] and George Hanson (Presbyterian church of England); and Mr. George Morgan.

As to the teachers, I have noted some who served in a visiting capacity. Among others who did so were F.B. Meyer, who, from 1887 travelled from Leicester, where he was minister of Melbourne Hall, for the purpose. Among early regular tutors was John Barfield. Among other things he escorted the students through Xenophon's *Anabasis* II, Euclid I and II, and Wayland on ethics. In Ancient History the objective was to study the Bible in relation to the *History of Rome* and the *Decline and Fall of the Roman Empire*, in such a way as to illustrate the outworking of prophecy. English essays were written, and "In the Elocution Class every attempt to form an artificial style is carefully avoided; on this account there are no recitations."[37] Meanwhile the Senior Tutor, the Revd. Anson J. Towell,

---

33 W. Darlow Serjeant (1842–1905) joined W.H. Tindall (who had received entire sanctification at the Keswick Convention) and others in founding the Methodist holiness convention at Southport in 1885. This serves to illustrate the fact that Grattan Guinnes could co-operate with evangelicals of a variety of kinds, for he opposed the "Keswick" teaching—despite which fact he did address a special Mildmay Conference in 1874. For Serjeant see Wesleyan *Minutes of Conference*, 1905, 141–42. For the holiness question see further D.W. Bebbington, *Evangelicalism in Modern Britain*, Ch. V.

34 *Minutes of Harley Institute/College Council 1896–1910*, list precedes p. 1.

35 Ibid., 57.

36 I cannot forbear to mention that Johnstone's obituary informs us that he was "possessor of a beautiful voice—it was a joy to hear him recite the Pied Piper." *Presbyterian Messenger*, March 1963. Hanson, Hay and Morgan were introduced to readers of *Regions Beyond*, June 1903, 179–81.

37 See J. Barfield's report in [Fanny Guinness], *The Regions Beyond: or, The Story of Our Fourth Year at the East End Training Institute, and at Hulme Cliff College, Curbar*, London: S.W. Partridge [1877], 32–33.

was responsible for English grammar and history, Bible and Church history, the Greek Testament, Hebrew (the seniors reading in Joshua, Psalms and Isaiah, and learning Old Syriac; the juniors reading Deuteronomy), and theology. Grattan Guinness had charge of theology "in its more evangelistic and pastoral aspects."[38] We later learn from Barfield that the students read Paley on natural theology and imbibed the theology of (probably A.A.) Hodge.[39]

The association of the Revd. J.S. Morris with Harley College appears to have begun in the early 1880s.[40] Morris, an artist's son, was born at Hackney in 1840. His parents belonged to Mare Street Baptist chapel, where Morris was baptised at sixteen years of age. He was soon found preaching at street corners, and evangelising the neighbourhood of his home; and for a while he worked under the auspices of the Evangelization Society. In 1863 he entered Pastor's College, and in 1866 was called to Romney Street Baptist chapel, Westminster. Twelve years later he accepted the pastorate at Leyton, associating his work there first with a lectureship, and then, from October 1889, with the Principalship of Harley College. In a report published in 1893, Morris refers to forty-eight mission stations in the London area which had been served by Harley students preaching as appropriate in English, French, Swedish, Norsk, Hindustani, Portugese, German, Arabic, Italian and Hebrew.[41] Of Morris Pastor Archibald G. Brown wrote,

> Our brother needed knowing. His was not a character that could be measured and sounded in a conversation. The back warehouse was out of all proportion to the front window, and it was wonderfully well stocked . . . "Saturated with Scripture" would be a fair description of the man. . . . [His lectures] were solid, massive productions, that told of years of studious thought, yet given with the simpicity of a child. . . . He was pre-eminently *a man of prayer.*[42]

---

38 See the report of Anson J. Towell, ibid., 33.

39 See Mrs. H. Grattan Guinness, The Story of Our Sixth Year [1878–1879], London: Hodder & Stoughton [1879], 41.

40 At this point the reports are in conflict. In the text I follow "A Brief Sketch" of Morris which was contributed to *Regions Beyond*, November 1895, 450–52, shortly after his death. But in ibid., January 1893, 36, an editorial introduction to his Principal's Report states that he was at Leyton for fifteen years *before* undertaking the superintendency of Harley College *ten years ago.* Published information is supplemented by a clipped set of papers, "Items of Interest," in a box labelled "Early Documents and Letters."

41 *Regions Beyond*, January 1893, 39.

42 Ibid., November 1895, 448–50.

Morris died in August 1895, the funeral service being held at Leyton. Dr. Harry Guinness recalled that during his last illness Morris had said,

> Oh what a comfort the Atonement is! I think I've read every book and pamphlet that has been written about it on either side of the Atlantic. But it isn't the *theory* of the Atonement, it's the blessed *fact*. I love the very words, "The blood of Jesus Christ." Call it the "Gospel of the Shambles" if you will, but I love the very words.[43]

The service closed with "the Harley favourite," "Like a river glorious. . . ."

In 1896 the *Minutes of the Harley Institute/College Council* begin. At the first meeting, held on 2 October, the Council reviewed the cases of eight weaker candidates whose probationary period was up. Of a Mr. Cranham it is said that "his age (24) together with his slight physique and his poor mental attainments left the Council with no other course than to reject him. He was urged to continue his good work in the villages." While a Welshman, Mr. J.R. Lewis, had money to pay his way, "he was rejected on the ground of his inexperience and extreme ignorance. We did not find any deep spirituality or force of Christian character about him, and it was felt he would be no credit to the college, and his future would be very uncertain." As for Mr. Werman, "This Jewish brother was warmly recommended by the Barbican Mission to the Jews, who would probably accept him for future work. He had, however, a very unprepossessing appearance, and seemed altogether not exactly the man we should care to have in the college. Under the circumstances, it was decided that if he could make arrangements to live outside we would give him the option of attending college lectures."[44]

Perhaps the most pressing issue at this date was the vacant Principalship. On 30 October it was agreed that for the time being Grattan Guinness should have the title, with Harry Guinness as Vice-Principal. The Reverend George Downs Hooper[45] was approached, but declined, as did the Revds. Walter Hackney and

43 Ibid., 447.

44 *Minutes of Harley Institute/College Council 1896–1910*, 7–8.

45 A collateral descendant of the martyred John Hooper (d. 1555), Bishop of Gloucester and Worcester, Hooper (1848–1908) was reared in the Church of England. In 1876 he joined the Baptists: "As a Churchman he had been a zealous and out-spoken advocate of the Establishment, and when his views changed he was both able and willing to give the reasons that led to the change." See his obituary, *The Baptist Handbook*, 1910, 487–88.

James Stephens. The latter, having declined the Principalship of the Pastor's College, felt that he could not now accept Harley. Hooper and another Baptist, the Revd. James Douglas, did, however, offer biblical and theological lectures, and the Revds. F.B. Meyer and G.H.C. MacGregor also came to the College's aid.[46] During this period Mr. Cosbie C. Brown was also a regular tutor, continuing in that office until 1903.[47] A minute of 12 February 1900 states that Silas Mead, formerly of Adelaide, who had served as acting Principal since the death of Morris,[48] was now to be relieved of his duties. The same meeting devised its list of "Qualifications of Principal":

> In the consideration of a new man for the Principalship, it was felt that not only should he be strong, healthy, and vigorous, but that he should be a spiritual force. He should undoubtedly be a Bible student, and able thoroughly to expound the entire Scriptures. It is of primary importance that he should accept con amore the Divine authority of the Word of God from Genesis to Revelation. He should further be missionary hearted and sympathetic, with a love for teaching and for young men. It was thought unwise that he should be permitted to occupy a pastorate at the same time, although he should be free to employ his Sundays in preaching here and there.[49]

In 1901 the Revd. Forbes Jackson, who had been travelling from Reading to give lectures since the previous year, took up residence in London as Principal of Harley College. Born in Fife on 7 November 1858, Jackson's early education was rudimentary, and he went to work in a linen factory at Kirkcaldy. He was baptized by the Revd. John Urquhart, and became a member of Whyte's Causeway Church. He became active in Christian work, and in 1880 entered Glasgow University, from which he graduated M.A. in 1884. During the summer months he took the classes of the Baptist Union of Scotland, whose first tutor had been James Culross.[50] Because of his admiration for Culross he proceeded to Bristol Baptist College,

46 *Regions Beyond*, January 1897, 5. Hooper noted that "In Systematic Theology we have fairly covered the course of [presumably A.A.] Hodge's Outlines, making liberal variations where needed, especially in Eschatology." Ibid., 6.

47 Ibid., 6.

48 Though the "Items of Interest" typescript states that he served in this capacity from 1897, and that he retired in 1901.

49 *Minutes*, 51.

50 See J.M. Gordon, "The later nineteenth-century," in *The Baptists in Scotland. A History*, ed. D.W. Bebbington, Glasgow: The Baptist Union of Scotland 1988, 61–62.

passed the first part of the St. Andrews B.D., but did not complete the course owing to his call to North Leith, where he began his ministry on 5 January 1886. Pastorates at Worcester (1890–1895) and King's Road, Reading (1895–1909) followed, and then he assumed his duties at Harley College.[51]

Meanwhile the work at Hulme Cliff College was becoming increasingly difficult to sustain. It had started well under the leadership of Mr. Dening of Bath, with an early tutor, Julius Rohrbach, writing enthusiastically of the courses held and of the commitment of the students.[52] Around 1880 Mr. William Rattray, who had been headmaster of Charlotte Street School, Aberdeen, became Principal of Cliff, serving until his death at the age of seventy-four, on 22 April 1895. Of him one of his former students wrote, "Mr. Rattray was a Calvinist, but so united man's free will with God's ordaining purpose, that he inspired us to plead with men as though all rested with them, and also to pray for souls and plead with God for the outpouring of His spirit as if all belonged to Him."[53] During the session 1891–1892, the Cliff students studied the books prescribed by the Presbyterian Church of England and the Christian Evidence Society. One of them, James Watson, gained a first prize for his work on Robert Flint's *Theism*.[54] Rattray was succeeded by a Congregational minister, John Francis Tooke Hallowes (1846–1917), who had taken first class honour in the Moral Science Tripos at Cambridge, and then completed six months of theological training at the Nottingham Institute. Following pastorates in Bakewell, Gloucester and Barnsley he spent nine years as a mission preacher, and then assumed his duties at Cliff College.[55] In October 1901 Cliff closed—it was hoped temporarily,[56] but in fact it did not reopen under Guinness auspices. Hallowes went to India, where he spent thirteen years as a missionary, and Cliff's long-serving tutor, Mr. F.W. Schofield, transferred to Harley College.

---

51 For Jackson see further *The Baptist Handbook*, 1914, 481–82.

52 See [Fanny Guinness], *The Regions Beyond; or, The Story of Our Fourth Year*, 33–34.

53 Quoted by Lucy E. Guinness, "Holding the ropes at home. No. VI. The life-work of our friend William Rattray. . . ." *Regions Beyond*, June 1895, 253. For Rattray's description of life at Cliff see ibid., January 1896, 46–48.

54 *Regions Beyond*, July–August 1892, 335.

55 For Hallowes see *The Congregational Year Book*, 1919, 74–75. He is here said to have become Principal of Cliff College in 1894. Rattray, however, "died in harness" in 1895, as we have seen. For Hallowes's account of the work at Cliff see *Regions Beyond*, September–October 1897, 374–75.

56 See the notice in *Regions Beyond*, October 1901, 280.

Among the reasons for the closure of Cliff were declining funds, and the reduction of the number of applicants for missionary training owing to the Boer War. Harry Guinness was, however, delighted that in 1903 the Wesleyan, the Revd. Thomas Cook, was able to take over Cliff as the base for the Joyful News Mission, which had been founded by the Revd. Thomas Champness; and that, with the co-operation of the Revd. Samuel Chadwick of Leeds, village missioners were still to be trained there.[57]

Under the strong leadership of Forbes Jackson, Harley College prospered academically. In July 1907 we find him appealing for additional study bedrooms, and for a new library and common room. A year later the foundation stones were laid.[58] As well as being needed for the work, the extensions were intended to meet the requirement of London County Council when the land was acquired, that new building must be under way by 1908. By 1909 Jackson was not quite so buoyant in spirit. He lamented that not many readers of *Regions Beyond* were interested in the training of students—and he granted that "No one cares to listen to the 'tuning up' of violin players." He proceeded to change the metaphor to a clay pit, and presented Harley's work as that of turning clay into presentable objects. He illustrated by reference to "a bit of raw material which dumped itself down upon us four years ago by way of Finland, Norway and far Zululand. A rough sailor, deck hand and ship carpenter the lad had been. . . ." At the end of his first year the student requested a further period of study on the ground that "I seem to know less now than when I came last October." "Oh yes," replied Jackson, "if you are growing more ignorant you had better stay." Eventually the "clay" became a competent medical missionary to Africa.[59]

But the writing was on the wall. As early as 22 October 1908 the Directors of the RBMU had held a Special Meeting at Devonshire House Hotel with a view to considering the defecit on operations,

---

57 See *Not Unto Us*, 16–17. See further, Amos S. Cresswell, *The Story of Cliff*, Calver, Sheffield: Joyful News Bookroom 1965; Norman G. Dunning, *Samuel Chadwick*, London: Hodder & Stoughton 1935; David H. Howarth, "'Joyful News' (1883–1963). Some reflections," *Proceedings of the Wesley Historical Society*, XLIV pt. 1, May 1983, 2–15; idem, *Samuel Chadwick and Some Aspects of Wesleyan Evangelism, 1865–1932*, unpublished M.Litt. thesis, University of Lancaster, 1978. The first minister the present writer remembers is Howard Belben (then at Cranleigh, Surrey), who taught at Cliff for twenty-three years—for the last twelve of them as Principal—until his retirement in 1977. See *Methodist Recorder*, 14 July 1977, 9.

58 See *Regions Beyond*, June 1907, 145–46; June 1908, 113–14.

59 F. Jackson, "Outward bound from Harley," *Regions Beyond*, July 1909, 130–32.

and over the next few years a number of such meetings took place.[60] Various solutions were proposed, and buyers were sought, to no avail. On 2 June 1910 the Harley Council decided "not to attempt to open [the College] to new candidates until, at the earliest, October, 1911."[61] In the latter year, and as a result of rising costs, the overseas work in Peru and Argentina was transferred to another body, while that in the Congo and Behar was retained. In the meantime, and not unconnected with the difficulties faced by the College and the reduction of the course from four to two years, Forbes Jackson had accepted a call to Crown Terrace Church, Aberdeen. A presentation was made to him,[62] and he was elsewhere described as one whose "gifts amounted to genius. As a preacher he was arrestive, virile, flinging out massive thoughts in concrete symbols and never in dim [?] and abstractions. As a teacher and leader of men he was magnetic, and won the lasting devotion of his students. As a pastor he was sympathetic and kindly, wise in counsel and courageous in rebuke."[63]

On 12 January 1911 the Directors of the RBMU determined not to reopen the College until the debt was entirely removed;[64] on 16 July 1915 they resolved in principle "to promote the resuscitation of Harley College under their own auspices," but at the same meeting agreed that it would be inexpedient to attempt this while the War lasted. A message to this effect was communicated in *Regions Beyond*.[65] In the meantime the College was used as a hostel for War refugees from Belgium. On 14 September 1917 a Committee was appointed, comprising the Revd. D.F. Mackenzie, Pastor Findlay, Mr. Wilson Heath, Dr. Meyer, Sir Andrew Wingate who, together with Dr. Stuart Holden, Dr. Maxwell and Mr. Sloan, were to consider the possibility of resuscitating the work of the College. Their ensuing report made it clear that while an evangelical missionary training institute was a dire necessity, it should not be under the auspices of the RBMU, and it should be housed elsewhere than at Harley. The report was adopted, and in consultation with the Charity Commissioners Harley was put on the market, with the proviso that funds accruing should be devoted to the objects for

---

60 See the RBMU *Minute Book 1908–1915*, 18–19; 133ff.; 160ff., etc.

61 *Minutes of Harley Institute/College Council*, 65.

62 See *Regions Beyond*, March 1910, 48–49.

63 *The Baptist Handbook*, 1914, 482.

64 RBMU *Minute Book 1908–1915*, 160–61.

65 Ibid., 252, 254; *Regions Beyond*, July–August 1915, 41.

which the RBMU existed.[66] In 1918 the premises were purchased for use as a warehouse for spices.

III

What, finally, of the Congregational alumni of Harley College? It has proved impossible to trace the careers of all of them.[67] Some have only their first appointment listed in *The Congregational Year Book*, and thereafter no more is heard of them. No doubt some proceeded to other missions, even to other careers.[68] Perhaps some went astray. Certainly Dr. Harry Guinness capitalised on one such at the Keswick Convention in 1910. He "told how he met in Tasmania a doctor who was dying, and who had been successful in his profession. In early days he had been a student at Harley House, with the intention of being a Missionary, but he had turned aside, and now as he lay dying he felt that all his worldly success was to him but 'dust and ashes.'"[69] The elusiveness of some notwithstanding, there is enough material available to demostrate something of the variety of service performed by the Congregational "Harley men." We shall briefly refer to some who served in the foreign, colonial and home mission fields.

Among those who served with the London Missionary Society was Oliver Fellows Tomkins. Born on 5 March 1873 at Great Yarmouth, he sailed for Papua on 8 December 1899. On his arrival the veteran missionary with whom he was to work, James Chalmers, sent a message home: "He will do; send us two more of the same

66 RBMU *Minute Book 1915–1920*, 72–79; 98.

67 For example, letters to the appropriate authorities have failed to produce information concerning A. Rivett, whose ministry began in 1881 in Australia; Samuel Roberts, who was at Bussleton, Western Australia in 1911; and William Tanner, who was at Waipu, New Zealand in 1910.

68 Michele Guinness provides no evidence for the assertion that, from about 1908 onwards, "Harley students offered themselves not to the China Inland Mission or to the Regions Beyond Missionary Union, but to the big denominational missions who would pay them more." See *The Guinness Legend*, 287–88. As we have seen, some were members of the "mainline" denominations, and it was natural that they should think in terms of the mission bodies of their own church families. It is, moreover, possible with integrity to have reservations concerning the faith mission principle on which some of the other organizations were conducted.

69 Quoted by Walter B. Sloan, *These Sixty Years. The Story of the Keswick Convention*, London: Pickering and Inglis [1934], 66.

sort."[70] The plan was to place Tomkins in charge of the Torres Straits Mission, but scarcely had he settled into the work when he, Chalmers and twelve students were killed at Dopima on 7 April 1901. At a meeting in the Royal Albert Hall in May of that year Dr. W. G. Lawes said, "What can I say of him who was the sharer of [Chalmers's] martyrdom, except that he had won all hearts, and that we expected great things from him for many years to come? . . . He was to [Chalmers] what Timothy was to Paul, his 'dearly beloved son.'"[71]

In 1902 it was reported that there were twelve Harley men holding Congregational pastorates in the British colonies;[72] and two years later D. Burford Hooke, Secretary of the Colonial Missionary Society, described their work.[73] James Middleton, Edwin A. Rumball and Hugh MacDermott were with the Fortune Bay Mission, Newfoundland. To his normal duties Rumball added lectures on hygiene, for which he was commended by one hearer who proudly declared that he always took a bath each year in June! Middleton, born in Sheffield in 1874, served for ten years in Newfoundland and then went to Halifax N.S. There, in 1915, he was received into the Presbyterian Church in Canada, and continued a Presbyterian after the formation of the United Church of Canada in 1925. He had four pastorates in New Brunswick, one in Saskatchewan, and was in England from 1922 to 1931. He died, highly esteemed, on 8 July 1944.[74]

---

70 Richard Lovett, *James Chalmers. His Autobiography and Letters*, London: Religious Tract Society 1912, 457. For Tomkins, see *The Congregational Year Book*, 1902, 204; James Sibree, *London Missionary Society. A register of missionaries, deputations etc.: from 1796 to 1923*, London: London Missionary Society, 4th edn., 1923, no. 1103; A. Peel, *The Noble Army of Congregational Martyrs*, London: Independent Press 1948, 70; Clyde Binfield, *So Down to Prayers. Studies in English Nonconformity 1780–1920*, London: Dent 1977, 223–30. For the LMS see Richard Lovett, *The History of the London Missionary Society*, London: H. Frowde, 2 vols., 1899; Norman Goodall, *A History of the London Missionary Society 1895–1945*, London: OUP 1954.

71 R. Lovett, op. cit., 457–58. For William George Lawes see Joseph King, *W.G. Lawes of Savage Island and New Guinea*, London: Religious Tract Society 1909; Albert Peel, *The Congregational Two Hundred*, London: Independent Press 1948, 226–27.

72 *Regions Beyond*, January 1902, 22.

73 See D. Burford Hooke, "Harley men in colonial fields," *Regions Beyond*, September 1904, 236–38. For this Society see Ralph Calder, *One Commonwealth for God*, London: Independent Press 1966.

74 See *Acts and Proceedings of the Seventieth General Assembly of the Presbyterian Church in Canada*, 1944, 304. For MacDermott, see Ralph Calder, op. cit., 23–24, 76.

Southern Africa was well served by Harley men. Among them was James Ramage, ordained in 1882, who, in 1901 was unanimously elected Moderator of the Congregational Union of South Africa. Another was Charles Thomson, whose ministry began in 1887, and who was at Ladysmith throughout the 121-day siege of 1899–1900, serving the Gordon Highlanders as well as his own congregation. In a letter Thomson wrote,

> Our church was commandeered for a hospital, and during five months we worshipped at the manse, most of the time under an awning erected at the end of the building . . . I have often read about the glories of war, but here we have seen much of the other side. On two occasions our church was filled with wounded men as they were brought in from the hills, and it just looked like a slaughter-house. . . . Surely nations can find some more humane way of settling their quarrels than this![75]

Frederick H. Tapp was also in Ladysmith throughout the seige. The first time we hear of him is in connection with the review of Harley probationers in 1896. He was permitted to continue his studies, but it was remarked that "he should be curbed and never put in the front as his tendency to vanity was somewhat marked."[76] Tapp made out well in the end, however. Having remained at his post in Ladysmith, he afterwards died of enteric fever.[77] Burford Hooke afterwards recalled: "The other day a young man came to me offering himself for work in the Colony of Natal. He had been trained at Glasgow University, but what prompted his offer to go out? Years ago, in Devonshire, Mr. Tapp had led him to a knowledge of the truth, and he wanted to labour in the same colony and carry on similar work."[78]

Thomas Gamble served at Heidelberg, South Africa, from 1883 to 1897, when he removed to Rose Lane, Uitenhage, Cape Colony, where he remained until his death in 1931. The church building at Heidelberg was too small to contain the congregation which gathered for his ordination, so the Dutch Reformed premises were used, with ministers of that Church taking a prominent part. During the early years of Gamble's ministry the church saw revival: "European

75 Quoted by John Brown, *The Colonial Missions of Congregationalism. The Story of Seventy Years*, London: The Colonial Missionary Society/The Congregational Union of England and Wales 1908, 101.

76 *Minutes of Harley Institute/College Council 1896–1910*, 11.

77 John Brown, op. cit., 100–01.

78 D. Burford Hooke in *Regions Beyond*, September 1904, 238.

as well as Coloured people were swept by the tide of the Spirit."[79] The church was enlarged, but a long drought seriously reduced the population of the area, and Gamble was forced to leave Heidelberg, "much to the regret of the whole town."[80]

If relations with the Dutch Reformed Church were cordial in Heidelberg, the same could not be said of the situation at Upington when Alexander Stewart went there from Heidelberg in 1902. Alban Heath writes: "Situated on the fringes of the Kalahari, eight hundred miles from Cape Town, [Upington] enjoys an isolation more real than blissful." The congregation there had formerly been under the Dutch Reformed Church, but during the Second Boer War (1899–1902) the members applied for admission to the Congregational Union. The Union's Executive Committee approach the DRC to no good effect, high court action ensued, and it was determined that the property belonged to the DRC. Stewart offered to withdraw if the people wished to remain with the DRC, but they did not. Accordingly, "With splendid enthusiasm they set themselves to build a new church, which was opened in December 1904. . . . Despite his isolation in the wilds, Mr. Stewart keeps a cheery disposition and, ably assisted by his devoted wife, is doing a work which makes the whole Union his debtor."[81]

Of James Reginald Truscott it may be said that his pilgrimage was both missionary and ecclesiastical. He served at Gwelo, Rhodesia and Que Que from 1900 to 1906. At the time the town was rising from the original mining camp, and Truscott established both a day and a Sunday school in his church. He then returned to England, became an Anglican, and graduated B.A. (1909) and M.A. (1912) of the University of Durham. Ordained deacon in 1909 and priest in 1910, he served at St. Andrew, Bishop Auckland (1909–1913), and then returned to South Africa. He ministered at Umzinto (1913–1922), and was Vicar of Dundee, Natal, from 1922. He last appears in *Crockford's Clerical Directory* for 1940.

We turn finally to six ministers who may represent the Harley Congregationalists who served in the British Isles, and we take them in chronological order. Philip Davis, born at Verwood, Dorset,

---

79 See George P. Ferguson, *CUSA. The Story of the Churches of the Congregational Union of South Africa*, Paarl: printed by A.H. Fisher 1940, 113. Gamble refers to the 1884 *Year Book* of the CUSA.

80 Alban E. Heath, *Congregationalism in South Africa. A Souvenir of the Congregational Union 1859–1909*, CUSA, [1909], 26. Heath, himself a Harley man, ministered at Paarl (1901-1906), Vryburgh (1906–1910), Florida Road, Durban (1910–1914), and Uitenhage. He served as Secretary of CUSA.

81 Ibid., 23. Cf. Ralph Calder, *One Commonwealth for God*, 66–67.

was ordained at York Street, Dublin in 1878, and served at Kilmainham, Dublin from 1881 to 1944, in which year he died. Of him it was written, "The best tribute, perhaps, to his character and to his devotion, is to be found in his long-sustained ministry and oversight of one small church."[82] There could scarcely be a greater contrast in the ministry of the native Irishman, James Cregan, who was born at Hillsborough on 16 November 1857. He resolved upon the Christian ministry under the influence of D.L. Moody, whom he met at the age of nineteen, and he began his work at Albert Bridge, Belfast, in 1882. In 1897 the old building was replaced by one capable of seating 1,200 people; three Sunday schools and a mission hall were conducted from the church. Cregan was held in high regard as preacher, pastor and organiser—not least by Roman Catholics. He served a term as Chairman of the Irish Congregational Union. In 1904 Cregan accepted the call to Cavendish Street, Manchester. An Institute was formed in 1908, and the church became known for its wide variety of social activities. But all were the outworking of a solid preaching and pastoral ministry:

> The Ministry of James Cregan, whatever happened in the way of organisation, was first and last and all the time a ministry of friendship. In lived with and for his people. Into Cavendish he brought a new atmosphere of comradeship. Men and women learned to know each other as they had never done before. He himself knew everyone. When he went into the homes of his own folk, he remembered all about them, where they had come from, how long they had been there, the names of their children, their ages, and their illnesses. He was elected to the Chair of the Lancashire Congregational Union in 1913, and when he visited a little country church, he talked to its rustic congregation in a spirit of exhilaration and hopefulness. Before he came away he shook hands with the caretaker, asking him all about his work, and the caretaker went home feeling that to sweep out the Church, and stoke up the boiler, was the biggest and best calling in the world. There was good preaching at Cavendish, for James Cregan was himself in the pulpit, and spoke with great human emotion and sincerity about the evangelical faith; he did it all in his own way, and it carried conviction. In the end he went to Paddington, and he left behind him a strong Church greatly in love with him.[83]

82 *The Congregational Year Book*, 1945, 454.

83 T.T. James, *Cavendish Street Chapel Manchester. Centenary Commemoration 1848–1948*, 1948, 28. For Cregan we also draw upon *The Congregational Year Book*, 1936, 650; *Regions Beyond*, November 1904, 306.

In 1914 Cregan removed to Paddington Chapel, London. There he spent the seventeen years until his retirement in 1931. He served as Chairman of the London Congregational Union, and of Board of Directors of the Colonial Missionary Society. He died on 16 November 1935.

Edmund George King, who always "spoke with enthusiasm of Dr. Guinness and the inspirational value of his college," was a staunch friend of James Cregan from Harley days onwards. King was born at Offham, near West Malling, Kent, in 1859. He ministered at Dunstable (1882–1888), Grange, Sunderland as assistant to J.K. Nuttall (1888–1891), Edge Hill, Liverpool (1891–1902), and Darwen Road, Bolton (1901–1916). He then retired to Thornton le Fylde, but took charge of Bethesda, Blackpool, from 1920 to 1923. Like Cregan, he exercised a wide-ranging ministry. During his ministry at Edge Hill the P.S.A. (Pleasant Sunday Afternoon) "became second only to Great George Street [Liverpool]—the greatest Brotherhood on Merseyside;" and a large schoolroom was opened in 1893 at a cost of £2,000 (including the land). King had "an instinct for public life," and served on the Thornton Cleveleys Council for nine years, for four years as Chairman. He continued on the Education Committee until June 1932. "[W]hen sometimes reminded of his successful ministry, 'Laus Deo' was his almost invariable reply." He died on 10 July 1932.[84]

Thomas James Worrall was born at Smethwick on 29 January 1869. He preached his first sermon at the age of seventeen, and after training at Harley College, he ministered at Cannock and Hednesford (1894–1897), Castlecroft, Bury (1897–1909) and Allerton Bradford (1909–1922). He died on 3 February 1922, aged 53. Possessed of a fluent pen, Worrall contributed to *The British Weekly*, wrote articles and short stories, and a play entitled, *A Modern Pharisee*. Among his writings is a collection of *Prayers for Use in the Home*. Published in 1914, it is dedicated "To my dear people of the Allerton Congregational Church. . . ." In a "Foreword" Worrall pleads for the reintroduction of the practice of family worship, and expresses the hope that "the father, or if not the father, the mother, at some convenient moment, may read the prayer allotted for each day." The prayers are simple and moving, as may be seen from the conclusion to that for Saturday: "Bless our home and all our dear ones, present and absent, and when we come to the close of life, as we now come to the close of this another week, may our eyes open upon the Eternal Sabbath which awaits the children of God." There

84 See *The Congregational Year Book*, 1933, 238–39; Benjamin Nightingale, *Lancashire Nonconformity*, Manchester: Heywood [1893], VI, 191.

is appended a "Prayer for the Present Hour." In time of war Worrall invites his people to confess the sins of the nation; to pray that "the experiences through which we are now passing may have a chastening and illuminating effect upon us as a people"; to remember the wounded, the rulers, the churches, the Allies, and the enemies—"They are Thy children and our brethren." Shortly before he died Worrall's sacred song, "The bugle call," was set to a tune specially written by the celebrated evangelical organist and composer, W.H. Jude. There are five stanzas and a running chorus. The opening gives the flavour of the whole:

We'll fight! we'll fight for Jesus!
We'll battle for His Cross,
We'll follow where He leadeth,
Whate'er may be the cost;
We'll fight against injustice,
'Gainst sin of ev'ry kind,
We'll make this precious counrty,
A 'Home' for all mankind.

Fight on! Fight on for Jesus!
The Bugle call obey,
Now to a mighty conquest,
Let's win a glorious day.

Of Worrall it was said, "He was a great soul, and to know him was to love him. Three young men from his pastorates Hednesford and Bury are in our ministry today."[85]

Hugh Cunningham Wallace, born at Hurlford, Scotland on 4 May 1873, would seem to be atypical of Harley men in that he and his co-pastor at Anerley, Surrey, Dr. Joseph Warschauer, were found propagating something less than the full-blooded evangel. As Edward Cleal delicately put it: "The present ministers have excited public attention as exponents of theological views differing considerably from those usually prevalent in Congregational churches. A secession took place in 1907, the prospects of which it is still too

85 See *The Congregational Year Book*, 1923, 121. *Prayers for Use in the Home*, printed in Bradford, was published by Allerton Congregational Church and Sunday School in 1914. For a copy of this, and of "The Bugle Call" (London: Reid Bros. 1921), and for other information I am indebted to T. James Worrall's granddaughter, Mrs. Mary Shaw of Bradford, with whom I was put in touch by Mrs. Catton, church secretary of Allerton Congregational church. For W.H. Jude see his *Music and the Higher Life*, London: Reid Bros. 1904.

early to estimate."[86] The culprit was "The New Theology." R.J. Campbell's book of that name had appeared in 1907, and in the same year Warschauer, a firebrand against Calvinism, published *The New Evangel.* It is likely that he first met Wallace in Bristol. Wallace, having begun his ministry at Westgate, Burnley (1897–1901), proceeded to the David Thomas Memorial church, Bristol (1901–1905). Meanwhile Warschauer, who had been a Hibbert Scholar, was Unitarian minister at Oakfield Road, Bristol (1899–1905). In 1905 they both moved to Anerley, where Warschauer remained until 1910, before moving to Horton Lane, Bradford (1910–1914). In October 1915 there was a second, and a different kind of storm. It erupted at the Congregational Council meeting in North Shields. Warschauer was accused of misconduct with Wallace's wife, but nothing was proved. Wallace continued at Anerley until 1941, when he removed to St. Austell (1941–1953), and thence to Woodham Ferrers (1953–1957). He died on 1 December 1958, modestly leaving instructions that no tribute was to appear in *The Congregational Year Book.*[87]

The words used of James Alfred Kaye are "Great Heart," "gallant servant of Jesus Christ," "Christian warrior" and (so Sydney Berry at Kaye's memorial service) "a real man's man." The words are well chosen. Kaye was born in Brechin on 24 May 1886, and educated at the Grove Academy, Broughty Ferry. He was converted at the age of fifteen, and became a member of the Free Church, Broughty Ferry, where his father was an elder, and whose minister from 1886 to 1897 was James Denney (who, though no fundamentalist was far removed from "The New Theology"—pardon the anachronisms).[88] While working as a traveller for a firm of Dundee merchants, Kaye became involved in Christian Endeavour and the Y.M.C.A., and shortly entered Harley College. According to Principal Jackson, Kaye hoped to serve as a missionary—probably in East or Central Africa. In the event, however, he completed his student pastorate at Theale (1909–1911), and remained in the English ministry.[89] He served at

86 Edward E. Cleal, *The Story of Congregationalism in Surrey*, London: James Clarke 1908, 116.

87 See *The Congregational Year Book*, 1958, 433; John W. Grant, *Free Churchmanship in England 1870–1940*, London: Independent Press n.d., 133–34.

88 For Denney see Alan P.F. Sell, *Defending and Declaring the Faith. Some Scottish Examples 1860–1920*, Exeter: The Paternoster Press, and Colorado Springs: Helmers & Howard 1987, ch. IX.

89 In *The Congregational Year Book* for 1910 Kaye is found in ministerial List B (that is, the non-collegiate roll), and Harley is not mentioned. In CYB 1914 he is on List A, having passed the Congregational Union Examination; and in CYB 1916 "Harley and Cong. U. Exam" appears by his name.

Park Institute, Reading (1911–1913), as assistant at Christ Church, Westminster Bridge Road, London (1913–1916), and as an Army chaplain (1916–1917). He then went to High Cross, Tottenham (1916–1924) and New Court, Tollington Park (1924–1941). During the Second World War he became superintendent minister (or "bishop" as he was affectionately known) of the Guildford group of churches. At his Induction Service Dr. A.M. Chirgwin, General Secretary of the London Missionary Society delivered the charge to the incoming minister, while Leslie Weatherhead delivered the charge to the church. Kaye was full of good works: Chairman of the London Missionary Society in 1931; founder of the Guildford and District Free Church Council, President of the Surrey Congregational Union in 1947, President of his local Rotary Club, and a member of the Education Committee of Surrey County Council. A much-travelled preacher, Kaye was awarded an honorary D.D. by Ursinus College, Pennsylvania, in 1953. On returning home he used his new hood as a visual aid in a children's address. The colours are old gold over black, with a red chevron—the colours which predominate in the coat of arms associated with the Heidelberg Catechism, a standard of the old German Reformed Church, within whose borders Ursinus had been established.[90] To Dr. Kaye, however, the colours signified that we proceed from the blackness of sin to the brightness of salvation by the blood of the Cross. He was a compelling preacher with a resounding voice, and when one heard him open a prayer with one of his favourite phrases (complete with the rolled "r" of Scotland), "Eternal and ever-blessed God . . ." one knew that one was on holy ground. James Alfred Kaye was one of the last of the old-style "princes of the pulpit." When he entered the room the members of the lay preachers' class stood, and called him "Sir." Yet he was the friend of all, and ever the missioner. Hence his delight when a new church was opened in 1958 in the needy suburb of Stoke Hill. He presided at the opening service on 4 October, and died suddenly in harness on 1 November. His wife, Beatrice Mabel (née Young) died a few weeks later, on 15 December.[91]

---

90 See Calvin D. Yost, *Ursinus College. A History of its First Hundred Years*, Collegeville, PA: Ursinus College 1985, 39. By a happy coincidence the writer was similarly honoured in 1988.

91 Before she died, Mrs. Kaye gave me her husband's cassock which, after sizeable tucks, I wore until it disintegrated. A cassock is no longer a part of my wardrobe. For Kaye see *The Congregational Year Book*, 1959, 424–25; Forbes Jackson in *Regions Beyond*, July 1909, [illegible]34; Joyce Reason, *A Fellowship of Churches 1662–1962*, privately printed 1962, 18–19.

IV

In 1908, just as the position of Harley College was about to become precarious, it was reported that during the twenty-one years from 1887, 786 students had passed through the training institutions of the RBMU, and were associated with more than forty denominational and other agencies.[92] Of these approximately five per cent left Harley College for service under Congregational auspices. Possessed of diverse talents they served in a wide variety of spheres. The tribute to one of them, Robert Miller (1864–1941), may be the tribute for most: "He was a man of simple faith, marked devotion to his Lord, intensely zealous in his work, and a fervent, earnest preacher, through whom many were converted. He had broad sympathies, was generous to the poor, deeply interested in God's work at home and overseas."[93] This is the epitome of the "Harley man," and those who owe anything to the English Congregational tradition may be glad that such were to be found within its ministerial ranks.

In Memoriam James Alfred Kaye

92 *Not Unto Us*, 56–57.

93 *The Congregational Year Book*, 1942, 439.

Appendix: Harley Alumni Who Served within Congregationalism

In each case the place where they first ministered is noted. In the case of those who remained within Congregationalism and died in the British Isles, the year in which their obituary appears in *The Congregational Year Book* is appended in brackets. Owing to ambiguities in the records, it is not claimed that this list is exhaustive.

AITCHISON, SAMUEL, Natal.
ANDERSON, G.B., Pacaltsdorp, South Africa.
ANDERSON, ISAAC, Battles Bridge, Essex.
ASHFORD, DUDLEY BRIGHT, Kawhia, New Zealand.
BAINE, FRANCIS HERBERT, Greenock Mission. (1902)
BIGNALL, PERCY EDWARD, Heidelberg, South Africa.
BRIDGER, ERNEST ALBERT, Auckland, New Zealand. (1946)
COLLINS, WILLIAM, Pine Grove, Ontario, Canada.
CREGAN, JAMES, Albert Bridge, Belfast. (1936)
DAVIS, PHILIP, Kilmainham, Dublin. (1945)
DERRY, CHARLES, Westminster Road, Birmingham, (assistant). (1941; began in Peru under EUSA)
DOWNHAM, THOMAS, Sebakwe, South Africa.
DOWNHAM, WALTER, North Street, Brighton (Countess of Huntingdon's Connexion)
FANSTONE, JAMES, Canada. (1938)
GAMBLE, THOMAS, Uitenhage, South Africa.
GROVES, WILLIAM, Sierra Leone.
HEATH, ALBAN ERNEST, Paarl, South Africa.
HORSCROFT, THOMAS, Uniondale, South Africa.
JAMES, JOHN EVANS, Guildford district. (1953)
JOB, HENRY ALLEN, Kawhia, New Zealand. (1948)
KAYE, JAMES ALFRED, Theale. (1959)
KING, EDMUND, Dunstable. (1933)
MACDERMOTT, HUGH J. A., Pool's Cove, Fortune Bay, Newfoundland.
MACKENZIE, J.H., New Zealand.
MIDDLETON, JAMES, Fortune Bay, Newfoundland.
MILLER, ROBERT, Irish Evangelical Society, Galway. (1942)
MORGAN, CONRAD, Mayville, South Africa. (1914)
MOWLL, WALTER JOHN, Whitby Road, Eastbourne (1967–1968)

NEWTON, E., Dysseldorp, South Africa.
NUTTER, HENRY CECIL, Central Africa.
PARKER, GEORGE FRANK, Ladysmith, South Africa.
PELLS, H.W., Worcester, South Africa.
PLEDGER, JOHN ROBERT FITCH, Hackney, South Africa. (1944)
RAMAGE, JAMES, Paarl, South Africa.
RIVETT, A., Beechworth, Victoria, Australia.
ROBERTS, SAMUEL, Bussleton, Western Australia.
ROGER, G., New Labrador.
RUMBALL, EDWIN A., Pool's Cove, Fortune Bay, Newfoundland.
RUMPUS, FREDERICK A.A., South India. (He also attended Hackney College)
SEARS, G.F., Little Bay, Newfoundland.
STEWART, ALEXANDER, Heidelberg, South Africa.
TANNER, WILLIAM, Waipu, New Zealand.
TAPP, FREDERICK H., Ladysmith, South Africa
THOMPSON, CHARLES, Ladysmith, South Africa.
TOMKINS, OLIVER FELLOWES, Papua. (1902)
TRUSCOTT, JAMES REGINALD, Gwelo, Rhodesia.
TYLER, T.W., Fourpaths, Jamaica.
WALLACE, HUGH CUNNINGHAM, Westgate, Burnley. (1959)
WATSON, JOHN BROWN, Pretoria, South Africa.
WEEKS, ERNEST RICHARD, Colonial Missionary Society, London. (1959)
WORRALL, THOMAS JAMES, Cannock and Hednesford. (1923)

XIII

Theology for All: The Contribution of H.F. Lovell Cocks

"I was about sixteen when I decided to enter College and had never entertained serious thoughts of any other sphere of labour than the ministry." So said H.F. Lovell Cocks near the beginning of his "Ordination Statement" made at Winchester Congregational church on 31 May 1917,[1] and his deep commitment to the Christian ministry, which fuelled his later work in theological education, never left him. As the centenary of his birth approaches I shall review the theological contribution of one who, though adept in scholarly philosophical and theological discussion, never lost the common touch. Summoned to preach on great occasions, he was equally at home addressing children in church, or multitudes over the radio. Appropriately presented according to his hearers' or readers' needs, his was a theology for all.

I

Harry Francis Lovell Cocks was born at Uxbridge on 28 February 1894 into a Christian home.[2] In his "Ordination Statement" he expresses gratitude for the support of his parents, and the guidance

---

1 I am most grateful to Mrs. Doris Caulfield, Lovell Cocks's daughter, and her husband, who provided hospitality in their home while I examined Lovell Cocks's papers, and who allowed me to borrow many of them. Mrs. Caulfield also read the first draft of this paper with great care, made most helpful comments upon it, and expressed her pleasure that this account of her father had been written. By the kind consent of Mrs. Caulfield and her brother, Lord Cocks of Hartcliffe, the Lovell Cocks papers are now housed at Dr. Williams' Library, London. In what follows *LCP* refers to a manuscript or typescript among the Lovell Cocks Papers. The "Ordination Statement" referred to is among these, and the quotation is from its first page.

2 For a brief obituary notice (here supplemented by *LCP*) see the *Year Book* of the United Reformed Church in the United Kingdom, 1984, 258–59.

of his minister, the Reverend F. L. Riches Lowe, who served at Providence Chapel, Uxbridge, from 1903 to 1933. At Riches Lowe's funeral service in 1960, Lovell Cocks recalled, "He was so very patient with me and my contemporaries in his Bible Class. We were the 'angry young men' of those days and he was generous and understanding in all his dealings with us."[3] Lovell Cocks honed his debating skills at school and church, began to preach in a nearby village church, and, in 1912, two years after passing the matriculation examinations of London University, entered Hackney College, whose Principal was P.T. Forsyth:

> I shall never cease to regard it as a signal act of Divine Providence that it was to Dr. Forsyth that I was led to be instructed. I am deeply indebted to all my professors for the knowledge they have so freely imparted to me; and to Dr. [Herbert Thomas] Andrews in particular for his readiness to help me on all occasions when I needed advice and interest. But it is difficult for me to speak of my debt to my Principal in language which will not seem extravagant. . . . It has been Dr. Forsyth who, under God, claimed me for the ministry, and made me a preacher of the Gospel he gave me to preach.[4]

Lovell Cocks never lost his sense of indebtedness to Forsyth and when, on 16 June 1977 he gave the address at the closing of New College, London (with which Hackney College had been united in 1924), he reiterated his view of sixty years before: "During my lifetime I have learned much from many teachers, but it is to Peter Forsyth that I owe my theological soul and my footing in the Gospel."[5] As he elsewhere wrote,

> We students were crude and slow, and there was much in [Forsyth's] teaching that was beyond us. Yet we never found him obscure. He gave us many a jolt with his paradoxes, but we understood him. His epigrams stuck in our thick hides like harpoons.

3 Quoted in the obituary of Frank Livingston Riches Lowe (1875–1960), *Congregational Year Book* 1961, 443.

4 H.F. Lovell Cocks, "Ordination Statement," 4–5; *LCP*.

5 Idem, "New College," 12; *LCP*. Lovell Cocks opened his address in characteristic style thus: "A speaker sometimes begins his address by wondering why he has been invited to give it—a risky gamut which only too often sets his hearers wondering too. I am not tempted to run that risk. We all know why I have been asked to address you. It is because I am a museum piece—not perhaps a collector's item, but still an exhibit whose undoubted authenticity may make a modest contribution in helping you to imagine what life was like at 527 Finchley Road in those far-off days before the first World War."

> When, for example, he told us that the first duty of a Christian Minister is not to entertain the passengers but to navigate the ship, he made his point with the dullest of us.[6]

Lovell Cocks was particularly impressed by Forsyth's mid-week devotional services. Attired in velvet doctor's cap and Geneva gown he would open with prayer. Then, guided by a few scraps of paper propped against the pulpit Bible, he would think aloud for about forty minutes: "Sometimes he would take a play of Shakespeare or Ibsen or a poem of Wordsworth and sink his well in it, digging deeper and deeper until he found the living water."[7]

We are fortunate in having Lovell Cocks's opinions of his other teachers:

> The Dr. [Herbert Hayes] Scullard I knew—a Christian gentleman if ever there was one—was a prodigious scholar of a humility so deep that he seemed to be apologizing for the weight of learning he carried. . . . Then there was H.T. Andrews, a truly inspired and inspiring interpreter of the New Testament and a preacher of great power. I think, too, of W[illiam] A[rchibald] Davies, a loveable man, who taught us Hebrew and possessed that unimpeachable passport to Paradise, the language of Zion, spoken with a Welsh accent. And what shall I say of Dr [Alfred Ernest] Garvie? We students admired him and his encyclopaedic range of erudition and we loved him too—but not always. . . . [H]e used to lecture on what he called Elementary Theology . . . [we] were expected to take it all down, dictated at the speed of an express train. But we had ways of applying the brakes and shunting the train into a siding. Notable among these was total abstinence. Once launched upon this, Garvie would wind himself up to a burst of impassioned eloquence, and at the first sign of his running down our loud 'hear hears' and desk-poundings would set him off again. . . . Full justice has yet to be done to Garvie's work and influence as a bold pioneer of ecumenical thought and action. . . . He was a fine scholar and a great Christian, and we who were privileged to know him cherish his memory.[8]

In addition to their formal course work, students were expected to preach on Sundays—notably in the mission stations of the Village Itinerancy Society. Considerable portions of their journeys were on foot, these hikes being made no more pleasant by the frock coats,

---

6 Idem, "A nineteenth-century prophet. Peter Taylor Forsyth," 2–3; *LCP*.

7 Ibid., 4. Lovell Cocks gave a thirty-five minute talk on Forsyth on the BBC Third Programme, 20 July 1948.

8 Idem, "New College," 7–9.

top hats and starched collars in which they were dressed. Lovell Cocks recalls a prayer meeting at one such place, during the course of which an old deacon addressed the Almighty thus: "'O Lord, this 'ere Kaiser's a-breathin' out threatenin's and slaughter. *You* deal with 'im, Lord—just you *deal* with 'im.' And then, by who knows what association of ideas, he went on: 'And this young man who's come from the College, O Lord, *save* 'im!'"[9]

Lovell Cocks earned the degrees of M.A. and B.D. of the University of London, with first class honours in Biblical and Historical Theology and Philosophy. Later he was awarded London's D.D. for a thesis which was published in abbreviated form under the title *By Faith Alone*.[10]

The foundations (intra- and extra-mural) laid, Lovell Cocks was, as we saw, ordained at Winchester in 1917. There followed pastorates at Hove, Sussex (1922–1927) and Headingley Hill, Leeds (1927–1932). From 1932 to 1937 he held the Chair of Systematic Theology and Christian Social Philosophy at Yorkshire United Independent College, Bradford. Here he gave courses in the philosophy and psychology of religion, and lectured at the School of Art and other venues in the neighbourhood. Among his papers are sets of lecture notes on "Fundamentals of the Christian Faith," "Plato's Republic," "The Reformation," "Troeltsch's *Social Teaching of the Christian Churches*," and "Epistemology." In this last he deals with the coherence theory of truth, F.C.S. Schiller, the American new realism, Samuel Alexander, Bertrand Russell and others. As an example of his later extra-mural work we may note a course of lectures given in the Department of Adult Education of Bristol University on *Man: His Origin, Duty and Destiny* (? 1956).There is also an exercise book labelled "Seed Plot," containing jottings for possible sermons.

Already known as preacher and pastor, he was now increasingly in demand as guest lecturer and conference speaker. Indeed, in his "An Impression" of The Ninth Theological Conference of Congregationalists held at Westminster College, Cambridge, 8–11 July 1935, Albert Peel declared that "Perhaps the most effective newcomer was Prof. H.F. Lovell Cocks, who not only read the opening paper, but took an active part in debate."[11] The conference was on the theme, "The Christian Doctrine of Man," and Lovell Cocks's topic was "God, man, and natural law."

---

9 Ibid., 6.

10 Published in 1943 by James Clarke.

11 Albert Peel, "An Impression," *The Congregational Quarterly* XIII, 1935, 510.

From 1937 to 1941 Lovell Cocks was Principal of the Scottish Congregational College, and lecturer in the postgraduate School of Theology of the University of Edinburgh; from 1941 until his retirement in 1960 he was Principal of Western College, Bristol, where he succeeded R.S. Franks, and whence his reputation as a dispenser of grounded yet gracious theology spread throughout and beyond English Congregationalism.

Lovell Cocks was a signatory to a manifesto *To the Ministers of Christ's Holy Gospel in the Churches of the Congregational Order*, which was drafted by B.L. Manning and sent to all ministers on 12 March 1939.[12] The authors declared that "The numbing pressure of secularism in our own country, as of paganism and militant atheism elsewhere, emphasizes the central place of the visible, organized Church in the purpose of God in history." Thus the cue to a call to Gospel faithfulness and to the ardent practice of the Congregational order. This same call was the inspiration of the series of Forward Books which began to appear under the general editorship of John Marsh during the second World War—among them Lovell Cocks's incisive volume on *The Nonconformist Conscience* (1943).[13]

In 1950–1951 Lovell Cocks was Chairman of the Congregational Union of England and Wales. His Address from the Chair, *A Church Reborn*,[14] was delivered on 15 May 1950, and to it, as to his other numerous publications, we shall refer in due course. As a trusted speaker on significant occasions we find Lovell Cocks addressing the United Service of Tribute to King George the Sixth in the Central Hall, Bristol, on Friday, 15 February 1952: "We thank God Who gave us so human a King, so kingly a man. . . . King George was a Christian believer and trusted in Jesus Christ for his salvation, just like any other justified sinner."[15] The following year found Lovell Cocks at St. Andrews, where he addressed the Seventh International Congregational Council, called to study the theme of "Congregational Churchmanship," on "The Foundation in Christ."[16] In 1955 he gave his Drew Lecture on Immortality, *The Hope of Glory*, at New

12 There is a copy of the manifesto in *LCP*. The other signatories are Sydney Cave, J.D. Jones, B.L. Manning, Nathaniel Micklem, E.J. Price, John Short and J.S. Whale.

13 Published by Independent Press.

14 Published in 1950 by Independent Press.

15 H.F. Lovell Cocks, *An Address delivered at the Central Hall Bristol . . . on the occasion of a United Service of Tribute to King George the Sixth*, 5, 9; *LCP*.

16 See *Proceedings of the Seventh International Congregational Council*, Boston and Chicago: The Pilgrim Press and London: Independent Press 1953, 45–57.

College, London.[17] For the first two years of its life (1958–1960) he served on the commission which produced *A Declaration of Faith* (1967) of the Congregational Church in England and Wales, one of the most substantial twentieth-century documents of its kind. A Cromwell enthusiast, Lovell Cocks gave the address at the Cromwell Association Annual Service in front of Cromwell's statue at Westminster on 3 September 1959, in which he presented Cromwell, mild and reluctant dictator though he was, as fundamentally a champion of religious liberty.[18] In the following year there appeared his study of *The Religious Life of Oliver Cromwell.*[19] Taking his cue from the fact that many historians had shown what Independency owed to Cromwell, Lovell Cocks set out to make plain Cromwell's indebtedness to Independency's concept of the gathered church.

As already noted, Lovell Cocks retired from the Principalship of Western College in 1960. In his final "Principal's Report" he recalled the coming of himself and his wife to the bomb-damaged premises in 1941; and spoke of the influx of students after the War, of the subsequent decline in numbers, and of the welcome fact that there were now more students on the roll than at any time in the previous history of the College. With characteristic modesty he said, "As I look back on my 19 years as Principal I am conscious that I have not achieved all I set out to do. But I am thankful for what I have been able to accomplish. . . ." He paid tribute to his colleagues, and to his wife, without whose "keen interest and shrewd judgment I could not have done half so much." Finally, he commended his successor, Basil Sims, to the College and its constituency.[20] In 1961 Lovell Cocks returned to Bristol to deliver the College's Valedictory Sermon in Highbury Chapel, his text being II Corinthians 4:7–10.[21] In the same year he was the Founder's Day preacher at Bristol University. On this occasion he preached on John 3:21.[22]

1962, the year in which the tercentenary of the Great Ejectment was marked, found Lovell Cocks on the national stage again—this time as Moderator of the Free Church Federal Council. His moderatorial address, *1662–1962: Free Church Witness, Then—and Now?*

---

17 Published by Independent Press; reprinted in Charles S. Duthie (ed.), *Resurrection and Immortality. A Selection from the Drew Lectures on Immortality*, London: Samuel Bagster 1979.

18 See "Oliver Cromwell," *LCP*.

19 Published by Independent Press, 1960.

20 Western College *Report*, 1960, 13–14.

21 Ibid., 1961, 10–11.

22 *LCP*.

was published by the Council. On 24 August of the same year he preached the sermon at the 1662 commemoration service at City Temple. His text was Hebrews 13:7f, and he reminded his hearers in no uncertain terms that their nonconformist forebears' "primary concern was not that *they* should be unfettered but that the Word of God should not be bound."[23]

More domestically, it fell to Lovell Cocks's lot to deliver the charge to John Huxtable on his induction as Minister Secretary of the Congregational Union of England and Wales. This service was held at the City Temple on 9 November 1964. On 6 November 1975 he spoke at the memorial service to Howard Stanley, John Huxtable's predecessor in office, uniting the words "integrity" and "kindness" as the epitome of the man. By that time, the United Reformed Church for which John Huxtable and (eventually) Howard Stanley[24] had worked so hard has been constituted in 1972. But it was Lovell Cocks who, on 14 March 1972, delivered the sermon at Argyle Church, Bath, at the last meeting of the Council of the Congregational Church in England and Wales. His text, "By faith Abraham . . . left home, without knowing where he was to go," gave him ample opportunity for pulling no punches: "*Follow Me means* press on; it doesn't mean *dig in.*"[25]

In the meantime Lovell Cocks had returned to Western College in 1968 to preach at the closing "Service of Thanksgiving and Faith" of that institution. Expounding Hebrews 13:14, "Here we have no lasting city but we seek the city which is to come," he acknowledged the "sharp pang" which all felt at the closing of the College, but exhorted his hearers to go forward confident in the God who, by the Cross, makes all things new.[26]

Lovell Cocks died, full of years, on 15 January 1983, leaving the children of his first marriage. Over two hundred people attended the funeral service at Amersham, and John Huxtable preached a memorial sermon in Redland Park Church, Bristol.

---

23 The sermon is printed in full in *The British Weekly*, 30 August 1962, 1, 5. A copy is in *LCP*. Our quotation is at p. 5 col. i.

24 Howard Stanley had opposed the Presbyterian-Congregational union proposals of 1947.

25 The texts of the addresses mentioned in this paragraph are in *LCP*.

26 Western College *Report*, 1968, 20–23.

II

> The new Principal of Western College comes to England at a time of high opportunity for leaders of Christian thought. The temptation of the ministry in the immediate future, we may guess, will be either to adventure too recklessly or to fall back too sombrely upon a sort of theological classicism. In Principal Cocks it will have a teacher, not of the "middle way," but of a doctrine and an emphasis founded upon two rocky bases—a deep and instructed loyalty to evangelical truth, and a clear-eyed awareness of the acutal needs of man and society.

Thus E.H. Jeffs in *The Christian World* of 18 July 1940.[27] As we proceed to examine Lovell Cocks's thought we shall find Jeffs's assessment amply borne out. We shall encounter one who placed his philosophical and theological learning at the service of the Gospel conceived as entailing both the proclamation of God's free grace and the struggle to alleviate the ills of church and world alike. His commitment in all of this was the greater because of the legacy of P.T. Forsyth, and because the horror of two World Wars and their aftermaths. We may properly begin with his major theological contribution, *By Faith Alone* (hereinafter *BFA*). We shall then indicate his position on further major doctrines of the Christian faith, and on socio-ethical questions. Our final main section, on worship and preaching, will be followed by a concluding assessment. Even as we thus systematise our intentions we are prompted to draw attention to the false impression which may thereby be created. For though his platform and hence his form varied, Lovell Cocks's content was all of a piece. He was not telling an essentially different story when addressing an academic audience from the one he told to eager hearers in the country chapels he loved so well. Indeed, the message he proclaimed so held him that there is more than a little preaching in the published version of his D.D. thesis, as the following summary will prove.[28]

"What is *saving faith?*" This is the question with which the "Author's Note" prefixed to *BFA* opens, and it is Lovell Cocks's preoccupation throughout the book. Since our human response of faith

---

27 P. 3. Copy in *LCP*.

28 We offer a fairly extensive summary both because Lovell Cocks's theological position is more completely adumbrated there than elsewhere, and because *BFA* is already rather scarce. 2,113 copies of the book were printed, of which a few remained thirty years on in 1974. For this information I am indebted to Mr. Adrian Brink, Managing Director of James Clarke & Co. Ltd., Cambridge.

is "conformed" to the object it acknowledges, namely, the living Word of God, the question cannot be answered by psychology or philosophy, but only by theology. The old, metaphysically grounded natural theology having failed, Schleiermacher and Kant threw the apologetic emphasis upon psychological and epistemological considerations; but now the "'prepared positions' to which the discomfited theologians were able to retreat" must themselves be called into question, for they have issued in a theological humanism which has been attacked by Barth and his school, and blighted by the harsh climate of the contemporary world. Where saving faith is concerned, theological humanism's error has been to equate it with the natural faith of human beings, with a view to justifying it to religion's "cultured despisers." By contrast, "Our own thesis . . . is that while saving faith presupposes natural faith (since it presupposes man with all his powers and interests), it is yet by no means continuous with it—as, for example, natural faith come to full self-consciousness or to its highest point of development—but exists in another dimension, being no innate human capacity but a gift to man through the Word of God."[29] While agreeing with Schleiermacher that religion is an affair of the whole person, Lovell Cocks objects to the apologetic use made of this insight: a use which, no less than the Enlightenment rationalism against which Schleiermacher protested, grounds religion and hence apologetics in human nature. Likewise for Kant the moral law is authoritative because it is *my own* self-legislated law. Moral faith is thus "the exercise of [man's] own sovereign rationality."[30]

We proceed to a discussion of theories of faith as postulation (Kant) and as valuation (Ritschl, Herrmann). These theories only throw into relief the gap between their understanding of faith and the "invincible certainty" of religous faith as we actually know it. They do, however, raise the question, "May not our intuition of value be itself an intuition of God?"[31] But this requires that there be "a specific vision of God as God,"[32]—hence to the religious *a priorism* of Troeltsch and Otto. Deficiencies of such positions notwithstanding, "If the awe we feel in the presence of the moral imperative seems to wear a numinous aspect, is not this a hint too plain to be disregarded? . . . May not this feeling of the numinous,

29 *BFA*, 9.

30 Ibid., 12.

31 Ibid., 21.

32 Ibid., 25.

this basic intuition, be *faith*?"[33] Onward to a discussion of such idealists as Edward Caird and W.E. Hocking, who sought to square the basic intuition with religion's rational element, and did so by asserting that our self-consciousness, our knowledge of other minds, and our knowledge of nature are possible only because of that objective order which enables us to say that the all-knowing God is the source of all our awareness. Lovell Cocks's verdict is blunt: "So far from being a gospel of deliverance, this shows our case to be desperate. If religion embraces the whole of our experience—since all our awareness is awareness of God—our religion is as chaotic as the world. And if every experience is a revelation of God, God also is chaos. . . . [W]e end as we began—*in postulates*. Apriorism is only an elaborate expression of this human necessity to postulate God."[34] Is there a way forward? If the facts can be described only in such paradoxical statements as that "Faith is a knowing yet not knowledge; a seeing, yet not sight; and though it has its reasons it is not reasoning,"[35] it is not surprising that humanist accounts of natural faith fail to satisfy, and that any theory which seeks to resolve the paradoxes must be false. The possibility remains, therefore, that saving faith may be non-identical and non-continuous with natural faith.

Lovell Cocks proceeds to argue that humanism is powerless to resolve three major crises. The first is the crisis of the moral consciousness, for notwithstanding Kant's assertion of radical evil, for example, idealism's optimism holds no remedy for the reality and pain of guilt: "No doctrine of immanence, no hierarchy of values, no 'vision,' no 'moral earnestness,' can be the rock of our salvation, but only the Word that judges us and wins from us the confession of guilt and impotence, coming to us amid the ruins of our fallen temples with the promise of a house not made with hands for an eternal habitation."[36] Secondly, the crisis of religion turns upon the false equation of revelation with our religious experience. In fact, however, "true religion is saving faith—the gift of God and the creation of His Word."[37] As if in anticipation of our present-day discussions of Christianity vis-à-vis the several faiths by which people live, Lovell Cocks inserts an important note in which he explains that while God's power, grace and presence may not be de-

33 Ibid., 28.

34 Ibid., 30–31.

35 Ibid., 31.

36 Ibid., 40.

37 Ibid., 49.

nied to those who are not Christians, "in the non-Christian faiths the *proclamation* of [the revelation in Christ] is unclear and the understanding of it defective. . . . [W]e affirm that it is still the God we know in Christ who comes to men, and still Christ in whom he comes; and above all that only in the Word as it is in Jesus, and by the faith that receives it, is the *truth* about the encounter of God and man revealed and acknowledged."[38] Thirdly, there is the crisis of mortality. Once again, humanism fails, for with its theory of natural immortality it only evades the fact of human finitude: "The Gospel we need is not an assurance that we are worthy of immortality, or that we may earn it by our virtue, but that God will raise us, not to the condemnation our sin deserves, but to an eternal life of communion with Himself."[39] Humanity, created in God's image for covenant relationship with God, has defaced that image at the Fall (though the divine image is not utterly destroyed—otherwise we should not be human or capable of sin). Accordingly, while we "have no *a priori* reason for believing that natural faith will fail to reach God with its philosophies," we must affirm that it fails *de facto*, not because man is finite, but because he is a sinner who "loves the abstractions he can admire or manipulate rather than the living Truth that menaces his egoistic pride."[40]

This is the human predicament which saving faith alone can remedy. Like knowing in general, faith is not a feeling, but a verdict. The relation between our human faith and the Word is not symmetrical, for the former is always dependent upon the creative grace of the latter. Faith is trust and worship; its opposite is not ignorance, but unbelief. It is prayer, obedience, communion with God. It is at the same time God's gift and the believer's act. By it the person becomes a new creature in Christ, and is called to lead a new life.[41]

Saving faith is created by the Word of God, and this is not a book, but a person, Jesus Christ. Revelation consists in the saving act of God in history, not, as with Enlightenment thinkers, in the identification of revelation with timeless truths at the expense of history. The Word is mediated by events and subsequently by the record of the events, retold through the ages so that God may address believers contemporaneously, and challenge their response/decision of commitment. Hence the importance of the

38 Ibid., 51.

39 Ibid., 59.

40 Ibid., 68.

41 This paragraph consists of a bald summary of *BFA* chs. VII, VIII.

Church's preaching, which God can transform into "the sacramental event of His coming."[42] Those whose faith is in Christ continue to be conscious both of sin and of their sonship, though as to the former Lovell Cocks does well to protest against the "'spatializing' of the evangelical experience. . . . [T]he believer is not *first* convicted of sin and *then* assured of pardon, nor does he *first* realize his need of Christ and *then* find that need satisfied. No true conviction of sin is possible apart from faith in saving grace. But equally there can be for us no faith in saving grace that is not also a confession and renunciation of our sin."[43]

There follows a discussion of justification by faith which is, rightly, construed as being primarily concerned with God's free grace in declaring righteous, for Christ's sake, sinners who have no righteousness of their own. It redefines our standing before God, and it is appropriated by our faith—which appropriation is not to be construed as a "work" of ours, but as the exercise of a gift of God. Saving faith is thus different in kind from faith as assent to a body of doctrines. It is the product of regeneration by the Spirit, who brings the Word home to the individual. In contrast with this, any relation of divine immanence conceived as direct, and not mediated by the verdict-demanding Word, is defective; indeed, any doctrine of "'degrees of immanence' is merely pantheism in its Sunday-best."[44]

In the last three chapters of *BFA* Lovell Cocks presents his understanding of the meaning of our fellowship with Christ. He writes first of Christ our righteousness, arguing that "We do not begin to approach the truth about the Atonement until we see the penal satisfaction and moral influence theories as not mutually exclusive but as complementary. The divine love in Christ is the heaviest judgment the sinner can receive."[45] Elaborating upon our faith-union with Christ he emphasises its uniqueness and its distinctiveness from all other *I–Thou* encounters, for here the human meets the divine. Then comes "the culminating point in our attempt to show how faith is conformed to the Word it knows. The believer is conformed to Christ, regenerated in His image, incorporated into His life, by receiving Christ's mind—Christ's faith, Christ's confession of holy love, Christ's judgment upon sin. All this has been *for* the believer as the ground of his justification. And now by the Holy

42 *BFA*, 113.

43 Ibid., 130.

44 Ibid., 151.

45 Ibid., 167.

Spirit an answering faith, confession and judgment, are offered *in* the believer and *by* him."[46] Even so, as Lovell Cocks insists in his concluding chapter, the relationship between the believer and Christ is not univocal, it is analogical; the believer's faith is not a replica of Christ's. That the believer's faith exists at all is a witness to the freedom of divine grace. This grace is electing grace, and to this the believer may and must witness: to this—not to a speculative doctrine either of double decree or of universalism. The believer knows reconciliation to God as fact; final redemption as promise. The believer's faith, though individual, is not isolated, but entails life in the fellowship of the Church. The new life, enjoyed now, is the foretaste of that victorious resurrection life beyond the grave.

So much for a summary of Lovell Cocks's major work. How was *BFA* received, and how shall we assess it now? Bound up with this question is another: "How does Lovell Cocks stand in relation to Barth's theology of the Word which was burgeoning in his day?" We may approach our answer to the former question *via* the latter, bearing in mind the important consideration that Barth had by no means run his full course when *BFA* appeared, and that Lovell Cocks and his reviewers have (and could only have) what we might now describe as the earlier and middle Barth in mind.

The verdicts of the original reviewers upon the relation of Lovell Cocks to Barth are interestingly diverse and, as often happens with reviews, they tell us something about the reviewers themselves. Thus, E.L. Allen wishes it to be understood that his "quarrel is not with the author but with the Barthian school in which he has enrolled himself."[47] On the other hand, and in the same publication, Nathaniel Micklem, thinly disguised under the pseudonym "Ilico," writes, "Dr. Cocks would, I think, repudiate the title 'Barthian.' He certainly is not of the strait sect of the Barthians." Nevertheless a later reference to "the Barthian school" is followed by the words, "(in which I venture to include Dr. Cocks)."[48] The Methodist, C. Ryder Smith, qualifying one slippery term and introducing another, seems to agree: "Dr. Cocks is not a complete Barthian but he is an 'existentialist'"; and he thinks that *BFA*'s "value lies in its largely successful attempt to deliver Barthianism from its negations."[49] To the Baptist A.C. Underwood, however, "The book will not please everybody as it may be taken almost as a manifesto

46 Ibid., 183.

47 E.L. Allen, *The British Weekly*, 10 February 1944.

48 Nathaniel Micklem, ibid., 23 March 1944.

49 C. Ryder Smith, *London Quarterly Review*, 1944, 279.

from the Barthian, Neo-Calvinist Group within Congregationalism." While applauding Lovell Cocks's spirit of urgency and devotion to Christ, and thanking him "for a fine piece of work in philosophical and systematic theology, whose assumptions, however, [those of his own theological persuasion] cannot share," Underwood and others "will remain unconvinced and it will not be due simply to their dislike of being labelled theological humanists and semi-Pelagians, on account of their inability to pronounce certain shibboleths. They would gladly accept the first label if it placed them in the same school as, say, Phillips Brooks and Dean Church. Semi-Pelagians they have never been, and never will be; they are, however, Synergists."[50] In the hinterland of these remarks is the venerable albeit intermittent debate within Baptist circles over Calvinism and Arminianism and, in particular, over the matter of human ability in relation to salvation. Over this we must here draw a veil.[51] More to our present purpose is the observation that Lovell Cocks appears to have touched a raw nerve with his critique of theological humanism which, as we have seen, was carefully constructed, and was far more than a matter of the hurling of shibboleths. W.A. Whitehouse might almost have had Underwood in mind when he concluded his review of John Hick's *Faith and Knowledge*, thus: "This book will delight readers whose prescription for religion is the 'theological humanism' represented by the last chapter, the limitations of which were ably diagnosed by Dr. Lovell Cocks in *By Faith Alone*."[52]

In a more balanced way than Underwood, the Congregationalist W.B. Selbie put his finger on a point of importance. He refers to Lovell Cocks's view (quoted above) that saving faith presupposes, but is not continuous with, natural faith—it is not an innate human capacity, but a gift through the Word. Selbie remarks: "Here Dr. Cocks seems to take away with one hand what he gives with the other. If there is such a thing as natural faith it would seem to involve necessarily some sort of native capacity in man for receiving and responding to the gift and revelation of God. This may be humanism, but it is well to remember that there is a true as well as a false humanism."[53] It is this ambivalence which makes it difficult to place Lovell Cocks in relation to Barth. Those reviewers who take him seriously on the presupposition of natural faith cannot

50 A.C. Underwood, *The Baptist Times*, 2 March 1944.

51 Though see Alan P.F. Sell, *The Great Debate. Calvinism, Arminianism and Salvation*, Worthing: H.E. Walter (now Bletchley: Word Books) 1982; Grand Rapids: Baker Book House 1983.

52 W.A. Whitehouse, *The Congregational Quarterly* XXXVI, 1958, 171.

53 W.B. Selbie, *The Congregational Quarterly*, XXII 1944, 171.

enrol him absolutely in the Barthian 'camp'; while those who emphasise the discontinuity he posits between saving faith and natural faith (especially if they dislike it) have no difficulty in so categorising him.

At a number of significant points Lovell Cocks distances himself from Barth. We have noted his opposition to the view that by reason of the Fall the image of God is utterly destroyed in human beings.[54] Elsewhere he reinforces the point with specific reference to Barth: "Man is made in God's image, and it will not do to say—as Karl Barth seems to say—that sin has wholly destroyed that image in us."[55] In the same place, and in the course of repudiating philosophy's assumption that, while God may be "a problem on the horizon of our thought," we at least know what man is, he writes, "I am not going the length of the Barthian theology. I am not suggesting we know *nothing* of man apart from Jesus Christ—which would be patently absurd. Our psychologies and sociologies most certainly give us knowledge that is relevant. But until we know the pattern of human life, their contributions are as unrelated as the heaped pieces of a jig-saw puzzle."[56] Similarly, we know something of God apart from Jesus Christ. This is why, although the Gospel cannot be made acceptable to natural man by argument, there remains the apologetic task of challenging rationalisations of the refusal of grace, and clearing away irrelevancies.[57] In the course of welcoming Nels Ferré's book, *The Christian Understanding of God* (1951) because of its positive apologetic value Lovell Cocks wrote: "The philosophia perennis still has its devotees and the Neo-Thomists are active amongst us. But in the Reformed Churches the philosophical theologians have walked delicately, like men engaged in dubious enterprise. . . . First it was Ritschl's influence and later Barth's [which] seemed to put the speculative method out of bounds to Christian thinkers. Yet faith is not to be identified with timidity or lazy-mindedness, and to think rigorously about what we believe is not necessarily intellectual arrogance. . . . Indeed, the theologian who is afraid of philosophy is almost certain to be unconsciously dominated by it."[58]

---

54 See further his article, "Doctrine of Man. The divine image in man," *The Expository Times* LXI, no. 2, November 1949, 43–46.

55 H.F. Lovell Cocks, "Reinterpretation of the fact of Christ," 7; *LCP*.

56 Ibid., 10.

57 *BFA*, 118–119.

58 Draft of a review of Ferré's book; *LCP*.

With this we come to the vexed question whether, apart from God's gift of saving faith, there is a point of contact for the Word of God. Lovell Cocks appraises the celebrated debate between Barth and Brunner as follows. First, he dislikes the metaphor "point of contact," since God is in contact with us at every point. Secondly, he awards marks to both sides: "Barth is right, surely, when he says that God must create His own point of contact with sinful man, and that we must take regeneration seriously. Yet Brunner is right when he urges that we cannot be accused of not taking regeneration seriously when we point out that it is man that is regenerated and not a stone or a fish. . . . Faith is an activity of the whole man." Thirdly, "Instead of asking where the point of contact may be found, let us rather ask the question—to what in man is the Gospel relevant? The only answer is that it is relevant to his entire situation as creature, son and sinner."[59] By none of which was the Dominican Victor White persuaded: "It is no answer to the [Barth–Brunner] dilemma to assert that by faith God is in contact with man at *every* point, if we cannot say why at every point of *man*, and not of 'stone or fish'; nor to say that the Gospel is relevant 'to the entire human situation as creature, son and sinner,' if we ignore the fact that the possibility of being son or sinner is a distinctively *human* situation."[60] But is not White answered by Lovell Cocks's extended treatment of the *imago Dei?*

On the other side, Lovell Cocks expresses agreement with Barth at many points. For example, with Barth he regrets that the Reformers did not resolve the tension between the doctrine of election as they expounded it and its pastoral uses; and he agrees that they failed "because they allowed their thinking to be deflected from the path marked out for them by their fundamental insight into the cardinal Scriptural truth that it is [in] Christ, and in Christ alone, that we know anything concerning the God who elects and the Man who is elected."[61] But above all, he agreed with Barth that "Christian theology is a Theology of Crisis, essentially and inevitably." But he immediately points out that "Karl Barth did not invent the phrase or the thing. It is not a modern pathological development of Christian thinking, compact of the disillusionment and despair of the defeated nations and the bewilderment and frustration of the victors. It is merely an attempt to take seriously what God is saying in His Gospel, and reiterating in the tragedies of a

59 *BFA*, 68–69.

60 Victor White, *The Journal of Theological Studies*, XLVI, 1945, 111.

61 H.F. Lovell Cocks, in a review of Barth's *Church Dogmatics II. The Doctrine of God, Part 2*, *The Congregational Quarterly* XXXVI 1958, 268.

world in flames—that the strategy of redemption is not evolutionary progress but judgment and crisis."[62] In all of which, Lovell Cocks thought, Barth had been pre-empted by P.T. Forsyth:

> [Forsyth] is a theologian of crisis. . . . Forsyth has been called "a Barthian before Barth." The label has been given him by those who prefer proprietary brands in theology. Yet it is misleading. It is true that the main emphases in Barth had been anticipated in Forsyth. Some will maintain that what Barth is saying in our day, Forsyth had already said in his—and said better. But whether Forsyth says it better or not, he says it differently. He speaks in a British and not a continental idiom. And many who will have no truck with Barth may find Forsyth a more congenial teacher.[63]

In all of which there was something in which A.C. Underwood could concur: "P.T. Forsyth said years ago all that is valuable in Barthianism."[64] Lovell Cocks did not, however agree with those who said that Forsyth, neglected during his lifetime, was discovered only later as "the Barthian before Barth. Not only discerning Anglicans like J.K. Mozley, but his fellow Congregationalists were well aware of his stature. Whenever a theological issue arose in our denominational assemblies, the cry of 'Forsyth,' shouted from all parts of the hall, would summon him to the platform."[65]

We may conclude this section by adverting to some reviewers' comments on particular points. Victor White may seem to go too far in saying that while asserting that faith is a divine gift, Lovell Cocks "strangely denies that it is a human possession (strangely, for it is a poor gift that does not become the possession of the receiver);"[66] for Lovell Cocks, grounding on the New Testament, affirms: "The Christian believer, in unison with the New Testament, declares that his faith is God's gift to him through the Word; yet it is none the less *his* act, and the only act wherein he is truly man and wholly free. . . . The paradox remains: faith is my act, truly mine, truly free; yet it is not my act in the sense of being a product of my human powers, but is a new creation in me."[67] But Lovell Cocks does say that faith is not our sure possession. He explains that

---

62 Idem, "The message of P.T. Forsyth," *The Congregational Quarterly*, XXVI 1948, 219.

63 Idem, "A nineteenth-century prophet," 2.

64 A.C. Underwood, *The Baptist Times*, 2 March 1944.

65 H.F. Lovell Cocks, "New College," 10; *LCP*.

66 V. White, *Journal of Theological Studies*, 112.

67 *BFA*, 81, 86.

faith, which is not so much "decision for life" as "*Life-as-Decision*," is not generated by ourselves, and that we have no power to determine when the Word will address us.[68] The root problem is that White is not at ease with paradoxical utterances concerning possession and non-possession which Lovell Cocks deems the facts of the case to require.

But White persists: "If [faith] is not possession, it is not life, and A.R. Whatley's [*sic*] criticism of Barth to the effect that 'If faith lies only in acts of decision, it would seem to be like the telegraph posts without the wires', remains unanswered."[69] But in answering Whately, Lovell Cocks (and Barth) insist on the psychological continuity of faith with the rest of our human experience: "The believer is a new man in Christ Jesus, but is not on that account a new field for psychological investigation and a unique datum for scientific observers."[70] The Christian believer's life in Christ is "a veritable life of faith, and not merely a series of *acts* like lightning flashes against impenetrable darkness."[71] In a subsequent explanation of the same point Lovell Cocks reiterated his view that "The abiding background of faith, the continuity of the believer's life and experience, is not any capacity in himself but the unfailing love and mercy of God"; and then proceeded to distinguish the act of faith from all other human acts thus:

> It is a decision, but it is not to be reckoned among other decisions. Even when we say that faith is "decision for Christ," we do not reach the heart of the matter. The ground of our faith is God's decision concerning us, declared and made effective in His Word. And the human analogue of this divine decision—our faith—is not the choosing of Christ above other lords, or the Kingdom of God above other causes, though such a choice, repeated again and again, is entailed by it and manifests it. When the Word of God is truly heard and acknowledged, our human existence stands revealed as being in itself decision. Not a series of isolated acts of decision, but life-as-decision—this is the essence of faith.[72]

In this decision certitude is to be found. To the believer, faith is not an hypothesis, and where the claim to absolute knowledge is

68 *BFA*, 89.

69 V. White, op. cit., 112, quoting A.R. Whately, *The Focus of Belief*, Cambridge: Cambridge University Press 1937, 12.

70 *BFA*, 90.

71 *BFA*, 89.

72 H.F. Lovell Cocks, "The faith that saves," in *Reformation Old and New*, ed. F.W. Camfield, London: Lutterworth 1947, 170.

not made, "faith is not faith."[73] This was too much for E.L. Allen: "[W]hen Dr. Cocks declares outright that a faith which does not claim 'absolute knowledge' is not faith, I fear me that he leaves us with fewer believers than there were righteous men in Sodom."[74] Here, once again, is the attempt to smooth out the paradox, though it must be admitted that Allen was tempted by the term "knowledge." In the next line Lovell Cocks uses "absolute certainty" as a synonym, and this is better in the sense intended. For on the one hand it does seem that believers do not go through life for ever wondering whether their faith-as-hypothesis will be overturned. They are recipients of a gift, not followers of hunches. On the other hand, their knowledge of God now is partial—then it will be face to face (I Corinthians 13:12).

III

We begin our sketch of Lovell Cocks's position on some further major Christian doctrines by noting two general characteristics of all his writing. First, he grounds upon the Bible. Lovell Cocks did much of his writing in the heyday of the so-called "biblical theology" movement. Accordingly, he declares that the Bible "*is* a whole. The Old Testament points forward to the New and finds its completion there. The New looks back to the Old and is not to be fully understood except against that background."[75] Consistently with this, and although Lovell Cocks was not primarily a technical biblical scholar, we find numerous analyses of Hebrew and Greek terms in his writings, and especially in his lecture notes. Secondly, much of his doctrinal writing is pastorally prompted and practically orientated. Thus, just as much of his ecclesiology is developed with a view to addressing the Church's current situation, so some of his deepest thought on the doctrine of God is prompted by concern for those who are puzzled by prayer—and with this we may begin.

In an article entitled, "The meaning and value of prayer," Lovell Cocks contends that "Prayer in all its forms, from the crudest to the most perfect, is, fundamentally, simply the consciousness and ex-

---

73 *BFA*, 73.

74 E.L. Allen, *The British Weekly*.

75 H.F. Lovell Cocks, *Man: His Origin, Duty and Destiny* (Tutorial course, Department of Adult Education, Bristol University, ? 1956), 2; *LCP*. Many subsequent biblical scholars have questioned whether it makes sense to speak of an overall theology in the Bible; some, not least Jewish scholars, regard the "biblical theology" stance as the imposition of a Christian perspective upon Hebrew materials; most agree that the New Testament cannot be understood apart from the Old.

pression of [the] attitude of dependence upon God and surrender to His will."[76] Not, indeed, that God's will is to be construed along crude predestinarian lines, according to which God's omnipotence is understood as the personification of the uniformity and law of nature as promulgated by nineteenth-century science. Certainly, prayer involves "a particular view of God and the world," but "at its highest this prayer-relation is that of redeemed to Redeemer."[77] That is to say, "Prayer arises in the redemptive relation; it is made from the standpoint of the Cross; it is in a real sense the fellowship of the sufferings of Christ. The mightiest prayers are prayed under the shadow of Golgotha. . . . The prayer-relation is sacramental. The true sacrament of divine grace is redeemed and sacrificial personality."[78]

Implicit here is the understanding of God as both transcendent and immanent. Indeed, immanence implies transcendence, for God could not be in anything unless he were other than that thing.[79] But, consistently with his attack upon "humanism," he elsewhere writes in fuller explanation of this point that "I am very sure that however we are to understand it, we must not be led to identify the Holy Spirit with our human psyche . . . [F]or all his indwelling [the Holy Spirit] remains inviolably and sovereignly Himself."[80] He then proceeds to qualify what he wrote in *BFA*:

> I still believe—on New Testament warrant—that it is through the Word of God that the Spirit influences us and creates faith in us. And I still believe that faith in its typical and mature form and exercise is a conscious knowing, and a conscious surrender to grace. But in my book I have fallen into the mistake of so much evangelical theology of assuming that the whole drama of salvation is played out on the stage of daylight awareness; that all decisions must be conscious decisions; and that the unconscious and the involuntary are the same thing. It is always hazardous to talk about "assured results" in a science so young, vivacious and wayward as modern psychology shows itself to be. But I will risk laying down three propositions and claiming for them the general agreement of the warring schools.
>
> First, that the human soul or psyche is much deeper and

76 H.F. Lovell Cocks, "The meaning and value of prayer," *The Congregational Quarterly*, III, 1925, 299.

77 Ibid., 302.

78 Ibid., 305.

79 H.F. Lovell Cocks, *BFA*, 150.

80 H.F. Lovell Cocks, "The divine life in man. Some aspects of the work of the Holy Spirit," 21; *LCP*.

richer than the empirical self through which it finds conscious expression. . . .

Then, too, this hidden psyche is dynamic—exercising choices and making decisions of which the daylight self is often completely unaware.

Finally . . . the psyche is never wholly passive or entirely plastic to suggestion. . . .

Now let us think of the Holy Spirit as the living God Who has revealed Himself in His Word, Jesus Christ. He is present to the human psyche. But are we to say present *to* or present *in*? Present *to*, surely, for there is no point in saying *in*. Of course God is present in the psyche, but He can be known by the psyche only as present *to* it. Yet, note, this does not mean he is necessarily present to consciousness. But to the psyche as a whole he is assuredly present. And although the phenomena of conversion, of the rise and progress of religion in the soul, can be described without residue in terms of psychology, this is entirely without prejudice to the theological interpretation that these things take place, that the man believes unto salvation, surrenders, and grows in grace through the influence and presence of the Holy Spirit.[81]

In yet another place Lovell Cocks reiterates his view that

A God wholly immanent is no God at all, but a mere name for the sum-total of things or else for some sub-personal Life-Force. . . . Our deepest experience of His transcendence defines that transcendence as preeminently moral and spiritual. God, that is to say, is the Holy One Whose pardoning love receives sinners into fellowship with Himself. Between Him and us a great gulf is fixed which can be bridged only from His side. But it is not primarily a gulf of metaphysical disparateness, or even the eternal distinction of the Creator from His creatures; it is a moral chasm and its name is sin. Across that gulf we see God coming to us in Christ; and in the abolition of that enmity the world becomes our Father's house, and the Cross, which otherwise were only the crowning proof of the hopeless irrationality of things, becomes the pledge of our pardon and the promise of our eternal life.[82]

In these words we have a summary of the way in which Lovell Cocks's understanding of God flows into his anthropology, soteriology and eschatology. Since we have rehearsed these themes in our discussion of *BFA* we shall note supplementary points only.

In view of the Fall, and in the wake of Paul and others, Lovell

81 Ibid., 22–23.

82 Idem, "The authority of the preacher," 11; *LCP*.

Cocks considers that humanity is in dire straits, and that "humanism" simply evades the issue: "Our *sin*, our heart of sinning, is that we identify ourselves with our 'better self,' trusting in him, instead of trusting and hiding in the infinite mercy of God."[83] This is not the way to sonship, which can be ours only by grace, not by nature. Not indeed that sin was transmitted by Adam to his descendants (which Paul does not teach). What is inherited is sinfulness and sin's penalty—death; and this is the clear teaching of Paul.[84] All of which throws into relief the fact that the ground of our faith is forgiveness. It is this which gives us a Gospel; for "[T]he principal thing in the relation between God and man is not the sin that ruptures [the relationship], but the grace that created and restores it. It is also true that grace means more than forgiveness and redemption, more than the reconciliation of the sinner to God. It is not only sin from which Christ saves, but fear and world-weariness."[85] We here stand at the threshold of Christology and soteriology.

On the opening page of *The Wondrous Cross* Lovell Cocks makes his starting-point plain for all to see: "We begin, as we must, with the unity of the Father, Son and Spirit in that divine love by which we are redeemed. The Atonement is the work of the triune God."[86] He proceeds to rebut a number of inadequate ideas: "The idea that God is in some way incomplete or unfulfilled apart from the beings He creates is not a Christian idea at all. . . . The Bible gives us no warrant for believing that God needs us *in the same way* that we need Him."[87] Again, "Christ did not die on the Cross to turn God from hatred to love. . . . Christ did not die to make God love us; He died because God had always loved us." Yet again, "If there has been no Incarnation there can be no Atonement. No *man* [in the sense of the best, bravest, purest man who ever lived—not in the sense of the Proper Man] can redeem us."[88] Moreover, given that we live in a sinful world "that stands under the judgment of God" we should not be surprised that God's Son suffered and died on the Cross. With respect to the historical events leading to the Cross we must never forget that organised religion was the primary culprit: "Let it be written in indelible letters in the offices of denominational headquarters and in all places where leaders of Christian churches

83 Idem, in *Reformation Old and New*, 168.

84 Idem, "Man: his origin, duty and destiny," 3–4, 26, 48.

85 Idem, "Reinterpretation of the fact of Christ," 6; *LCP*.

86 Idem, *The Wondrous Cross*, London: Independent Press 1957, 7.

87 Ibid., 13.

88 Ibid., 17.

gather, that it was ecclesiastical vested interests that crucified the Son of God."[89] But the supreme reason for the Cross is "rooted in the gracious purpose of God in His dealing with a sinful race. . . . Our sin is deadly serious; for it is more than the transgression of the Law. It is the flouting of divine love. The Christian Gospel is not that sin does not need to be paid for; but that it is God Himself in Christ who pays for it. The forgiveness that is freely offered to us is costly indeed. The Cross of Christ is the revelation of its infinite price."[90] Accordingly, it will not suffice to say that the life, ministry and death of Christ reveal the love of God for sinners. God's love is holy and must be satisfied; it is the divine judgment on our sin. Hence the Cross as sacrifice for sin. Here Christ is our substitute, in the sense that he does what we ought to do, but never can except in him as Mediator. He is also our representative, but not in the sense that he "steps forward from our ranks to treat with God as the spokesman we have chosen." ". . . The Cross is not the place where humanity rises to the peak of its capacity. . . . It is the place where God offers His best to us."[91] Christ does not and cannot repent for us, and he needs no repentance himself (a veiled critique of McLeod Campbell's theory here), but he "offers the pledge and promise of our repentance, so that the Father accepts us even while we are yet sinners when by faith we identify ourselves with His beloved Son."[92]

In order to point up the radical nature of human need, Lovell Cocks was ever zealous to distinguish between suffering and sin. The latter is a much deeper tragedy than the former, for "My suffering is something that happens to me, but for my sin I am responsible. In the one case I am merely the victim, in the other the creator of evil."[93] The Cross, therefore, is not simply the depiction of One who suffers alongside us, but is the place where God in Christ, once and for all, wins a victory of cosmic significance.[94]

---

89 Ibid., 39.

90 Ibid., 42, 50.

91 Ibid., 58–59.

92 Ibid., 59.

93 Idem, "By faith alone," (a lecture), 12; *LCP*.

94 For examples of the way in which this point is still contested see Alan P.F. Sell, *Aspects of Christian Integrity*, Calgary: University of Calgary Press 1990, and Louisville: Westminster/John Knox Press 1991, ch. II, espec. 42–45. Because of the climax of *The Wondrous Cross*, to which we here allude, H.H. Williams was less than accurate in saying "[Lovell Cocks] directs our eyes so steadfastly at Adam, that we have difficulty in hearing the trumpet note in 'Christus Victor.'" See *Baptist Times*, 14 March 1957. Interestingly, Williams trained for the minis-

It is of great importance to Lovell Cocks (and to Christian theology) that this victory was won on the stage of human history. In a set of lectures on Christology he makes short work of Lessing and his dictum that "Historical truth, which is accidental, can never become the proof of the truths of reason, which are necessary." He denies that historical truth is accidental; on the contrary, history "is the very sphere in which the reality of things is made manifest. . . . Moreover, history can be declared accidental or contingent only under the presupposition that God is not to be found there."[95] But this would be to beg the question. Finally, the assumption that the truths of religion are necessary truths of reason reflects the non-historical, static rationalism of the eighteenth century, and that route is no longer open to us. No account of the historical facts on which Christianity grounds will be complete which does not accommodate both the fact of the crucifixion and the fact of the Pentecostal faith in the risen Lord: "We can refuse to accept this apostolic verdict, but I do not see how we can deny that it was given, or that any interpretation of Christ's Person that sets it aside in favour of a purely humanitarian conception has broken with the N.T."[96] Clearly, in the confession, "Thou art the Christ, the Son of the living God," there is a value judgment, but "By this is not meant that it is not also a judgment of fact, but only that *this* fact cannot be apprehended in its fulness apart from what it makes of us. What Christ is can only appear in what He has done for us."[97] We have seen what Lovell Cocks thinks Christ has done for us; who, then, is he?

Following A.E. Garvie,[98] Lovell Cocks finds the Chalcedonian two-nature doctrine of the person of Christ inadequate. The terms in which it is expressed are ambiguous, and it does not satisfactorily preserve the unity of the Godhead. He quotes Garvie with approval: "If we use the term person in the same sense as regards the Godhead as we do as regards Christ, we deny the divine unity and fall into tritheism. If we use the word substance in the same sense as regards Christ as we do as regards the Godhead, we deny the unity of His person and fall into dualism."[99] Further, the doctrine

---

try under A.C. Underwood at Rawdon College, Leeds—not, indeed, that students are always clones of their principals!

95 Idem, "Is our problem historical?" 1; *LCP*.

96 Idem, untitled paper on Christology, 6; *LCP*.

97 Ibid., 3.

98 A.E. Garvie, *The Christian Doctrine of the Godhead*, London: Hodder & Stoughton 1925, 130–36.

99 H.F. Lovell Cocks, appended note to "Is our problem historical," final page; quoting A.E. Garvie, op. cit., 135–36.

involves the life of the historical Jesus in an incredible dualism; we have "Either two personalities or an impersonal manhood"; and the impersonal categories (being, substance) employed divert us from the religious and ethical datum of the communion of Jesus with God.[100]

It must be said that a more generous appreciation of Chalcedon is possible, though this is not the place to argue for it in detail. Briefly, the Chalcedonian fathers intended to maintain the unity of the Godhead, however much the available intellectual currency (and what else could they have used?) may seem to militate against it. Their definition makes a brave attempt to block off untoward exits into heresy. But, above all, they were making a serious effort to witness to the truth that none can save but God, and that the only mediator between sinful humanity and God is (in Luther's later term) Proper Man.[101] But, as we have seen, this is precisely what Lovell Cocks wishes to hold. In his own words: "The man Jesus is the Son of God incarnate—the Son of God or Logos revealed within the forms and limitations of our finite temporarl experience. That is to say, Jesus Christ is not a man indwelt by the Spirit of God or human nature assumed by the Logos. He is the Son *as man*. This conception may be as full of heresies as a sponge of holes, but it does seem to give full value to the formula that the Word became flesh."[102]

IV

"The Bible knows nothing of an individual salvation in isolation from one's fellow men. We are saved from isolation and incorporated into the life of a community."[103] With this we come to ecclesiology, and we may say at the outset that Lovell Cocks was a staunch churchman, and that he espoused a "high" doctrine of the Church. By this we mean that for him the Church is not one human society among many: "[T]he true church is constituted by believers whom the Holy Spirit has gathered and over whom Christ presides; yet the believers constitute the church not as an aggregate of 'saved' indi-

100 Lovell Cocks learned this point from P.T. Forsyth. See his "P.T. Forsyth's 'The Person and Place of Jesus Christ,'" *The Expository Times* LXIV, no. 7, April 1953, 195–98, espec. 194 (ii).

101 See further, Alan P.F. Sell, *A Reformed, Evangelical, Catholic Theology. The Contribution of the World Alliance of Reformed Churches 1875–1982*, Grand Rapids: Eerdmans 1991, 41–43.

102 H.F. Lovell Cocks, "Reinterpretation of the fact of Christ," 10.

103 Idem, "Man: his origin, duty and destiny," 49.

viduals, but as a living fellowship or commonalty which seeks in all its acts of worship and witness to acknowledge the sovereign authority of its Lord."[104] This position he worked out in a variety of ways—not least in contrast to ideas of the Church which, he felt, undermined the Gospel and were false to the Christian facts. Thus he insisted upon the catholicity of Christianity, with the strong proviso that "The real Catholic Church—as distinct from any denominational representative of it—includes all who are 'in Christ.' Outside its fellowship is no salvation—since the very meaning of salvation is that the believer is incorporated into that fellowship."[105] By this understanding, the Roman Church is at fault, for it illegitimately circumscribes the body of the faithful, and sustains itself by an untenable view of ecclesial authority: "Papal infallibility, like the Divine Right of Kings, is an instrument of despotic authority masquerading as an article of faith."[106]

These are blunt—even polemical—words, which were written as long before Vatican II as we are after it. It must be said that some of Lovell Cocks's negatives make us a little uneasy; but in his positive points there remains a good deal of grist for the mill of ecumenical discussion. For example: "[A]lthough the visible Church in all its manifestations is the *intermediary*, it is never in any of them the mediator of the Word. It is always the channel, never the fount of grace. The Word of God is not bound either to the Sacraments or to the Church which dispenses them."[107] Again, "[t]he Protestant objection to the doctrine of transubstantiation is not that such a change, being miraculous, is impossible, but that, being unnecessary, it would be meaningless. . . . [T]he assembled believers . . . 'make' the sacrament, not by changing bread and wine into the divine substance, but by a moral surrender in the inward parts."[108]

On the relation between sacraments and ministry Lovell Cocks had a good deal to say. The Protestant, he declares, is not against bishops as such, but against the theory which makes the bishop "essential to the being of the Church. It is Catholicism—let it be said with the utmost plainness—which is standing in the way of the catholicity of the gospel."[109] To the members of the Seventh Inter-

---

104 Idem, "The Gospel and the Church," in *Congregationalism Today*, ed. John Marsh, London: Independent Press 1943, 37.

105 Idem, "The reformation of the Church," 4; *LCP*.

106 Idem, *The Faith of a Protestant Christian*, London: Independent Press 1932, 17.

107 Idem, "The reformation of the Church," 5.

108 Idem, *The Faith of a Protestant Christian*, 49.

109 Ibid., 46.

national Congregational Council (1953) he said, "Perhaps we may even find in the apostolic succession, when we come to share it, a very eloquent symbol of the continuity of the Church's life across the centuries. But I trust we shall go on denying, as we now deny, that it *constitutes* that continuity. By God's grace we already stand in the real apostolic succession, for it is in the contemporary Christ, the living Lord, that the Church's life across the centuries is summed up and secured."[110] As he more curtly expressed it in a unpublished address: "If Jesus was dead—so that all we could do was to execute His will according to the directions he had given us; if Jesus the great Shepherd of the sheep had left us: why then it might be necessary to have officers in the church who could rightfully claim to represent Him, and produce some sort of documentary evidence that they did so."[111] As to the possibility of the reordination of non-episcopally ordained ministers: "That a faithful minister of the Gospel whose preaching and pastoral work has been manifestly blessed by God should be excluded from his ministerial functions and his ministry regarded as null and void until a bishop's hands had been laid upon his head, seemed to [the men of 1662]—and seems to us—not only contrary to common sense but perilously close to the sin against the Holy Spirit. If and when we take episcopacy into our Free Church system, it is not to be expected of us that we can swallow with it a theory which practically denies the New Testament doctrine of grace."[112]

The same principle applies where laypeople are concerned. When properly authorised by the church, they may both preach and administer the sacraments, for these tasks are the privileges of the church, the body of believers, they are not "the prerogative of a sacerdotal caste."[113] There can be no question of defectiveness or "invalidity" here.[114]At the same time he regretted that "[S]o many of us forget all about the priesthood of believers except when we invoke it to establish the right of a layman to preside at the Lord's Table—an application of the principle, by the way, which would have scandalised the ejected ministers of 1662. But this misses the point altogether. The question is not who is to preside at the Communion Table in church but who is to take the sacrament to the

110 Idem, "The foundation in Christ," 53.

111 Idem, "The rock from which we were hewn," 5; *LCP*.

112 Idem, "The men of 1662 and what they stood for," 6; *LCP*.

113 Idem, "The ordinances of the Gospel. The Lord's Supper," 3; *LCP*.

114 Idem, *The Faith of a Protestant Christian*, 48.

world outside."[115] Elsewhere he summed the matter up thus: "The Minister is a man who preaches the Word of God. He is a layman, who, by being called by Christ and set apart by the Church, stands over against the Church as being in some sense the embodiment of what the Church is in the mind of its Lord. To the local church he symbolises the Great Church of which that local church is organically a part. He is an apostolic and a catholic man. In short he is a bishop—who within the local church represents the Church universal. And as he represents the Great Church to the local church, so he represents the Great Church to the world."[116]

While denying that the Church was essentially an institution, Lovell Cocks had little patience with the view that the Church is simply a "spiritual" society with no visible embodiment. Such a view, he declared was no more viable than the doctrine of a wholly spiritual Incarnation.[117] The church comprises believers, though we must never forget that "[W]hat constitutes the Church is not the covenant we make with one another, but the covenant, mediated through Christ, which our faith can but acknowledge and receive."[118] He was equally opposed to those (not excluding some Congregationalists) who rejoiced or charged that Congregationalism has no creed: "Never was there a greater mistake or more serious misunderstanding of our witness. A Congregational Church fellowship, so far from not having a creed, is a creed made visible." Not only in its public worship, but in its "sacred and joyful Church Meeting" Congregationalism proclaims that Jesus Christ is the risen Lord who lives and reigns amidst his people.[119]

Not indeed that Lovell Cocks viewed "this sacred and joyful" gathering entirely through rose-coloured spectacles: "I once heard a Church Secretary, whose articulation of final consonants left much to be desired, announce that on Thursday at 7:30 the Church Meeting would be hel'. Alas! he may have been right at that."[120] Not only in practice, but also in their theory of Church Meeting, Congregationalists have frequently missed the way: "It cannot be said too strongly or too often that our Church Meeting is not a democracy. A democracy expresses and makes effective the sover-

115 Idem, "1662–1962: Free Church witness, then—and now?" 10.

116 Idem, "The Church and mission," (apparently a much re-worked draft); *LCP*.

117 Idem, "The reformation of the Church," 15.

118 Idem, "Where two or three," *World Congregationalism* III, no. 8, May 1961, 33. Cf. idem, "The foundation in Christ," 48–49.

119 Idem, "The foundation in Christ," 46–47; cf. idem, "The reformation of the Church," 12.

120 Idem, Congregational Council Sermon, 15 March 1972, 4.

eignty of the people. The Church Meeting, on the other hand, expresses and makes effective the sovereignty of Christ."[121]

Important though the Church Meeting is, it does not follow that Congregationalists have any justification for isolationism vis-à-vis the wider Church: "If, as we maintain, the local fellowship is the catholic Church of Christ outcropping in a particular place, so also is the synod and any other fellowship of Churches gathered through their responsible representatives under the authority of the Lord Christ and in order to do His Will."[122] Neither may Congregationalists suppose that they can justifiably shun wider ecumenism. In his ordination statement Lovell Cocks said, "Our Independency must not lead us to imagine that we are released either from the authority of Christ or from our responsibility to the great Church,"[123] and from this position he never wavered. As an expression of this responsibility he advocated intercommunion: "Surely the living unity of Christians at the Lord's Table would prove the most powerful solvent of ecclesiasticism and all its works!"[124] It would also promote mission: "[T]he royal priesthood of believers loses half its effectiveness when the priests appear to be serving rival altars."[125] Following his attendance at the Third World Conference on Faith and Order (Lund, 1952), he looked for the time when Anglo-Catholics and Congregationalists could agree that they are still divided within the Church; for then it would be plain that neither episcopacy nor the Church Meeting are essential to the existence of the Church.[126] But when reviewing the proceedings of that Conference he could only conclude: "There seems to be universal agreement that we shall not come closer together until we have learned to enter far more deeply into one another's traditions of worship; but how can we do that so long as it is still impossible for

121 Idem, *A Church Reborn*, 21.

122 Idem, "The foundation in Christ," 54; cf. idem, "Where two or three," 34–35; Sermon at the Induction of John Huxtable, 6; *LCP*. This view was contested by Russell H. Stafford at the same International Congregational Council. His point in brief was that, unlike members of a local church, members of a council do not dwell together in Christian intimacy; hence a council is not a church. But can we say that if councils and local churches invoke the guidance of the Holy Spirit the former will always be denied that guidance while the latter will always receive it? See further, Alan P.F. Sell, *A Reformed, Evangelical, Catholic Theology*, 98–99.

123 H.F. Lovell Cocks, "Ordination statement," 11.

124 Idem, *The Faith of a Protestant Christian*, 45.

125 Idem, "1662–1962: Free Church witness, then—and now?" 12.

126 Idem, "Lund—1952," 4; *LCP*.

us all to meet at the Table of the Lord? It is all very disheartening."[127] Forty years on, it still is. And at the root of the sorrow is the denial of catholicity which current practice entails. As Lovell Cocks wrote, "The catholicity we covet is union with our brethren in celebrating the all-sufficiency of Christ to supply the needs of His Church and to redeem His world from darkness and despair."[128]

V

This reference to the needs of the world brings us naturally to socio-ethical matters, on which Lovell Cocks had much to say, and of which his *The Nonconformist Conscience* (hereinafter *NC*) is the epitome. In that work he describes the development through history of Nonconformist social, ethical and political attitudes, with 1662 as his *terminus a quo*. Following the Ejectment the church-chapel distinction gained increasing prominence in England,[129] "as the theological significance of the Establishment seemed to decline its social importance increased."[130] The "weaker brethren" among the Nonconformists succumbed to the blandishments of the Establishment, for "if bigotry has slain its thousands, snobbery has slain its tens of thousands,"[131] while the "moral tonic" of those who remained true to their convictions seemed "unnecessarily bitter to the English palate"—though this was not unconnected with the "Anglican arrogance [which] was one of its ingredients."[132] His smouldering resentment encouraged the Nonconformist to regard his Nonconformist Conscience as "the mark of a spiritual aristocracy, a counterblast to coronets and mitres."[133] Excluded from state office, Nonconformists gave themselves to trade and industry and—which was of special significance—to the ministry. Their political inheritance, rooted in Calvin, was shaped by Locke and Rousseau—though, as mediated by Priestley: it was the Rousseau of the social contract who looked back to Locke, not the Rousseau

127 Idem, *The Congregational Quarterly* XXII, no. 2, April 1954, 177.

128 Idem, untitled paper on the Anglican volume *Catholicity* (1947), presumably written for the group of Free Churchmen which produced *The Catholicity of Protestantism*, eds. R. Newton Flew and Rupert E. Davies, London: Lutterworth 1950, 5. Lovell Cocks was a member of this group of thirteen, the other Congregationalists being John Marsh and Nathaniel Micklem.

129 See further, ch. V above.

130 H.F. Lovell Cocks, *NC*, London: Independent Press 1943, 14.

131 Ibid., 15.

132 Ibid., 16.

133 Ibid., 17.

of the organic community and the general will who looks forward to Hegel and Marx. From 1832, under the reign of *laissez-faire*, Nonconformists for the most part did not press the claims of justice beyond legal rights, and certainly did not challenge the offences against love which were entailed by private ownership as such. The individualistic morality of the Enlightenment, with its exclusion from consideration of iniquities which cannot be laid at the door of individuals, only made matters worse.[134] Hence, "nonconformist diagnoses of social evils have always tended to come to rest in the conclusion that drink, gambling, and thriftlessness, rather than bad housing, unemployment and soul-deadening working conditions, are responsible for the misery and degradation of the poor."[135] As he strongly put it:

> We look in vain for a genuine theology of politics. Here, at any rate, the Free Churches had lost their Calvinistic footing. . . .
>
> [T]he "individual" of the new democratic philosophies was the natural, egoistic man, possessing value and making claims in his own right, and not the rational but sinful creature whose earthly titles stand only in the soverign will of a creating and redeeming God. . . .
>
> What [Nonconformists] failed to see was the blatant denial of the Christian doctrine of human community that lies at the heart of *laissez-faire*. Repudiating the medieval conception of Natural Law, *laissez-jaire* had retained and distorted one element in it—natural rights. The right of property, which for medieval theology had been squarely based upon the social function of property [? and] was to discharge as well upon the well-being of the individual personality to which it was to minister, had been roughly torn out of its community context and made absolute. In Locke's theory, far from property rights serving society, it is society, or at least the State, that comes into existence to serve them. . . . The result is to destroy the basis of any organic doctrine of human community. Society, it seems, rests upon the miraculous confluence and harmony of individual egoisms. The assertion that God is the author of this

134 We must, however, raise an eyebrow when he writes that eighteenth-century rationalism "hardly touched [Nonconformists'] theological orthodoxy." See his "The social thought of 19th century English Nonconformity," *Christianity and Society* X, no. 3, Summer 1945, 17. The Presbyterians were mightily touched by it, as were the General Baptists; and while most Congregationalist churches remained orthodox a number of prominent Congregational individuals did not. See Alan P.F. Sell, "Presbyterianism in eighteenth-century England: the doctrinal dimension," *Dissenting Thought and the Life of the Churches*, ch. V.

135 H.F. Lovell Cocks, *NC*, 39.

> pre-established harmony and of the self-regarding mechanism of economic man is wholly in line with deism but irreconcilable with Christian theology.[136]

It was over the bridge of municipal, rather than State, socialism that "Nonconformists passed from the arid land of individualism to new prospects and vistas of communal life and service,"[137] and Lovell Cocks illustrates this progress in some detail. There remained obstacles, however, and "The Education Act of 1902 [which was designed to make Anglican schools a charge on local rates] was the signal for the last [and ultimately successful] great battle for the War of the English Sects."[138] Subsequently Nonconformist political activity has been widened in scope, and it is essential that Christians are engaged in politics. But since politics is a "realm of relative untruth and sin, where counting heads is more immediately important than changing hearts . . . their political activity is in ceaseless tension with their evangelical witness."[139]

But at the root of the socio-political problem is an ecclesiological weakness: just as Enlightenment rationalism had separated "rational religion" from the particular world faiths; and just as the Evangelical Revival's individualistic message had separated the Gospel from the visible church and introduced missionary agencies and undenominational Christanity, so now the social gospel was to be proclaimed by churches which were not conceived as "local auxiliaries of the world missionary society," but as "centres of social service and branches of the Kingdom-of-God political party."[140] He elsewhere points out that socialist Nonconformists "drew their Christian inspiration from the Sermon on the Mount rather than the creed, not because they rejected the theology of the Incarnation, but because they had not learned its relevance to their task."[141] What needs to be recovered by evangelicals and social gospellers alike is the other half of the answer to the question, "What is the Church?": "The Church is indeed the fellowship of witness to the Gospel that makes men new, but she is also and primarily the Body of Christ, the witness to the new humanity of which he is the Head. . . . In the end our Christian social ethics and our doctrine of human community depend upon our doctrine of the Church, and

136 Idem, "The social thought of 19th century English Nonconformity," 19, 20–21.

137 Idem, *NC*, 48.

138 Ibid., 67.

139 Ibid., 75.

140 Ibid., 85.

141 Idem, "The Free Churches and social responsibility," 8; *LCP*.

this in turn is dictated by our conception of the nature of the Gospel."[142] Or again: "Because it is concerned with man in all his relationships Christianity cannot ignore man's politics and economics; but precisely because it is concerned with man in his deepest and most tragic existence it can never be primarily a political Gospel or an economic programme but must be a word of forgiveness."[143] We need "united witness to the Word that wrestles with principalities and powers for the souls of men and nations," and "a political doctrine that shall be neither bourgeois nor proletarian but uncompromisingly Christian."[144] Why? Because "We are faced with the necessity of rebuilding human community from the bottom upwards, and if we cannot do it in a Christian way it will most certainly be done for us in a totalitarian way."[145] Meanwhile, "the Free Churches have ample warrant for believing that those organs in their polities that, like the Congregational Church Meeting, give expression to the personal responsibility of the individual Christian for the Church's corporate obedience to Christ, are essential both to the fulness of the Church Universal and to the health of secular society."[146] Indeed, in his reprinted article, *The Church in the Atomic Age*, Lovell Cocks, when contemplating the totalitarian possibility, declared:

> [U]nder the great tribulation the Church Meeting would manifestly be the most significant gathering in the world. None but believers would attend it, for it would be too unhealthy for the time-servers, the quislings, and all fair-weather Christians. Since its decisions would be no mere paper resolutions but would commit those who made them to immediate and, perhaps, dangerous witness for Christ, no time would be wasted in trivialities, but there would be much prayer and earnest waiting upon God. And would not Christ be there, giving to His servants grace for their need, subduing their egoisms and fears, quickening their faith, reviving their hope, and enlarging their love? Would not believers long for the Church Meeting as hungry men crave for food? And would not the little company seek out other fellowships of Christ's people and rejoice in a common loyalty to Him? Would not the World-Church be for them a far more vivid and vital reality than as yet it is for us?[147]

142 Ibid., 85–86.

143 Idem, "By faith alone," 4.

144 Idem, *NC*, 91–92.

145 Idem, "The social thought of 19th century English Nonconformity," 22.

146 Idem, *NC*, 90. Lovell Cocks spoke to the same effect at the Lund Conference on Faith and Order of 1952. See the Lund *Report*, 142–43.

147 Idem, *The Church in the Atomic Age*, London: Independent Press n.d., 20–21.

We thus see that although Lovell Cocks stoutly upholds the Christian's political obligation, he does not think that the Church as such should engage in party politics. Christians, however, should, for political opportunities constitute ways of loving our neighbours, and of holding together love and justice. The only thing the Church as such has to request from a democratic state is the opportunity to preach the Word. Since sin cannot be legislated out of the human heart, or sinners be made good by Act of Parliament, we must not be surprised if the state uses force to compel defaulters to mend their social manners and to preserve the freedoms of others. Nor, when justice is to be served, should Christians baulk at seeking votes with those whose basic convictions differ widely from their own.[148]

Was Lovell Cocks finally an optimist or a pessimist where the affairs of the world were concerned? Certainly he was no facile optimist: "We have outgrown, let us hope, the naïve idea that, as Dean Inge has said, people who travel at sixty miles an hour are five times as civilised as those who travel at twelve."[149] But he was not a pessimist either, for he believed that moral progress is possible, at a price. The price is that of the contributions individuals make, not indeed in with a view to their own self-realisation, but in terms of self-sacrifice and service. Why is moral progress so slow, while science proceeds so rapidly? Because whereas the scientist builds upon the work of predecessors, "in the moral race everybody starts from scratch, and moral progress depends upon new victories won by individual Smiths over the ancient temptations. . . . No wonder the ordinary man is important, for in Smith the human race makes a new beginning and this old world gets a new chance. . . . It is the virtue of spare parts to be exactly similar and interchangeable; but it is the virtue of selves to be irreplaceable."[150]

VI

Lovell Cocks could never forget the Smiths of the world.This was what urged him to respond positively to preaching invitations on all possible occasions—indeed, he was preaching until a few months

148 The points in this paragraph are culled from a brief manuscript paper on "The Christian and politics," and from another, unpaginated, on the same theme; *LCP*.

149 H.F. Lovell Cocks, "The individual and moral progress," *The Congregational Quarterly* XXIV, 1930, 30.

150 Ibid., 33, 34. Cf. idem, *Congregationalism and Personal Responsibility*, Leeds Congregational Council, n.d.

before his death. But there was a more theological motive too in his conduct of worship. He believed that our most important work is worship. Not, indeed, that in worship we struggle to make contact with God; rather, worship is the miraculous response we are enabled to make to God's supreme revelation in his Word. By the preaching of the Word the sacramental symbols are brought into conformity with the Word. Baptism and the Lord's Supper are neither greater nor lesser than preaching: they bear witness to the same Gospel as that which is preached, and they do not supply a grace which the preaching lacks. Biblical preaching is both expository and topical at the same time.[151]

Lovell Cocks did not construe his conviction that "The Holy Spirit is the only preacher"[152] to mean that the human preacher may take his ease. For all the importance of the socio-ethical *fruit* of the Gospel, he deeply regretted that

> [O]ur preaching has largely ceased to be theological and has become ethical in tone. . . . [P]eople are not being fed by our views on current events. It is necessary on occasion to preach peace and social reconstruction; it is necessary, on occasion, to castigate public evils like drink and gambling. But if we do nothing else we are not preaching the Word. We realise this and sometimes we sit down in our study and prepare to handle a great theme like the Atonement or Justification by Faith. But the fire of inspiration will not burn; we cannot make the doctrine live even to ourselves, and the whole subject remains wooden and abstract. At last we find we have nothing to say and we fall back on a neat little address all about Martha and Mary, or a thoughtful essay on the psychology of habits. Here we are at home, for are not our shelves crammed with little books by Fosdick and Weatherhead?[153] And meanwhile the people come Sunday by Sunday—Oh! so patiently—waiting for the Word. God help us!—have we nothing to say?[154]

Lovell Cocks knew that "Only a forgiven man can preach the forgiveness of God,"[155] and he knew that true preaching would reach deeply to meet that need. For this reason he warned his students against the kind of sermon which is a platform, rather than a pulpit, utterance. In such a sermon the aim might be to demonstrate

---

151 The points in this paragraph are culled from H.F. Lovell Cocks, "The place of the sermon in worship," *The Expository Times* XLIX, 1937–1938, 264–68.

152 Ibid.

153 For this we might today read "self-help" and even "New Age"!

154 H.F. Lovell Cocks, "By faith alone," 18.

155 Idem, Charge to Horace Sharp, Healey, 30 March 1936, 2; *LCP*.

that Christianity is our only hope, and this is done by showing that salvation cannot come by science, education, economic development, and so on. But the people who might believe that it does are not in Church! Such preaching is familiar, vague and, above all it deals only with ideas, not with souls.[156]

Lovell Cocks took his own advice. Biblically grounded and theologically aware, his sermons were intensely practical. It has proved possible to gather thirty-three of his sermons, of which three were broadcast, twenty-three were published—some in *The Christian World Pulpit*, but most in *The Expository Times*. The earliest to hand is "God's peace terms" (Luke 2:14), which was preached on 23 December 1917; the last to appear in *The Expository Times* (July 1964) is on "The good Shepherd" (Mark 2:17). Since the available sermons represent only a fraction of Lovell Cocks's homiletic output, and since many biblical references are scattered through them, the following statistics must not be taken with undue seriousness. It is, however, the case that of the available sermons two only have no texts; two texts only are from the Old Testament (both from Psalms); seventeen texts are from the Gospels (nine from John), six are from Paul's epistles, three from Hebrews, and one each from Acts, James and I Peter.

Among the broadcast sermons is one delivered in Highbury Chapel, Bristol, which was prerecorded on 28 September 1945 and aired on 7 October, in which the theme was God's peace which passes understanding. Lovell Cocks broadcast a Good Friday address on 15 April 1945; and on 3 March 1953 he was again in the studio to reflect theologically upon the devastating floods which had just struck the West country.[157]

Lovell Cocks was never more down to earth than in the short talks broadcast by the BBC under the title, "Lift up your hearts." The talks were heard on the six week-day mornings, and the Independent Press published the following: *Love Came Down at Christmas* (1951); *The Love of the Father* (1952); *Happiness Day by Day* (1955); *The Way We Talk About God* (1955); *Behold, Thy King Cometh* (1956); *Loving Our Neighbours As Ourselves* (1958); *The Lord's Prayer* (1959); and *The Things We Say* (1961). Something of the flavour of these always difficult assignments is suggested by chapter titles taken randomly from the last-mentioned pamphlet. Thus the chapter "Be your age!" leads to reflections on growth in grace, while that entitled, "Was my face red!" concerns God's reaching out to us when we are ashamed of ourselves.

---

156 Idem, "Lectures on preaching," V; *LCP*.

157 For the texts of these broadcasts see *LCP*.

Most moving, and most courageous of all is the first of a series of three talks transmitted on 5 April 1966. The opening words are, "A few weeks ago my dear wife died. I have suffered other bereavements, yet none as sharp and searching as this. But Easter is coming, and it is with Easter in his mind that Paul tells us that Christians are not to grieve as those who have no hope."[158] The series thus proceeds through the problem of suffering, to the idea of resurrection, and thence to the sacraments as memorials. Here, for a wide and largely unknown audience, he reiterated the theme of his Drew Lecture on Immortality, in which he had said with equal plainness: "In heaven we shall be nearer to our friends than ever we were on earth."[159]

VII

Of his beloved and revered teacher Lovell Cocks wrote, "[I]f Forsyth lacked the precision of thought and the power of systematization that are the recognized virtues of the professor, he possessed something we prize even more highly—a prophet's piercing vision and embattled word."[160] Lovell Cocks, like his mentor, could produce the striking epigram, though his pages were not peppered with paradoxes to the extent that Forsyth's were. He had the same prophetic word to proclaim, though his method was more systematic. Lovell Cocks's message was consistent throughout his life, and although he packaged it differently according to his audiences or readership, the basic evangelical notes are sounded throughout. His ability to reach churched and (especially through the wireless) unchurched alike is not shared by all theologians, or even by all pastors.

On a few occasions his writings have raised qualms. With post Vatican II hindsight some of his claims concerning the Roman Church require modification. While fully agreeing that the Chalcedonian Formula does not provide a satisfactory account of the way in which the two natures are united in Christ, and that its terminology is problematic, we nevertheless find it possible to be more generous in our appreciation of the Formula than was he. And we could wish that he had grounded his soteriology, ecclesiology and social thought more *explicitly* in the doctrine of the Trinity. But the

158 The text of these talks is among *LCP*. Lovell Cocks's second wife predeceased him in September 1981.

159 H.F. Lovell Cocks, in *Resurrection and Immortality*, 161.

160 Idem, *The Congregational Quarterly* XXXI, 1953, 76.

outstanding thing is the continuing freshness of so much of what he wrote. To the extent that the present-day Church does not heed him on the heart of the Gospel of forgiveness, on the nature of the Church and the challenges of Christian fellowship, on the anti-sectarian implications of Christian oneness in Christ (especially challenging at the Lord's Table), and on the Christian hope, the present-day Church is the loser.

There we might have left matters. But there is one thing more. We have sought to present Lovell Cocks as having a theology for *all*. He loved children; and from the notes of a children's address written on a postcard headed "Headingley Hill Congregational Church, Leeds," it would appear that Belinda Bunny, Marcus Mole and Tom Tortoise all had trouble with Harry Hedgehog. Why? Because he was such a prickly person. We too can be prickly to others by hasty words, angry looks and thoughtlessness. It will not suffice to behave in those ways and then say, "I didn't mean it." *Don't do it.*[161]

161 As the writer's "anecdotage" looms ever closer, it may not be out of place to record an experience which occurred during my only meeting with Lovell Cocks. The then venerable man came to preach the Church Anniversary sermons at Worcester. He arrived at the manse, where he was to stay, during the Saturday afternoon. Reaching the door before us, our younger daughter, then aged four, threw it open and, in an excess of pastoral concern, and with some well-intentioned exaggeration said, "Good afternoon Dr. Cocks. What do you like doing on Saturdays? We *always* watch the wrestling on TV!" "I enjoy that too," he declared. And for the next hour the two of them, separated in age by some seventy years, hollered at the "baddies" and cheered on the saints of "grunt and groan." To which the moral is: Lovell Cocks's was not simply a theology for all. He was a theologian for all—which is far better.

XIV The Congregational Lecture for 1991

Rhetoric and Reality: Theological Reflections on Congregationalism and its Heirs

I am delighted to have been invited to contribute to the series of Congregational Lectures which has been wending its spasmodic way since 1833. The first series (1833–1851) was sponsored not by the Congregational Union of England and Wales, but by individuals associated with the Memorial Hall Library. The second series, which began in 1873, was under the auspices of the Union. Now the lectureship is under the Memorial Hall Trust, and thus the original connection is preserved. If the Congregational Lectureship had bequeathed nothing but R.W. Dale's *The Atonement* (1875) and P.T. Forsyth's *The Person and Place of Jesus Christ* (1909), it would have served us well, and humbled all subsequent lecturers.

Not the least of the pleasures in being invited to give this Lecture is the reminder that by grace I have been engrafted into a communion of saints with whom I share more than an ecclesiological inheritance. Thus Ralph Wardlaw, who opened the first series of Congregational Lectures with *Christian Ethics; or Moral Philosophy on the Principles of Divine Revelation* (1833), was in the territory of my earliest researches; though I should not feel quite as confident as he in declaring, "Deny God and you annihilate both" God and morality.[1] Other lecturers included Robert Vaughan (1834), who was to become the first president of my theological college, Lancashire Independent, and Henry Rogers (1873), its second president. Then there was George Redford who, like Vaughan, preceded me in the pastorate of Angel Street, Worcester (though what either of them would have thought of that noble building's present use as a night club, I shudder to think). George Payne, who lectured on *Original Sin* (1845), was at that time teaching at Western College,

1 Ralph Wardlaw, *Christian Ethics; or Moral Philosophy on the Principles of Divine Revelation*, London: Jackson and Walford, 2nd edn., 1834, vi.

whither he had gone from Blackburn Academy, Lancashire's predecessor.

Four out of the first series of fifteen lectures, and two out of the first ten of the second series, concerned the nature, authority and inspiration of the Scriptures. The subjects of the second series, from 1873, reveal a concern to undermine Anglo-Catholic pretensions and to shun sacerdotalism, as witness Enoch Mellor's *Priesthood in the Light of the New Testament* (1876), and John Brown's *Apostolical Succession in the light of History and Fact* (1897).

According to the Library Committee's original Advertisment, the lectures were designed to partake "rather of the character of *Academic prelections* than of popular addresses."[2] If things academic are properly judged by the yard or by weight, many of the lecturers triumphantly met the stated objective. George Redford devoted 608 pages to *Holy Scripture Verified* (1837), while Richard W. Hamilton squeezed out 555 pages on *The Revealed Doctrine of Rewards and Punishments* (1847). I propose to be briefer.

It is interesting to observe that few of the lecturers in the nineteenth century used their platform to promote Congregationalism as such. One who did so was Samuel Davidson, yet another teacher at Lancashire Independent College. In the preface to his lecture on *The Ecclesiastical Polity of the New Testament* (1848) he advises us that he does not appear as an apologist for Congregationalism, but as a student of Scripture. As it turns out, however, the New Testament has a decidedly congregational ring.

As a Congregational Lecturer Davidson stood in a very different position from myself. In the first place, I am very much on our side of modern biblical criticism—that criticism which Davidson helped to pioneer, and for which he was removed from Lancashire College in 1857, President Vaughan following him a month later.[3] Secondly, whereas Davidson was able to look forward to continued expansion of Christianity and to yet more glorious days for Congregationalism, I must reckon with the fact that in the West at least, Congregationalism and its heirs occupy the declining territory of the so-called mainline churches in a post-Constantinian world. Thirdly, any enthusiasm I might have for commending the Congregational Way must of necessity be tempered by the fact that as a distinct

---

2 Prefixed to the early volumes.

3 See Joseph Thompson, *Lancashire Independent College, 1843–1893*, Manchester: J.E. Cornish 1893, 145–46. For the general context see Alan P.F. Sell, *Theology in Turmoil. The Roots, Course and Significance of the Conservative-Liberal Debate in Modern Theology*, Grand Rapids: Baker Book House 1986, ch. II.

entity much of Congregationalism is no more, quite frequently because of its openness to union with those of other traditions, and occasionally because here and there it has gone Unitarian. (I do not overlook the fact that the congregational polity with various refinements and accretions is shared by many others—notably by Baptists and Pentecostalists of the Assemblies of God; but here I have the Congregationalists as such in mind).[4] As to the unions which have taken place: a number of them have been transconfessional in nature—the United Church of Canada (1925), the United Church of Zambia (1965), and the Uniting Church in Australia (1977), for example; other unions have been of the inner-Reformed variety, as in the case of the United Church of Christ in the U.S.A. (1957). These, together with America's Unitarian Universalists, are among the heirs of Congregationalism that I shall have in mind as I proceed to offer some theological reflections upon three characteristically Congregational slogans:

> We believe that the Church comprises gathered believers;
> we believe in the priesthood of all believers;
> we believe in freedom.

How much of this is mere rhetoric? Do the slogans describe the reality of church life? Have they any significance in the changed circumstances I have sketched?

I

"We believe that the Church comprises gathered believers." Another way of saying this is that the Church is a covenant community. God graciously calls people to himself and gives them to one another in love and fellowship. By the Holy Spirit those who believe are called under the preaching of the Word, and are enabled to respond. Negatively, God does not address one here and one there and leave them isolated from each other. They are gathered; they are, to use the traditional term, "visible saints." They are, to use the classical term, regenerate. They have been born again, as Jesus told Nicodemus he

4 In this connection it is strange that so careful a scholar as B.R. White, in a generally favourable review of my book, *Saints: Visible, Orderly and Catholic. The Congregational Idea of the Church*, Geneva: World Alliance of Reformed Churches and Allison Park, PA: Pickwick Publications 1986, should have chided me for seeming to be unaware of non-Congregationalists who share congregational polity; for on p. 4 I write that I do not "deny the polity to Baptists, to the Pentecostals of the Assemblies of God, and to others." See B.R. White in *The Baptist Quarterly*, XXXII, no. 2, April 1987, 94.

needed to be; they have new life in Christ—but, again, not as atoms; for the New Testament is full of corporate terms: household of faith, royal priesthood, multi-limbed body.[5]

What a host of things can go wrong in practice with this biblical yet fragile idea of the Church as God's gathered saints! With the passage of the centuries the idea has been historically, theologically and sociologically vulnerable. For example, whereas there is a line of local church covenants stretching from the Separatist forebears of Congregationalism to the early decades of the nineteenth century, we find a quite sudden diminution of local covenant-making from about 1820 onwards.[6] This, I believe, is attributable in large part to the Evangelical Revival, which placed the emphasis upon the proclamation of the Gospel and conversion, and which brought into the churches many whose understanding of the faith was sketchy indeed, and whose experience and appreciation of the covenant family was negligible. Let me not appear churlish concerning a great movement of the Spirit. It is far better that multitudes be reached with the Gospel than not—always provided that the methods and manner are consonant with the Gospel. But if mission be the task of the Church, we do need a continuing Church, not unrelated atoms, to undertake that task. In its unfortunate aspect, the Evangelical Revival, with its emphasis upon my sin, my guilt, my soul, my redemption, is disturbingly like Enlightenment individualism gone religious.[7] Deprived of the ecclesial experience the newly converted are cheated; and it is not surprising if religion comes to be understood as helping oneself, and if, in consumer societies, the churches come to be regarded as competing enterprises whose goods may be selectively bought or passed by.[8] In America the

5 For some illuminating reflections upon congregational ecclesiology by Mennonite Brethren scholars see *Direction*, XV, no. 2, Fall 1986.

6 For a full account of this phenomenon see Alan P.F. Sell, *Dissenting Thought and the Life of the Churches. Studies in an English Tradition*, Lewiston, NY: Mellen Research University Press 1990, ch. I.

7 Not, indeed, that I wish to indulge in the currently fashionable sport of "Enlightenment-bashing"! It ill behoves those who use modern commentaries when preparing their sermons to participate in such entertainment. A discriminating approach to the Enlightenment is required. If reason is not almighty we need not be driven to enthrone irrationalism. Moreover, as a legitimate protest against the imposition of conscience-denying authorities, whether papal or biblical, Enlightenment individualism was a necessary foil, and has played a valuable part.

8 See further on this theme Alan P.F. Sell, *Aspects of Christian Integrity*, Calgary: University of Calgary Press 1990, and Louisville: Westminster/John Knox Press 1991, ch. VI.

problem was exacerbated when the separation of Church and state flowing down from the Constitution and the Bill of Rights of 1791 made its impact upon established Congregationalism. With few exceptions the Church Meeting was no longer the town meeting, and over against the organised state there grew up the organisations of Christian voluntary societies. At first interdenominational, and a pragmatic response to the challenges of the frontier, they have frequently taken on a life of their own and are often not ecclesiastically accountable.

Small wonder that the concept of church membership was gradually weakened. Richard Baxter, of course, had never approved of the notion of the gathered church:

> I will never join with them that will have but one Form in Christ's School. I would have the A B C taught there as well as the profoundest Mysteries. 'Tis no sign of the Family of God to have no Children (what if I said Infants) in it, but strong Men only: Nor of the Hospital of Christ, to have none Sick; Nor of his Net to have no Fish, but good; nor of his Field, to have no Tares: Flesh and Blood hath ticed me oft to Separation, for Ease; but its too easy a way to be of God.[9]

Had Baxter tried the way of separation he might not have found it so easy! But, more seriously, his words contain two challenges to those who inherit the Congregational Way. First, if exclusive emphasis is placed upon the Church as comprising regenerate, professed saints, whose testimony is deemed adequate by the local church, and whose walk is sufficiently godly to raise no saintly eyebrows, is not the status of baptised infants and children—the seed of believers, thrown into question? What is required is an understanding of Christian initiation as a process encompassing several moments: baptism, nurture, profession of faith and reception/confirmation; with regeneration and conversion, simultaneously or not, at the will of the Spirit and prior to profession. It is not without significance that with the post-Revival emphasis upon the experience of conversion infant baptism suffered a further setback in churchly circles, and got its own back, so to speak, by becoming ever more definitely a rite of passage in the general populace. That this was the emerging situation even as the Revival went its way is clear from the *Divinity Lectures* of 1777 delivered by John Conder at the Old College, Homerton. He advises his students: "Baptize the Children of those who are not Members privately and

9 Richard Baxter, *Reliquiae Baxterianae*, 1696, ed. M. Sylvester, App. iii, 62.

not in the Church—which cases you will find much the most numerous."[10] It is tempting to read between the lines the implication that while the Lord is omniscient the saints, mercifully, are not. Equally significant is the view of Robert Mackintosh, no sacerdotalist he, that infant baptism "stands as the one bulwark against the destruction of the Church in favour of the evangelistic committee."[11]

The second challenge posed by Baxter's words is to that "Pelagianism" which ever threatens Congregationalism. A genuine concern for a pure heart and the fruit of the Spirit—as experienced by Theophilus Lobb and John Pye Smith, for example, when they were contemplating making their profession of faith,[12] can topple over into an unhealthy introspection which so focuses attention upon one's "worminess" (to use a term beloved by our forebears of yesteryear, its slander against a worthy species notwithstanding) as to remove the eye from Christ. Having passed to the membership roll it could be but a step to a doctrine of merit. There is irony in the fact that those who did not wish to bind the conscience by confessional subscription sometimes had fewer qualms about lashing it to a code of prohibitions including card playing and the like. In the pungent words of Mackintosh, "Doctrinally and emotionally [the Puritan convert] was to live by grace; but his conduct was to be exactly the same *as if he expected to be justified by works*."[13] Thence to Baxter's complaint that the gathered church had a place only for the doctrinally and morally fit and healthy. The wheat and tares argument had rumbled on over the centuries, and the early Congregationalists were so concerned to ensure the purity of the visible church that they were inclined to overlook what the Bible says about milk for babes and stronger meat for the more mature. Moreover, the only way in which they could succeed was by diligent policing of the saints. They could be petty; but at their best they knew that it mattered who the saints were and what they did. They did not so readily draw the conclusion that the visible saints

10 *Divinity Lectures delivered by the Revd. John Conder DD., Tutor at the Old College, Homerton, and transcribed by the Revd. W.L. Bishop*, New College, London, Library at Dr. Williams's Library, London, MSS. L28.1.2., 533.

11 Robert Mackintosh, *The Insufficiency of Revivalism as a Religious System*, bound with his *Essays Towards a New Theology*, Glasgow: Maclehose 1889, 28. See further Alan P.F. Sell, *Robert Mackintosh: Theologian of Integrity*, Bern: Peter Lang 1977, ch. III.

12 See Alan P. F. Sell, *Dissenting Thought*, 18–22.

13 R. Mackintosh, *Insufficiency of Revivalism*, 8.

comprise an earthen vessel.[14] This goes far towards explaining the puzzlement of Congregationalism's heirs at Bernard Thorogood's question: "We [of the United Reformed Church] try to be broad in our sympathy and membership. We don't like rigidity in Church discipline. We are not by nature heresy hunters. How then do we deal with people who are on the edge of our fellowship either by conduct which many consider to be immoral or by preaching what many see to be contrary to our basis?"[15]

It seems clear to me that church discipline can never be entirely absent from churchly life. Primarily it is discipline under the Gospel, and it entails the *positive* equipping of the saints for mission and service, and in this respect it finds a prominent focus at the reception or confirmation of a member. It is of great importance that the challenge of the Gospel be presented to those contemplating this step. I cannot forget the rueful lament of a writer to *The London Christian Instructor, or Congregational Magazine* of 1821: "No person used to be admitted into the church without being examined as to knowledge and experience publicly, before a considerable congregation; and, yet, it was scarcely ever known, that any person was deterred from offering himself as a candidate for communion, on account of the strict mode of admission."[16] By that time it had become common practice for candidates for membership simply to write a lettter of application, or to have one written on their behalf. Later still the letter was dispensed with, and the favourable report of the minister or deacon(s) began to suffice. There were those, among them Robert Vaughan, who cautioned against undue reliance upon specific hurdles to be surmounted by those to be received as members, for "While resolved not to open the doors of the church to the worldly, we should be careful that we do not close them against Christians."[17] But this was a plea against legalistic procedures; Vaughan was all for presenting the challenge of church membership to those preparing for it.

To come to our own time: in the year in which I was ordained, 1959, there appeared a new *Book of Services and Prayers*. In the "Service for the Reception of Church Members on Profession of Faith" there are questions to candidates of monastic rigour:

---

14 See further Alan P.F. Sell, *Guidelines on Church Discipline*, London: The United Reformed Church 1983.

15 Bernard Thorogood, quoted in *Newshare*, no. 73, March/April 1990, 12.

16 *The London Christian Instructor, or Congregational Magazine*, IV, 1821, 338–39.

17 Robert Vaughan, *Congregationalism: or, The Polity of Independent Churches, viewed in relation to the State and Tendencies of Modern Society*, 2nd end. revised and enlarged, 1842, 200. Cf. Alan P.F. Sell, *Dissenting Thought*, 30–31.

> Do you acknowledge Jesus Christ as your Lord and Saviour, and do you confess the Christian faith as it is taught in the Holy Scriptures?
>
> Do you promise to obey God's holy will, and to walk according to his commandments all the days of your life? Do you resolve to fulfil the duties of membership in the Church, joining regularly in public worship, in the Communion of the Lord's Supper, and in the Church Meeting; and, being faithful in Bible reading and in prayer, in giving and in service?
>
> Do you promise to live and witness as a Christian believer, to seek the peace and welfare of Christ's Church, and, with all the followers of Christ, to work and pray for the coming of his kingdom in the world?[18]

The analogous questions in the current *Service Book of the United Reformed Church*, one of Congregationalism's heirs, are grounded more adequately in Trinitarian belief, but are much less specific as to the precise duties enjoined upon members: "Do you promise, trusting in God's grace, to be faithful in public and private worship, to live in the fellowship of the Church, to share in its witness?"[19]

It may be that the lack of specificity is influenced by the sociological fact that the population is more mobile than ever before; some United Reformed churches act as *quasi*-parish churches, and others are constituents of local ecumenical projects. People are less likely than hitherto to remain with the church of their childhood and youth—if indeed they have such a church. I have to say, however, that I prefer the older, more specific, list of duties to the more recent truncated list, and this not least because of the clear reference to the Church Meeting. To this matter I shall return; but first I must address a more fundamental theological question, changing opinions on which cannot but influence the viability of the slogan "We believe that the Church comprises gathered believers."

The emphasis now is not upon the "gathered" but upon the "believers." Congregationalists used to be among the charismatics, however little boisterousness they may have shown. To some extent they subsequently sold the pass to others. Be that as it may, from Calvin, the great theologian of the Spirit, they learned of the work of the third Person in what used to be called "the application of redemption." In particular they learned that regeneration, the new birth, is that gracious divine act by which they had passed from death to life, and to which their human response, whether concur-

18 *A Book of Services and Prayers*, London: Independent Press 1959, 55.

19 *Service Book. The United Reformed Curch in the United Kingdom*, Oxford: Oxford University Press 1989, 42.

rent or subsequent, was enabled by the same Spirit. Calvin, of course, borrowed all of this from Paul. With Paul the Congregationalists spoke of being "in Christ," and their entire ecclesiology was founded upon the fact and the experience. It was to this that they testified when making their profession of faith, believing that there was a distinction of eternal significance between those who were Christ's and those who were not.

There may be many reasons why Congregationalists and their heirs have softened their teaching on regeneration. To the extent that regeneration was equated with conversion conceived in stereotyped ways Nevin and his fellow Mercersburg theologians were right to protest in the middle of the last century, and we should still be right to protest today. It may be that on the one hand we have become a little respectable, and do not wish to be as other men, or even as those television evangelists and others, whom we have allowed to hijack the term "born again" and to apply it in sectarian ways. It may be that in a time of growing ecumenical dialogue with people of many faiths we feel that emphasis upon Christian distinctiveness would be downright rude.[20] Or it may simply be that we have succumbed to that egalitarian spirit which makes a virtue out of the blurring of all important distinctions. I shall return to this matter in my conclusion. But now we must pass to the second piece of characteristically Congregational rhetoric.

II

"We believe in the priesthood of all believers." I do not think I need spend time in slaying the heresy that this means that in the church anyone can do anything he or she pleases. While every Christian is privileged to have access to the Father through the one mediatorial High Priest, Jesus Christ, there is more than one individual in the priesthood. What is properly in view, then, is that corporate ministry of confession, praise, prayer, and service which, in Congregationalism at its best, has found its fuel in the conjunction of Word, sacraments and Church Meeting. It is upon the last that I now focus. I make no apology for reminding you of R.W. Dale's now classic affirmation:

> To be at a church meeting—apart from any prayer that is offered—any hymn that is sung, any words that are spoken, is for me one of the chief means of grace. To know that I am surrounded by men and women who dwell in God, who have received the Holy Ghost,

20 On this question see further Alan P.F. Sell, *Aspects of Christian Integrity*, ch. V.

> with whom I am to share the eternal righteousness, and eternal rapture of the great life to come, this is blessedness. I breathe divine air I am in the New Jerusalem which has come down out of Heaven from God, and the nations of the saved are walking its streets of gold.[21]

You may be inclined to think that this is an unattainable ideal. An ideal it is; unattainable it is not. For I have been privileged to be in Church Meetings of the kind Dale had in mind—supremely, if I may so testify, some of those conducted by Sydney Morgan at Perry Hill church, Worplesdon; and I have had the great good fortune of conducting meetings like it myself. But, worms in earthen vessels that we are, we have no cause to become starry-eyed. I do not think my ears deceived me when, on walking up the path to Church Meeting, I heard a deacon mutter in tones of mixed determination and glee, "I'm going to stick my oar in tonight!" And did not the same R.W. Dale say of Church Meetings that, in the absence of any disciplinary connection with the Lord's Supper, "'Church meetings' are, I believe, very often, precisely of the same character as the weekly meetings for prayer, which any person who likes may attend; or else they are meetings for the transaction of formal business, in which no rational man can feel any intense interest?"[22] Many of us have experienced Church Meetings of that kind and, indeed, it must be said that the career of Church Meeting has been, to say the least, chequered throughout Congregational history.[23] The fault may, however, be rather with the saints than with the polity.

Certainly the ways in which the idea of Church Meeting can be vitiated are legion. Perhaps foremost among them is by the equation of Church Meeting with democratic government. Before coming to the main point three things must be said. First, the term "democratic" has been used in more than one way in Congregational circles. In the middle years of the nineteenth century the Secretary of the Congregational Union of England and Wales, Algernon Wells, denied that Congregationalism was democratic.[24] This denial, however, was inspired by distress prompted by the determination of some Congregational ministers to reach out to the working classes. It was all of a piece with Robert Vaughan's advice to the

21 R.W. Dale, "The evangelising power of a spiritual fellowship," in D. Macfadyen, *Constructive Congregational Ideals*, London: H.R. Allenson 1902, 136.

22 Idem, *Essays and Addresses*, London: Hodder & Stoughton 1899, 141.

23 See John H. Taylor, "The survival of the Church Meeting 1691–1901," *Congregational Historical Society Transactions* XXI, no. 2, December 1971, 31–44.

24 See ibid., 42–43, referring to *The Congregational Year Book* 1847, 47.

socially elevated that, notwithstanding Congregationalism's reputation for being "a rude commonwealth," "Distinguished laymen who take their place frankly among protestant dissenters, need not be apprehensive that the respect shewn to their civil rank elsewhere, will be wanting on the part of their new friends."[25]

Secondly, as John Taylor has reminded us, the historical fact is that it was as Dissenters became enfranchised, and began to play their part in civic life, that the Church Meeting began to emerge from the doldrums into which it had so frequently fallen.[26]

Thirdly, some of Congregationalism's apologists have been less than prudent concerning democracy. Thus the distinguished American Congregational historian H.M. Dexter declares that "CONGREGATIONALISM is the democratic form of Church order and government." True, he goes on to say that "It vests all ecclesiastical power (under Christ) in the associated brotherhood of each local Church, as an independent body,"[27] but "under Christ" is within brackets and could be overlooked—as by J. Guinness Rogers who, in his Congregational Lecture applauded Dexter for truly describing Congregationalism as democratic.[28] A dozen years or so before Dexter wrote, J.W. Nevin was found inveighing against Puritanism (his rude name for New England Congregationalism gone rationalistic):

> Theoretically and practically, Puritanism treats the actual church as a simply human institution, the work of man's hands, and of divine force at the last only as civil government is of such force, or in the sense rather of the republican maxim, "The voice of the people is the voice of God. . . ." . . . It is made the glory of Christianity to be purely and intensely democratic. . . . The people are the fountain of right, and the basis of all order and law. Congregationalism completes itself in full Independency. All thus comes to the platform of common sense; all goes by popular judgment and popular vote.[29]

---

25 Robert Vaughan, *Congregationalism*, 175, 181. Cf. Alan P.F. Sell, *Dissenting Thought*, 31.

26 See John H. Taylor, "The survival of the Church Meeting," 42.

27 H.M. Dexter, *Congregationalism: What it is; Whence it is; How it works; Why it is better than any other form of Church Government*, 4th end. revised and enlarged, Boston: Noyes, Holmes 1874, 1.

28 J. Guinness Rogers, *The Church Systems of England in the Nineteenth Century*, London: Hodder & Stoughton 1881, 628.

29 J.W. Nevin, "Early Christianity," *The Mercersburg Review* III, no. 6, November 1851; reprinted in *Catholic and Reformed. Selected Theological Writings of John Williamson Nevin*, eds. Charles Yrigoyen, Jr., and George M. (*sic*) Bricker, Pittsburgh: The Pickwick Press 1978, 232–33.

Of the earliest group of Congregational Lecturers Samuel Davidson saw as clearly as anyone else how important it was to take the Christological reference out of Dexter's brackets, and give it primacy. In reply to the Wesleyan systematician Richard Watson, who had referred to the anomaly of "referring every decision to numbers and suffrages, and placing all that is good, and venerable, and influential among the members themselves, at the feet of *a democracy*," Davidson wrote,

> This objection to Congregationalism is virtually based on the assumption of the system being *a pure democracy*. But it is a mistake to think so. The highest or legislative power is not vested in the people. They are not the rulers. Christ alone properly governs, inasmuch as He is lawgiver. . . . Carson long ago termed the government of an independent church a *Christocracy*, an expression far more indicative of its nature than a *democracy*.[30]

As Dale was later to say,

> The whole power of a church depends upon whether its action is Christ's action or not. He is not bound by majorities. In any action in which Christ takes part His will is necessarily supreme. To maintain the supremacy of the will of Christ in the Church is to maintain that the Church is a Divine society of which Christ is Founder and Lord, and in whose assemblies Christ is present.[31]

The objective, then, is not simply majority rule, but unanimity in Christ. The method is not "one person, one vote," but the earnest seeking of the mind of Christ. Consequently, as Daniel Jenkins saw,

> The Church Meeting . . . needs the scriptures open in the midst and it needs to hear the voice of the Spirit-guided Church through the ages in interpreting scripture. Because of this it needs the service of the ministry. It is sometimes said that the minister is merely a chairman in the Church Meeting and that any other person could be chosen to take his place if the meeting saw fit.

---

30 Samuel Davidson, *The Ecclesiastical Polity of the New Testament Unfolded*, London: Jackson and Walford 1848, 411, 412. Davidson quotes Watson's *Theological Institutes*, but gives no page reference.

31 R.W. Dale, *A Manual of Congregational Principles*, London: Hodder & Stoughton 1884, 36.

> Such a notion is alien to the conception of the Church Meeting, implying that the meeting is its own master and in no sense bound by the Word of God.[32]

Happily, Dr. Jenkins does envisage that in cases of emergency other steps may be taken; but I believe the main thrust of his argument to be utterly sound. The Church Meeting is a continuation of worship. It is, as Lovell Cocks urged, a credal act. It is where Congregationalists and certain of their heirs proclaim that "Jesus Christ is Lord" of the whole witness and mission of the church.[33] It is where those who have sat under the preaching of the Word and received the bread and wine at the Lord's Supper gather to do their contextual theology in fellowship, and by the Spirit through the Word. I find it hard to imagine that believers would not wish to do this. The truth is, however, that many do not. They are not, perhaps, entirely to blame. Church Meeting has not universally lived up to its high objectives, or been so rich in fellowship, so lively in debate and so productive of good that members would not willingly absent themselves. At the same time, obligations remain even when the way is dull and the air polluted by discord. Then, especially perhaps, the credal witness needs to be made. It is precisely because I do not wish the United Reformed Church to forget the practical pastoral and missionary implications of the creed confessed in worship, or to lapse into uncatholic atomism, that I regret that the latest set of questions addressed to members at confirmation, to which I referred earlier, are not more specific as to the obligations of membership. For the same reason I feel saddened by a sentence in a report from the Eastern Province of the United Reformed Church: "the time has come to acknowledge that for many deeply committed people in our churches, the part of membership which turns them on least is attending meetings, debating and voting."[34] As I read this I hear down the years the lament of R.F. Horton of Lyndhurst Road, Hampstead, Congregational Church: "They do not know what a Church Meeting is. In fifty years I have failed to teach

---

32 Daniel T. Jenkins, *The Church Meeting and Democracy*, London: Independent Press 1944, 29.

33 See H.F. Lovell Cocks, *A Church Reborn. An Address from the Chair of the Congregational Union of England and Wales delivered in Westminster Chapel, London on May 15th, 1950*, London: Independent Press 1950, 21; and ch. XIII above.

34 Quoted by Norman Hart, "When is a member not a member?" *Reform*, October 1990, 5.

them."[35] The remedy proposed in the Eastern Province document is even more disquieting. In fairness, they are not entirely at ease with it, but they propose that there be members and "governing members," the latter of whom would commit themselves to the Church Meeting.[36]

Let it be said at once that restorationism, whether with respect to the first century or the sixteenth does not and cannot work, and can deny the Spirit; and let it also be said that confronted by actual situations Christians are not called upon to be entirely witless or unadaptable. Certainly Congregationalism has always been a variegated phenomenon in which some have given primacy to spiritual fellowship, others to local autonomy;[37] and the fact that in some contexts it proved impossible to organise upon Congregational lines—at least initially—is clear. Thus, of missionary endeavour in Samoa Norman Goodall wrote, "The special local responsibility of church members was emphasized, but the nature of Samoan village life made it almost impossible to give reality to the separated church meeting in the Congregational sense."[38] In a word, there can be a godly pragmatism.

To return to the Eastern Province's suggestion of two classes of member. More important than the fact that some believers are not "turned on" by Church Meeting is the fact that over the years, and not uninfluenced by ecumenical discussion, there has been a change in what may be called the order of initiation. The order used to be baptism, nurture, profession of faith, reception as a member, participation in the Lord's Supper. But the renewed emphasis upon baptism, the fact that some people feel ready to profess their faith at a younger age than was normal in the past—even before the age of ten, and the discussion in many parts of the world of the participation of children at the Lord's Supper[39]—all of this has conspired to leave the Church Meeting hanging in the air. If the Church Meeting is not all it ought to be, it is not surprising if a person should say, "I have been baptised; I have made my profession; I am

35 Quoted in A. Peel and J.A.R. Marriott, *Robert Forman Horton*, London: Allen & Unwin 1937, 186.

36 Ibid.

37 See Alan P. F. Sell, *Saints, passim.*

38 Norman Goodall, *A History of the London Missionary Society 1895–1945*, London: Oxford University Press 1954, 367. Of course, the objective of the London Missionary Society was not to plant polity, but the Gospel—as its Constitution made clear. See ibid., 3.

39 See, for example, Alan P. F. Sell, "The Lord's Supper in the Reformed family," *The Reformed World*, XXXIX, no. 2, June 1986, 518–27.

entitled to receive the Lord's Supper; I can serve in various ways, and join church groups in which I am interested—but why should I attend boring Church Meeting? Let those who wish to govern do so." It is not surprising, but it is sad, and this for a number of reasons.

First, the person has been speaking like an individualistic consumer. This is a very serious matter in the West at this time. The Canadian sociologist Reginald Bibby has, in many works, documented the evidence for his assertion that group life "is being threatened. . . . Religious groups . . . have frequently catered to individualism, providing Canadians with an array of items in response to what amounts to consumer demand."[40] Or, in the words of William Willimon of Duke University, "I believe the day is coming, has already come, when the church must again take seriously the task of making Christians, of intentionally forming a peculiar people. . . . The Church is not rejecting the world when it says that Jesus Christ is Lord, rather it is serving the world by attempting to tell and show the world what the world otherwise cannot know."[41]

Secondly, acquiescence in a two-tier membership surrenders the church to all the perils of the corporate model, if not to elitism and gnosticism. People really do begin to speak in terms of boards and business meetings; churches can become collections of more or less unrelated, and sometimes competing, interest groups. What is then required is the manager, and I was not surprised to see that the most prominent volumes in one American pastor's office were on business management. Very soon the concept of vocation is under threat—and even the language used shows it, as when church officers refer to the "hiring and firing of staff" without realising that they are saying anything odd. Hear the rueful comment of an American Baptist historian: "Looking back over fifty years, we find it hard to know which came first, managerial pastors or apathetic congregations."[42]

Thirdly, consider the reponsibilities laid upon the Church Meeting by the United Reformed Church in the United Kingdom:

---

40 Quoted in *Canada Lutheran*, March 1990, 27. See also Reginald W. Bibby, *Fragmented Gods*, Toronto: Irwin Publishing 1987.

41 William Willimon, "Making Christians. The Fox Theater and Christian formation," *Canada Lutheran*, February 1990, 15, 16.

42 Bruce L. Shelley, "Congregationalism and American culture," *Fides et Historia*, XXI, no. 2, June 1989, 47. Cf. Alan P.F. Sell, *Aspects of Christian Integrity*, ch. VI.

Concerning the outgoing of the Church:

i. to further the Church's mission in the locality;
ii. to develop local ecumenical relationships;
iii. to further the Church's compassionate ministry in the locality and throughout the world;
iv. to consider and support the wider work of the Church at home and abroad;
v. to consider public questions in relation to the Christian faith;
vi. to bring concerns for consideration by the Elders' Meeting and wider councils of the Church.

Concerning the nurture of the fellowship:

vii. to call a minister with the concurrence of the District Council(s) concerned . . .;
viii. to elect elders and officers, determining their number and period of service, and representatives to wider Councils;
ix. to admit and transfer members, to maintain standards of membership, and to suspend or remove names from the membership roll, always on the advice from the Elders' Meeting;
x. to adopt financial reports;
xi. to receive reports and proposals from the Elders' Meeting, District Council, Synod and General Assembly and to authorise appropriate action;
xii. on the recommendation of the Elders' Meeting to make or provide for the making of arrangements for the proper maintenance of buildings and the general oversight of all financial responsibilities of the local church;

And generally:

xiii. to do such other things as may be necessary in pursuance of its responsibility for the common life of the Church.[43]

As befits a structure document, there is a legal air to these words, but that they are inspired by missionary, pastoral and fellowship ideals is plain for all to see, and all of these matter to the whole church. How could professed believers not be excited about all of this? How could they willingly leave it all to "governors?" Do they not care how the church's mission will proceed? Who are to be baptised, received as members, married? Have they no thought for the wider family of Christ, or concern to make a concerted witness in God's world? The really surprising thing in the directions is the

43 *Manual*, London: The United Reformed Church 1973, 21–22.

statement that the Church shall meet "at least once a quarter." I should have thought that a weekly meeting would be more in keeping with the specified obligations. We might hope that even the most bureaucratically minded of the saints would be hard put to fill weekly meetings with business, and that then the primary purposes of contextualising the Gospel and forming the saints for witness and service would take precedence. It would be self-contradictory indeed if, having agreed that mission is the task of the Church as a whole, the United Reformed Church were at the same time to embrace the view that reflection and action upon the Church's mission is something with which some, but not all professed church members need be concerned. Accordingly, if pre-teenagers are to receive the Lord's Supper on profession of faith, or even prior to it, continued nurture should make it plain that the obligations and privileges of full responsibility in the church still lie ahead, and a liturgical way of marking the progression to these should be found; but this for all the believers, not for self-selected "governors" only.

The term "wider family of Christ" prompts me next to recall a phrase I used earlier. I referred to the fact that at Church Meeting Congregationalists and *some* of their heirs confess that "Jesus Christ is Lord." My point here is that, sadly, Church Meeting has not been carried with enthusiasm into all of the united churches into which Congregationalism has gone; and my case is that unless we have the strongest possible understanding of the priesthood of believers in its local expression, any attempted practice of mutual *episcope* as between the more local and the wider foci of churchly life will be vitiated, for the wider body will have an inadequate partner with which to relate. Thus, at the time of the formation of the United Church of Canada, it was realised "That while the officers and courts of the negotiating Churches may bear different names, there is a substantial degree of similarity in the duties and functions of these officers and courts."[44] As J.W. Grant has noted, in keeping with the nature of Canada itself as a mosaic of cultures and traditions, "The same mosaic pattern is conspicuous in the Basis of Union [of the United Church of Canada]."[45] As H.H. Walsh explains: "It became a matter of redistributing a plurality of familiar names to the officers and courts of the united churches. The highest court was to be known as the General Council (a Congregational term), presided over by a moderator (a much venerated Presbyterian title). Next in order were to be eleven territorial conferences to be

---

44 *Basis of Union Together with a Brief Historical Statement*, Toronto 1922, 18.

45 J.W. Grant, *The Canadian Experience of Church Union*, Richmond: John Knox Press 1967, 37.

made up of three or four hundred ministers and an equal number of laymen, elected from the sessions and official boards of local congregations, exercising authority over the ministry in the matter of admission and discipline; below the conference was to be a presbytery to maintain oversight of pastoral charges, to superintend the education of candidates for the minisry and to license, induct and to have oversight of ministers within its area."[46] Were the Congregationalists, like Baal of old, asleep, or on a journey? They did not think so. They believed that they had stood up for their principles in the degree of autonomy accorded to local congregations,[47] and in reducing the obligation upon ministers from formal assent to a written form of words to "essential agreement" with the Basis of Union. It is, nevertheless, significant that Church Meeting does not appear in Walsh's list of organisations to be harmonised, and it is possible that it was not a universally lively forum in pre-union days. The current situation is that local congregations of the United Church are required to meet annually, as in many branches of Presbyterianism, and may meet more frequently if they deem it advisable[48]—as, for example, when a minister is to be called. One of my United Church informants hazarded the guess that local congregations may average one additional meeting per annum, but none of them thought that monthly congregational meetings were held. Interestingly, J.W. Grant, reflecting on the disadvantages of the composite method by which union was achieved, writes, "With its emphasis on working together as the purpose of unity, it is apt to leave unanswered some questions about the terms on which Christians live together."[49] In an ideal world the Canadian Congregationalists might have raised precisely those questions, but there is little evidence that they did. The same J.W. Grant has more recently posed a resulting problem to his own people: "the main issue is not whether the rights of the membership are being denied, or whether in a conciliar system the courts have the constitutional right to speak for the church, but what efficacy can attach to decisions, that do not, at least in the long run, carry the wholehearted concurrence

---

46 H.H. Walsh, *The Christian Church in Canada*, Toronto: Ryerson Press 1956, 292–93.

47 See G. Stanley Russell, *The Road Behind Me*, quoted by Claris Edwin Silcox, "Canadian Congregationalism and the United Church of Canada," in *The Congregational Quarterly* XXII, no. 2, April 1954, 141–42.

48 See the *Basis of Union* of the United Church of Canada, 5.8.3.

49 J.W. Grant, op.cit., 37.

of the community."[50] It would appear that in the absence of virile local ecclesial realities partnership and mutual *episcope* as between the several foci of churchly life are threatened, and mutual suspicion and even secession can be sad consequences.

As we turn to Australia, let us hear the chilling words of Hugh Jackson concerning the early decades of this century:

> The church meeting, the embodiment of the Congregational ideal of the gathered-church, was a particular cause of concern. In his chairman's address to the Australian Union in 1904, the Rev. Dr. John Fordyce said that one had to be a hero to defend the church meeting to an audience of Congregationalists. "I suppose no institution today is really less popular amongst us." Between 1913 and 1916 a confidential survey was made of Congregational ministers in Australia and New Zealand, asking them for suggestions about denominational reforms. From the ministers' returns there emerges a general and deep dissatisfacton with the church meeting. One minister wrote that only ten per cent of members believed in the church meeting and even they would not grieve to give it up. Another replied he had not held a church meeting for seven years. A third was laconic: "The Church Mtg is a failure, try postal voting." It would be wrong to suggest that the church meeting had ever been popular with Australian Congregationalists but such disquietude had been unknown a generation earlier.[51]

There may not have been disquietude, but a note supplied by Jackson reveals that there was considerably less than full enthusiasm for the Church Meeting: "In 1894 Rev. James Rickard conducted a survey in Victoria and found that nearly three times as many members attended the monthly communion service as attended the church meeting."[52] It is scarcely surprising that when, in 1912, the Congregational churches of Victoria were asked for their views on union with Presbyterians and Methodists, thirty-four out of fifty-

50 Quoted by Gordon Harland in his review of *Voices and Visions: 65 Years of the United Church of Canada*, Toronto: The United Church Publishing House 1990, in *Touchstone*, IX, no. 1, January 1991, 53. Cf. Alan P.F. Sell, *Aspects of Christian Integrity*, ch. III, espec. 68–71.

51 Hugh Jackson, "Religious ideas and practice in Australian Congregationalism 1870–1930: Part I," *The Journal of Religious History* XII, no. 3, June 1983, 274. The sources of the author's two quotations are: *Volume of Proceedings* of the Congregational Union of Australia and New Zealand, 1904, 15; and A.J. Griffith's notebook, "Abstract of Ministers' Answers to Questions, January 1916," Congregational Union of Australia Records, 3145. 2.

52 Ibid., 274 n. 22, quoting *Victorian Independent*, August 1894.

five churches failed to vote on the issue.[53]

Despite all of this it would appear that in Australia the practice of Church Meeting was deemed sufficiently important for Congregationalists to secure its anchorage in the basis of the Uniting Church. The former Australian Congregationalist, Geoffrey Barnes, writes: "In [the Uniting Church's] written statements and its rules and regulations the congregation has its place as a council of the Church along with the parish council, the elders council, presbytery, synod and assembly. The congregation should meet regularly to build the members up in faith and be concerned for the mission of Christ in the community and the world beyond. . . . However, it is doubtful if in many places congregations are meeting as regularly as was hoped."[54] The explanation given is that of balancing the logistics of meetings at various levels. The Uniting Church is still young, and perhaps a friendly observer may express the hope that should organisational pruning ever be contemplated, the opportunity should be taken of strengthening the local Church Meeting in the interests of mutual *episcope* between it and whatever wider councils are retained.

As a final example I would cite that inner-Reformed union between the American Congregational Christian Church and the Evangelical and Reformed Church in 1957. Here the local church has considerable autonomy but, as Robert Paul has pointed out, the spiritual authority on which such autonomy is based is not spelled out in the Constitution of the Church.[55] In similar vein Louis H. Gunnemann writes, "It is of no small significance that although the covenant concept is interwoven with the histories of both predecessor bodies of the UCC, the word covenant is not used in either the *Basis of Union* or the early editions of the Constitution and Byelaws . . . the UCC covenantal style emerged as a *juridical* expression of

---

53 Ibid., 275, citing typescript "Minutes of Meeting of Standing Committee on Church Union . . . 21st October 1912," Victorian Congregational Union Records, 9239,10/2, at La Trobe University.

54 G.L. Barnes, "Reflections of an erstwhile Congregationalist ten years into the Uniting Church," *Church Heritage. Journal of the Church Records and Historical Society (Uniting Church in Australia—NSW Synod)*, V. no. 2, September 1987, 85. It is not unduly fanciful to attribute the survival (however vestigial) of Church Meeting at all to such stalwarts as A.J. Griffith. See Clyde Binfield, "A letter from Australia," *The Journal of the United Reformed Church History Society* III, no. 8, May 1986, 348–55. On the other hand, and for the view of a continuing Australian Congregationalist, see John Wheeler, "Congregationalism in Australia," *Congregational Journal* XIII, no. 1, September 1987, 10–34, espec. 20.

55 Robert S. Paul, *Freedom with Order. The Doctrine of the Church in the United Church of Christ*, New York: United Church Press 1987, 56.

the covenant relationship, with little or no elaboration of the implicit *theological* dimensions affirmed in paragraph 2 of the Preamble of the Constitution: 'The United Church of Christ acknowledges as its sole head, Jesus Christ, Son of God and Savior.'"[56] There is no evidence that Church Meeting was enthusiastically offered by Congregationalists to the new Church. Rather the impression is that as a regular gathering it was largely extinct within Congregationalism itself at the time of union; and the fact is that erstwhile Evangelical and Reformed churches have not been rushing to adopt it. As the historian of that union has noted, "The goal of developing a new form of the visible church was deprived, from the beginning, of a clearly articulated ecclesiology."[57] No doubt this goes some way towards explaining why, in the Constitution of the United Church of Christ the covenant idea is couched in social-contractual language.[58]

I have suggested that quite apart from its intrinsic theological merits and its challenges to fellowship and witness, Church Meeting should be revitalised as a check upon individualistic consumerism and the corporate model of churchly life; and as a means of enhancing that mutuality of *episcope* which is a clear implicate of the Gospel. In all of this there is a word of relevance to any who may be contemplating conversations with Methodists, whose *raison d'être*, unlike that of the Congregationalists, was not ecclesiological.[59] But by far the deepest significance of Church Meeting is in its nature as a confessional act. If we are not to be hypocrites, we need to say "Lord, Lord" in Church Meeting as well as in Sunday worship. For in Church Meeting we seek to know what the Lord would have us do, and to receive the strength he imparts for mission and service.

III

So to our final piece of Congregational rhetoric: "We believe in freedom." In introducing this subject I finally succumb to the temptation to quote Bernard Lord Manning. Agreeing that liberty is "the native air of Congregationalists," he asks,

> But what sort of liberty? Freedom from all those things that used to rouse violent emotions in our liberty-loving breasts: freedom

56 Louis H. Gunnemann, *United and Uniting. The Meaning of an Ecclesial Journey*, New York: United Church Press 1987, 137. Cf. R.S. Paul, op. cit., 58.

57 Ibid., 133.

58 Ibid., 166–67.

59 See further, Alan P.F. Sell, *Dissenting Thought*, ch. XXI.

> "from the bishop of Rome and all his detestable enormities"; from hierarchies, from priestcraft, from councils, from creeds, from tradition, from dogma? You know the whole bagful of bogeys whom we habitually defy. But when, to-day, you say that liberty is the distinctive possession of us Congregationalists, do you seriously mean liberty from these things and the like? If so, you have no liberty but such as falls to the lot of all men. If this be your liberty, it is the liberty of the beasts that perish. Why, it is the freedom of Mr. Bertrand Russell, of Mr. Joad, of Mr. Llewellyn Powys, of Mr. Mencken: they all enjoy this freedom, with a freedom from all knowledge of Church history thrown in. This is a freedom enjoyed by all this sad, despondent, dying world. It is a freedom that leaves the man in the street exactly where you found him. Freedom from dogma, from tradition, from priestcraft, from creed, from an infallible Book: with a small price he has obtained *this* freedom, with the price of a two-seater car or a Sunday excursion ticket. . . .
>
> No: our distinctive contribution is liberty, but it is Christian liberty: liberty not from the Church, but in the Church. . . .
>
> What was it that made us assert the rights of individual independent congregations. . . . Was it a love of petty societies, of primary assemblies, of theoretic democracy? Nonsense: it was a doctrine of grace. . . . We found grace in the independent congregations to which (if the Church were to rule its own house) historical accident had driven us. . . . Where we found grace we recognized the one catholic and apostolic Church which with all Christians we confessed.[60]

There you have it. Fundamentally, the freedom of Congregationalists, as of all Christians, is freedom by and in that Gospel which has freed them. They are no longer captives to sin; the grave cannot hold them; and the last enemy, death, has been vanquished. They are released and empowered for witness and service. Hence P.T. Forsyth's reiterated insistence that ours is a "FOUNDED FREEDOM. Not freedom alone is our genius; for freedom alone is but caprice, atomism, and anarchy in the end. But it is freedom created and founded and reared by an authority which cannot be either evaded or shaken; and which creates our emancipation, in the very depth and crisis of our soul, by the eternal redemption at the heart of all history in Christ's cross."[61]

---

60 Bernard Lord Manning, "The place of Congregationalism in the living Church: Our distinctive contribution," *Proceedings of the Fifth International Congregational Council*, London: Congregational Union of England and Wales 1930, 253–54; reprinted in idem, *Essays in Orthodox Dissent* (1939), London: Independent Press 1953, 107–09.

61 P.T. Forsyth, *Faith, Freedom and the Future* (1912), London: Independent Press 1955 347; cf. ibid., 289–90.

But although the positive basis and thrust of our freedom in the Gospel must be emphasised, there are implications, some of them negative, attaching to it, and these are important. The problem arises when, as has sometimes happened, they are elevated to the supreme position. Let us briefly examine some of the implications of our Gospel freedom.

First, we are free from the world. We do not owe our freedom to the world, that is, to the prevailing culture around us, and it is quite clear that our forebears sometimes thought of themselves in the first instance as being separated from the world. This separation was part and parcel of their positive calling to be God's *holy* priesthood—a people separated unto the Lord. The Puritan Thomas Watson put the challenge to holiness in strongly trinitarian terms: "A Christian's heart is to be the presence-chamber of the blessed Trinity; and shall not holiness to the Lord be written upon it? Believers are children of God the Father, members of God the Son, and temples of God the Holy Ghost; and shall they not be holy? Holiness is the badge and livery of God's people."[62] But if, at certain periods, our way of being in the world but not of it has led us to quietistic withdrawal, our problem today—at least in the West—is rather that of undue identification with the prevailing culture to the extent that we lack the ability to challenge it without hypocrisy. Hear the United Church of Christ theologian Gabriel Fackre: "Self-conscious attention to culture is basic . . . to a world-formative faith. . . . But . . . it is one thing to relate to culture, and another to capitulate to it. To let the world set the agenda is very bad advice if it means that the culture's answers to its own questions become the church's answers. Or more subtly: the world's formulations of its questions (with its implied answers) are accepted uncritically by the church as *the* questions."[63] How are we to have the elbow-room which prophets need if all distinctions are blurred? Let us be warned by William Willimon:

> A stark reality for many of us liberal, mainline churches is that there is no way for us to form people into a body that has no boundaries, no integrity of its own. We must define our beliefs and attitudes, the integrity of our community. No one ever lived or died for "pluralism." We live in a society in which individualism is

62 Thomas Watson, *A Divine Cordial*, Grand Rapids: Sovereign Grace Publishers 1971, 79–80.

63 Gabriel Fackre, "A conversation continued," *The Unitarian Universalist Christian* XLII, no. 4, Winter 1987, 17. Cf. Susan Brooks Thistlethwaite, "Theological ferment in the United Church of Christ," *The Chicago Theological Seminary Register*, LXXV, no. 2, Spring 1985, 45.

> valued over community and in which personal autonomy and freedom mean more than truth. So the chief North American virtues are tolerance and affirmation, virtues which the liberal church has absorbed to its peril. One reason why formation has been deemed unimportant by many of our churches is that we assumed that our community was roughly continuous with the society as a whole.[64]

We need take no false comfort from the fact that Willimon is a Methodist who lives in America. The challenge presses: what does it mean in practice that we are freed both from, and for, the world?

Secondly, in England the Congregational tradition still witnesses alongside an established Church and, traditionally, we have declared that we are free from the control of the Church by the state. And so we are. However, now that the disabilities attaching to Nonconformity are almost entirely removed, we may be tempted to think that the battle is won. In an important sense, however, it has not yet begun. As P.T. Forsyth said bluntly, "What we protest against is not the abuses but the existence, the principle, of a national Church."[65] My point is that after four hundred years of chequered and variously formulated ecclesiological witness as to the nature of the Church, the "crown rights of the Redeemer in his Church," and the incompetence of the state to order the worship and life of Christ's Church, there has been no theological discussion with the Church of England of the points at issue.[66] The 1989 tercentenary of the Toleration Act might have provided an occasion for serious consideration of the question; the quatercentenary in 1993 of the martyrdom of Barrow, Greenwood and Penry may yet provide the occasion, though at present I have few grounds for optimism that it will.

I by no means suggest that our testimony has been universally honourable and consistent even when we have offered it. Though pleased enough to have their own freedom, the New England Congregationalists refused to grant Roger Williams his on his adoption of baptist views, and banished him to Rhode Island. As one of Oliver Goldsmith's characters noted, "No man is so fond of liberty himself as not to be desirous of subjecting the will of some individuals in society to his own."[67] Again, Robert Paul has made it quite clear that the Congregationalists at the Westminster Assembly were

64 W. Willimon, "Making Christians," 17.

65 P.T. Forsyth, "The evangelical basis of Free Churchism," *The Contemporary Review*, LXXXI, January–June 1902, 693.

66 See further, Alan P.F. Sell, *Dissenting Thought*, ch. XXII.

67 Oliver Goldsmith, *The Vicar of Wakefield* (1766), London: Collins 1953, 140.

remarkably reticent concerning toleration until it became clear that, given the Presbyterian majority, they might lose their own freedom unless they waxed vocal on the matter.[68] But at the present time our reluctance to testify at all on these matters simply allows members of the Church of England to continue in ignorance. In witness whereof I call Bishop Hugh Montefiore, who denounced the British Liberal Democratic Party's motion for the disestablishment of the Church of England as a "repudiation of Christianity in this country."[69] My distinct impression is that this was not an example of episcopal humour. Since it would be ungracious to charge one of the Lord's shepherds with arrogance, we ought to resort to such terms as myopia or "cloud cuckoo land." For these are the words of one who can neglect the history and witness of all who have managed not to opt into, or to repudiate, the Establishment while remaining Christian. I do not, of course, say that Bishop Montefiore is representative of all bishops, and his facility for provocative utterance has been in evidence on other occasions, and on quite different matters. But so long as there are Church of England Bishops of this erasing kind, Nonconformists will not need to rely upon Korea's Minjung theologians for reminders concerning the "underside of history." Again, the Bishop's words are those of one whose Church's Sunday attendance at worship out of some thirty-five million baptised and eleven million confirmed members is approximately 1,165,000.[70] I do not rejoice in this statistic; it does, however, throw into relief the questions, Is it true that to be a Christian is to be visibly of the Church? If so, what are we to make of millions of incomplete Christian initiations? Surely these cannot all be the result of pastoral failure. May not some be indicative of the repudiation of Christianity? With people of many faiths and of none in our midst, and with many Anglican parish churches acting as *de facto* gathered churches, it must surely be dawning upon all that, as Robert Browne saw long ago, "the kingdom off God Was not to be begun by whole parishes, but rather off the worthiest, Were thei neuer so feuve,"[71] and that the question of the nature of the Church in a pluralistic society is urgent.

Thirdly, Congregationalists have believed that local churches have all that is required to order their life and witness, for they have

---

68 See Robert S.Paul, *The Assembly of the Lord*, Edinburgh: T. & T. Clark, 103.

69 H. Montefiore, quoted in the [Canadian] *Anglican Journal*, December 1990, 4.

70 The figure is as given in the [London, U.K.] *Daily Mail*, 7 December 1990.

71 Robert Browne, A True and Short Declaration, c. 1583, in Albert Peel and Leland H. Carlson, *The Writings of Robert Harrison and Robert Browne*, London: Allen and Unwin 1953, 404.

Christ as their Head. Hence the emphasis upon the autonomy of the local church. Down the centuries comes the affirmation of the Savoy Declaration of Faith and Order (1658): "Besides these particular Churches, there is not instituted by Christ any Church more extensive or Catholique entrusted with power for the administration of his Ordinances, or the execution of any authority in his name."[72] This did not preclude advisory synods or councils, and as he reflected on the history A.J. Grieve roundly declared that "It is a libel to say that the local churches had no dealings with one another."[73] It cannot be denied, however, that autonomy has sometimes been construed to mean that freedom entails our being free from all other Congregationalists, and free to do as we please. This has led to caricatures of the tradition by others. Thus, for example, John Congram, the editor of the [Canadian] *Presbyterian Record* writes, with reference to the pre-1925 Canadian Congregational Union, "Our denomination [that is, the Presbyterian Church in Canada] is in danger of replacing it. Increasingly, congregations are only interested in themselves."[74] In the course of administering a gentle corrective, I could only admit that since, like all polities, the Congregational is worked by sinners, there is point in the old adage that "Congregationalism may be the polity of heaven, but on earth the saints sometimes *deserve* Presbyterianism!"[75] But much more serious than the caricatures of others is the fact that Congregationalists have sometimes been slow to appreciate and give expression to the catholicity which is inherent in their claim that the Church

---

72 *The Savoy Declaration of Faith and Order 1658*, ed. A.G. Matthews, London: Independent Press 1959, 122, art. VI. See further Alan P.F. Sell, *Saints*. In referring to this work Alan Argent took me to task for denominating the period 1640–1690 that of "Classical Congregationalism." Erik Routley had earlier characterised the years 1600–1649 thus. See A. Argent, "Albert Peel: the restless labourer," *The Journal of the United Reformed Church History Society* IV, no. 5, October 1989, 328 n. Undeniably, I needed a chapter heading between "The prehistory of Congregationalism" and "Towards evangelical Congregationalism"! But I defend my title (and my period over against Routley's) negatively, because between 1600–1640 English Congregational witness was, for legal reasons, necessarily skeletal; and positively, because the period 1640–1690 saw Cromwell, the Cambridge Platform, Savoy, the Dissenting exodus of 1660–1662, such prominent apologies for the polity as those of John Owen and Thomas Goodwin, the shaping of the polity under persecution, and the Toleration Act of 1689. All of which, I think, suffices to justify my form of words.

73 A.J. Grieve, "The Congregational tradition," An address at Carr's Lane Church, Birmingham, 1 June 1948, quoted by Charles E. Surman in his *Alexander James Grieve*, Manchester: Lancashire Independent College 1953, 47.

74 John Congram, editorial in *Presbyterian Record*, July–August 1990.

75 Alan P.F. Sell, letter in ibid., October 1990, 7.

comprises a holy priesthood of believers called and gathered by God. They have even invoked their freedom in practical denial of this claim.

It is worthwhile to underline this point. Not for nothing have Congregationalists been in the van of ecumenical developments during this century. To mention only the deceased, A.E. Garvie, Leslie Cooke, Norman Goodall, John Huxtable, Douglas Horton, H.S. Leiper—these are but a few of the names which come to mind when Congregational catholicity is in view.[76] Moreover, there are the united churches into which Congregationalism has gone; and there is the World Alliance of Reformed Churches—that union in 1970 of the World Presbyterian Alliance with the International Congregational Council—which to this day remains the only international union of two Christian world communions.[77] *De facto* sectaries they may be, but sectarian on principle—never! They know that God calls one Church, and they know that there is no such thing as a "Christian in general." That is to say, that one's rootage in the Church catholic is inseparable from one's rootage in the local church. Membership in the latter is membership in the former. They also know, as Samuel Davidson pointed out in his Congregational Lecture of 1848, that "The only scriptural representation is, *the church universal* consisting of all saints on earth and in heaven; and *a particular church* composed of Christians usually assembling in the same place."[78]

In our own lifetime we have seen how this principle can be variously construed in practice. On 16 May 1962, when less than three years into my ministry, I seconded a motion at the Annual Assembly of the Congregational Union of England and Wales, which was designed to encourage further thought prior to the taking of a decision that the Union be renamed "Church." The proposer was Reginald Cleaves. He and I were at one on the biblical point made by Davidson long ago; but whereas Mr. Cleaves emphasised the autonomy of the local church, my concern was rather that to take the name "Church" for the denomination would be a sectarian act. I believe that our catholicity entails the conviction that denominations are aberrations with which we have been landed by history,

---

76 See further, Norman Goodall, "Some Congregational pathfinders in the ecumenical movement," *Transactions of the Congregational Historical Society* XX, no. 6, October 1967, 184–99.

77 See further Alan P.F. Sell, *A Reformed, Evangelical, Catholic Theology. The contribution of the World Alliance of Reformed Churches 1875–1982*, Grand Rapids: Eerdmans 1991, espec. ch. IV.

78 S. Davidson, *The Ecclesiastical Polity of the New Testament Unfolded*, 131.

and that we should not do things which would make them more fortress-like than they already are. I do not, of course, deny that God the Holy Spirit can address assemblies just as easily as a local Church Meeting; I am utterly persuaded that mutual relations between churches are not only useful, but right; and when it became clear that "Church" in the denominational sense was not being defended on biblical grounds, and that *mutual episcope* as between the local and wider foci (I do not say "levels") of churchly life was in view, I was able to go forward with the Congregational Church in England and Wales, whereas Reginald Cleaves felt that he could not, and became a leader of the Congregational Federation.[79] From my point of view as just sketched, it can only be regarded as regrettable that a pseudonymous letter-writer to *Reform* should so misunderstand our catholicity as to wish to be a member of the United Reformed Church, but *not* of a local church.[80]

But perhaps the worst way of construing Congregational freedom is to suppose that it means freedom to believe as we please. It cannot be too firmly stated, however, that when our forebears resisted confessional subscription it was not because they did not believe very much, or because they were unwilling to testify to their beliefs. Certainly they did not wish to foster hypocritical assent. They did not wish to risk the elevation of particular forms of words above the Word in Scripture. With John Owen they sometimes insisted that the Holy Spirit's continual leading might render specific acts of subscription redundant; with Richard Baxter they sometimes saw confessional subscription as a badge of sectarianism threatening their catholicity; and they were universally opposed to subscription required by the state, for the control of doctrine was not the state's business.[81] But by far the larger part of them saw themselves as standing in the heritage of the catholic faith of the ages. However, with the weakening of the checks and balances provided by the closely knit covenant community; with the rise of the idea of the inalienable rights of conscience; and in the wake of the challenges of scepticism and the advent of modern biblical criticism;

79 See further Alan P.F. Sell, *Saints*, 114–15; idem, "Commission I: from the camp of the bewildered," *The Christian World*, 9 November 1961, 8; R.W. Cleaves, *The Story of the Federation. Congregationalism 1960–1976*, Swansea: John Penry Press 1977. See also Louis H. Gunnemann, *The Shaping of the United Church of Christ*, New York: United Church Press 1977, 40.

80 "Nonconformist" in *Reform*, December 1990, 23.

81 See further Alexander Mackennal, *Life of John Allison Macfadyen*, London: Hodder & Stoughton 1891, 184; Geoffrey F. Nuttall, *Congregationalists and Creeds*, London: Epworth Press 1966; Alan P.F. Sell, *Dissenting Thought*, 57–59; idem, *A Reformed, Catholic Evangelical Theology*, 79–83.

the anchorage in catholic doctrine could be strained to breaking-point, so that in his day P.T. Forsyth, for example, felt constrained to protest that where doctrine was concerned "Too many are occupied in throwing over precious cargo; they are lightening the ship even of its fuel."[82]

At this point the career of those other heirs of Congregationalism (who still retain the polity), the American Unitarian Universalists, is instructive. Thomas D. Wintle has described the three successive waves which have swept over American Unitarianism since Emerson resigned from the Second Church in Boston in 1832. First, Emerson and the Transcendentalists proclaimed an *unmediated* acquaintance with the immanent God. Secondly, in the last three decades of the nineteenth century there arose the liberal Christians on the one side and the non-covenantal theists and exponents of the free development of moral character on the other. Thirdly, in this century there arose the humanists who seek religion and religious fellowship without God. And Dr. Wintle has sufficient grace and humour to quote against his own denomination (though he is himself a convinced Unitarian Christian) an assertion possibly attributable to Martin Marty, namely, that American Unitarianism provides "a half-way house between Methodism and the golf course."[83] An Episcopalian observer of that denomination has referred to a "parent who would not let her daughter attend her UU Sunday School class because the curriculum was entitled 'Adventures of God's Folk.' She didn't want her daughter exposed to that G-word, and by avoiding saying it or experiencing it, she thought 'it' would go away." The observer wryly comments, "It remains unclear how this kind of reaction fits into a UU's claim to openness, tolerance, and inclusion as basic tenets of her faith."[84] Assuredly, there is no intolerance like liberal intolerance!

That the waves which have lashed American Unitarianism have

---

82 P.T. Forsyth, *The Principle of Authority* (1913), London: Independent Press 1952, 261.

83 Thomas D. Wintle, "Seeing ourselves: A UU Christian perspective," *The Unitarian Universalist Christian* XLII, no. 4, Winter 1987, 52–54. It is interesting to note the analogous trends within Quakerism. It is not uncommon to meet Christian Friends, evangelical Friends, humanist Friends, universalist Friends, unitarian Friends, Buddhist Friends, and Friends whose motivation for allegiance to the Society is pacific or ecological. The last prompt the insistence of some Quakers upon their full designation, *The Religious* Society of Friends. See, for example, John Punshon, *Letter to a Universalist*, Pendle Hill Pamphlet no. 285, 1989; and the review of it by Audrey Fenner in *The Canadian Friend* LXXXVI, no. 1, January–February 1990, 30–33.

84 Gwen Langdoc Buehrens, "Finding the common spiritual task," in ibid., 12.

at least dampened some of Congregationalism's ostensibly more orthodox heirs is clear from the comment of W. Widick Schroeder of the United Church of Christ. He writes:

> Many who prize congregational autonomy would not affiliate with a religious institution having any other form of polity, for they believe that the voluntary associational principle is the most fitting form of religious association. They hold that this principle reflects the primacy of persuasion and liberty in religious matters and sustains most fittingly a collegial style of religious leadership. They also believe congregational polity legitimates diversity of belief and practice in different gathered communities who voluntarily will to relate to other congregationally based communities. . . . A common sharing of awareness of the Divine immanence is an adequate basis for the unifying facet of religious expression.[85]

Emerson lives! Now the most troubling result of all of this is that it provides fuel to conservatives who wish to call everyone to heel—even to the point of subscription. I have made it clear that those who stand in, or who are heirs of the Congregational Way will not willingly take that route. On the other hand, P.T. Forsyth was right to caution that "There must surely be in every positive religion some point where it may so change as to lose its identity and become another religion."[86] For me the standing ground is that of the earliest Christian creed, "Jesus Christ is Lord." Since the church comprises saints, but saints of many differing opinions and degrees of Christian maturity, there must be room for people to grow in knowledge as they grow in Christ. If the most a new Christian can say is "Jesus is my Master and I try to follow him," I am not going to be so sectarian as to trounce such a person for being a benighted old-fashioned liberal, or so "Pelagian" as to suggest that assent to full-blooded Chalcedonianism is the condition of salvation. But I firmly believe that as we probe what is going on beneath the Congregational rhetoric we shall not wish to stop short of the classical trinitarian confession of faith.

For what is the reality which underlies the slogans concerning the Church catholic as comprising believers gathered by and to God and therefore given to one another, a holy priesthood, a freed people? The answer can only be the electing grace of the triune God, whose Son said, "You did not choose me, I chose you" (John 15:16).

---

85 W. Widick Schroeder, "The United Church of Christ: the quest for denominational identity and the limits of pluralism," *The Chicago Theological Seminary Register* LXXXV, no. 2, Spring 1985, 25–26.

86 P.T. Forsyth, *The Principle of Authority*, 219.

As a new millennium approaches, Congregationalists and the heirs of Congregationalism would do well to address this question: Is it true that the Church comprises all those whom the Father calls, regenerates, frees and gathers by the Spirit, on the ground of the Son's finished work? An enthusiastic affirmative answer will (without any recourse to subscription) fuel the continued proclamation of the Gospel. A churchly life consistent with that same Gospel will be one in which all the saints participate, and by which they are nourished, disciplined and equipped for witness and service. From the pulpit, at the Table and in and through the covenant family's institutions (including, it may fervently be hoped, the kind of Church Meeting which none would willingly avoid, and the adoption of which on grounds of mission and enacted confession those of other traditions may even wish to consider) the catholic confession will be joyfully made and zealously practised: "Jesus Christ is Lord."[87]

87 It was recently reported that a North American Lutheran adjunct professor had been warned that he would no longer be permitted to teach his seminary course on ecclesiology if he persisted in calling Jesus Christ the "Lord" of the Church, for this was unacceptable hierarchical language. It is, however, characteristic of the Gospel that the world's terms and values are turned upside-down and that, in this case, the Lord is one who takes a towel and does slaves' work (John 13:3–17). Nothing could be less hierarchical. I can testify to the strength which many East European Christians derived from the knowledge that the dictators who strutted the several stages behind the iron curtain (now happily removed) were not real lords at all. Such consolation should not readily be denied by those who sit in relative ease. The example I have given is by no means isolated. More widely, trinitarian language, such as I have just used without apology, is being called into question, especially by some feminist writers. For a provocative response to this see Donald G. Bloesch, *The Battle for the Trinity*, Ann Arbor, Michigan: Servant Books 1985. See also Alvin F. Kimel, Jr., (ed.), *Speaking the Christian God. The Holy Trinity and the Challenge of Feminism*, Grand Rapids: Eerdmans, forthcoming. My suggestion that our ecumenical partners may wish to contemplate something in the nature of a regular meeting of the Church is made with some diffidence since those of the Congregational heritage do not always realise the full potential of Church Meeting—where that institution still exists. I fully realise that when speaking of the local meeting of the priesthood of believers, much turns upon the definition of "local"; and I am aware that in theory the local Church for Anglicanism is the diocese, and for Presbyterianism, the presbytery. However, I do not see that episcopal or presbyterial polity would be adversely affected by monthly or quarterly meetings of professed local church members for reflection upon their life and mission, with a view to hearing and responding to reports of their officers, and as a means of testifying to Christ's Lordship over the whole of their churchly life. It is well known that Presbyterian church members have traditionally met intermittently in order to approve the budget, elect elders, and call ministers.

Index

Biblical and fictional names are not included. See also the list of Harley College alumni, pp. 301–302. See ch. XII for references to many London districts.

Abbott, Judith B. A., 340
Abbott, W. C., 119
Abel, Richard, 65
Aberdeen, 149, 288, 290
Abernethy, 175
Aberystwyth, 211
Abingdon, 136
Act of Uniformity, 125, 126–130, 140, 166
Adelaide, 287
Africa, 53, 92, 293, 294, 298
African theology, 53
Afro-American theology, 52, 55
Aikin, John, 66
Airthrey, 186, 188
Albury Park, 192
Alexander, Archibald B. D., 107
Alexander, Samuel, 306
Alföldi, A., 96
Allen, E. L., 101, 315, 321
Allen, J. H., 240
Alloa, 281
Altham, 125, 132
Ambrose, 96, 156, 159
America, 42, 48, 68, 122, 251, 279, 343, 344, 355, 360–361, 364
American Bible Society, 251
American Sunday School Union, 251
Anabaptists, 33, 47, 100, 105, 106, 125, 179
Anderson, Anthony, 113
Andrews, H. T., 305
Anerley, 297, 298
Angier, John, 131
Anglicans, 42, 44, 47, 62, 123, 136, 187, 257, 294, 369, 371. *See also* Church of England
Anicetus, 153
Anne, 140, 173
Annesley, Samuel, 67
Antigua, 76
Antinomianism, 40, 167, 278
Apostles' Creed, 273
Appleby, 133
Argent, Alan, 366
Argentina, 290
Arianism, 16, 143, 172, 185, 191, 194, 196, 203, 207, 208
Aristotle, 230
Arminianism, 16–17, 80, 150, 167, 172, 194, 196, 200, 202, 204, 278, 316
Arnold, Denis, 276
Ascham, Roger, 61
Ashe, John, 137
Assemblies of God, 343
Associate Reformed Presbyterian Church, 165

Athanasius, 5, 153
Atherstone, 65
Atonement, 263–271, 286, 324–325
Auchterarder, 167
Audland, John, 63, 133
Augustine, 96, 97, 100, 104, 107, 147, 154, 156, 157
Austad, Torleiv, 101
Australia, 42, 279, 291, 359–360
Authority, ch. I
Ayers, John, 136
Aylesbury, 135

Bacon, Francis, 231, 247
Bagshawe, William, 137, 176
Bahner, F. F., 250, 269
Baker, Frank, 79
Bakewell, 288
Bakewell, Robert, 184, 201, 204
Baillie, Donald M., 81
Baillie, John, 81
Bain, Alexander, 233
Balfron, 174
Balmaghie, 171
Bampfield, Francis, 128
Banbury, 133
Baptists, 7, 15, 16, 19, 56, 58, 123, 125, 127–128, 134–135, 137, 138, 140, 143, 144, 188, 193, 202, 206, 282, 284, 316, 343, 355
Baptist Union of Scotland, 287
Barbados, 76
Barbican Mission to the Jews, 286
Barbour, Hugh, 64
Barclay, Robert, Sr., 149
Barclay, Robert, 71, ch. VI
Barfield, John, 284, 285
Barlow, William, 122
Barmen Declaration, 102–103
Barnardo, Thomas, 280, 282, 283
Barnes, Geoffrey, 360
Barnsley, 288
Barrie, J. M., 219
Barrow, Henry, 107, 110–113, 116, 121, 364
Barth, Karl, 55, 103, 311, 315, 316, 319
Bartlett, William, 126
Basle, 189
Bates, William, 35, 37, 129
Bath, 283, 288, 309
Baxter, Beatrice, 33
Baxter, Margaret, 34, 35
Baxter, Richard, ch. II, 78, 122, 128, 130, 132, 133, 138–139, 156, 181, 345–346, 368
Bayle, Pierre, 183
Baynes, N. H., 96
Beard, J. R., 202
Bebbington, D. W., 84, 219, 279, 284, 287
Beddome, Benjamin, 66
Bedford, 132
Bedfordshire, 131
Beedel, F., 279
Behar, 290
Belben, Howard G., 289
Belden, Albert D., 101
Belfast, 279, 295
Belgium, 102
Bellhouse, G. T., 50
Bender, Ross T., 104, 271
Bennet, Gervase, 72
Bennett, T., 140, 141
Benson, George, 209
Bentham, Jeremy, 223, 233
Berg, H. G. vom, 105
Berg, Joseph F., 251, 254
Berger Hall, 283
Berkeley, George, 222, 227, 229, 230, 231, 238, 239, 245, 246, 247
Berlin, 193
Bermuda, 76
Bernard of Clairvaux, 95
Berne, 189, 190
Berry, Sydney, 298
Betjeman, John, 249
Beynon, Tom, 47, 81, 180
Beza, Theodore, 191
Bibby, Reginald W., 87, 355
Bible, 4, 7, 13–19, 26–29, 36, 39, 47, 49–51, 54, 71, 72, 76, 78, 83, 92–95, 107, 112, 136, 154, 155, 156, 161, 191, 195, 196, 199, 205, 209, 273, 281, 285,

Bible (*continued*)
321, 327, 338, 342, 368
Bideford, 126
Binfield, Clyde, 292, 360
Birmingham, 9, 115, 281, 366
Bishop of St. David's. *See* Jenkinson, John Banks
Bishop, W. L., 346
Bishop Auckland, 294
Blackburn Academy, 342
Blackpool, 296
Blandshard, Brand, 147, 160
Blaykling, John, 63
Bloesch, Donald G., 371
Boehme, Jakob, 71
Boesak, Allan A., 53
Bogue, David, 186, 194
Bohemia, 254
Böhler, Peter, 68
Bolam, C. G., 220
Bolton, 296
Bomberger, George H., 250
Bomberger, John Henry Augustus, ch. XI
Bomberger, Mary Hoffmeier, 250
Bonar, Horatius, 169
Bonhoeffer, Dietrich, 102
Boniface VIII, 97
Booth, S. H., 19
Bost, Ami, 183, 184
Boston, Thomas, 166, 167, 168
Boston, U.S.A., 369
Botting, Thomas, 136
Bourn, Samuel, 202
Boylan, Henry, 275
Bradbury, Malcolm, 91
Bradbury, Thomas, 141
Bradford, 296, 298, 306
Bradford, (G. Fox's cousin), 65
Braine, J. J., 212
Braithwaite, W. C., 125, 131, 133, 134, 140, 149
Bray, Gerald, 97
Brechin, 298
Brecknockshire, 112
Brecon, 214
Brecon Academy, 214
Brent, Colin, 136
Brentall, John M., 176
Brethren, 42
Brethren (Plymouth), 282
Bricker, Florence M., 250
Bricker, George H., 51, 264, 351
Bridge, William, 122
Bridgnorth, 33
Briggs, J. H. Y., 18, 19
Brigham, 77
Brink, Adrian, 310
Brinkerhoff, Merlin B., 87
Brinton, Howard H., 147, 162
Bristol, 19, 128, 133, 135, 217, 279, 298, 307, 308, 309
Bristol Baptist College, 287
Britain, 192
British and Foreign Bible Society, 8, 42
British Broadcasting Corporation, 338
Brockett, Allan, 132
Bromley Hall, 283
Brooks, Phillips, 316
Brooks, Thomas, 126
Broomhall, M., 280
Broughty Ferry, 298
Brown, Archibald G., 284, 285
Brown, Cosbie C., 287
Brown, John, 48, 132, 293, 342
Brown, John, of Wamphray, 154–155, 156, 157, 158
Brown, Thomas, 223, 228, 229
Browne, Robert, 110, 121, 365
Bruce, A. B., 24
Bruen, Rev. Mr., 193, 194
Brunner, Emil, 318
Buckinghamshire, 131, 132, 135
Buehrens, Gwen Langdoc, 369
Bullinger, Heinrich, 168
Bulmer, John, 211, 213, 217
Bunyan, John, 48, 57, 76, 77, 83, 132, 142, 146
Burleigh, J. H. S., 166
Burleigh, Lord, 113
Burne-Jones, Edward, 9
Burnley, 298
Burrough, Edward, 133
Burroughes, Jeremiah, 122
Bury, 281, 282, 296, 297

Bury St. Edmunds, 109
Butler, Joseph, 143, 219, 230, 238
Busher, Leonard, 123
Bussleton, 291

Cadbury family, 85
Cadbury, H. J., 125
Caird, Edward, 219, 241, 243, 312
Caird, John, 242
Calamy, Edmund, 127, 128, 131, 135, 139
Caldecott, Alfred, 220, 244
Calder, Ralph F. G., 188, 292, 294
Calkins, A. B., 9
Calver/Curbar, 283, 284
Calvin, John, 5, 100, 104–105, 107, 108, 114, 168, 190, 191, 271, 349
Calvinism, 16–17, 40, 47, 80, 81, 127, 135, 150, 154, 167–170, 177, 179, 185, 186, 195, 197–198, 201, 202, 204, 205, 207, 266, 298, 316, 333
Calvinistic Methodism, 47, 80, 81, 179, 185, 200
Cambridge, 15, 65, 109, 110, 112, 135, 141, 160, 306
Cambridge Platform, 366
Cambridge Platonists, 71, 160, 163
Cameronians. *See* Reformed Presbyterian Church
Campbell, G. W., 209
Campbell, John, 59, 216
Campbell, J. McLeod, 325
Campbell, R. J., 298
Canada, 42, 279, 357–359
Canadian Mennonite Brethren Conference, 62
Candlish, R. S., 264
Cannock, 296
Canterbury, 126
Cape Colony, 293
Cape Town, 294
Carlson, Leland H., 109, 111, 113, 365
Carlyle, Thomas, 91, 207, 223, 224
Carnell, E. J., 50, 180
Carnock, 167
Carpenter, J. Estlin, 220, 222, 223, 224, 228, 235, 242
Carpenter, Lant, 19
Carruthers, Mr., 282
Cartwright, Thomas, 35, 108
Catholic Apostolic Church, 192, 207
Catton, Mrs., 297
Caulfield, Doris, 303
Caulfield, James, 303
Cave, Sydney, 307
Cefn Brith, 112
Chadwick, Samuel, 289
Chalcedonian formula, 326–327
Chalmers, James, 291–292
Chalmers, Thomas, 173, 229, 230
Champness, Thomas, 289
Chandler, Samuel, 209
Channing, William Ellery, 224, 244
Chantrye, Richard, 136
Chapelle du Témoinage, 196
Charles I, 64, 122
Charles II, 124, 125, 126, 130, 134, 136, 137, 138, 150
Charterhouse, 67
Cheadle, 276
Cheare, Abraham, 135
Cheltenham, 276, 277
Chenevière, Jean-Jacques-Caton, 184, 191, 194, 196–201, 202, 203, 204, 205, 206, 207, 208
Cheshire, 276
Chester, 125, 133
Chesterton, G. K., 10
Chicago, 283
Chillingworth, William, 28
China, 280, 281
China Inland Mission, 280, 291
Chirgwin, A. M., 299
Christ, Carol P., 51
Christ Church, Oxford, 67, 191
Christian Endeavour, 298
Christology, 263–271, 326–327

Chrysostom, John, 159
Church, 38–39, 159, 265–266, 268–269, 272, 274, 327–332, 340, 343–349, 367; authority of, 8–14, 26–27; order, 175, 328–332, 349–361; and society, 332–336; and state, ch. IV, ch. V, 173–175, 179, 202, 344–345, 368; unity of, ch. II
Church, R. W., 316
Church Meeting, 330–331, 335, 345, 348, 349–361, 368, 371
Church Missionary Society, 8
Church of England, 4, 7, 8–9, 16, 34, 36, 37, 39, 45, 56, 79, 108–109, 125, 128–129, 135, 138, 139, 140, 143, 147, 179, 209, 282, 284, 286, 332, 334, 364, 365
Church of Scotland, 107, ch. VII. 187–188, 193, 209
Cicero, 161
Civil War, 33
Clarke, Samuel, 143, 232, 233
Cleal, Edward E., 297, 298
Cleaves, Reginald W., 367–368
Clement of Alexandria, 152, 161
Cliff College, 283, 288–289
Cliff House. *See* Cliff College
Clifton, 276
Cochrane, A. C., 103
Cocks, H. F. Lovell, ch. XIII, 353
Cocks, Lord, of Hartcliffe, 303
Cocks, Lottie Violet Mary, 308, 339
Cocks, Edith Ethel, 339
Coke, Thomas, 194
Colchester, 132
Cole, John, 136
Coleraine, 279
Coleridge, S. T., 223, 224, 225, 229, 232, 238, 263
Coley, 130
College of Geneva, 192, 195
Collegeville, 254
Collins, Anthony, 223
Collins, G. N. M., 172
Collins, Robert, 130
Colonial Missionary Society, 292, 296
Comte, Auguste, 228, 229
Conder, John, 345
Condillac, E. B. de, 232
Condy, W. H., 284
Cone, James H., 52
Congar, Y., 14, 49
Congo, 290
Congram, John, 366
Congregational Church in England and Wales, 368
Congregational Federation, 368
Congregational Fund Board, 201, 214
Congregationalism/Congregationalists, 7, 15, 37, 39, 41, 42, 47, 56, 110, 123, 125, 127, 128, 135–136, 137, 143, 144, 186, 188, 193, 201, 202, 206, ch. IX, 271, ch. XII, 282, 283, 284, ch. XIII, ch. XIV
Congregational Lectures, 341–342, 352
Congregational Union of Australia, 359
Congregational Union of England and Wales, 216, 298, 307, 309, 341, 350, 367
Congregational Union of Ireland, 295
Congregational Union of Scotland, 212
Congregational Union of South Africa, 293, 294
Conscience, 12, 19–26, 29–30, 234–236, 247
Constantine, 95
Contextual theologies, 51–55
Conventicle Act, 125, 129, 132, 136, 141
Conway, Anne, 71
Conway, John S., 103
Cook, Thomas, 289
Cooke, Leslie E., 367
Copleston, F. C., 97
Copping, John, 109
Cornhill, 166

Corporation Act, 125, 126, 137, 141
Council of Trent, 13
Cousin, Victor, 226, 229, 240
Cragg, G. R., 133
Coventry, 33
Cramer, Jacob, 276
Cramer, Johann Baptist, 276
Cramer, Wilhelm, 276
Cramer, William (*sic*), 276
Cranham, Mr., 286
Cranleigh, 289
Crauford, Alexander, 24, 220
Creasey, Maurice A., 148, 163
Creeds and confessions, 48, ch. VIII, 308, 362, 370
Cregan, James, 295–296
Creighton, Louise, 4
Creighton, Mandell, 4
Cresswell, Amos S., 289
Crieff, 167
Crisp, Tobias, 40, 169
Croft, William, 69
Cromwell, Oliver, 40, 119, 120, 121, 122, 123, 124, 129, 144, 308
Crosby, Thomas, 135
Cudworth, Ralph, 232, 233
Cuff, W., 284
Cullmann, Oscar, 13, 94
Culross, James C., 282, 283, 287
Cumberland, 77, 133
Cumberland and Westmorland Association, 39
Cuming-Brown, J., 284
Cyprian, 154, 156
Cyril of Alexandria, 153, 161

Daillé, John, 151
Dale, R. W., 115, 341, 349–350, 352
D'Alembert, Jean LeR., 183, 194
Dalfsen, Gerardina L. van, 147
Daly, Mary, 51, 52
Dalberg-Acton, J. E. E., 93
Darlington, 281
Darlow, T. H., 219
Davenport, John, 127
Davidson, Samuel, 342, 352, 367
Davidson, Thain, 282
Davie, G. E., 245
Davies, Horton, 220
Davies, Rees, 47, 179
Davies, Rupert E., 332
Davies, William Archibald, 305
Davies, W. T. Pennar, 113
Davis, Philip, 294–295
Dawson, Albert, 86
Dean, Peter, 82
Declaration of Breda, 124
Deism, 196, 221, 228, 238, 242
Delamotte, Charles, 68
Dell, William, 48
Dening, Mr., 283, 288
Denmark, 103
Denney, James, 271, 298
Derby, 19, 72, 134
Derbyshire, 134, 176, 283
De Sach, Herr, 193
Descartes, René, 229
D'Esterre, J. N., 275–276, 278
D'Esterre, Jane Lucretia, 275–276, 277, 278
Devonshire, 126, 131, 133, 293
Devonshire Association, 38
Dexter, H. M., 351
Dickie, John, 220
Diderot, Denis, 194
Diet of Worms, 100
Disciples of Christ, 42, 44
Discipline, 347–348
Dissenting academies, 138, 140, 143
Docetism, 273
Doddridge, Philip, 66
Dodwell, Henry, 36
Doeuff, Michèle le, 52
Dopima, 292
Doric Lodge, 283
Dorner, I. A., 258
Dorset, 67
Downgrade Controversy, 18–19, 29
Drayton-in-the-Clay, 64
Dru, A., 86
Drummond, A. L., 192
Drummond, Henry, 184, 191–192, 197, 205, 207, 209

Drummond, James, 22, 23
Drummond, John, 167
Dryburgh, 166
Dublin, 19, 275, 276, 277, 279, 295
Dudley, 33
Duke of Alva, 7
Duke University, 355
Duncan, Captain, 186
Dundee, 186, 298
Dundee, Natal, 294
Dunfermline, 166, 178
Dun Laoghaire, 276
Dunning, Norman G., 289
Dunstable, 296
Durant, John, 126
Durban, 294
Dury, John, 37
Dutch Reformed Church (South Africa), 294
Dutch Reformed Church (America), 251
Duthie, Charles S., 308
Dyke, Daniel, 128

East London Institute, 280–282
Easton, 251
Eaton-Constantine, 33
Edinburgh, 42, 167, 174, 186, 222, 245, 276, 281
Education Act, 334
Edwards, Jonathan, 223, 226, 229
Edwards, Thomas, 124
Eeg-Olofsson, Leif, 148, 163
Église du Bourg-de-Four, 183
Église du Témoinage, 183
Egypt, 279
Ejectment of 1660–1662, 126–129, 332
Ejerfelt, Lennart, 99
Eliot, John, 147
Elizabeth I, 107, 108, 121
Ellis, J. J., 19
Ellwood, Thomas, 89, 132, 162
Emerson, Ralph Waldo, 369
Empaytaz, Henri-Louis, 183, 184, 185, 189, 197, 204
Endy, Melvin B., Jr., 160
Enfield, William, 66
England, 106, 107, 119, 138, 139, 145, 176, 257, 277, 279, 294
Enlightenment, 163, ch. X, 311, 334, 344
Epistemology, ch. X
Epworth, 66, 67
Erskine College and Seminary, 165
Erskine, Ebenezer, ch. VII, 185
Erskine, Henry, 165–166
Erskine, Ralph, ch. VII, 185
Escott, Harry, 186, 188
Essex, 108
Ethical theism, ch. X
Ethics, 55–56
Europe, 92
Eutyches, 255
Evangelical Alliance, 16, 42
Evangelical and Reformed Church, 360
Evangelical Faculty, Geneva, 190–191
Evangelical Revival, 83–84, 144, 188, 334, 344, 345
Evangelization Society, 285
Evangelism, ch. III
Evans, R. P., 184
Ewing, Greville, 186
Ewins, Thomas, 128
Exeter, 132
Experience, ch. III
Eyam, 134

Faber, Frederick William, 86
Fackre, Gabriel, 50, 54, 363
Fairbairn, A. M., 11, 145, 183, 220
Faith, 310–321
Farel, Guillaume, 191
Farnham, Lord, 283
Fatio, Olivier, 183
Fawcett, John, 176–177
Feeling, 82
Fell, Margaret, 75
Fell, Thomas, 75
Feminist theology, 51–52, 54, 55, 371
Fenner, Audrey, 369

Fenny Drayton. *See* Drayton-in-the-Clay
Ferguson, George P., 294
Ferré, Nels F. S., 317
Ferrier, J. F., 237, 245, 247
Fichte, J. G., 227
Fife, 287
Fifth Monarchy Men, 125
Findlay, Pastor, 290
Finland, 99, 289
Finney, C. G., 88, 251
Fiorenza, Elisabeth Schüssler, 54
Firmin, Giles, 75
Fischer, Andrew, 106
Fisher, Edward, 166
Fisher, James, 175
Fishwick, Henry, 125
Fitz, Richard, 121
Fitzgerald, Fanny. *See* Guinness, Fanny
Five Mile Act, 125, 129, 138, 141
Flannery, Austin, 12, 43
Flavell, John, 128
Flavell, Richard, 128
Flew, Antony G. N., 82
Flew, R. Newton, 332
Flint, Robert, 288
Flintham, 135
Flood, James, 148
Florence, 76
Flossenberg, 102
Fordyce, John, 359
Forney, Edward O., 257
Forsyth, P. T., 23, 25, 27, 29, 57, 81, 82, 83, 85, 88, 89, 97, 101–102, 145, 220, 222, 271, 273, 304, 305, 310, 319, 327, 339, 341, 362, 364, 369, 370
Fort Wayne, 253
Fosdick, H. E., 337
Foulk, J. S., 258
Fox, Christopher, 64
Fox, George, 57, ch. III, 124, 125, 132, 149
Fox, Mary, 64
France, 76, 188, 191, 192, 277
Frankfurt, 108
Frankland, Richard, 138
Franklin, Robert, 133
Franklin and Marshall College, 250, 251
Franks, R. S., 307
Fraser, Alexander Campbell, ch. X
Free Church Federal Council, 308–309
Freedom, 361–371
Freiday, Dean, 152
French Revolution, 186–187
Froude, J. A., 207
Fry, Elizabeth, 85
Fuller, Thomas, 123
Fullerton, W. Y., 279

Galland, Pastor, 189, 190
Gamble, Thomas, 293–294
Garbet, Francis, 33
Gardiner, Captain, 280
Garvie, A. E., 305, 326, 367
Gassendi, Pierre, 232
Gaussen, F. S. R. L., 190, 191, 192
Gaussen, Louis, 183
Gee, Henry, 125, 139
Gelasius, 96
Geneva, 76, 105, 108, ch. VIII
Genevan Church, ch. VIII
Genevan Revival, ch. VIII
George VI, 307
Georgia, 68
German Reformed Church, ch. XI, 299
Gib, Adam, 178, 180
Gibbs, John, 131
Gill, John, 29, 80, 177
Gilley, Sheridan, 9
Gillies, Donald, 50
Glasgow, 172, 228, 283
Glasgow Missionary Society, 188
Glebe-Moller, Jens, 103
Gloucester, 286, 288
Godber, Joyce, 132
Godley, Eleanor, 112
Goethe, J. W. von, 263
Goldsmith, Oliver, 24, 25, 364
Gooch, W. Fuller, 284
Good, James I., 260–261, 262
Goodall, Norman, 42, 187, 292, 354, 367

Goodwin, Thomas, 38, 122, 366
Gordon, Mr., 283
Gordon, Alexander, 34, 35, 128, 149, 157, 164
Gordon, J. M., 287
Goring, Jeremy, 223
Gosport, 186
Grace, W. G., 219
Graham, John W., 77
Grant, Mr., 282
Grant, John W., 298, 357, 358
Great Yarmouth, 133, 291
Greaves, R. L., 135
Grebel, Conrad, 105
Green, J. R., 128
Greenwood, John, 107, 109–113, 116, 121, 364
Gregory, Benjamin, 20
Gregory I, 5, 153
Gregory VII, 5, 96, 100
Gregory of Nazianzus, 156
Grieve, A. J., 366
Griffith, A. J., 359, 360
Grosart, A. B., 35
Grosz, Elizabeth, 52
Grotius, Hugo, 148, 150, 157
Grubb, Edward, 163
Grundy, John, 19
Guers, Emil, 183
Guinness, Fanny, 279, 281, 283, 285, 288
Guinness, Frederick William, 276
Guinness, Grace, 280
Guinness, Harry Grattan, 280, 283, 284, 286, 289, 291
Guinness, Henry Grattan, 275–283, 284, 285
Guinness, John Grattan, 275, 276
Guinness, Lucy Evangeline, 280, 288
Guinness, Mary Geraldine, 280
Guinness, Michele, 275, 276, 291
Guinness, Paul Grattan, 280
Guinness, Robert Wyndham, 276
Guldin, John Craig, 251
Gunnemann, Louis H., 360, 368
Guyon, Madame (Jeanne Marie Bouvier de la Mothe), 74
Gwelo, 294
Gwyn, Douglas, 71, 76, 78

Hackney College, 304
Hackney, Walter, 286
Hadow, James, 167, 168
Hageman, Howard, 260, 264
Haldane, Alexander, 185, 186, 189, 193, 194
Haldane, James, 186, 187
Haldane, Katherine, 189
Haldane, Robert, 184, 186–194, 197, 204, 205, 207, 208, 209
Halifax, 130
Halifax, Nova Scotia, 292
Hall, Douglas John, 30
Hall, Francis B., 148, 163, 164
Hallowes, John Francis Tooke, 288
Hamilton, James, 173
Hamilton, Richard W., 342
Hamilton, William, of Strathblane, 173
Hamilton, William, 226, 229, 230, 237, 240
Hampson, Daphne M., 51, 52
Hampstead, 353
Hancox, Edward, 82
Hanson, George, 284
Hanson, R. P. C., 13, 14
Harbaugh, Henry, 253, 267
Hardcastle, Thomas, 128
Hardman, Keith, 88, 251
Hardwicke's Marriage Act, 141
Hardy, William John, 125, 139
Harland, Gordon, 358
Harley College, ch. XII
Harley, Robert, 140
Harmati, Béla, 99
Harries, N., 214
Harries, T., 212–213
Harris, Howel, 47, 81, 83, 179, 180
Harris, John, 277
Harrity, Grant E., 250
Harrow, 191
Hart, Norman, 353
Hartlepool, 276
Hartley, David, 19, 223
Haseley, 112

Haverfordwest, 211, 215
Hay, Robert Wright, 284
Hayes, George Passmore, 148
Heads of Agreement, 39
Healey, 337
Heath, Alban E., 294
Heath, Wilson, 290
Hebden Bridge, 177
Hednesford, 296, 297
Heffenstein, Jacob, 251
Hegel, G. W. F., 226, 229, 231, 263, 333
Heidelberg, 293–294
Heidelberg Catechism, 270, 273, 299
Heitzenrater, Richard P., 70, 74
Helfenstein, Samuel, 256
Helwys, Thomas, 123, 138
Henderson, A. R., 136
Henderson, Henry F., 166, 167
Henge Lane, 136
Henley, W. E., 263
Henry IV, 96
Henry, Philip, 127, 128, 133
Heraclitus, 161
Hereford, 34
Heron, Alasdair I. C., 221
Heron, Alastair, 162
Herrmann, Wilhelm, 311
Hervey, James, 167
Herzog, J. J., 253
Hewett, M., 131
Heyer, Jean, 183
Heywood, Oliver, 130, 137
Heywood, T., 131
Hick, John, 316
Hildebrand. *See* Gregory VII
Hill, Alan G., 11
Hill, Rowland, 187, 215
Hillhouse, Mr., 189
Hillsborough, 295
Hinkle, Gerald H., 250, 251–252, 261, 263
Hoadly, Benjamin, 143
Hobbes, Thomas, 232, 233
Hobson, Paul, 128
Hocking, W. E., 312
Hodge, A. A., 285, 287
Hodgkins, John, 113
Hog, 167
Holcfort, Francis, 135
Holden, J. Stuart, 284, 290
Holland. *See* Netherlands
Holmes, Kenneth, 280
Holt, R. V., 244
Holy Spirit, 322–323
Homerton College, 201, 215
Hooke, D. Burford, 292, 293
Hooke, William, 127
Hooker, Richard, 106, 107
Hoole, Rev. Mr., 130, 131
Hooper, George Downs, 286
Hooper, John, 286
Hopkey, Sophia Christiana, 68
Hopkins, Mark T. E., 18
Horace, 152
Horle, W. Craig, 132, 134
Horne, C. Silvester, 187
Horner, Francis, 10
Horton, Douglas, 367
Horton, Robert Forman, 283, 353
Houghton, Frank, 280
Hove, 306
Howard, John, 84–85
Howarth, David H., 289
Howe, John, 40, 131, 138, 181
Howgill, Francis, 63, 133
Hubberthorne, Richard, 124, 133
Huber, Wolfgang, 101, 103
Hügel, F. von, 86, 87
Hughes, Clive, 211
Hughes, Thomas, 58
Hulme Cliff College. *See* Cliff College
Hulme, J. H., 283
Hulme, Mrs. (later Mrs. David Robertson), 283
Hume, David, 82, 172, 222, 229, 232, 238, 243
Hunter, Joseph, 127, 131
Huntley family, 85
Hurditch, Grace. *See* Guinness, Grace
Hurlford, 297
Husset, Joseph, 40
Huston, Marion Elizabeth, 254
Hutcheson, Francis, 173, 228, 233

Hutchison, Matthew, 188
Hutton, Susanna, 275
Huxley, Julian, 81
Huxtable, W. John F., 309, 331, 367
Hyde, Edward, 125–126
Hymnals, 216

Ibsen, H., 305
Idealism, ch. X
Ignatius Loyola, 86
Immanence, ch. X
Ince, Peter, 59
Independents. *See* Congregationalism/ Congregationalists
India, 288
Inge, W. R., 336
Ingham, Benjamin, 68
Ingham, Richard, 132
Innes, D. J., 166, 167
Innocent III, 97
International Congregational Council, 307, 328–329, 331
International Missionary Council, 42
Inward Light, 71–72, 76–78, ch. VI
Ireland, 139, 228, 276, 278, 279
Irenaeus, 13
Irving, Edward, 192, 207
Isleham, 15
Italy, 76

Jackson, A. W., 220, 241, 242
Jackson, Alvery, 66
Jackson, Forbes, 284, 287–288, 289, 290, 298, 299
Jackson, Hugh, 359
Jacobi, F. H., 227
Jamaica, 76
James I, 121, 122
James II, 138
James, John, 135
James, Mr., 189
James, T. T., 295
James, William, 73, 86
Janeway, Abraham, 129
Jay, William, 59
Jeffs, E. H., 310
Jenkins, Daniel T., 352–353
Jenkinson, John Banks, 212
Jerome, 152, 153–154
Jerusalem, 76
Jessey, Henry, 128, 134
Jesspo, T. E., 86
Jews, 139, 141, 196
Joad, C. E. M. , 362
John Paul II, 49
Johnson, Francis, 112
Johnston, J. Horace, 284
Jollie, Thomas, 125, 131, 132, 135
Jones, A. H. M., 96
Jones, Beti, 211
Jones, Henry, 220, 243, 244
Jones, Ifano, 211
Jones, J. D., 307
Jones, R Tudur, 126, 128, 130
Jones, Rufus M., 70, 71, 160
Jones, Samuel, 215
Jones, T. Canby, 72
Jouffroy, T. S., 226
Jowett, Benjamin, 264
Joyful News Mission, 289
Jude, W. H., 297
Julian, John, 176, 220
Justin Martyr, 161, 215

Kalahari Desert, 294
Kant, Immanuel, 82, 226, 227, 228, 229, 230, 231, 232, 234, 240, 311, 312
Kaye, Beatrice Mabel, 299
Kaye, James Alfred, 298–299, 300
Keble, John, 106
Kee, Alastair, 96
Keeble, Neil, 37
Keech, Benjamin, 135
Keillor, Garrison, 180, 181
Keith, George, 147–148, 153, 157, 159, 161–162
Kelvedon, 15
Kendal, 281
Kent, 296
Kent, John, 279
Kenworthy, Fred, 25
Ker, I. T., 11

Keswick Convention, 284, 291
Kidderminster, 33, 34
Kierkegaard, S. A., 86
Kilmainham, 295
Kilmarnock, 281
Kimel, Alvin F., 371
King, Edmund George, 296
King, Joseph, 292
King, Rachel Hadley, 72
King's Head Society, 201
Kinross, 174
Kirkcaldy, 287
Klein, H. M. J., 253, 254
Knox, John, 108, 191
Korea, 365
Kossen, H., 105
Kruedener, Barbara Juliana Freifrau von, 185, 189, 197
Krüger, G., 185, 186
Kumm, Karl, 280
Küng, Hans, 6, 14
Kurtz, J. H., 253

Labouderie, Abbé, 197
Lachman, David C., 166
Lactantius, 161
Ladysmith, 293
Lambeth Conference, 62
Lancashire, 63
Lancashire Congregational Union, 295
Lancashire Independent College, 341, 342
Lancaster, 132
Lancaster, PA, 250
Lancaster Theological Seminary, 250
Langan, 215
Langmore, 217
Larcombe, Geoffrey, 275
Latin America, 51, 52, 53
Latitudinarians, 143
Laud, William, 122
Lausanne, 42
Law, William, 8, 74
Lawes, W. G., 291
Leary, William, 82
Lee, Edward Dunn, 112
Leeds, 289, 306, 326, 340
Leger, Jean, 119
Lehmann, H. T., 100
Leibniz, G. W., 222, 232, 239
Leicester, 120, 284
Leicestershire, 64, 120
Leighton-under-Wrekin, 33
Leiper, H. S., 367
Leo XIII, 9
Leominster, 71
Leuenberg Agreement, 44
Lewes, 136
Lewis, J. R., 286
Liberation theology, 51, 55
Liddon, H. P., 4
Lincoln College, Oxford, 67
Lincolnshire, 66, 134
Lindsay, James, 226, 238
Lippmann, Walter, 50
Littlejohn, Jerome, 130
Liturgy, 255–260
Liverpool, 19, 20, 223, 224, 279, 281, 282, 296
Llanboidy, 179
Llanelli, 214
Llangamarch, 112
Lobb, Theophilus, 346
Locke, John, 18, 45, 139, 219, 222, 226, 230, 231, 232 238, 244, 332–333
Loewen, Harry, 105
Loewen, Howard John, 105
Lollards, 64
London, 10, 20, 34, 35, 39, 110, 121, 125, 126, 132, 134, 135, 166, 177, 201, 206, 223, 234, ch. XII, 304, 308, 338
London Congregational Union, 296
London Missionary Society, 187, 194, 215, 291–292, 299, 354
Long, Edwin M., 252
Longfellow, Henry Wadsworth, 91, 92
Loukes, Harold, 73, 78
Lovett, Richard, 187, 292
Low, George D., 166
Lowe, F. L. Riches, 304
Lucinius, 154
Ludlow, 33

Lull, Timothy, 103
Lund, 331, 335
Lundie, Lady, 186
Luther, Martin, 5, 69, 91, 92, 100–101, 102, 105, 114, 327
Lutherans, 44, 45, 99–101, 102, 371
Lutheran World Federation, 99
Lutterworth, 64
Lyall, Leslie T., 280

Macaulay, T. B., 139
McCrie, C. G., 166
McCulloh, G., 220
MacDermott, Hugh, 292
MacEwen, A. R., 169, 174, 182
Macfadyen, D., 350
McGinn, Donald J., 113
MacGregor, G. H. C., 284, 287
Macintyre, Alasdair, 82
Mackennal, Alexander, 368
Mackenzie, D. F., 284, 290
Mackenzie, J. S., 22, 23
McKerrow, John, 166, 188
Mackintosh, C. W., 280, 281
Mackintosh, H. R., 242
Mackintosh, James, 228–229
Mackintosh, Robert, 56, 263, 346
McLachlan, Herbert, 143, 201, 202
MacLean, Donald, 166
MacLeod, John, 166, 167, 173
Macmillan, Donald, 227
Macmillan, John, 171
Macquarrie, John, 221
Madan, Falconer, 120
Madstard, William, 33
Maine de Biran, F. P. G., 226
Mair, Thomas, 175
Malan, Caesar, 183, 184, 191, 192, 193–196, 198–199, 202, 203, 204, 205, 206, 207, 208
Malan, C. (the Younger), 193
Maldon, 108
Mancetter, 65
Manche, Alfred de, 6
Manchester, 20, 224, 281, 282, 295
Manchester College, Oxford, 222
Manchester College, York, 19
Manchester New College, 20, 223, 224, 234
Manning, Bernard Lord, 56, 307, 361–362
Manning, John, 135
Mansfield, Lord, 141
Mantle, J. Gregory, 284
Manton, Thomas, 129
Mantua, 76
Manz, Felix, 105
Marriott, J. A. R., 283, 353
Marrow Controversy, 166–168
Marseilles, 192
Marsh, John, 328, 332
Marshall College. *See* Franklin and Marshall College
Martin, David, 191
Martin, Charles B., 82, 83
Martin, Henry, 109
Martindale, Adam, 131, 136
Martineau, James, ch. I, ch. X, 266
"Martin Marprelate," 112–113
Martinsburg, 253
Marty, Martin E., 369
Marx, Karl, 333
Mary, 107
Mason, John, 169
Mason, John Mitchell, 193, 194
Massie, J. W., 279
Mather, Eleanor P., 147
Matthews, A. G., 121, 122, 127, 128, 130, 134, 366
Maurice, F. D., 223, 224, 263, 264
Maxwell, Dr., 290
Maxwell, J. L., 280
Maxwell, Jack Martin, 255, 258–259, 261, 262
Mead, Silas, 287
Mechie, Stewart, 166
Medway, John, 201, 206
Mellone, S. H., 23, 220, 235
Mellor, Enoch, 342
Memorial Hall Library, 341
Memorial Hall Trust, 341
Mencken, H. L., 362
Menzies, John, 151

Mercersburg, 250
Mercersburg theology, ch. XI, 349
Merle D'Aubigné, J. H., 183, 190
Merlin's Bridge, 214
Methodism/Methodists, 42, 44, ch. III, 196, 199–200, 204, 206, 284, 359, 364, 369. *See also* Calvinistic Methodism; Wesleyans
Merthyr Tydfil, 214
Mexico, 276
Meyer, F. B., 284, 287, 290
Meyer, Lewis, 250
Meynell, Hugo, 11
Micklem, Nathaniel, 307, 315, 332
Middleton, James, 292
Miles, John, 128
Mill, James, 223, 228
Mill, John Stuart, 223, 226, 228, 230
Miller, Allen O., 99
Miller, Larry, 105
Miller, Robert, 300
Milne, Dr., 284
Milne, A. A., 3
Milton, John, 119, 124
Minjung theology, 52–53, 55
Mirbt, D. Carl, 47
Moderatism, 171–174, 185, 186, 188, 207
Moncrieff, Alexander, 175, 180
Monilaws, 166
Monod, Frederic, 190, 191
Montauban, 189, 191
Montefiore, Hugh, 365
Moody, Dwight L., 283, 295
Moon, Norman S., 128, 283
Moore, E. W., 284
Moorhouse, 133
Moravians, 67, 68–69, 75, 183, 185, 196
More, Henry, 71, 149, 163
Morgan, George, 284
Morgan, G. Campbell, 87, 284
Morgan, G. Sydney, 350
Morgan, J. L., 215
Morgan, James, 279
Morgan, Richard, 215
Morris, J. S., 285–286, 287
Morris, Richard, 215
Morris, Thomas, 9, 10
Mottram, Eric, 91
Moulinié, Pastor, 189
Mozley, J. K., 319
Muirhead, J. H., 222, 227, 243
Murray, John, 169
Murton, John, 123
Mysticism, 70–75

Naseby, 33
Nash, Robert, 14, 27, 28
Natal, 293, 294
Neal, Daniel, 38
Neill, Stephen C., 42
Neff, Felix, 183
Nelson, John, 139
Nesti, Donald S., 148
Netherlands, 7, 111, 122, 139
Nevin, J. W., 50–51, ch. XI, 349, 351
Newark, 135
New Brunswick, 292
Newbury, 217
Newcastle, 281, 282
New College, London, 277, 304
Newcome, Henry, 131
New England, 116, 124
Newfoundland, 76, 292
New Haven, 127
Newman, Francis, 10, 28
Newman, Jay, 95
Newman, John Henry, ch. I, 149, 221, 224, 266, 272
New Measures, 252–253, 255, 261
New Theology, 298
Newtown, 214
New York, 193
New Zealand, 291
Nicholls, Michael, 18
Nichols, J. H., 255, 265, 266
Nickalls, John L., 63, 124
Nicol, Iain G., 104, 271
Nicoll, W. Robertson, 219
Nicolson, M. H., 71, 149
Nightingale, Benjamin, 296

Nikkel, James, 61
Ninth Theological Conference of Congregationalists, 306
Noble, Thomas, 178, 179
Nonconformist conscience, 332–336
Nonconformist Relief Act, 141
Nonconformity, ch. XIII, 364
Norfolk, 109, 110, 132
Norris, John, 160
Northampton, 112
Northamptonshire, 112, 131
North Leith, 288
North Shields, 298
Northumberland, 166
Norway, 76, 289
Norwich, 142
Nottingham, 19, 134, 135, 136, 204
Nottingham, Earl of, 139
Nottingham Institute, 288
Nottinghamshire, 64, 135
Nutt, Thomas, 136
Nuttall, Geoffrey F., 37, 38, 64, 71, 77, 78, 96, 101, 128, 153, 156, 160, 201, 206, 368
Nuttall, J. K., 296
Nye, Philip, 38, 122
Nygren, Anders, 101

Oakley, Henry, 284
Oddy, Joseph, 131
Offham, 296
Okullu, J. Henry, 106
Olney, 131
Orr, J. Edwin, 279
Orthodox Churches, 50, 57
Outler, Albert C., 62, 68, 74
Otto, Rudolf, 311
Owen, John, the Anglican, 33
Owen, John, the Congregationalist, 38–39, 71, 128, 131, 144, 156, 366, 368
Owen, W. T., 202
Owens, B. G., 128, 130
Oxford, 4, 8, 9, 33, 65, 67, 120, 141, 191, 192, 222

Paarl, 294
Paine, Thomas, 186
Palatine, 76
Palestine, 279
Paley, William, 226, 285
Palmer family, 85
Palmer, Alfred Jabez, 284
Palmer, S., 131
Pantheism, ch. X
Papua, 291
Paris, 149, 189, 234
Parker, Irene, 143, 201
Parker, Joseph, 86
Parkinson, R., 131
Parnell, C. S., 275–276
Pastor's College, 287
Pattison, Mark, 4
Paul, Robert S., 123, 360, 364
Paulinus, 152
Payne, Ernest A., 18, 128
Payne, George, 341
Payne, John B., 250, 261, 268
Peake, A. S., 29
Peake, Leslie S., 29
Peasants' Revolt, 100
Peek, Mr., 276
Peel, Albert, 109, 112, 121, 143, 283, 292, 306, 353, 365, 366
Peirce, James, 209
Pelagianism, 150, 152, 156, 161, 181, 194, 208, 316, 346, 370
Pembroke, 212
Pembrokeshire, 179, ch. IX
Pembrokeshire Congregational Magazine, ch. IX
Pendle Hill, 63
Penn, W., 282
Penn, William, the Quaker, 64, 140, 142, 153, 162
Penney, Norman, 132
Pennington, Isaac, 125
Pennsylvania, 299
Penry, Comfort, 113
Penry, Deliverance, 113
Penry, John, 107, 112–114, 116, 364
Penry, Safety, 113
Penry, Sure Hope, 113
Perkins, William, 33
Perret, Edmond, 209

Perrin, J. P., 119
Perth, 174, 175
Peru, 290
Philadelphia, 251
Pianezza, Marquis di, 119
Pictet, Benedict, 190
Piedmont, 119–120, 142, 145, 192
Pierce, William, 112, 122
Pietism, 101, 183
Pius IX, 9, 46
Pius X, 6
Plato, 189, 190, 232, 306
Plymouth, 135
Plymouth Rock, 122
Polycarp, 153
Pope-Levison, Priscilla, 84
Portmoak, 166
Powell, Vavasor, 128
Powicke, F. J., 40, 109, 110, 143
Powys, Llewellyn, 362
Prayer, 321–322
Preaching, 170, 278–279, 336–339
Presbyterianism/Presbyterians, 35–37, 42, 45, 47, 56, 124, 126, 127, 128, 129, 130, 136, 137, 139, 142, 144, 147, 154, ch. VII, 201, 202, 206, 209, 251, 271, 282, 284, 288, 292, 309, 333, 359, 366, 371
Preston, 281
Preston Patrick, 63
Price, E. J., 307
Price, Richard, 227, 233
Priestley, Joseph, 8, 68, 223, 226, 233, 332
Primitive Methodists, 29
Princeton, 49
Pringle-Pattison, A. S., 23, 219, 220, 222, 238, 242, 243, 246, 247
Pronier, C. L., 191
Prosper of Aquitane, 157, 158–159, 161
Protestant Ministers of the Three Denominations, 206
Punshom, John, 369
Pusey, E. B., 8, 257
Pyt, Henri, 183, 190

Quakers, ch. III, 107, 123, 124, 125, 132, 133, 134, 136, 137, 138, 139–140, 141, 142, 143, 144, ch. VI, 204, 369
Que Que, 294

Rack, Henry, 70
Radley, Mr., 134–135
Radstock, Lord, 284
Rahner, Karl, 14
Ramage, James, 293
Ramsey, I. T., 45
Rankin, Catherine, 19
Ranters, 123
Rattenbury, J. Ernest, 74, 75
Rattray, 288
Ratzinger, Joseph Alois, 6
Rauch, Frederick A., 250
Raven, Charles E., 101
Rawdon College, Leeds, 331
Rawlinson, Abram, 76
Reading, 279, 287, 288, 299
Reardon, B. M. G., 221
Reason, Joyce, 299
Redford, George, 341, 342
Reformation, 29, 261
Reformed Church in Canada, 45
Reformed Churches, 102
Reformed Presbyterian Church, 165, 171, 188
Regions Beyond Missionary Union, 280, 289, 290, 291
Reid, J. K. S., 49
Reid, Thomas, 219, 222, 226, 232, 238, 239, 246
Religious Society of Friends. *See* Quakers
Reuther, Rosemary Radford, 51, 52
Rhode Island, 123, 364
Rhodesia, 294
Rhydwilym, 47, 179
Riale, Joshua, 258
Rich, Robert, 109
Richards, G. W., 250, 253, 255
Richardson, Alan, 14
Richmond, 131

Richter, Richard P., 250
Rickard, James, 359
Rieu, Charles, 189
Ritschl, Albrecht, 311, 317
Rivett, A., 291
Roberts, Arthur O., 64
Roberts, Samuel, 291
Robertson, David, 283
Robinson, John, 176
Robinson, N. H. G., 22
Robinson, Richard, 63
Rochford, 109
Rogers, Henry, 28, 181, 341
Rogers, J. Guinness, 351
Rohrbach, Julius, 287
Roman Catholicism/Roman Catholics, 5–6, 7, 8, 9–14, 20, 28, 31, 38, 39, 43, 47, 50, 57, 75, 86–87, 88, 107, 108, 119, 123, 124, 132, 134, 137, 139, 196, 197, 252, 255, 257, 295, 328, 361
Rome, 10, 76, 95, 96
Ross, James, 186
Rotherham Academy, 202, 211
Rotterdam, 204
Rouse, Lady, 33
Rouse, Ruth, 42
Rousseau, J.-J., 183, 196, 332–333
Routley, Erik, 366
Rowe, Kenneth E., 74
Rowell, Geoffrey, 224
Rowton, 33
Royer-Collard, Pierre Paul, 226
Rugeley, 217
Rumball, Edwin A., 292
Russell, David, 213
Russell, Bertrand, 306, 362
Russell, G. Stanley, 358
Russell, Letty M., 51
Russia, 191
Ruxton, 217

St. Andrews, 307
St. Austell, 298
St. David's, 212, 215
Salmond, S. D. F., 235
Saltmarsh, John, 167
Samoa, 354
Sandemanians, 81
Sarjeant, W. Darlow, 284
Saskatchewan, 292
Satigny, 190
Savoy Declaration, 365–366
Savoy, Duke of, 119, 120
Sayce, A. H., 4
Scandinavia, 99, 100
Scapula, 146
Schaff, Philip, 57, 208, 251, 263
Scheewind, J. B., 220, 235
Schelling, F. W. J. von, 227, 229
Schillebeeckx, Edward, 6
Schiller, F. C. S., 306
Schleiermacher, F. D. E., 5, 82, 263, 311
Schleitheim Articles, 105
Schofield, F. W., 288
Scholes, Percy A., 276
Schopenhauer, A., 229
Schroeder, W. Widick, 370
Schultz, Robert C., 100
Scotland, 36, 139, ch. VII, ch. VIII, 212, 224, 228, 229, 277, 297
Scott, Richenda, 71, 72
Scott, Thomas, 8
Scottish Congregational College, 307
Scottish intuitionism, 226, 239–240
Scougal, Henry, 73
Scullard, Herbert Hayes, 305
Secession Church, 165, 173–180
Sechêron, 191, 192
Second Boer War, 294
Secretariat for Promoting Christian Unity, 43
Sectarianism, 32, 36, 46–59, 177–181, 367
Seekers, 64
Segundo, Juan Luis, 51
Selbie, W. B., 145, 316
Sell, Alan P. F., 7, 16, 17, 28, 40, 43, 47, 55, 56, 63, 66, 79, 80, 82, 84, 104, 110, 115, 121, 134, 138, 143, 144, 145, 166, 176, 186, 200, 202, 220, 221,

242, 245, 250, 263, 264, 271, 272, 289, 298, 316, 327, 331, 333, 341–342, 343, 344, 346, 347, 349, 351, 354, 355, 358, 361, 364, 366, 367–368, 371
Sellers, Ian, 202
Seneca, 190
Separatists, 106–114, 116, 121–122, 144, 344
Servetus, Michael, 204
Seth, James, 237–238, 239, 244, 247
Seventh-Day Baptists, 128
Shaftesbury, Anthony Ashley Cooper, 233
Shakespeare, 305
Sharp, Horace, 337
Shaw, Duncan, 166
Shaw, Mary, 297
Sheffield, 281, 282, 292
Shelley, Bruce L., 355
Shepard, Thomas, 32
Sherlock, William, 36
Shindler, Robert, 18
Shinn, Roger L., 99
Shipdham, 110
Short, H. L., 220
Short, John, 307
Shrewsbury, 33
Shriver, George, 208
Shropshire, 131
Sibbes, Richard, 33
Sibree, James, 292
Sidgwick, Henry, 23, 235
Silcox, Claris Edwin, 358
Simeon, Charles, 187
Simms, T. H., 201
Simprin, 167
Simson, John, 168, 172
Simpson, Sidrach, 38
Sims, Basil, 308
Sin, 323–325
Skinner, John, 128
Sloan, Walter B., 290, 291
Smethwick, 297
Smith, Barbara, 220
Smith, C. Ryder, 315
Smith, Francis, 135
Smith, J. W. Ashley, 143
Smith, John Pye, 184, 201–206, 209, 346
Smith, William, 134
Société des Amis, 185
Société Évangélique, 183, 190, 191
Society for the Propagation of the Gospel, 187
Socinians, 38, 39, 123, 139, 155, 172, 183, 194, 195, 203, 208, 214
Solemn League and Covenant, 126, 127, 178
Socrates, 161, 189
South Korea, 48, 52, 180
Southport, 284
South Wales English Congregational Union, 217
South Wales Congregational Church Aid Society, 217
Southwark, 15
Soviet Union, 62, 92
Spain, 108
Spangenberg, Gottlieb, 68, 75
Spinoza, Benedict de, 222
Spurgeon, Charles Haddon, ch. I, 279, 283
Spurgeon, James, 15
Spurgeon, John, 15
Spurr, F. C., 284
Stafford, Russell H., 331
Stanley, A. P., 4
Stanley, Howard S., 309
Stanley, Thomas, 134
State, ch. IV, ch. V, 173–175, 179, 202, 344–345, 368
Stephens, James, 287
Stephens, T., 214
Stewart, Alexander, 294
Stewart, Dugald, 226, 228
Stillingfleet, Edward, 39, 181
Stirling, 166, 174, 283
Stockholm, 42
Stoke Hill, 299
Stordy, Thomas, 133
Stoughton, John, 59
Stouppe, Jean-Baptiste, 119
Strachan, G. C., 192
Strathblane, 173

Stunt, Timothy, 184
Sudan United Mission, 280
Suffolk, 135
Sundback, Susan, 99
Sunderland, 281, 282, 296
Surinam, 76
Surman, Charles E., 366
Surrey, 113, 192, 289, 297, 299
Surrey Congregational Union, 299
Sussex, 136, 306
Svaglic, Martin J., 8
Sweden, 99
Swedenborgianism, 261
Sylvester, M., 34, 345
Systematic theology, 55

Tallents, Francis, 131
Tanner, William, 291
Tapp, Frederick H., 293
Tasmania, 291
Tauler, Johann, 73
Tavard, G., 14
Tayler, John James, 241
Taylor, Adam, 135
Taylor, F. H., 280
Taylor, James Hudson, 280, 283
Taylor, Jeremy, 67, 73
Taylor, John, 142, 143, 202
Taylor, John H., 350, 351
Tenby, 212
Terra del Fuego, 280
Tertullian, 13, 146, 152, 215
Test Act, 125, 137, 141
Teversham, 15
Thacker, Elias, 109
Theale, 298
Theodosius, 97
Theological education, 55
Thistlethwaite, Susan Brooks, 363
Thom, J. H., 227, 234
Thomas à Kempis, 73
Thomas Aquinas, 97
Thomas, J. M. Lloyd, 36, 123
Thomas, Roger, 57
Thomas, W. H. Griffith, 284
Thompson, Albert R., 250, 273
Thompson, Arthur P., 250
Thompson, Bard, 57
Thompson, John, 135
Thompson, Joseph, 342
Thomson, Charles, 293
Thornaby, William, 131
Thornborough, John, 33
Thornton Cleveleys, 296
Thornton le Fylde, 296
Thorogood, Bernard, 347
Thouless, R. H., 83
Throckmorton, Job, 112, 113
Thurian, Max, 43
Tierney, Brian, 97
Tillard, J. M. R., 49
Tindall, W. H., 284
Tipperary, 276
Tolbert, Mary Ann, 52
Toleration, ch. V
Toleration Act, 35, 39, 139–140, 143, 144, 364, 366
Tombes, John, 71, 128
Tomkins, Oliver Fellows, 291–292
Toplady, Augustus Montague, 80
Torrance, James B., 32, 46
Torres Straits Mission, 292
Toulmin, J., 38
Tourn, Giorgio, 119, 145
Towell, Anson J., 284
Towgood, Micaijah, 202, 209
Tradition, 12–14, 19, 26–29, 273
Traill, Robert, 169
Trappe, 253
Trendelenberg, F. A., 226, 227
Trevelyan, G. M., 139
Trible, Phyllis, 52
Trinity College, Dublin, 277
Troeltsch, Ernst, 306, 311
Trosse, George, 129
Trueblood, D. Elton, 148, 151, 160, 163
Truscott, James Reginald, 294
Turkey, 76
Turner, G. Lyon, 129, 137, 235
Turner, Henry, 19
Turner, William, 19, 202
Turretin, Françoise, 190
Turretin, Jean-Alphonse, 209
Tuscany, 76
Tuttle, Robert G., 74
Two kingdoms, 100–101, 114
Tyerman, Luke, 89, 177, 178

Uitenhage, 293, 294
Umzinto, 294
Underhill, Evelyn, 73
Underwood, A. C., 315–316, 319, 326
Union des Églises Évangéliques, 190
Unitarians, 19–20, 25, 57, 75, 141, 190, 196, 202, 203, 204, 209, 224, 227, 244, 298, 369
Unitarian Universalists, 343, 369
United churches, 102
United Church of Canada, 6, 45, 343, 357–359
United Church of Christ, 360–361, 363, 370
United Church of Zambia, 343
United Reformed Church, 309, 347, 348, 353, 355–357, 368
United States. *See* America
Uniting Church in Australia, 343, 359–360
Unity, ch. II
University College, London, 10
University of Calgary, 82, 87
University of Cambridge, 109, 110, 112, 141, 288
University of Durham, 294
University of Edinburgh, 186, 222, 245, 307
University of Geneva, 190, 192
University of Glasgow, 173, 293
University of Lethbridge, 87
University of London, 304
University of Oxford, 8, 128, 141, 192
Upington, 294
Upton, C. B., 22, 23, 220, 226, 227, 234, 236, 242, 243, 246
Urquhart, John, 287
Ursinus College, 250, 253, 258, 299
Urwick, William, 275, 276, 277, 278
Ussher, James, 36
Utilitarianism, 235
Uxbridge, 303, 304

Valentinus, 155
Vatican I, 12
Vatican II, 14, 31, 43, 328, 339
Vaughan, Robert, 120, 341, 342, 347, 350, 351
Venerable Company of Pastors, 194–196, 203
Venner, Thomas, 125
Vernet, Jean-Jacques, 195
Victoria, Australia, 359
Vigne, Randolph, 119
Vincent of Lérins, 13
Vischer, Lukas, 105
Vocation, 175–177
Voges, Friedhelm, 171, 185
Vola, Giorgio, 119
Voltaire (Françoise-Marie Arouet), 196
Vossius, Gerard Jan, 148, 150, 157
Vryburgh, 294

Waddington, John, 110, 114
Wadsworth, Kenneth W., 202
Wainsgate, 177
Waipu, 291
Waldegrave, Robert, 112, 113
Waldensians, ch. V
Wales, ch. IX, 277
Walker, James, 166, 168
Walker, Patrick, 172
Wallace, Mrs., 298
Wallace, Hugh Cunningham, 297–298
Waller, Ralph, 20, 220, 221, 224, 244
Walsall, 82
Walsh, H. H., 357–358
Ward, R., 71
Ward, Seth, 133
Wardlaw, Ralph, 212, 341
Warfield, B. B., 49
Warner, John, 166
Warschauer, Joseph, 297–298
Warwickshire, 65
Waterbeach, 15
Watson, James, 288
Watson, John, 220, 221
Watson, Richard, 352
Watson, Thomas, 128, 129, 363

Watt, Hugh, 173
Watts, Isaac, 215
Watts, Michael R., 105, 121, 133
Wayland, F., 284
Waynesboro, 251
Weatherhead, Leslie D., 299, 337
Webb, C. C. J., 242
Webster, James, 167
Weir, J., 279
Wells, Algernon, 350
Wendt, Pastor, 193
Werman, Mr., 286
Wesley, Charles, 68, 69, 80, 200
Wesley, John, 17, ch. III, 170, 194, 200
Wesley, Samuel, 67
Wesley, Susanna, 67
Wesleyans, 143, 282, 284, 352. *See also* Methodism/Methodists
Western College, Bristol, 307, 308, 309, 310, 341
Westley, Bartholomew, 67
Westley, John, 67
West-Linton, 174
West Malling, 296
Westminster Abbey, 123–124
Westminster College, 306
Westminster Shorter Catechism, 150
Westmorland, 63, 64
Whale J. S., 307
Whalley, Edward, 33
Whately, A. R., 320
Wheeler, John, 360
White, B. R., 128, 136, 343
White, Edward, 17
White, John, 67
White, Joseph Blanco, 224
White, Victor, 318, 319–320
Whitefield, George, 80, 138, 177–179, 186, 199
Whitehead, John, 125
Whitehouse, W. A., 316
Whitgift, John, 108, 112
Whiting, C. E., 133
Whitley, H. C., 192, 207
Whitley, W. T., 125, 127, 132, 134
Wickstead, Richard, 33
Widgery, A. G., 235
Wieser, T., 84
Wilberforce, Robert Isaac, 266
Wilberforce, William, 84
Wilcox, Richard, 185
Wilde, Oscar, 61
Wiles, Maurice, 161
Wilkinson, Wilfred R., 73
William/William and Mary, 35, 120, 121, 138, 140, 145, 171, 173
Williams, Daniel, 138
Williams, David, 112
Williams, Edward, 202, 211
Williams, George H., 106
Williams, H. H., 325–326
Williams, J. B., 127
Williams, Roger, 123, 364
Willimon, William, 355, 363, 364
Willingham, 131
Wilson, John, 229
Wilson, William, 175
Wiltshire, 133
Winchester, 303, 306
Wingate, Andrew, 290
Winslow, 135
Wintle, Thomas D., 369
Wiseman, N. P. S., 192
Witherspoon, John, 172
Wolff, G. Dering, 257
Wood, H. G., 162
Woodham Ferrers, 298
Woolf, S. J., 120
Worcester, 33, 286, 288, 340, 341
Worcestershire, 37, 38
Worcestershire Association, 37–38
Wordsworth, William, 223, 305
World Alliance of Reformed Churches, 43–45, 208, 367
World Conference on Faith and Order, 42
World Council of Churches, 31, 42, 43, 84, 88
World Missionary Conference, 42
World Presbyterian Alliance, 42, 254, 367
World War II, 102
Worplesdon, 350
Worrall, Thomas James, 296–297
Wragge, J. Philip, 147, 148

Wright, Julia Aymer, 254
Wright, W. J. Payling, 120
Wroxeter, 33
Wyclif, John, 64

Xenophon, 284

Y.M.C.A., 42, 298
Yarmouth. *See* Great Yarmouth
Yates, James, 208–209
York, 137
York, PA, 250
Yorkshire, 131, 177
Yost, Calvin D., 250, 253, 299
Yrigoyen, Charles, Jr., 51, 251, 264, 351

Zaller, R., 135
Zambia, 42
Zanchius, Hieronymus, 168
Zululand, 289
Zürich, 105
Zvomunondita Kurewa, J. W., 53
Zwingli, Ulrich, 105, 114